JUNIOR CYCLE SECOND & THIRD YEAR

FIRE AND ICE

2

PAULINE KELLY • DEIRDRE MURPHY

TOMÁS SEALE • MARY-ELAINE TYNAN

GILL EDUCATION

PK: For my children's godparents, Danny, Mags and Sean.
DM: For my sisters and brother: thanks for the encouragement and the many books you passed on.
TS: For my father, who showed me the importance of being a good communicator and orator.
MET: For Bernie Verdon and John Fahy — inspirational English teachers whose passion and enthusiasm were infectious.

Gill Education
Hume Avenue
Park West
Dublin 12
www.gilleducation.ie

Gill Education is an imprint of M.H. Gill & Co.

ISBN: 978-0-7171-69832

Design and layout: Anú Design
Cover design: Martin O'Brien
Illustrations: Derry Dillon and Brian Fitzgerald
Audio recording: Millbrook Studios

At the time of going to press, all web addresses were active and contained information relevant to the topics in this book. Gill Education does not, however, accept responsibility for the content or views contained on these websites. Content, views and addresses may change beyond the publisher or author's control. Students should always be supervised when reviewing websites.

The paper used in this book is made from the wood pulp of managed forests. For every tree felled, at least one tree is planted, thereby renewing natural resources.

17010431VP

Contents

Assessment Focus
p. 447

Acknowledgments

Introduction

Fire and Ice 2 is a second and third year textbook designed to meet all the requirements of the new **Junior Cycle English Specification**. There are thirty-nine learning outcomes in the Specification across the three strands: **Oral Language (OL)**, **Reading (R)** and **Writing (W)**.

In line with the Specification, *Fire and Ice*, Books *1* and *2* ensure that over the three years of Junior Cycle, students have a wide and varied experience of texts that **stimulate**, **engage**, **inspire** and **challenge**.

Fire and Ice 2 takes a dual approach with both thematic and genre chapters (or 'collections'). **Thematic** collections (1–5) are based around a theme and a variety of texts is given for each theme, allowing for a contextual approach to teaching and learning. Engagement with texts is central to the development of language and literacy. The *Fire and Ice* series uses a wide variety of texts — **oral, aural, written, visual, digital and multi-modal** – in the lessons.

The **genre** collections (6–10) are designed to accompany the periods when working on the studied texts. In these collections **Exam Focus** exercises ensure that students learn the correct terminology for **short story**, **poetry**, **drama**, **novel** and **film**. Everything taught is related to the studied texts, covering learning outcomes asterisked for the final examination (e.g. R4 *Use an appropriate critical vocabulary while responding to literary texts*). Students will explore and appreciate both classical and contemporary texts, including examples of well-loved poetry, fiction and drama alongside the best of new writing.

With the new emphasis on the development of oral language, the *Fire and Ice* series place a strong focus on oral proficiency. The **Oral Communication** chapter provides invaluable information and guidance on completing the Classroom-based Assessment 2: Oral Communication.

Finally, to bring all elements of the course together, the **Assessment Focus** chapter explains the various elements of assessment and how to prepare for them through sample answers and helpful tips.

Using this Book

Learning Outcomes
OL5, OL7, OL9, R8, R12, W3, W4, W13

The **learning outcomes** are referenced for the teacher at the beginning of each collection. These have been translated into easy-to-follow **spidergrams** for the student. All thirty-nine learning outcomes for Junior Cycle are covered across the series.

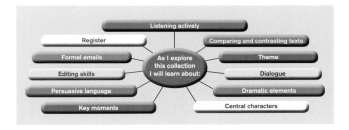

In the thematic collections students are then shown the **summative written task** and **oral communication** that they are working towards in the collection. The learning in each collection has been carefully designed to scaffold the students toward those tasks to ensure the greatest chance of success.

For my writing task I will:
Write a news broadcast about a missile attack on a city

For oral communication I will:
Speak my news broadcast as if I were a radio or television newsreader

In the genre collections students are encouraged to relate what they are learning/doing to their **studied text** (short story, play, novel, film).

I will relate everything I learn about drama to my **studied play**

What I will learn:

to use adjectives and verbs; to state and explain my opinion about my experience in a new school; to use the five senses to describe something

SHOW WHAT YOU KNOW

Every lesson has a strong AfL focus, beginning with a student-friendly skills-based learning intention, **What I will Learn**, to involve the learner in the whole process of learning and assessment.

Each collection culminates in **written tasks and oral communication** that prepare the student for assessment.

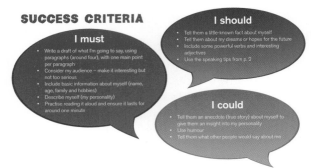

Exam Focus

Lennie and George's relationship changes many times throughout the novel.

1. Choose one important relationship from a novel you have studied. Map the high moments where things are going well, and the low moments when the relationship is struggling. Draw a graph to represent these moments.

2. Present the graph to your class, explaining a key moment and why it is important in the chosen relationship.

3. Imagine you are working on the film adaptation of this novel. Make a list of all the props you would need to get in order to shoot this scene. Explain the significance of one of the props in terms of the character, the setting and the plot.

The genre collections also include **Exam Focus** sections with questions and sample answers to ensure that students are familiar with what is required in the final written examination.

These activities are scaffolded with clear **success criteria** to prompt the student to fully address the task and to encourage self- and peer-assessment and assist students in their reflection notes.

Final **Exam Focus**

Pick a key moment from your studied film and discuss the use of two of the following elements: costume, shots and angles, lighting and special effects, music.

The Poetry, Drama, Novel and Film collections end with a **Final Exam Focus** consolidating all the learning from the collection in an exam-related task.

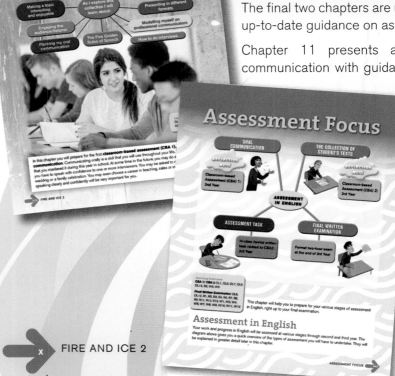

The final two chapters are unique to the *Fire and Ice* series as they provide up-to-date guidance on assessment:

Chapter 11 presents a comprehensive preparation for the oral communication with guidance, tips and exercises to lead students in an enjoyable way to the second classroom-based assessment. Also included are step-by-step diagrams that demonstrate the research, planning, shaping and delivery process.

Chapter 12 focuses on the various types of assessment the student will encounter in second and third year. With advice, tips and sample answers, it provides a guiding hand through what's required.

Throughout the book you will see various easy-to-follow symbols:

Other features to help the student in Fire and Ice 2:

Prepare
This section precedes texts, using AfL strategies to encourage students to explore their prior knowledge and to predict before they read/listen/watch.

Mind Your Language
These sections concentrate on the nuts and bolts of language – grammar, punctuation, spelling, etc.

Top Tips
These boxes contain important definitions and examples to assist the student in their understanding of the topic.

Remember
Something the student has come across before in the book that will help here.

PIE
The **PIE** symbol appears wherever this strategy will help the student to answer a question, prompting them to fully develop their points by illustrating and explaining them.

The 5Ws
Reminds the student to ask 'who', 'what', 'where', 'when' and 'why' when reading an article or watching a news clip.

Research Zone
Students are prompted to go beyond the textbook to research a topic or theme.

Additional ideas for teachers:

Audio Available
When the aural symbol appears without the word 'Listen', it indicates that the poem or piece of prose is available to listen to in the ebook (and on www.gillexplore.ie for teachers), though it's not integral to a lesson.

Groupwork/Pairwork
These symbols appear within any of the other sections as a methodology within them.

Think Pair Share
This activity encourages higher-order thinking that involves students thinking individually, then pairing with a partner, then sharing ideas with the wider group.

Worksheet
This symbol appears where there is a suitable (photocopiable) worksheet for the lesson.

Note on film/video: Wherever possible, film/video has been embedded within the ebook for offline use. This is indicated by the 👁 and 🎧 icons. Where permission was unavailable, or where there is audio/digital material that will be of further interest to students, we have directed you to a source on **You Tube**. Students will need to be online to play YouTube clips. A full listing of all YouTube clips and links is available on **GillExplore.ie**.

Fire and Ice
by Robert Frost

Some say the world will end in fire,
Some say in ice.
From what I've tasted of desire
I hold with those who favor fire.
But if it had to perish twice,
I think I know enough of hate
To say that for destruction ice
Is also great
And would suffice.

Friendship

Comprehension strategies

Key scenes and moments

Reviewing

Using photos to inspire a story

Characterisation

As I explore this collection I will learn about:

Advertising

Idioms

Oral language conventions

RAFT

SHOW WHAT YOU KNOW

The skills you learn in this collection will enable you to **show what you know** in your final tasks at the end of this collection.

For my writing task I will:
Write a review (positive or negative) about a book/film/play/article/advertisement/poem/album/documentary/website/CD/video game

For oral communication I will:
Choose an interesting photograph from my/someone's life and present it orally, telling an anecdote about the person/people in the photo

Learning Outcomes
OL1, OL3, OL5, R6, R7, W3, W6, W8

Exploring the Theme – Friendship

Theme *n.*
Definition: Central idea or message that runs through a text
Synonyms: idea, message

Friendship *n.*
Definition: The relationship between friends; the state of being friends
Synonyms: friendly relationship, attachment, alliance, bond, tie, link

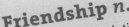

'Friends and good manners will carry you where money won't go' – **Margaret Walker**

'A friend in need is a friend indeed' – **Proverb**

'Friendship is a single soul dwelling in two bodies' – **Aristotle**

'The enemy of mine enemy is my friend' – **Proverb**

'Don't walk in front of me, I may not follow
Don't walk behind me, I may not lead
Walk beside me, and be my friend' –
Albert Camus

'The only way to have a friend is to be one' – **Ralph Waldo Emerson**

'A true friend never gets in your way unless you happen to be going down' – **Arnold H. Glasow**

'Anyone can sympathise with the sufferings of a friend, but it requires a very fine nature to sympathise with a friend's success' – **Oscar Wilde**

After reading the quotes on page 2, answer these questions.

1. Choose your favourite quote about friendship. Pair up with another student and explain why you like the quote you chose.

2. Find some other quotes about friendship.

3. Make up a saying or quote of your own about friendship.

4. Now write your quotes out nicely, decorate them and make a collage with them. You might like to add photos of your friends to the collage.

   Some other information you could put on your collage:

   ✱   A good friend is …

   ✱   A good friend is not …

   ✱   A good friend does …

   ✱   A good friend does not …

   Alternatively you can do a digital design, adding quotes, drawings or images/photos.

Lost at Sea

Imagine you have been lost at sea with your best friend. You are on a lifeboat trying to find land or someone who can rescue you. On the next page is a list of items that you may keep on the boat.

1. Read the list carefully and choose ten items which you wish to keep. Rank the ten in order of importance (with '1' being the most important item).

2. Pair up with a classmate and compare your lists.

3. Now join another group. Share and discuss your lists. Then agree on a final ten items to keep, ranking them in order of importance again.

Add three other items to the list that you think might be necessary to survive at sea.

Everyone in the group must have a responsibility in this discussion. Possible roles are:

a)   A person to keep the discussion focused, monitor the time and make sure that everyone gets a chance to speak (chairperson)

b)   **A person to note down the group's decisions (minute-taker)**

c)   **A person to feed back the decisions made to the rest of the class (reporter)**

d)   A person to check all details are correct before you finish, i.e. that there are only ten items on the list, in the order the group have agreed on, as well as three extra items (secretary)

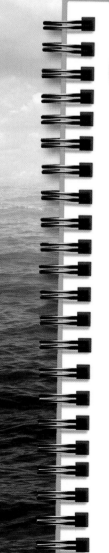

List of items

A plastic pack containing a map
of the Atlantic Ocean and a compass

A baseball cap

A 5 litre can of petrol

A whistle

A 20 litre drum of fresh water

A small radio with batteries

A video game with batteries

A can of shark repellent

Two large bars of chocolate

An ocean fishing rod and bait

Five hand flares

Three life jackets

Two large wool blankets

A sewing kit with straight and curving needles and strong white thread

A notebook with 98 lined pages

Two black ink ballpoint pens

Two sea anchors

A first aid kid in a waterproof plastic case

A large square of mosquito netting and 20 ft of thick rope

EXPLORE

1. What skills did you use in this activity (mention at least two)?

2. What personal qualities were important for completing it?

3. As a team, what would you do differently the next time?

4. What did you learn from working with your classmates during this activity?

Poetry

What I will learn:

to revise and identify the parts of speech; to analyse how the themes of friendship and love are explored in a poem

REMEMBER

A **noun** is a naming word: a person, place, thing, animal or quality. 'Friend' and 'friendship' are both nouns.

A **pronoun** is a word used in place of a noun, e.g. 'I', 'he', 'she', 'they'. (There are different types of pronouns. These are examples of **personal pronouns**.)

An **adjective** describes the noun, e.g. We have a very **strong** friendship.

A **verb** is a doing or action word. e.g. to **love** (infinitive), we **fought** (past tense), we **will drive** (future tense).

An **adverb** gives us more information about the verb, e.g. She ran **slowly**.

 Identify the noun, pronoun, adjective, verb and adverb in this sentence (there may be more than one in some cases).

As Marcus jogged casually towards his oldest friend, he grinned from ear to ear.

Now write your own sentence that includes at least one noun, pronoun, adjective, verb and adverb. Ask another student to identify each element.

READ

You will now read a famous poem called 'He Wishes for the Cloths of Heaven', by W. B. Yeats. It was written in 1899 for Maud Gonne, a woman that Yeats was friends with (although he hoped for a more romantic relationship with her). You could argue that this is a poem about love as well as friendship.

Poetic Devices

You'll remember that a **stanza** is a number of lines grouped together (like a verse in a song). Some poems only have one stanza, as in the poem you will read by W. B. Yeats. **Alliteration** is another device used by writers and poets. It is the repetition of consonant sounds, e.g. 'Peter Piper picked a peck of pickled peppers' ('p' sound repeated). **Assonance** is the repetition of vowel sounds, e.g. 'Try as I might, the kite didn't fly' ('i' sound repeated). To remember which is which, note that the word 'alliteration' ends with a consonant, and the word 'assonance' ends with a vowel.

He Wishes for the Cloths of Heaven

by W. B. Yeats

Had I the heavens' embroidered cloths,
Enwrought with golden and silver light,
The blue and the dim and the dark cloths
Of night and light and the half-light,
I would spread the cloths under your feet:
But I, being poor, have only my dreams;
I have spread my dreams under your feet;
Tread softly because you tread on my dreams.

EXPLORE

W1.2

P I E

1. How would you describe the mood of the poem? You may use one of the words below or suggest your own.

optimistic	**fearful**
carefree	bitter
careless	**poignant**
cautious	hopeful

Mood *n.*

Definition: A temporary state of mind or feeling

2. Identify a line in the poem where the poet uses (a) assonance and (b) alliteration. Explain how the usage affects the meaning of the poem and you, the reader, e.g. does it improve the rhythm, does it make you slow down when reading, does it create harsh sounds?

3. The poet describes himself as 'poor'. What do you think he means by this? (*Hint:* there are several possible meanings.)

4. Choose your favourite image from the poem. Explain how it relates to the theme of love and friendship, and why you like it.

P I E

5. What do you think is the main message of this poem? **P I E**

CREATE

Think about a dream or goal that you have. Imagine that you are asked to talk about this for one minute. Plan what you would say (write in bullet points) and then practise in front of a classmate.

Give each other feedback, listing two things you liked and one thing they could improve on in their presentation. What did you learn from working with a classmate?

An Article

to explore the theme of friendship by reading an article;
to think critically about the power of advertising; using RAFT

To 'think critically' about something does not mean to criticise; rather it means to analyse something and to look at the positive and negative aspects with a view to suggesting improvements.

PREPARE

Every year we celebrate Mother's Day, Father's Day, Valentine's Day … but did you know that in some countries they celebrate Friendship Day?

1. Before you read about it, imagine that you were planning a Friendship Day in your school. What would you do for one of your friends to mark the occasion?

2. Now come up with a symbol that everybody could wear for the day to mark the occasion. For example, in Ireland, people wear daffodils to raise awareness about cancer on Daffodil Day, and shamrocks on St Patrick's Day, while in the United Kingdom they wear poppies for Remembrance Day (which is why it's also known as Poppy Day).

READ

National Friendship Day

This week millions of people celebrated 'National Friendship Day' in countries around the globe, exchanging gifts, cards and celebrating the importance of friendship.

The **brainchild** of Joyce Hall, the founder of Hallmark Cards, he <u>tested the waters</u> in 1930 when he chose August 2nd as the day when friends would mark their friendships by sending cards.

Cynics criticised Hall's **innovation**, suggesting that it was just another **manipulative** marketing ploy by the greeting card industry

to pressurise people to buy cards, pointing out that this time of the year represented the quietest sales period for the greeting card industry, with there being a **lull** between holiday celebrations. National Friendship Day, as it was then, survived for a few years in the US but it <u>fell out of favour</u> in the 1940s.

The idea of a 'World Friendship Day' was then proposed by Dr Artemio Bracho on 20 July 1958 during a dinner with friends in

Puerto Pinasco, a town in Paraguay. From this small gathering of friends came the 'World Friendship Crusade', a foundation that promotes friendship and fellowship among all human beings. Since that time, Friendship Day has been celebrated on 30 July in Paraguay.

After **lobbying** the United Nations for many years to recognise the day, the 'World Friendship Crusade' finally succeeded, and on 27 July 2011 the General Assembly of the United Nations declared that 30th July would be the official 'International Friendship Day'.

Friendship Day has become very popular in Asia, largely due to the growth of the internet, especially in countries like India, Bangladesh and Malaysia where communication was very difficult in the past. Now computers and mobile phones make it easier to get in touch with old friends. In Asia, friends mark the day by exchanging flowers, cards and jewellery. In parts of South America, friends **acknowledge** each other by exchanging friendship bands.

While greeting card companies and florists obviously benefit, other multinationals have jumped on the bandwagon. For example, Coca-Cola designed a special 3.5 metre-high vending machine to celebrate the day in the Latin American market, which required friends to lift each other up in order to avail of the special '2 for 1' offer. While Friendship Day seems to have **bypassed** Europe, Coke has successfully created other campaigns in this part of the world by putting Christian names on bottles which friends can then buy for each other. The questions is, does anybody actually benefit from this other than Coke?

Some people would say that actions speak louder than words and that we should **boycott** such days. They argue that it's strange that we might be called on to celebrate our friends on one day of the year only, but the same argument could be made about Mother's Day or Father's Day. Sometimes it's nice to have an excuse to tell people how much they mean to us. **Corporate** giants like Hallmark and Coke certainly aren't complaining anyway!

EXPLORE

1. Choose one positive and one negative aspect of National Friendship Day from the article.

2. How do you think the writer of the article feels about National Friendship Day? Give reasons for your answer. **P I E**

3. Would you celebrate National Friendship Day if we had it in Ireland? Explain your answer. **P I E**

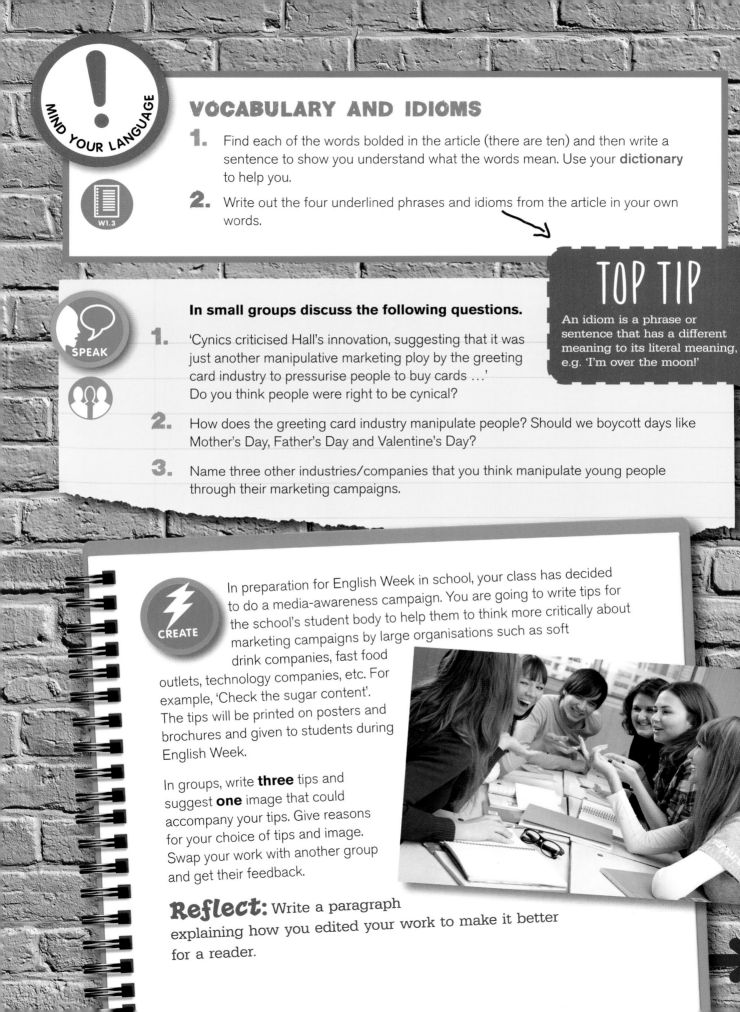

VOCABULARY AND IDIOMS

1. Find each of the words bolded in the article (there are ten) and then write a sentence to show you understand what the words mean. Use your **dictionary** to help you.

2. Write out the four underlined phrases and idioms from the article in your own words.

TOP TIP

An idiom is a phrase or sentence that has a different meaning to its literal meaning, e.g. 'I'm over the moon!'

SPEAK

In small groups discuss the following questions.

1. 'Cynics criticised Hall's innovation, suggesting that it was just another manipulative marketing ploy by the greeting card industry to pressurise people to buy cards …' Do you think people were right to be cynical?

2. How does the greeting card industry manipulate people? Should we boycott days like Mother's Day, Father's Day and Valentine's Day?

3. Name three other industries/companies that you think manipulate young people through their marketing campaigns.

CREATE

In preparation for English Week in school, your class has decided to do a media-awareness campaign. You are going to write tips for the school's student body to help them to think more critically about marketing campaigns by large organisations such as soft drink companies, fast food outlets, technology companies, etc. For example, 'Check the sugar content'. The tips will be printed on posters and brochures and given to students during English Week.

In groups, write **three** tips and suggest **one** image that could accompany your tips. Give reasons for your choice of tips and image. Swap your work with another group and get their feedback.

Reflect: Write a paragraph explaining how you edited your work to make it better for a reader.

Imagine that you are organising a Friendship Day for first years in your school.

1. Working in pairs, make a list of the events that could take place to help them settle in to their new school.

2. Design a poster/website/Facebook page advertising the event and encouraging students to take part.

Success Criteria

* This must include the date, location and what will happen on the day.

* You must choose an appropriate image to make it more interesting.

* You should use the **RAFT** structure when thinking about how to write.

* You should use persuasive language to encourage students to attend.

* You should use different types (sizes, colours) of font/text.

* You could also include a catchy slogan to get students' attention.

* You could provide a couple of tips to help those students struggling with the settling-in process.

3. When you have finished, complete the following sentences:

* To prepare for this task I … (include material used/accessed)

* I learned the following from creating this …

* The image I chose was … I chose this image because …

* I worked with my classmate to improve our work by …

Persuasive writing/ language *n.*

Definition: Writing or language that seeks to convince the reader/ listener/viewer of a certain point of view; it hopes to persuade them.

RAFT GUIDELINES

When you write, use the **RAFT** structure to help you.

ROLE OF THE WRITER

Who am I as the writer? What is my personality? How will I react to the information or situation? My role depends on the situation; for example, am I a film critic writing a review, or a customer writing a letter of complaint?

AUDIENCE

For whom am I writing? Who needs to read this? Who am I trying to persuade? What is the goal or purpose of writing? What type of emotional reaction do I want from the reader?

FORMAT

In what format am I writing? There are numerous possibilities, for example an article, a diary entry, a speech, an opinion piece.

TOPIC

What am I writing about? What is the subject I am covering? What information do I have to share? What is the focus of my chosen format?

A Poem for a Best Friend
by Emma Ronan

Our cheeks are rosy,
We're wrapped up cosy,
In blankets,
On your double bed.
Watching sci-fi,
Wasting Wi-Fi,
Surfing websites,
Limbs like lead.
Laughing loudly,
Pointing proudly
At the brothers
On the screen
We surf the channels,
Wearing flannels,
Like the brothers we look mean
One of them dies.
'It must be lies!!!'
You scream, I laugh,
It happens all the time.
But we're not like that,
Sister, friend.
I'll be with you
Till the end.

The author of this poem, Emma Ronan, is a student of Enniscorthy Vocational College. This poem was published in *The Irish Times Fighting Words Supplement* on 29 April 2015.

An Advertisement

What I will learn:

to critique advertising campaigns; to consider the use of idioms in everyday language

Friendship is such an important part of our lives that companies like Coca-Cola have designed numerous campaigns around the theme.

THINK Can you think of another product that could use the theme of friendship to increase their sales? How would they do this?

PAIR Working in pairs, discuss your ideas and choose one idea.

SHARE After one minute, join up with another pair of students and pitch your idea to them. Choose the best idea in every group of four and then share them with the class.

Coca-Cola 'Friendly Twist' Marketing Campaign

Now watch how a Coca-Cola advertisement used the theme of friendship to market their product. Look up 'Coca Cola Friendly Twist' on YouTube.

This advertisement was designed by Leo Burnett (a large advertising agency) and broadcast in Colombia in 2014. The target market was new college students (freshmen) and the theme was 'new friendships'.

You will watch the advertisement three times and answer the questions below after each viewing.

First viewing

1. What are the students doing at the beginning of the advertisement?

2. Explain the pun (play on words) in the line 'A Coke bottle like any other. But with a little twist'.

3. Describe the atmosphere among the students at the end of the advertisement.

4. Explain the idiom 'to break the ice'. Now use this idiom in a new sentence.

Second viewing

Pay attention to the text that appears on the screen and, working in pairs, see if you can fill in the gaps.

First day of college

A day when talks and _____ are reduced to zero.

So we thought of something _____ to make freshmen bond.

An _____ to break the ice

And make them start _____ .

A Coke bottle like any other,

But with a little _____ .

Coca-Cola presents:

The _____ Twist

A cap that can't be opened

Until you match it with _____ one.

Open a Coke.

Open a new _____ .

Coca-Cola – Open Happiness

TOP TIP

A **target market** is a particular group of people (consumers) at which a particular product/service is aimed. In this advertisement, the target market is new college students (freshmen).

Copy is what the advertising or media industry calls the text that accompanies their adverts or comprises their articles.

Tone is the attitude of a writer towards their subject or audience. Tone is usually shown through the choice of words or the viewpoint. The tone of this Coca-Cola advertisement changes through the course of the advertisement.

Final viewing

Watch the advertisement once more, this time paying attention to the music.

* Make a note every time the music changes, using one word to describe it.
* Consider how this affects the tone. For example:

  Fast, upbeat music → *Happy tone*

  Slow, sombre music → *Sad tone*

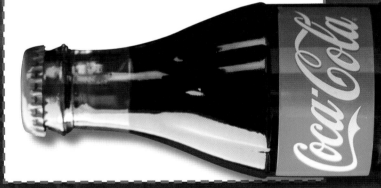

 As a group, discuss the following questions:

1. What did you think of this advertisement? Make a list of five adjectives to describe it, e.g. funny, boring, innovative.

2. Make a list of any persuasive language (words or phrases) used in the advertisement.

3. Think about how the **RAFT** structure (p. 10) would have been used to help the agency make this advertisement. In pairs, work out what the role of the writer was here, the target audience, the format they were using and the topic.

4. Imagine that you work for the advertising agency that made this ad. Find or design another image that you would use in a follow-up ad for the Friendly Twist campaign to remind people about it.

REMEMBER Persuasive langugage and writing hopes to convince the reader/viewer of a certain point of view; it hopes to persuade them.

TOP TIP

A podcast is a form of digital media, i.e. a piece of audio (sound recording, not video) that is broadcast online. It comes from the words iPod + Broadcast = podcast. Podcasts are very popular as they can be downloaded onto a phone and listened to from anywhere and at any time. There are many excellent and free podcasts available. If you have a smartphone, take a look in the app store – you might be surprised at how entertaining a podcast can be!

When making an advertisement, you might find the following websites and apps useful:

- To make animation-style ads – www.goanimate4schools.com

- To make mini-cartoons and mini-movies – www.creazaeducation.com

- To make short films – www.generator.acmi.net.au

- To make comic-style ads – www.bitstripsforschools.com

- To create a story arc (setup, conflict, challenge, climax and resolution) – the Toontastic app

- To make audio ads or podcasts – www.podbean.com

Making Advertisements Work

Advertisers realise that to entice consumers to buy their products, there are a number of steps most consumers go through before they actually make a purchase. This process may take a short time for cheap products (chocolate bars, clothes) or a long time for expensive products (cars, holidays). The process, from learning to buying, is referred to in the marketing industry as **AIDA**:

Attention – Learn about the product/service

Interest – Become interested in the product/service

Desire – Create a wish to buy the product/service

Action – Buy the product/service

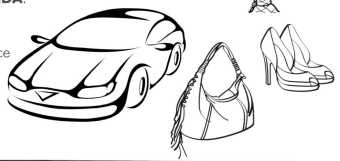

MIND YOUR LANGUAGE

IDIOMS

Remember how the Friendly Twist campaign used the phrase, 'to break the ice' – why do we say 'to break the ice' when we don't actually intend to break any ice? It's like saying 'to kick things off' when you don't actually intend to kick anything! Everybody knows what we mean by these expressions, but when we break down the words and analyse them, they seem quite strange. These puzzling and yet familiar expressions are called **idioms** and languages are filled with them.

In **FRENCH**, if you want to say that something is very expensive, you might say that it *coûter les yeux de la tête*, which literally means that it costs the eyes in your head, while in **ENGLISH** we might say that something 'costs an arm and a leg'. In **ROMANIAN**, an idiom for wasting time or doing nothing is *a freca menta*, meaning 'to rub mint'. In **POLISH**, when you want to say something is boring you can say, *Nudne jak flaki z olejem*, which literally means 'dull as tripe in oil'. Can you think of an equivalent English-language way of saying that something is boring?

1 MIN

1. Working in pairs, make a list of as many idioms as you can, e.g. to fly by the seat of your pants, to kick the bucket, etc.

2. Match the idioms on the next page with their meanings, which have been scrambled up. We have 'kicked things off' and done the first one for you.

$\longrightarrow$

Idiom	Meaning
Don't count your chickens before they hatch	Avoid facts and reality by pretending they do not exist
Bury your head in the sand	To be jealous
Bury the hatchet	Behave/do what you are told
Give someone the cold shoulder	Unfair
Green-eyed monster	Don't be too confident or make plans based on an outcome that may not happen
Give someone a leg up	Frustrate someone
Take the wind out of someone's sails	Ignore a person or treat them with noticeable disrespect
Toe the line	To help someone
Ruffle a person's feathers	Make up after an argument
Below the belt	To have annoyed someone, either on purpose or by accident

Working with a partner, look back at the English idioms you wrote down earlier. Choose five of them and try to find out their origins. You can then present some of these to the class.

If you speak any other languages, you might like to tell your classmates an idiom from that language and explain what it means. Try to find out its origin.

A Literary Extract

What I will learn:

to appreciate and critique literary fiction; to introduce a surprising detail into a conversation/story

Writers are often given awards for their writing. One of the most prestigious awards given to people who write fiction is the Man Booker Prize, given once a year to the writer of a new English-language novel. Since the inaugural (meaning 'first'; say: *in-aw-gral*) award in 1969, many Irish authors have been nominated for and won the Booker Prize, such as Anne Enright (*pictured*), who won in 2007. You can browse all nominations and winners of the Man Booker Prize on www.themanbookerprize.com.

Class Challenge

1. If the Booker Prize began in 1969, how many winners have there been to date?

2. Looking up the Booker Prize website, make a list of all the Irish authors who have been nominated since 1969. Where possible, mention the name of the novel that they were nominated for and the year of nomination.

3. Now pair up, compare your lists and combine them. When you are ready, compare your answers with the rest of the class and see who got the most correct.

The winner is ...

You get 1 point for every Irish Booker nominated/winning novel that you find.

You will get an extra mark if you can give the name of the novel that they were nominated for.

You will get one more point if you know the correct year of the author's nomination.

You should know that some authors have been nominated more than once ...

PS Your teacher will find all these answers in their Resource Book!

READ

The following two passages are taken from a novel called *We Are All Completely Beside Ourselves* by an American author, Karen Joy Fowler (*pictured*). It was one of the six novels nominated for the Booker Prize in 2014.

This novel is about the very complex relationships within a family: between brothers and sisters, sisters and sisters, parents and children.

In this extract from Part II, Chapter 2, the narrator, Rosemary, writes about her early childhood, and in particular about her sister, Fern, and her brother, Lowell. She also had an imaginary friend called Mary.

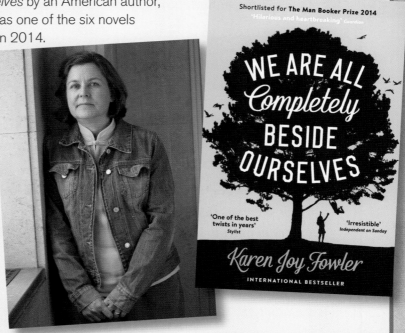

Shortlisted for **The Man Booker Prize 2014**
'Hilarious and heartbreaking' *Guardian*

WE ARE ALL
Completely
BESIDE
OURSELVES

'One of the best twists in years'
Stylist

'Irresistible'
Independent on Sunday

Karen Joy Fowler
INTERNATIONAL BESTSELLER

We Are All Completely Beside Ourselves
by Karen Joy Fowler

Part II, Chapter 2

In most families, there is a favourite child.
Parents deny it and maybe they truly don't
see it, but it's obvious to the children.
Unfairness bothers children greatly.
It's hard to always come in second.

It's also hard to be the favourite.
Earned or unearned, the favourite is a burdensome thing to be.

I was our mother's favourite child. Lowell was our father's. I loved our father as much
as our mother, but I loved Lowell best of all. Fern loved our mother best. Lowell loved
Fern more than he loved me.

benign: harmless

When I lay out these facts, they seem essentially benign. Something here for everybody.
More than enough to go around.

Part II, Chapter 5

There's something you don't know yet about Mary. The imaginary friend of my childhood
was not a little girl. She was a little chimpanzee.

So, of course, was my sister Fern.

Simian-ness: being a monkey (simian = monkey)

Some of you will have figured that out already. Others may feel it was irritatingly coy
of me to have withheld Fern's essential simian-ness for so long.

* STOP *

The narrator states that 'The imaginary friend of my childhood was not a little girl. She was a little
chimpanzee. So, of course, was my sister Fern.' How did you feel after reading this? *Now read on …*

In my defence, I had my reasons. I spent the first eighteen years of my life defined
by this one fact, that I was raised with a chimpanzee. I had to move halfway across the
country in order to leave that fact behind. It's never going to be the first thing I share with
someone.

But much, *much* more important, I wanted you to see how it really was. I tell you Fern
is a chimp and, already, you aren't thinking of her as my sister. You're thinking instead that
we loved her as if she was some kind of pet. After Fern left, Grandma Donna told Lowell

and me that when our dog Tamara Press had died, our mother had been devastated – just the way she was now, being the implication. Lowell reported this to our father and we were all so offended Grandma Donna had to give it right up.

[…] Until Fern's expulsion, I'd scarcely known a moment alone. She was my twin, my fun-house mirror, my whirlwind other half. It's important to note that I was also all those things to her. I would say that, like Lowell, I loved her as a sister, but she was the only sister I ever had, so I can't be sure; it's an experiment with no control. Still, when I first read *Little Women*, it seemed to me I'd loved Fern as much as Jo loved Amy if not as much as Jo loved Beth …

Fern and I were raised in as much the same way as was deemed rational. I'm sure I was the only chimp sibling in the country who had to decline all birthday party invitations, though this was mostly to prevent me from bringing colds home; little chimps are terribly susceptible to respiratory infections. We went to exactly one party in my first five years, and I don't even remember it, but Lowell told me there'd been an unfortunate incident involving a piñata, a baseball bat, and a lot of flying candy that ended up with Fern biting Bertie Cubbins, the birthday girl, on the leg. Biting someone who's not in the family – apparently, a really big deal.

[…] My very earliest memory, more tactile than visual, is of lying against Fern. I feel her fur on my cheek. She's had a bubble bath and smells of strawberry soap and wet towels. A few drops of water still cling to the sparse white hair on her chin. I see this, looking up from the shoulder I am leaning against.

I see her hand, her black nails, her fingers curling and uncurling. We must have still been very young, because her palm is soft and creased and pink. She is giving me a large golden raisin.

There is a dish of raisins on the floor in front of us, and I think they must have been Fern's and not mine, earned somehow in one of our games, but it doesn't matter, because she is sharing them with me – one for her, one for me, one for her, one for me. My feeling in this memory is a great contentment.

TOP TIP

The style of this text is casual and conversational. When a book is said to have a 'conversational style', it means that something is written in a casual style that sounds like the narrator is speaking directly to you – like in a conversation. It is a less formal way of writing, designed to draw you in and make you want to 'listen'.

A narrative arc is the way that the plot is structured – the opening, first point of conflict, climax and resolution. You will learn more about narrative arc in Collection 6.

?
EXPLORE

1. Describe the relationship between Fern and Rosemary (the narrator). **P I E**

2. How did other people react when Fern was sent away?

3. From your reading of the extract, what impression do you get of Rosemary's family?

4. How was the narrator's childhood affected by growing up with **P I E** a chimpanzee?

5. Did you enjoy reading this extract? Give a reason for your answer. **P I E**

Challenge Yourself

1. Which of these storytelling elements are present in this extract (give one quote to support each element which is present):

   suspense

   conflict   resolution   drama

   challenge   plot twist   strong characterisation

   climax   powerful descriptions

2. Why do you think this novel was nominated for the Man Booker prize?

3. In this extract, the main character is greatly affected by the loss of her 'sister' Fern. Thinking back to a previous novel you have studied, explain how a character was affected by an event (big or small) or another person in their lives. Describe how the event/other person affected the main character.

   Use the following headings to organise your answer:

   * Title of novel
   * Author
   * Name of the character you are writing about
   * In the novel I studied, this character was affected as follows: …

Working in pairs, do an improvised drama (where you make it up as you go along). Speaker 1 must reveal a surprising fact to Speaker 2. Speaker 2 must react to this, and the dialogue will continue from there.

Your surprising fact doesn't need to be true, but if you do make it up, be prepared and have thought about it in detail. Here are some useful questions and sentence starters to help you create an interesting dialogue.

Things that Speaker 2 could ask	Things that Speaker 1 could say
Tell me something interesting about yourself	You might find this strange but …
How did that happen?	It all started when …
What was that like?/Tell me more about …	It was …
What was the best/worst part?	The best/worst moment I remember was …
How did it affect you?	It made me realise that …
How do you feel about it now?	Looking back now, I think that …

Writing Reviews

People review books, films and a host of other things. The purpose of a review is to tell others about an experience. Some of the best reviewers are full of opinions and very personal in their writing.

Traditionally, reviews were printed in newspapers and magazines. Reviews are also broadcast on the radio and television, but since the advent (birth) of the internet, there are hundreds of reviewing websites. One such website is TripAdvisor, which allows travellers to read and write reviews of restaurants, hotels and other tourist attractions.

◎◎ tripadvisor®

Make a list of things that can be reviewed. Do you know of any other sites where people can read/post reviews?

Here are a sample of some reviews.

Concert Review

Ed Sheeran (Whelans) 24 June 2015

Ed Sheeran thrilled a small, exclusive crowd of 800 lucky fans at a secret gig in one of Dublin's most intimate and popular venues, Whelan's. The atmosphere was electric as fans waited in anticipation for him. One fan fortunate enough to get into the gig tweeted, 'Waiting for @edsheeran to take to the stage at @whelanslive...'

One hundred of those who had been promised a ticket were not given access as allocation was determined on a 'first-come-first-served' basis. The venue issued a statement explaining that they had no part in the ticketing process,

passing the blame on to ApplauseStore.com, a ticketing [...]
manages the tickets for events like The X Factor, Top Gear[...]

Following a tweet from Whelan's, 'Look who dropped in for a pi[...]
fans arrived on the scene, causing a frenzy on Wexford Street as they
chanted and begged to be allowed entry to the exclusive gig.

For the next two hours, those lucky enough to be inside sang and swooned
while the adored British singer-songwriter belted out some of his most loved
tunes and charmed them with his 'cheeky-chappie' personality. Leaving the
venue, one reveller commented happily: 'All my dreams came true tonight.
He's my idol and I was standing a few feet from him. He was incredible.'

Warming up the stage for Ed was UK singer-songwriter, Jamie Lawson, the
first artist signed by Ed to his new label, Gingerbread.

Before leaving, Sheeran signed a poster saying: 'To Whelans! Everything for
me started here, and I hope to always play here if you'll have me. Lots of love
Ed Sheeran.'

We certainly hope that you will be back Ed – you'll always be welcome in
Ireland!

> **REMEMBER**
> An adjective is a describing word, e.g. exciting, deafening.

? EXPLORE

1. Make a list of all the positive adjectives the reviewer uses in this concert review.

2. Choose five of these adjectives and change them to different adjectives that could be used in the same sentence.

3. Imagine you were the editor of the newspaper in which this review appeared and you had to select an appropriate image to accompany this article. Which of the three images below would you use? What impact do you think this would have on the way that the reader might respond to the article?

'All the Hip and Zip of Pixar, with Added Sorrow' ★★★★ **Tara Brady, www.irishtimes.com**

...ever have suspected that *Frozen*, its last major release, would have ...enomena of the age. Happily, by accident rather than **design**, it has ...actly the right sort of project: something completely different. Nodding ...manga, this beautiful film has all the hip and zip of a Pixar project, but it ...d gentle sorrow of a *Dumbo* or a *Bambi*.

Set in a perfect **amalgam** of two great cities that (no clues here) goes by the name of San Fransokyo, *Big Hero 6* concerns the sad, but promising life of a bright teenager named Hiro. The technical genius is wasting his talent on backstreet robot fights when his brother introduces him to **personnel** at the robotics lab in the city's university. Hiro is a very modern creation: the bright, sensitive kid who, though lost at school, comes alive when put among similarly focused digital brainboxes. A tragedy soon knocks him down again, but **redemption** is at hand.

> Brief description of the film plot. (Spoiler alert! Be careful not to spoil the film/book storyline. A 'spoiler' is a piece of information that would ruin it for anyone watching/reading it for the first time.)

> Good points

There is nothing at all wrong with the first half of *Big Hero 6*. Origin story to a cult Marvel posse, the film introduces Hiro to a hugely charming inflatable robot named Baymax. Triggering reminders of *The Iron Giant*, the two **meander** about a gorgeously realised city whose foliage blends the western US with eastern Asia. There are makings of a classic in that relationship.

Unfortunately, the film slips off the rails a little in its later stages as it turns into a fairly **conventional** superhero adventure (and goodness knows, we have enough of those), involving a noisy fight against a **bafflingly** uninteresting villain.

> Bad points

Still, *Big Hero 6* confirms the continuing strength of **mainstream** animation. If you want further evidence, be sure to arrive in time for the gorgeous Oscar-nominated short, *Feast*.

> Sum up your thoughts here

 EXPLORE Would you go and see this film on the basis of this review? Explain your answer. **P I E**

Create a glossary (a list of words with their definitions) for teenagers who read this review. Look up the following nine words in your **dictionary** and then write them out like a glossary.

Glossary

phenomena
design
amalgam
personnel
redemption
meander
conventional
baffling
mainstream

RESEARCH ZONE

Working in pairs, go online and find a poster advertising 'Big Hero 6' which could be shown to a group of second year students who were going to see the film.

* Make up a list of sample questions about the poster and give it to another group, while you answer their questions. Students should be able to find the answers from looking at the poster.

Note: If a question is too difficult for you to answer, then other students will probably find it difficult too!

LISTEN

Now listen to a conversation between a radio host and reviewer. While you listen, make a list of any positive and any negative points that the reviewer makes about the item being reviewed.

Positive points	Negative points

Listen to the conversation once more and now make a list of the questions that the radio host asked the reviewer.

Working in pairs, imagine that one of you is a television/radio host and the other is a reviewer. The reviewer will choose something they have seen, read or used recently and review it (e.g. a film, book, video game, website, etc.)

The reviewer will make notes to prepare, such as:

* The *title* of the film, book, etc. and key people involved (director, author, designer, actors)
* A quick *synopsis* of the story/main features, etc.
* The *best* and *worst* features
* Whether they would *recommend* it, and to whom
* A *star rating* (out of five stars usually)

To prepare for the interview, write **bullet points** on flashcards rather than a script. This will make the interview sound more natural and conversational. If you get nervous and forget your points, you can glance down at your flashcards to remind yourself.

The radio host/interviewer should make a list of the questions they plan on asking and give a copy to the reviewer so that they can be prepared to answer them.

Reflect: How did working with a partner help you? What did you learn?

Tips for Writing Questions

* When preparing to interview someone, avoid closed questions such as, 'Did you like it?' or 'Would you recommend it?' These questions get 'yes' and 'no' answers, whereas open questions such as, 'Tell me what you liked the most/least about the film/book' or 'Why would you (not) recommend this film/book?' will make the reviewer give you a more considered response.

* Write key words for questions on flashcards to help jog your memory if you forget some of the questions.

The interview can take place when you are both ready to act out the scene. The interviewer will ask questions and the reviewer will answer them. It may take a couple of run-throughs to get it right. It can then be recorded or acted out in front of a group of students/the class.

Important words

Flashcards = Fantastic

Large font

To remind you

A Short Film

What I will learn:

to view a film with the aim of reviewing it; to select a key scene or image from a film

Sometimes friendship comes in the most unexpected forms. The short film you will watch, *Lamb*, is set on a rural farm in Australia during a drought. The plot is simple but powerful. The seven-minute film centres around a farmer and his young son who finds solace (comfort) in his pet lamb, the last living animal on their farm.

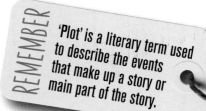

REMEMBER 'Plot' is a literary term used to describe the events that make up a story or main part of the story.

FUN FACT

A few weeks before films are released to the general public, reviewers are invited to a special advance screening, where they get to see the film before everyone else does.

WATCH

Lamb
(Emma Freeman, dir.)

A **key scene** is a memorable scene of special importance or great emotion. It may be a scene of great drama, conflict, or development of plot or character. It could be a turning point in the action, or it may reveal the truth about characters or relationships.

? EXPLORE

Watch the film and then answer these questions.

1. Name the title and director of the film.

2. Describe the plot of the film in fifty words or fewer.

3. Choose either a **key scene** or your favourite image from the film. Explain why you chose this and why it is important in the context of the film.

4. Friendship is just one of the many possible themes of this film. Name another possible theme and explain how it is presented. **P I E**

5. This film was the winner of Tropfest 2002, the world's largest short film festival. Why do you think the judges chose this film as the winner? Discuss this question with other students in a group.

Suggest other possible titles for this film. Share the best suggestions with the class and vote on the best one(s).

Every entry into Tropfest must include a 'Tropfest Signature Item (TSI)'. This is to ensure that the film was made that year specifically for the competition. In 2002 the signature item was a match. Can you remember where this item featured in 'Lamb'?

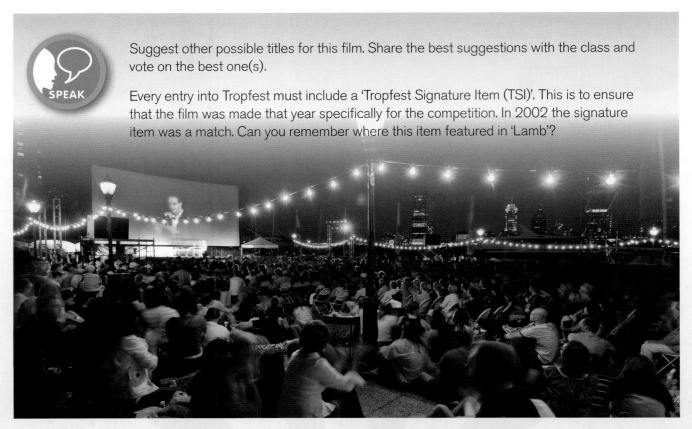

To see other short films, visit the Tropfest Junior website at www.international.tropfest.com/tropjr

The Irish Film Board also has an archive of short films at www.thisisirishfilm.ie/shorts/

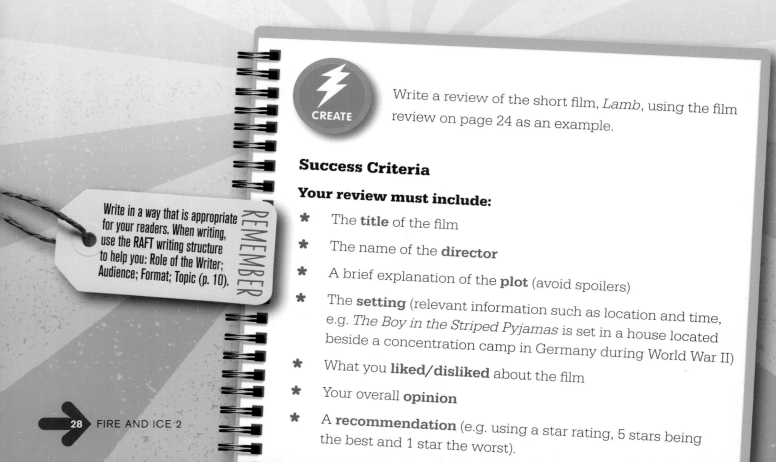

Write a review of the short film, *Lamb*, using the film review on page 24 as an example.

Success Criteria

Your review must include:

* The **title** of the film

* The name of the **director**

* A brief explanation of the **plot** (avoid spoilers)

* The **setting** (relevant information such as location and time, e.g. *The Boy in the Striped Pyjamas* is set in a house located beside a concentration camp in Germany during World War II)

* What you **liked/disliked** about the film

* Your overall **opinion**

* A **recommendation** (e.g. using a star rating, 5 stars being the best and 1 star the worst).

REMEMBER

Write in a way that is appropriate for your readers. When writing, use the RAFT writing structure to help you: Role of the Writer; Audience; Format; Topic (p. 10).

A Novel Extract

What I will learn:

to read an extract from a novel that explores the complexities of friendship; to read carefully and remember details; to think about characterisation in a novel

The Apple Tart of Hope, by Irish writer Sarah Moore Fitzgerald, is about Meg and her best friend and neighbour, Oscar. When Meg moves to New Zealand with her parents, Oscar goes missing and is presumed dead. The first extract you will read is told from Meg's perspective. Later you will read Oscar's side of the story.

> **PREPARE**
>
> What do you imagine is the relationship between the title, *The Apple Tart of Hope*, and its plot? Think about this for a few moments and then write down your ideas in one paragraph, starting with: 'I think the book is called *The Apple Tart of Hope* because …'

Extract 1 from *The Apple Tart of Hope* by Sarah Moore Fitzgerald

He came over all the time and we'd hang out. One day we sat under the kitchen table in my house and carved our names on it where nobody could see. And from then on that table was special because it had our secret underneath.

You don't notice yourself growing up, but one day, sooner or later, it's just not comfortable to sit under the kitchen table anymore. When we were old enough to be allowed out on our own, the first place we used to go was the harbour to throw stones into the water. We took it in turns to see who could skim theirs furthest. I always used to win, but he didn't care.

'Everyone has their special skills,' he'd say, 'and one of yours happens to be a strong intuitive sense of the aerodynamics and contact requirements of disc-shaped seashore skimming stones.'

He'd make me laugh almost all the time with the way he spoke, and the things he said.

We got to sitting at our windows, late at night, at the end of every day. He was different from anyone I'd ever met, and when Oscar was my friend, nothing was annoying or complicated. Everything was simple and enjoyable and fun. Everything made sense.

I don't remember now who took the photo of us, but I've had it in my room for years. We're leaning out of our windows and we're laughing at each other with a joyfulness purer

than anything to do with the polite smiling you get used to doing when you get older. That photo has the kind of proper smiles that happen when you're looking straight into the face of someone who's been your best friend for a long time.

During the weeks before the trip, our talks had taken on a new and mournful tone. I'd sit at my window sniffing while Oscar sat at his, looking at me with a tender kind of frown on his face. He had this way of swinging his legs from side to side with his hands on the window frame, holding on. I'd developed a habit myself that involved picking the loose plaster off our outside wall. It was a measly kind of rebellion – my resentful response to feeling so sorrowful and so misunderstood.

The nights before I left were hotter than I had ever remembered. But in our town, even on the stillest of summer nights, the cold is never far away.

I told him about how I didn't want to go – how my parents were robbing me of my most fundamental human right by making me do something that was completely against my will. I told him about what nightmares I was having because of the gigantically hard job it was going to be to get to know bunches of New Zealand people I'd never met, and who already had friends and weren't in the market for a new pale red-haired freckly one from Ireland.

Even though Oscar Dunleavy was my friend, it didn't mean he automatically agreed with everything I said, or believed the things I believed. And when it came to our trip, he was definitely on my parents' side. He told me I should embrace it, which is exactly what Mum and Dad had been saying the whole time too. Embracing it, he reckoned, was the only way anyone should treat an opportunity like the one that was being handed to me on a plate.

'It's really not something to complain about,' he had said, pointing out that I was going somewhere brilliant and different for half a year, and reminding me that I'd be living in a house that had a swimming pool in the garden and a fantastic lake nearby surrounded by mountains. He said that if I was grumpy about a trip like that, people would get jealous of me – they'd think I was taking for granted something that hardly anyone ever got a chance to do, which is to get away from the life they're living, and try a completely new one for a while.

According to him, it could be quite bad luck to have the evil eye of resentment following me around when I was in the middle of getting used to a whole different country.

I tried to explain to Oscar how dangerous and unrelenting the sun was going to be, and how, compared to the New Zealand people, I would look so pale that everyone was going to assume I had some serious illness or pigmentation-related disability. I was sure to be marked out as a misfit, and I was positive that no one was going to talk to me.

'They're going to be *dying* to talk to you,' he had said. 'Nobody's going to think there's anything wrong with you. You'll be exotic and fascinating and pretty much the whole population will want to be your friend. Plus, there are things that have been invented for hot climates, you know, like sun block. Air-conditioning. T-shirts. Meg, there's a solution to every problem. What you're doing right now is looking for reasons not to want to go.'

He told me that within a few short weeks I'd have forgotten all my unwillingness about the trip and that I'd be populating my Facebook page with photos of smiling sunny fantasticness.

Meanwhile, back here, he reminded me, the Irish winter would be sneaking up on everyone. The mornings would be growing colder and gloomier, and getting up for school would be the depressing activity that we both knew well. By the time October came everyone's teeth would be chattering, their hands fused in claw-like grips around the handlebars of their bikes because of the icy rain that would be pelting down from a great height.

'How many people do you know who have ever had the chance of a sunshine-filled expedition to a new bright land with white beaches and outdoor parties and surfing lessons?'

I kept doing my best to try to think that he was right. But there was an anger in me that seeped onto almost everything during those weeks before I left. My parents hadn't the decency to check with me, not even out of curiosity, whether the trip was something I was interested in. I couldn't stop thinking about that, and dwelling on it, and it had soured the air around me.

I'd wanted a mature discussion, which would have included me informing my parents – because it had obviously escaped their notice – that I wasn't cut out for New Zealand, what with my love of temperate climates and my prawn-like complexion.

EXPLORE

1. Make a list of Oscar's positive qualities, as described by Meg.

2. Oscar tries to convince Meg that her trip to New Zealand will be a positive one. List three of the reasons he gives her.

3. Which of these characters would you like to be friends with? Explain your answer, giving examples.

4. The style of this text is casual and conversational as it is written from a teenage girl's perspective. Can you find any evidence of this style? (See the Top Tip on page 19 to revise this style.)

5. **Characterisation** is the idea of creating characters from a narrative. Characters may be presented through descriptions, their actions, speech, thoughts and how they interact with other characters.

   The characterisation in this novel is very powerful. Choose three adjectives to describe each of the two characters you met in this extract. Back up your choice of adjectives with characterisation evidence from the story, e.g. speech, thoughts. For example:

Oscar is very intelligent. We see this through his speech when he uses a range of complicated phrases to describe something. For example, he describes Meg's 'special skills' by saying 'one of yours happens to be a strong intuitive sense of the aerodynamics and contact requirements …' He has used very complex and technical vocabulary here to describe his friend's good qualities when he could easily use simple language. This makes me wonder if he is trying to sound clever and perhaps hiding his insecurities behind big words. It's a really interesting character trait which made me think a lot about Oscar as a character.

SPEAK

Meg comments that, 'Even though Oscar Dunleavy was my friend it didn't mean he automatically agreed with everything I said, or believed the things I believed.'

In groups, discuss whether you think that this is the mark of a good or bad friend? Be able to explain your answer.

READ

Now read the second extract from the novel. This time, we hear what happened from Oscar's perspective. In this scene he is hiding out in the house of a local man (Barney), while everybody searches for him, presuming that he is dead.

Extract 2 from *The Apple Tart of Hope* by Sarah Moore Fitzgerald

Barney had asked me to start from the beginning.

'The beginning of what?' I asked him, and he said, 'Try to think of when things started to go wrong. Go back to the moment when you set off along this path, this path where you, you fine young fellow, you charming boy, thought a good option would be to drown yourself in the sea. Have a think about it before you start talking. I have plenty of time.'

And he rustled around the cluttered living room with the big soft broken chair in the middle of it, and he sat in another chair next to it and looked straight at me. He had no computer or phone or iPad or even a TV as far as I could see. Towers of dusty books surrounded us.

I could feel something that I hadn't felt for a long time. Something quiet and difficult to spot, but it was the feeling that you get when someone is listening to you. Really listening carefully. And it makes you want to tell things exactly the right way. It makes you want to take your time, and explain, and get it right.

I told him how much I'd missed Meg, but also how Paloma Killealy was a great new arrival in the neighbourhood and how everybody liked having her around and how nice her hair was and how everyone thought she was beautiful.

'Ok then, let's start with Paloma,' he'd suggested, which I suppose was as good a place as any.

'I may have taught her a lot of stuff that I am quite good at explaining, but she has taught me a lot too.

'In particular, the thing that sticks in my mind most is what she told me when she first arrived about a thing called The Ratio. It's a useful thing for anyone to be aware of, and if it hadn't been for her, I'd never have known about it.'

'The Ratio?' said Barney, quietly building up the little fire, slowly placing sticks in a pile and then balancing a big wooden block on top of them.

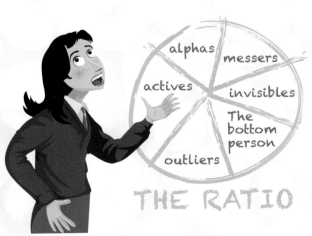

'Yes,' I replied. 'The Ratio. Paloma knew a lot about it because she'd moved a total of seven times since she started school. You learn stuff when you move around like that. Not everyone knows about The Ratio, but it's always the same, no matter what school you go to.'

Paloma said it was kind of **a universal rule**. If you've ever been at school, like ever in your whole life, you should have some inkling, some vague idea that it exists.

* STOP*

What does the word 'ratio' normally mean? Discuss this in your groups. Now think about what it could mean in the context of this story. *Now read on …*

For any class of average size, this is roughly the way it goes:

There'll usually be four or five alphas: top dogs, people like Andy and Greg, she told me. They'll walk in slow motion, like astronauts, and they never have to move out of anyone's way. Their lockers are always closest to the door. They don't have to wait in the queue and everyone looks at them when they pass by. Each of the alphas has one or two hangers-on but they are faithful and true in a way that alphas don't ever seem to deserve.

Invisibles are another group; around seven smart, decent, quiet, good kids who no one takes much notice of and whose name Paloma predicted everyone would forget within a year of leaving school. And then the 'actives' are five cheerful souls who never seem to notice **the underbelly that lurks like a watchful reptile in every class**. They throw themselves into ten-kilometre runs and colour days and events designed to make the place look like a wholesome, simple, happy, straightforward place.

There are three or four serious messers – their sequence on the ladder changes daily; they'll lose their popularity in a split second by flicking a spit ball at some target and accidentally hitting Andy Fewer.

There is a small bunch of outliers: the punky, kohl-eyed, T-shirted, pink-haired, black-booted, note-book writing, music-listening crew, never quite knowing where they fit in and not being sure if they ever want to.

And that's pretty much it. Except for one more. One other person. The person on the bottom. Nobody wants to be a member of this sad little one-man club, but somebody always is.

'Sounds complicated,' I'd said.

'That's because it is,' she'd replied. 'Knowing The Ratio is vital,' she claimed.

'Is it?' I asked her. I told her that our class was not like that. Everyone got on with each other. **We didn't have any outliers** and certainly nobody who was the 'bottom one'.

'Oh yes you do,' she said, 'or if you don't, you will.'

'Are you sure?'

'Yes, I am,' she replied

Even as we spoke, I'd already started to worry that I might be missing something. I kept suggesting that maybe The Ratio existed in other places, like the places she had been, but I hadn't seen any evidence of it here. And I remember she'd slid a flat stick of chewing gum out of its foil and pointed it at me as if it was a wand, to help emphasise the next bit of the lesson.

'Oscar, you're wrong. The Radio is everywhere. You need to challenge every single one of the things you think are true. **There are surface impressions and then there's**

the reality that sits beneath the surface. Someone like you might be innocent enough to think that studying Maths and English and Science and Geography and History are the most important things you need to do to get ahead at school. That's probably what you've been told.

'But listen to me, Oscar, I'm doing you a massive favour by telling you what I know: it's much, much more important to study The Ratio. That's what you really need to understand. It's where the power lies: it's all about who you can afford to annoy, and who you can't. Where you are, and how likely you are to move. How stable your position is. At the moment, that's up in the air for me because this is the beginning – because I'm new.

'You may think that a casual conversation with a harmless-looking person is of no consequence, but you've got to be incredibly careful. The decisions you make matter. They matter very much. And if you get in too deep, it's difficult to go back.

'No one's going to be able to help you if you get stuck in the wrong category. Look at me, Oscar,' she said and she held me by the shoulders and I could feel her slender fingers kind of digging into me – she spoke as if this was the most important thing I was probably ever going to learn.

'These things do *not* work themselves out. This will not pass. Do take notice. Take a *lot* of notice. This is the rest of your *life* we're talking about. This is not something simple.'

'So are you studying the form at the moment? Have you placed everyone in one of your categories already?'

'Me? Oh goodness no, Oscar,' Paloma replied, using this old-fashioned kind of voice and raising her perfect eyebrows in a high, indignant arch.

'This is the world order I'm talking about. This doesn't come from *me*! Come on, I wouldn't take it on myself to label anyone in that way. All I'm saying is that's what people do. But me? Don't you know me by now? Can't you see that I just want to be everyone's friend?'

* * *

Barney said that in his opinion, a thing like The Ratio only existed if people believed in it.

'I know,' I replied. 'I mean, I had completely thought that too. At first I'd thought she had it wrong. I thought she was applying some random set of rules to her new environment, the same way she had when she thought boys were supposed to take girls to The Energiser and stuff like that. I kept trying to tell her that The Ratio didn't exist here, but she kept telling me that it did. It was everywhere, she said; it's basically the way human beings work.

'And you see Barney, it turns out she was right. It turns out that there'd been a vacancy for the Person At The Bottom, and not long after she briefed me about it, I was the one who filled it. I must have been the näivest person on the planet – thinking that everyone got along with everyone else – liking the people in my class and assuming that they liked me. But our links with one another had been damaged and poisoned somehow, and it's funny, but no sooner had Paloma told me about The Ratio, than I started to notice it. You see, Barney, coincidentally, it was right then that everything started to go wrong.'

'Doesn't sound like a coincidence to me,' said Barney.

The Energiser: the local disco

1. Read the following statements and decide whether they are true or false, based on what you remember. **Do not** go back and check yet – this is a test of your memory. Tick the boxes on the left hand side to indicate if the statement is true or false.

Answer here from memory **after your first reading** of the extract			Answer these questions again **after re-reading** the extract	
True	**False**	**Statement**	**True**	**False**
		Barney does not have a lot of modern technology in his house		
		'The Ratio' was Oscar's invention		

Answer here from memory **after your first reading** of the extract			Answer these questions again **after re-reading** the extract	
True	False	Statement	True	False
		An alpha is someone at the bottom who is very unpopular		
		Outliers tend to have pink hair and write in notebooks		
		Barney believes The Ratio is true whether you believe it or not		
		The Energiser is the name of the local disco		
		Paloma says that she is one of the 'invisibles'		
		Oscar believes that people never liked him		

2. Re-read the text, and check your answers from the text, this time ticking the boxes on the right hand side.

3. Explain the terms or sentences bolded in the text, in your own words.

4. There are two new key characters introduced in this extract. Explore the role of one of these characters, explaining how they influence Oscar and the plot.

5. Choose a **key moment** in this section and explain how it affects one or more of the main characters.

6. Is this the type of book you would like to read? Explain your answer, mentioning features of the writing that influenced you – characterisation, language, drama, tension, narration, setting, etc.

Key moment *n.*

Definition: A moment of special importance or significance. It may be a moment of great emotional impact, a moment that throws light on our understanding of a character or a moment that marks a turning point in a story.

REMEMBER

Plot is a literary term used to describe the events that make up a story or main part of a story. Characters may be presented through descriptions, their actions, speech, thoughts and how they interact with other characters.

SPEAK

Discuss the following questions in pairs or groups.

1. What technique(s) does Paloma use to make Oscar doubt himself?

2. Does 'The Ratio' exist in Irish schools, in your opinion? If so, does it or would it have an effect on students? What kind of negative effects could this system have on students?

3. How can students work to ensure that systems like this don't become the norm in classrooms or schools?

CREATE

The Ratio is the kind of thinking that causes some students to be isolated/bullied. Make a short advertisement (for radio, print, TV or internet) which could be shown to secondary students during Anti-Bullying Week. The purpose of the advertisement is to emphasise the importance of treating everyone fairly and equally and to discourage bullying. For ideas that you might include, go to www.antibullyingireland.com

Bullying is a very serious issue and not tolerated in Irish schools. If you or someone you know is being bullied, please speak to an adult. Alternatively you can contact any of the organisations listed on www.antibullyingireland.com, such as **Childline** on **1800 66 66 66** (6 p.m.–10 p.m. daily) and **Samaritans Ireland** on **116 123**.

An Audio Piece

What I will learn:

to listen actively to get the gist of a story; techniques to learn spellings and new vocabulary

PREPARE

Look at this photo of a group of girls and imagine the relationship between them. How do they know each other, do you think? Now make up a scenario where three of them have a disagreement.

You will now listen to a tale told by one of the girls in the photo about an argument they had and you can see if you guessed correctly. This story is from *Sunday Miscellany*, a popular long-running radio series from RTÉ Radio 1. The show consists of short anecdotes that are written by listeners and then recorded in a studio by them. They are then broadcast on the radio. The stories are usually about small, commonplace events that had a big effect on the person telling the story.

TOP TIP

An anecdote is a short amusing or interesting story about a real incident or person.

'Picturing the Past' by Barbara McKeon

As you listen to this piece, 'Picturing the Past' by Barbara McKeon, answer these questions.

EXPLORE

1. What kind of friendship did the girls in the tale have?

2. What do you think the author is saying about the theme of friendship?

3. Did you like this piece? Explain your answer.

W1.7

MIND YOUR LANGUAGE

VOCABULARY AND SPELLING

Listen to the piece again and complete the following exercise.

1. In your copy, under these three headings, write down the words that arise under the relevant heading:

Words I already knew

Words I guessed from the context

Words I didn't understand

2. Now, compare this list with a small group of students and see how many you can work out between you. For any words you still don't understand or need to check the spelling of, use your **dictionary**.

3. When you are sure about their meaning and spelling, take five minutes to learn the spelling of as many of these words as possible, and then test each other by calling out the word and seeing who can spell it. Help each other out if you like!

TOP TIP

Use the Safe Spelling Code: **LOOK • COVER • WRITE • CHECK**

Look at the word and memorise the spelling. Now cover it so that you can't see it. Try to write it out from memory. Check to make sure you spelled it correctly. If you didn't spell it correctly you need to go through the process again until you know it.

SHOW WHAT YOU KNOW

You have learned many writing and speaking skills in this collection of texts.
Now it's time to *Show What You Know!*

My Writing Task

Your school has decided to publish a school magazine for the first time and it will include a review page.
Write a review for the magazine.

You can review anything that interests you (e.g. a book, film, play, article, advertisement, poem, album, documentary, website, CD or video game). Reviews should be 300–400 words in length. You might get some ideas from: www.juniorcycle.ie/NCCA_JuniorCycle/media/NCCA/Documents/Curriculum/ENGLISH/ FINAL_Suggested-Texts-05-2014_1.pdf

SUCCESS CRITERIA

I should
- Use the RAFT structure
- Mention things I would like to change about the item/product I reviewed/ways to improve it
- State whether I would recommend it to others (explaining why)
- Suggest what age groups would enjoy it
- Give it a star rating

I must
- Include the title of the book, film, CD, website, video game, etc.
- Mention who wrote/directed/made/designed it (e.g. writer, director, game designer, etc.)
- Use language appropriate for my target audience
- Include a brief summary of the content (in three sentences)
- State my general opinion (what I liked and didn't like)

I could
- Include an image to represent the review
- Mention quotes from or an interview with people who actually read/saw/ used the item/product

Here is a list of some vocabulary which might help you to write an interesting review.

In my opinion	I found this	I would (not) recommend	In my experience	Personally
director	designer	writer	playwright	artist
features	plot	furthermore	finally	however
engaging	interesting	dialogue	characters	special effects
challenging	educational	well-researched	attention-grabbing	predicable
uninspiring	dramatic	disappointing	entertaining	compelling

Reflection Note
If you choose to place this task into your **Collection of Texts**, complete a **reflection note**.
Hint: See the success criteria above to help you.

Self-Assessment

Re-read what you have written and then write down two things you think you did well and one thing you could improve on.

Redrafting

Reviewing the success criteria again to make sure you have met all the requirements, and taking into account your own self-assessment notes, you can now revise your blog to create a second draft. When you are happy with your review, you can put it in your Collection of Texts.

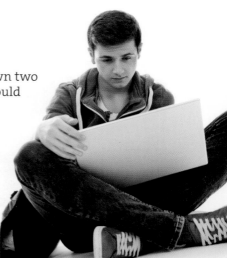

Oral Communication

Choose an interesting photograph from your life/from the life of someone you know personally/from a celebrity's life, and tell an anecdote (story) about the person/people in it.

SUCCESS CRITERIA

I must

- Use 'Picturing the Past', the *Sunday Miscellany* piece and other examples of oral storytelling (e.g. The Moth), to guide my research*
- Use a photograph and show it/project it onto a screen while I speak
- Describe an anecdote (real or imagined), which includes some or all of the people in the photograph
- Make bullet points of what I wish to say and then make changes after someone else has listened to me and made suggestions
- Speak for 2–3 minutes, varying my tone, pitch and pace. (See page 438 for more speaking tips.)

I should

- Include a beginning, middle and end to the story
- Introduce the person/people in the photograph (explain who they are and how they know each other)
- Try to draw on as many of the five senses as possible to enhance the description
- Practise speaking my anecdote until I know it and can perform it confidently

*For other oral storytelling examples, go to page 441

I could

- Use dialogue or humour, if appropriate
- Refer to the *Sunday Miscellany* website for guidelines: www.rte.ie/radio1/sundaymiscellany; or to The Moth website for storytelling tips: http://themoth.org/tell-a-story/storytelling-tips

Peer Assessment

Ask another student to listen to your work and to note two things that you did well and one thing you could change. This will help you to redraft your work.

Redrafting

After you have practised reciting your anecdote in front of someone, make a list of ways you can improve it. You should also review the success criteria again. At this point, make any necessary changes to your speech. When you are happy with it, you can present it orally or record and then present/submit it to your teacher.

Reflection Note

Now complete the **Oral Communication Template for Student Reflection.**

War

Formal language and proper vocabulary for news reports

Expressing personal opinions

Using a photograph to inspire a story

Proof-reading skills in punctuation and spelling

Infographics or 'Information Visualisation'

As I explore this collection I will learn about:

What register means

The use of satire to ridicule or make a point

How a writer develops characters

The use of puns in poetry

Four-part structure of a short story: setting/action/climax/resolution

A mind map for a dramatic performance of a poem

Listening to other students' work and giving helpful comments

SHOW WHAT YOU KNOW

The skills you learn in this collection will enable you to **show what you know** in your final tasks at the end of this collection.

For my writing task I will:
Write a news broadcast about a missile attack on a city

For oral communication I will:
Speak my news broadcast as if I were a radio or television newsreader

Learning Outcomes
OL5, OL8, OL12, R1, R6, R9, W2, W3, W13

Exploring the Theme – War

War *n.*

Definition: fighting between nations, groups or states, using weapons and armies, and causing vast destruction and loss of life

Do you read newspapers or listen to the morning or evening news? For the next few weeks, as you study this collection and to enable you to do the Writing and Oral tasks on pages 74 and 75, you will need to do both. Inform yourself about war in the world today.

You will also need to begin looking at some reliable news websites, e.g. RTÉ, *The Irish Times*, BBC, *The New York Times*, *The Guardian*, and those recommended by your teacher.

Using the map below, name three areas where war is happening today. If you can name the warring countries, peoples or armies, do so. This is the start of your war research.

Personal Opinions About War and Weapons

W2.1

Statement	Agree	Disagree	Because ...
There is never a good reason to go to war			
War is the only way to stop a country or group that threatens to attack			
War memorials are a waste of money			
Countries spend too much money on weapons			
Write a statement of your own about war with which you strongly agree or disagree			

Children in War

What I will learn:

how to make a point in an introduction to a newspaper article and then prove the point in what follows; to appreciate a letter written in a child's words; to improve my proof-reading skills by correcting punctuation, capital letters and spelling

Many stories have been written about children living through wartime, among them, *Goodnight Mr Tom*, *War Horse*, *Private Peaceful*, *The Diary of a Young Girl*, and *The Silver Sword*.

Can you name the authors of these stories? Do you know of any others?

Using one of these three photographs as a prompt, write an opening paragraph of a story. Suggest a title for your story.

Extract from *When the Children Came Home: Stories of Wartime Evacuees* by Julie Summers

Millions of British city children were evacuated to safer places during the Second World War. Some hated living away from their families – others didn't want to go home again.

The greatest evacuation of children in British history began on Friday, 1 September 1939. It was codenamed 'Operation Pied Piper'. Who on earth came up with that name? Not a mother, that is certain. After all, the Piper leads the children of Hamelin away from the town, never to return.

Over the six years of the war, more than two million children were sent away from their family homes. Most returned, but how they had changed and how the separation affected their relationships with their families is seldom considered.

What must it have been like to have been sent away from home at five, 10 or even 14, as some of the older ones were, and then come home months – or, more often, years – later and have to pick up where you left off? Is it even possible when your life has changed in all other respects? […]

Joan Risley is keen to emphasise the good points in her experience. She was evacuated twice. The first time, she went with her sister to Beccles, in Suffolk. They were home by the beginning of 1940 but when an invasion seemed likely, Joan announced that she wished to be evacuated again. None of her brothers and sisters wanted to go too, so she was sent alone, aged nine, to Northamptonshire. She lived there with a childless couple who loved and cared for her as their own.

When she returned in 1945 she found it difficult: 'I remember sitting on a sofa with a feeling of not belonging. By that time we were really poor. Dad was still ill and unable to work. My family all commented on how I talked different, so I had that strange feeling of not quite belonging yet wanting to be there because they were my family. I soon got used to being with Mum, and she got used to me. But with my siblings it was more difficult. They are my family and I am very fond of them but they never went away like I did, so they don't understand that I have had these two lives.'

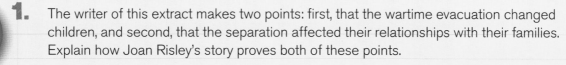

1. The writer of this extract makes two points: first, that the wartime evacuation changed children, and second, that the separation affected their relationships with their families. Explain how Joan Risley's story proves both of these points.

2. Joan lived through the war with 'a childless couple who loved and cared for her as their own'. Why do you think she found it hard to come back home?

Little Daisy Dobbins looked straight at the man with the camera, clutching the blanket in which Molly, her rag doll, lay asleep. Big sister Rosie stood smiling behind her and little brother Charlie stood shyly at the back. Their tiny house in London had no garden but Mother had told them they were going to a lovely farm in the country with hens and ducks and chickens. Cheerful Rosie, in her brand new hat, saw herself feeding the ducks and collecting eggs in the morning with the farmer's wife, like in her storybook. But Daisy and Charlie were worried because they were little and still had nightmares. Mother wouldn't be there to comfort them in the dark and whisper it was all right now.

CREATE

1. In this photograph there are seven evacuee children. Choose one of them and write 180–205 words about your chosen child as if you were a journalist who had interviewed this little boy or girl. Tick off each point in the grid below as you cover it.

Here is an example from a student who remembered to give the children old-fashioned names.

Checklist for Writing your Article

Point	Tick
Give the child a name and perhaps an age	
Say something about what he/she is wearing or holding	
Imagine what he/she is thinking	
Mention the home they are coming from and their image of where they are going	
Say something about their hopes or fears	
Add another idea of your own	

If you write a good article, you could keep it safely and then return to it at some point in the future to expand it into a good short story for your collection.

2. There are constant stories in the news about children living in warzones. Choose one such story that you have heard or read about on the news or in a newspaper or on a reliable website. Write a 3–4 sentence radio or TV news item presenting this story. Read your news item aloud.

Here are the opening sentences of articles written by students.

The body of an unidentified little boy has been found on a beach on the Greek island of Kos. It is believed that the child drowned in a failed attempt to sail from Turkey to Greece ...

In a terrifying night of bombing and shelling in the city centre, two children have been reported killed in an apartment block that collapsed following a mortar attack...

BRITONS

"WANTS"
YOU
JOIN YOUR COUNTRY'S ARMY!
GOD SAVE THE KING
Reproduced by permission of LONDON OPINION

READ

Lord Kitchener, British Secretary of State for War in 1914, was the face on the famous World War I recruiting poster, 'Join Your Country's Army'!

In 1914, at the outbreak of World War I, Alfie Knight, a nine-year-old Dublin boy, had a very innocent vision of war and of how he could play his part in it. He wrote a letter to Lord Kitchener asking if he could join the army. This letter is now on display in the Imperial War Museum in London.

Dear Lord Kitchner,

I am an Irish boy 9 years of age and I want to go to the front I can ride jolley quick on my bicycle and would go as despatch ridder I wouldint let the germans get it. I am a good shot with a revolver and would kill a good vue of the germans. I am very strong and often win a fight with lads twice as big as mysels. I want a uneform and a revolver and will give a good acount of myself. pleese send an anencer

Yours affectionately
Alfie Knight

A despatch rider was a military messenger who delivered urgent messages between headquarters and the army at the front.

EXPLORE

1. What skills and talents does Alfie offer in his letter?

2. Alfie has asked you to rewrite his letter correcting his spelling. Rewrite it, 'polishing it up'. Do not change his words or sentences because that would take away his personal style. Simply correct the spellings and insert capital letters and punctuation where they are needed.

CREATE

In a reply to Alfie, sent by his private secretary, Lord Kitchener thanked him for his offer but explained that he was 'not yet quite old enough to go to the front'.

Write the full letter of response that you think the private secretary would have sent to Alfie. Remember that he would have used formal language – in the style of official letters from government departments – but knowing that he was writing to a child, he would have kept his language simple.

Women and Armed Conflict – An Infographic

What I will learn:

how to read an infographic

Infographics or 'Information Visualisation'

An infographic (information graphic) lays out information, ideas, statistics, or even a story, in the form of a diagram, i.e. a mixture of pictures and words. It can present a large amount of data in images, which is an easy way for a reader to process information. It may use colour to highlight facts and figures. A good infographic is a powerful text that presents a topic in a clear, visual layout.

The infographic opposite was designed by the United Nations in October 2015. It explains how war has a damaging impact on the lives of women and girls. Not only do they suffer violence, but their health, education and legal rights are all damaged, even when the war is over.

This infographic has an advanced vocabulary. You will be better able to understand it if you match these words and their definitions before you begin.

Reconciliation	the process of putting a decision or plan into action
Consequences	make people who were fighting become friends and be at peace
Radicalisation	results of something that happens
Monitoring	relating to mothers
Maternal	talks to get compromise or agreement
Exacerbates	smaller figures added together to make the final figure
Aggregate figure	giving confidence, self-esteem and power
Negotiations	make a bad situation even worse
Implementation	checking to see that things are properly done
Empowering	make people become radical or extreme in their attitudes

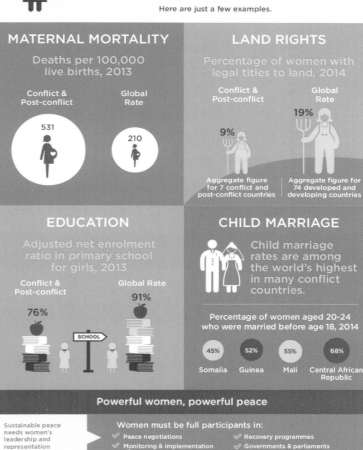

WOMEN & ARMED CONFLICT

"Women are the best drivers of growth, the best hope for reconciliation in conflict and the best buffer against the radicalization of youth and the repetition of cycles of violence."

— Phumzile Mlambo-Ngcuka, UN Women Executive Director

The destructive effects of conflict on women and girls: A snapshot

Women and girls bear the brunt of many of the harmful consequences of armed violence.

In the last two decades, the use of violence against women and girls during conflicts, and especially sexual violence, has become more visible.

But aside from increased sexual violence, conflict exacerbates many inequalities that can last well after a war ends.

Here are just a few examples.

MATERNAL MORTALITY

Deaths per 100,000 live births, 2013

Conflict & Post-conflict: 531
Global Rate: 210

LAND RIGHTS

Percentage of women with legal titles to land, 2014

Conflict & Post-conflict: 9%
Global Rate: 19%

Aggregate figure for 7 conflict and post-conflict countries
Aggregate figure for 74 developed and developing countries

EDUCATION

Adjusted net enrolment ratio in primary school for girls, 2013

Conflict & Post-conflict: 76%
Global Rate: 91%

SCHOOL

CHILD MARRIAGE

Child marriage rates are among the world's highest in many conflict countries.

Percentage of women aged 20-24 who were married before age 18, 2014

Somalia: 45%
Guinea: 52%
Mali: 55%
Central African Republic: 68%

Powerful women, powerful peace

Sustainable peace needs women's leadership and representation at all levels of decision-making.

Women must be full participants in:
- ✓ Peace negotiations
- ✓ Monitoring & implementation of peace agreements
- ✓ Post-conflict planning
- ✓ Peacekeeping missions
- ✓ Recovery programmes
- ✓ Governments & parliaments
- ✓ Security & justice sectors
- ✓ Administration of public services
- ✓ Transitional justice

"Protecting and empowering women during and after conflicts is one of the most important challenges of our time."

— Ban Ki-moon, UN Secretary-General

UN WOMEN

unwomen.org

@UN_Women   facebook.com/unwomen   gplus.to/unwomen

Sources: UN Maternal Mortality Estimation Inter-agency Group (MMEInfo); Population Division's World Fertility Data, Interpolated Annual Indicators, 2012 Land Rights Database, FAO, 2014; UNESCO Institute for Statistics (education data as of June 2015); Monitoring the Situation of Children and Women (Child Protection/Child Marriage), UNICEF; United Nations World Population Prospects, UN DESA, 2012
Quote: Side by Side - Women, Peace and Security, video (Ban Ki-moon)
Credits: Vector icons: Flaticon; Photo: UN Photo/Eskinder Debebe (Ban Ki-moon)

EXPLORE

Study the infographic on women and armed conflict carefully, then complete the following sentences using only the information provided.

1. Worldwide, in developed and developing countries, out of every 100 women, _____ own land.

2. In countries affected by war, out of every 100 women, _____ own land, either during war or when it is over.

3. For the year 2013, out of every 100,000 babies born, in countries affected by war, _____ died.

4. In the same year, the worldwide *survival* figure out of every 100,000 babies born was _____.

5. The country referred to in the infographic with the lowest figure for girls marrying before the age of 18 is _____.

6. In the Central African Republic, 32 out of every 100 women aged 20–24 were married before the age of 18. True or false?

7. In Somalia, a higher percentage of women marry before the age of 18 than in Mali. True or false?

8. Name the United Nations Secretary General who is quoted in the infographic. In your own words, explain what this person says.

Formal and Informal Register

What I will learn:

what 'register' means; how to use appropriate register in a news report

Register means style of writing or speaking, i.e. the words we use, how formal we are and even how careful we are in pronouncing words. We use formal register in speeches, newspaper editorials, reports, important letters, at very solemn moments and in legal documents. Alfie Knight used a child's register in his letter to Lord Kitchener, but read his letter again and you will notice how he did his very best to be formal.

We use **informal register** when we chat to our friends. We shorten words and speak casually in a way that might not be acceptable if we were addressing someone we weren't so familiar with. 'Hey' or 'Hi' are examples of casual, informal register, whereas 'Good afternoon' or 'Good evening' are formal.

A news report uses **formal register**. It will not use slang words. It aims to be precise and correct as it gives information to readers or listeners. An epitaph is written in a solemn, formal register, e.g. *in loving memory of …*

Epitaph *n.*

Definition: Words written on a tombstone or a memorial

Test your understanding of register by linking the extracts below with the correct text. In each case, say if the language is formal or informal.

Extract 1

This is Martin Brophy, standing before the shattered remains of government buildings in Mapalinda, which was struck at dawn by an air-to-ground missile attack.

a) Epitaph for the small force of three hundred Spartan (Greek) soldiers who, in 480 B.C., died, heroically defending the pass of Thermopylae against a huge invading Persian army.

Extract 2

Go, stranger, and to the Spartans tell
That here, obedient to their word, we fell.

b) Eyewitness speaking to an interviewer just after an explosion.

Extract 3

The ground broke open … it was just brutal, mad … black smoke all over the shop … everyone legging it, crashing into the street … windows smashed to bits …

c) TV journalist in a foreign city speaking to camera.

Read each extract aloud in the tone of voice you think appropriate.

The Language of News Broadcasts – A Vocabulary Test

Place the correct word beside its definition. Cross out each word as you use it. Some have been done for you.

	Correct word	Definition
ambush		Remove people from danger to safety
ammunition		People killed or injured
~~annihilate~~		Soldiers who are not part of an official army
~~arsenal~~		Vehicles or ships travelling in a line for safety
atrocities		Place where vehicles are stopped to be checked
barricades		Hole in ground to protect soldier from enemy fire
bombardment		A strike back after an attack
booby trap		Cruel, shocking, violent acts
casualties		Bullets, shells etc. fired from weapons
ceasefire	annihilate	Destroy completely
checkpoint		Heavy firing of bombs from aircraft
civil war	conquer	Defeat in battle, take control of country or people
civilian		Line of objects to stop people passing through
counter-attack		Object containing hidden explosive device
~~conquer~~		Another word for spying
conscription		Citizen who is not a member of the army
convoy		Being made to join the army or navy
curfew		A surprise attack by people waiting and hiding
espionage		Murder of all people of a race or religion
evacuate		An order for civilians to stay in their homes
foxhole		War between citizens of the same country
genocide		A temporary agreement to stop fighting
guerrillas	arsenal	A store or collection of weapons

In groups of three, **A** calls out the definition, **B** replies with the correct word, **C** holds the page to act as checker.

Place the correct word beside its definition. Cross out each word as you use it. Some have been done for you.

	Correct word	Definition
infantry		A small battle
informant	mortar	Large heavy gun that fires bombs high in the air
liberation		Abbreviation of 'prisoner of war'
massacre		Small group of infantry soldiers
~~mediation~~		Crush to small bits
mobilise		Someone who passes information to police
~~militants~~		Country with great power and influence
mine		Extra troops sent in to support an army
neutral		Bomb placed underground which explodes when touched
paramedic		Freeing of a city or people from military control
POW		Agreement to stop fighting
platoon		Death on a large scale
pulverise		Taking neither side in a war
refugees		Person who treats injured people before arrival in hospital
reinforcements	mediation	Attempts to get sides to meet and end a war
retreat		Order troops to move into a region or battle
~~mortar~~	militants	Fighters who do not belong to a regular army
superpower		Move backwards after a defeat
skirmish		People escaping from war or persecution
strongholds		Foot soldiers
truce		Place where the enemy has most soldiers

In groups of three, **A** calls out the definition, **B** replies with the correct word, **C** holds the page to act as checker.

A News Report

  This news broadcast gives a vivid picture of a city under attack.

Following a brief ceasefire, hostilities have resumed in the besieged town of Limenia, where fierce fighting and shelling shook the city overnight. Mortar bombs have caused massive destruction as panicked civilians tried to flee the city.

Orla Colvin, our correspondent in Limenia, has taken refuge in the central hospital, from where she sends us this report.

Good evening, Andrew.

Last night, the city of Limenia came under fierce bombardment. For hours, explosions lit up the sky, and when dawn broke, we could see that a whole area of the city had been reduced to rubble. This morning, thick, dark smoke rises above us.

A curfew has been put in place by the government. In this very tense atmosphere, where further bombing is expected, those who can do have already fled. Paramedics are taking the injured to the two hospitals that remain operational, and it is from one of these hospitals that I am bringing you this report. I can tell your listeners that the scenes here are chaotic, with medical supplies fast running out. A convoy of army trucks bringing essential supplies was wiped out in an early-morning ambush. Indeed, we are hearing reports that rebel troops are within hours of the capital.

Normally busy city-centre streets are deserted, apart from Red Cross vehicles. A strange silence and a fear hangs about us, with everyone wondering what the next few hours will bring.

This is Orla Colvin, reporting for the Fire and Ice News Agency in Limenia.

Read this report aloud slowly and clearly, as if you were on camera.

Write a short paragraph explaining in your own words what is happening in the city of Limenia.

Here is a news report written by a student who has used formal language and correct war vocabulary. He then read what he had written aloud and wrote a short reflection on the process.

DAY OF TERROR

The greatest city on the planet is in flames after a spectacular missile strike from the east. The bombardment of New York City began in the early hours of this morning with no warning to allow the city to be evacuated.

Skyscrapers have crumbled to ruins, whole streets are pulverised to rubble, and black clouds of smoke are rising high into the atmosphere. As the city plunged into darkness and chaos, panicked New Yorkers scrambled for their lives. Nowhere was safe. Public transport has ground to a halt and all airports have closed.

The Pentagon has put the country on a war footing and has ordered all military personnel to report for duty. The President is on Air Force One heading for a secret location from which she will direct operations and prepare for counter-attack. Her family has been evacuated to a safe, unidentified location.

Student Reflection

I wanted my report to give a dramatic picture of the destruction and the terror in the city of New York. My headline is good because it's short, eye-catching and factual. I remembered to say **what** happened and to explain **who**, **where** and **when**. The **why** is not known at this point.

I'm very pleased with my action verbs like 'crumbled', 'pulverised' and 'scrambled'. I think my vocabulary is good and I have shown that I know the correct register for a news report. My sentences are different lengths so they sound well when you read them out loud. I explained what is happening for ordinary citizens, but I also gave information about the government and military response to the terror.

I think I could have made it more realistic by naming different places in New York, for example 5th Avenue or Broadway. I definitely should have got an interview with an 'eyewitness', but overall I'm happy that I set out the information clearly in short paragraphs and that I used proper, formal language.

CREATE

In groups of three, write the first three or four sentences of a news report from a city in a war zone. Read your sentences aloud to the rest of your group as if you were a newsreader. Ask them to tell you what you did well and what you could do better.

Reflection Note

Write a short reflection on what you think you did well in the piece you wrote.

Poetry

What I will learn:

the meaning of 'pun' and 'satire'; how a writer uses comical alliteration and black humour to make a serious point

READ

The poet Siegfried Sassoon (*pictured*) fought in World War I and won the Military Cross for his courage in carrying one of his men to safety through heavy artillery fire. Although he was a hero, he was so angry at the fact that hundreds of thousands of men were being slaughtered in horrific battles that he began to write anti-war poems saying the army commanders were wasting soldiers' lives.

TOP TIP

A **pun** is a play on words that have different meanings. The title of this poem by Siegfried Sassoon, 'Base Details', has two puns. 'Base' is a military operations building; but 'base' also means low, disgraceful or shameful. 'Details' means military routines, but also refers to the facts and details of war.

Base Details
by Siegfried Sassoon

If I were fierce, and bald, and short of breath,
I'd live with scarlet Majors at the Base,
And speed glum heroes up the line to death.
You'd see me with my puffy petulant face,
Guzzling and gulping in the best hotel,
Reading the Roll of Honour. 'Poor young chap,'
I'd say – 'I used to know his father well;
Yes, we've lost heavily in this last scrap.'
And when the war is done and youth stone dead,
I'd toddle safely home and die – in bed.

TOP TIP

Satire uses humour or exaggeration to make something or someone look ridiculous. It criticises stupidity or corruption. It could be called 'angry comedy'. This poem is a satire. The **tone** is angry, bleak and savage but also funny. It makes the Major look ridiculous and it pities the soldiers.

Mind-Mapping 'Base Details'

Write 3–4 paragraphs about this poem as if you were directing it to be performed on stage.

Use the mind map to describe the characters, setting, scenery, costumes, lighting, colours and props.

Mind Map for Dramatic Performance of 'Base Details'

Task: To describe the backdrop, the lighting and colours, the scenery, the props, the costumes, how you would represent the soldiers, the words spoken, any music or sound effects you would use. Imagine how the Major looks, what he is doing, what he says, how he walks. The words and phrases you write in each box in the mind map can then become paragraphs in your longer piece of writing about the poem.

Backdrop
The sky lit up with flares?
World War I poster?

Characters
Who? Where?
Army Major/soldiers?

Costumes
In your own words, describe the Major and the soldiers: what colours and uniforms are they wearing? Rain-soaked shoes or shiny polished boots? Who is wearing ribbons or medals?

BASE DETAILS
by
Siegfried Sassoon

Closing moments
Imagine the closing moments of the scene as the Major walks off the stage: 'If I were fierce, and bald and short of breath ... I'd toddle safely home and die – in bed.'

Voiceover
Emphasise the alliteration in the lines spoken by a narrator: *guzzling* and *gulping*.
The rhythm and the rhyming words are fast and jingly as if it was all funny. The last line slows to show how serious and angry the poet is.

Sound effects
Clink of cutlery in restaurant? Voices? Heavy guns?
Battle sounds?

TOP TIP

Find out more about these elements of drama in Collection 8 Part 1.

The General
by Siegfried Sassoon

'Good-morning, good-morning!' the General* said   *a*

When we met him last week on our way to the line.   *b*

Now the soldiers he smiled at are most of 'em dead,   *a*

And we're cursing his staff for incompetent swine.   *b*

'He's a cheery old card,' grunted Harry to Jack   *c*

As they slogged up to Arras** with rifle and pack.   *c*

But he did for them both by his plan of attack.   *c*

General is one of the highest-ranking military commanders. His role is to be an intelligent strategist, planning large-scale military campaigns.

**158,000 men died at Arras, one of the bloodiest, most life-wasting battles of WWI.*

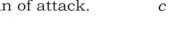

Perform a dramatic reading of this poem. **Tone** (the emotion in your voice), **volume** (loud or soft) and **tempo** (the speed of speaking) will be important.

SPEAK

Instructions

1. Appoint four characters: the General, Harry, Jack, and the narrator.

2. Readers take a few minutes to read the poem silently, preparing the tone of voice that is suitable for their character.

3. Jack and Harry will march together, stooped under imaginary backpacks, with Harry grunting his line, 'He's a cheery old card', when appropriate.

4. The General will pass by calling out 'Good morning, good morning' to them. (Think of his tone, volume and tempo. Imagine any movement or gesture you think he might make.)

5. The narrator will stand nearby and will be sure to pause for a moment before speaking the last line.

6. The class will write comments on the performance, giving each character two stars (two positive comments) and a wish (one suggestion for improvement) for their reading or performance.

The simple rhyme scheme of this poem (*a,b, a,b, c,c,c*) makes it easy to learn by heart. Try to learn it as quickly as you can. Raise your hand when you are ready to recite it. Remember to pause for a few seconds before the last line.

Epitaph on a Tyrant
by W. H. Auden

——————, of a kind, was what he was after,

And the —————————— he invented was easy to understand;

He knew human ————— like the back of his hand,

And was greatly interested in ————— and —————;

When he laughed, respectable ————— burst with laughter,

And when he ————— the little children ————— in the streets.

You can see W. H. Auden recite this poem, along with some powerful footage from World War II, if you look up the poet and poem title on Dailymotion.com

Tyrant: cruel ruler who has complete power

---

1. Some of the words have been removed from this poem. Choose the correct words from the lists below. When you have done this, rewrite the poem as you think it was written.

Line 1	Line 2	Line 3	Line 4	Line 5	Line 6
Love	machine	folly	literature	friends	died
Approval	poetry	habits	armies	relatives	passed away
Perfection	trick	faults	poetry	senators	cried
Fame	literature	intelligence	fleets	enemies	blubbered

2. Are there any words or phrases in this poem that surprised you? Explain.

3. Who are the characters in the poem? For each character, choose one adjective and quote a word, phrase or line from the poem to support your choice.

4. Explain the last line. How would the meaning change if 'died' and 'cried' were reversed?

5. What kind of a person do you think the man of the title was?

6. Can you think of any person (living or dead) who might resemble the tyrant of this poem? Justify your answer.

Pick a character from a poem, play or novel you have studied. Write a short epitaph for his or her gravestone. Remember to use formal language, which is appropriate for an epitaph.

A Short Story

What I will learn:

how a writer develops characters; story structure; an opening that makes readers want to read on; a powerful closing paragraph that makes them think deeply about the story

This short story by Irish writer, Frank O'Connor (*pictured*), is based on a true incident during the Irish War of Independence, a **guerrilla war** between the British forces in Ireland and the Irish Republican Army from 1919 to 1921. In the story, two English soldiers have been captured by Irish rebels and are being held captive in a remote farmhouse. Though their countries are at war, the men talk, play card games and get to know each other. When news of the execution of Irish prisoners comes through, however, the story darkens.

> Guerrilla soldiers are not members of an official army. They make surprise attacks on their enemies.

FUN FACT

This story has inspired two films and has been performed as a play in New York and other cities.

Cast of characters

Belcher: an English prisoner

Bonaparte: the Irish soldier narrator

Jeremiah Donovan: the officer in command of the group of Irish guerrilla fighters

Feeney: an Irish intelligence officer who brings news of the outside world to the farmhouse

Hawkins: the second English prisoner

Noble: the other Irish soldier guarding Belcher and Hawkins

The old woman: tends the house and feeds the men

'Guests of the Nation'
by Frank O'Connor

I

At dusk the big Englishman, Belcher, would shift his long legs out of the ashes and say 'Well, chums, what about it?' and Noble and myself would say, 'All right, chum' (for we had picked up some of their curious expressions), and the little Englishman, Hawkins, would light the lamp and bring out the cards. Sometimes Jeremiah Donovan would come up and supervise the game, and get excited over Hawkins's cards, which he always played badly, and shout at him as if he was one of our own, 'Ah, you divil, why didn't you play the tray?'

But ordinarily Jeremiah was a sober and contented poor devil like the big Englishman, Belcher, and was looked up to only because he was a fair hand at documents, though he was slow even with them. He wore a small cloth hat and big gaiters over his long pants, and you seldom saw him with his hands out of his pockets. He reddened when you talked to him, tilting from toe to heel and back, and looking down all the time at his big farmer's feet. Noble and myself used to make fun of his broad accent, because we were both from the town.

I could not at the time see the point of myself and Noble guarding Belcher and Hawkins at all, for it was my belief that you could have planted that pair down anywhere from this to Claregalway and they'd have taken root there like a native weed. I never in my short experience saw two men take to the country as they did.

They were passed on to us by the Second Battalion when the search for them became too hot, and Noble and myself, being young, took them over with a natural feeling of responsibility, but

Hawkins made us look like fools when he showed that he knew the country better than we did.

'You're the bloke they call Bonaparte,' he says to me. 'Mary Brigid O'Connell told me to ask what you'd done with the pair of her brother's socks you borrowed.'

For it seemed, as they explained it, that the Second had little evenings, and some of the girls of the neighbourhood turned up, and, seeing they were such decent chaps, our fellows could not leave the two Englishmen out. Hawkins learned to dance 'The Walls of Limerick', 'The Siege of Ennis' and 'The Waves of Tory' as well as any of them, though he could not return the compliment, because our lads at that time did not dance foreign dances on principle.

So whatever privileges Belcher and Hawkins had with the Second they just took naturally with us, and after the first couple of days we gave up all pretence of keeping an eye on them. Not that they could have got far, because they had accents you could cut with a knife, and wore khaki tunics and overcoats with civilian pants and boots, but I believe myself they never had any idea of escaping and were quite content to be where they were.

It was a treat to see how Belcher got off with the old woman in the house where we were staying. She was a great warrant to scold, and cranky even with us, but before ever she had a chance of giving our guests, as I may call them, a lick of her tongue, Belcher had made her his friend for life. She was breaking sticks, and Belcher, who had not been more than ten minutes in the house, jumped up and went over to her.

'Allow me, madam,' he said, smiling his queer little smile. 'Please allow me,' and he took the hatchet from her. She was too surprised to speak, and after that, Belcher would be at her heels, carrying a bucket, a basket or a load of turf. As Noble said, he got into looking before she leapt, and hot water, or any little thing she wanted, Belcher would have ready for her. For such a huge man (and though I am five foot ten myself I had to look up at him) he had an uncommon lack of speech. It took us a little while to get used to him, walking in and out like a ghost, without speaking. Especially because Hawkins talked enough for a platoon, it was strange to hear Belcher with his toes in the ashes come out with a solitary 'Excuse me, chum,' or 'That's right, chum.' His one and only passion was cards, and he was a remarkably good card player. He could have skinned

myself and Noble, but whatever we lost to him, Hawkins lost to us, and Hawkins only played with the money Belcher gave him.

Hawkins lost to us because he had too much old gab, and we probably lost to Belcher for the same reason. Hawkins and Noble argued about religion into the early hours of the morning, and Hawkins worried the life out of Noble, who had a brother a priest, with a string of questions that would puzzle a cardinal. Even in treating of holy subjects, Hawkins had a deplorable tongue. I never met a man who could mix such a variety of cursing and bad language into any argument. He was a terrible man, and a fright to argue. He never did a stroke of work, and when he had no one else to argue with, he got stuck into the old woman.

He met his match in her, for when he tried to get her to complain profanely of the drought she gave him a great comedown by blaming it entirely on Jupiter Pluvius (a deity neither Hawkins nor I had ever heard of, though Noble said that among the pagans it was believed that he had something to do with the rain). Another day he was swearing at the capitalists for starting the German war when the old lady laid down her iron, puckered up her little crab's mouth and said:

'Mr. Hawkins, you can say what you like about the war, and think you'll deceive me because I'm only a simple poor countrywoman, but I know what started the war. It was the Italian Count that stole the heathen divinity out of the temple of Japan. Believe me, Mr. Hawkins, nothing but sorrow and want can follow people who disturb the hidden powers.'

A queer old girl, all right.

GET TO KNOW THE CHARACTERS

Identify the character being spoken about in each case:

- He reddened when you talked to him, tilting from toe to heel and back, and looking down all the time at his big farmer's feet.
- They had accents you could cut with a knife …
- She was too surprised to speak …
- He had an uncommon lack of speech.
- He had too much old gab …

II

One evening we had our tea and Hawkins lit the lamp and we all sat into cards. Jeremiah Donovan came in too, and sat and watched us for a while, and it suddenly struck me that he had no great love for the two Englishmen. It came as a surprise to me because I had noticed nothing of it before.

Late in the evening a really terrible argument blew up between Hawkins and Noble about capitalists and priests and love of country.

'The capitalists pay the priests to tell you about the next world so that you won't notice what the bastards are up to in this,' said Hawkins.

'Nonsense, man!' said Noble, losing his temper.

'Before ever a capitalist was thought of people believed in the next world.'

Hawkins stood up as though he was preaching.

'Oh, they did, did they?' he said with a sneer. 'They believed all the things you believe – isn't

that what you mean? And you believe God created Adam, and Adam created Shem, and Shem created Jehoshophat. You believe all that silly old fairytale about Eve and Eden and the apple. Well listen to me, chum! If you're entitled to a silly belief like that, I'm entitled to my own silly belief – which is that the first thing your God created was a bleeding capitalist, with morality and Rolls-Royce complete. Am I right, chum?' he says to Belcher.

'You're right, chum,' says Belcher with a smile, and he got up from the table to stretch his long legs into the fire and stroke his moustache. So, seeing that Jeremiah Donovan was going, and that there was no knowing when the argument about religion would be over, I went out with him. We strolled down to the village together, and then he stopped, blushing and mumbling, and said I should be behind, keeping guard. I didn't like the tone he took with me, and anyway I was bored with life in the cottage, so I replied by asking what the hell we wanted to guard them for at all.

He looked at me in surprise and said: 'I thought you knew we were keeping them as hostages.'

'Hostages?' I said.

'The enemy have prisoners belonging to us, and now they're talking of shooting them,' he said. 'If they shoot our prisoners, we'll shoot theirs.'

'Shoot Belcher and Hawkins?' I said.

'What else did you think we were keeping them for?' he said.

'Wasn't it very unforeseen of you not to warn Noble and myself of that in the beginning?' I said.

'How was it?' he said. 'You might have known that much.'

'We could not know it, Jeremiah Donovan,' I said. 'How could we when they were on our hands so long?'

'The enemy have our prisoners as long and longer,' he said.

'That's not the same thing at all,' said I.

'What difference is there?' said he.

I couldn't tell him, because I knew he wouldn't understand. If it was only an old dog that you had to take to the vet's, you'd try and not get too fond of him, but Jeremiah Donovan was not a man who would ever be in danger of that.

'And when is this to be decided?' I said.

'We might hear tonight,' he said. 'Or tomorrow or the next day at latest. So if it's only hanging round that's a trouble to you, you'll be free soon enough.'

It was not the hanging round that was a trouble to me at all by this time. I had worse things to worry about. When I got back to the cottage the argument was still on. Hawkins was holding forth in his best style, maintaining that there was no next world, and Noble saying that there was; but I could see that Hawkins had had the best of it.

'Do you know what, chum?' he was saying with a saucy smile. 'I think you're just as big a bleeding unbeliever as I am. You say you believe in the next world, and you know just as much about the next world as I do, which is sweet damn-all. What's heaven? You don't know. You know sweet damn-all! I ask you again, do they wear wings?'

'Very well, then,' said Noble. 'They do. Is that enough for you? They do wear wings.'

'Where do they get them then? Who makes them? Have they a factory for wings? Have they a sort of store where you hand in your chit and take your bleeding wings?'

'You're an impossible man to argue with,' said Noble. 'Now, listen to me' – And they were off again.

It was long after midnight when we locked up and went to bed. As I blew out the candle I told Noble. He took it very quietly. When we'd been in bed about an hour he asked if I thought we should tell the Englishmen. I didn't, because I doubted if the English would shoot our men. Even if they did, the Brigade officers, who were always up and down to the Second

Battalion and knew the Englishmen well, would hardly want to see them plugged. 'I think so too,' said Noble. 'It would be great cruelty to put the wind up them now.'

'It was very unforeseen of Jeremiah Donovan, anyhow,' said I. It was next morning that we found it so hard to face Belcher and Hawkins. We went about the house all day, scarcely saying a word. Belcher didn't seem to notice; he was stretched into the ashes as usual, with his usual look of waiting in quietness for something unforeseen to happen, but Hawkins noticed it and put it down to Noble's being beaten in the argument of the night before.

'Why can't you take the discussion in the proper spirit?' he said severely. 'You and your Adam and Eve! I'm a Communist, that's what I am. Communist or Anarchist, it all comes to much the same thing.' And he went round the house, muttering when the fit took him: 'Adam and Eve! Adam and Eve! Nothing better to do with their time than pick bleeding apples!'

STOP

- How would you describe the differences in personality between Belcher and Hawkins?
- Explain the difference between a prisoner and a hostage.
- What does Bonaparte know there that would be no point in explaining the situation to Jeremiah Donovan? Why would there be no point?
- What change has happened between Section I and Section II of the story? *Now read on …*

III

I don't know how we got through that day, but I was very glad when it was over, the tea things were cleared away, and Belcher said in his peaceable way: 'Well, chums, what about it?' We sat round the table and Hawkins took out the cards, and just then I heard Jeremiah Donovan's footsteps on the path and a dark presentiment crossed my mind. I rose from the table and caught him before he reached the door.

'What do you want?' I asked.

'I want those two soldier friends of yours,' he said, getting red.

'Is that the way, Jeremiah Donovan?' I asked.

'That's the way. There were four of our lads shot this morning, one of them a boy of sixteen.'

'That's bad,' I said.

At that moment Noble followed me out, and the three of us walked down the path together, talking in whispers. Feeney, the local intelligence officer, was standing by the gate.

'What are you going to do about it?' I asked Jeremiah Donovan.

'I want you and Noble to get them out; tell them they're being shifted again; that'll be the quietest way.'

'Leave me out of that,' said Noble, under his breath. Jeremiah Donovan looked at him hard.

'All right,' he says. 'You and Feeney get a few tools from the shed and dig a hole by the far end of the bog. Bonaparte and myself will be after you. Don't let anyone see you with the tools. I wouldn't like it to go beyond ourselves.'

We saw Feeney and Noble go round to the shed and went in ourselves. I left Jeremiah Donovan to do the explanations. He told them that he had orders to send them back to the Second Battalion. Hawkins let out a mouthful of curses, and you could see that though Belcher didn't say anything, he was a bit upset too. The old woman was for having them stay in spite of us, and she didn't stop advising them until Jeremiah Donovan lost his temper and turned on her. He had a nasty temper, I noticed. It was pitch-dark in the cottage by this time, but no one thought of lighting the lamp, and in the darkness the two Englishmen fetched their topcoats and said good-bye to the old woman.

'Just as a man makes a home of a bleeding place, some bastard at headquarters thinks you're too cushy and shunts you off,' said Hawkins shaking her hand.

'A thousand thanks, madam,' said Belcher, 'A thousand thanks for everything' – as though he'd made it up.

We went round to the back of the house and down towards the bog. It was only then that Jeremiah Donovan told them. He was shaking with excitement.

'There were four of our fellows shot in Cork this morning and now you're to be shot as a reprisal.'

'What are you talking about?' snaps Hawkins. 'It's bad enough being mucked about as we are without having to put up with your funny jokes.'

'It isn't a joke,' says Donovan. 'I'm sorry, Hawkins, but it's true,' and begins on the usual rigmarole about duty and how unpleasant it is. I never noticed that people who talk a lot about duty find it much of a trouble to them.

'Oh, cut it out!' said Hawkins.

'Ask Bonaparte,' said Donovan, seeing that Hawkins wasn't taking him seriously. 'Isn't it true, Bonaparte?'

'It is,' I said, and Hawkins stopped. 'Ah, for Christ's sake, chum!'

'I mean it, chum,' I said.

'You don't sound as if you meant it.'

'If he doesn't mean it, I do,' said Donovan, working himself up.

'What have you against me, Jeremiah Donovan?'

'I never said I had anything against you. But why did your people take out four of your prisoners and shoot them in cold blood?'

He took Hawkins by the arm and dragged him on, but it was impossible to make him understand that we were in earnest. I had the Smith and Wesson in my pocket and I kept fingering it and wondering what I'd do if they put up a fight for it or ran, and wishing to God they'd do one or the other. I knew if they did run for it that I'd never fire on them. Hawkins wanted to know was Noble in it, and when we said yes, he asked us why Noble wanted to plug him. Why did any of us want to plug him? What had he done to us? Weren't we all chums? Didn't we understand him and didn't he understand us? Did we imagine for an instant that he'd shoot us for all the so-and-so officers in the so-and-so British Army?

By this time we'd reached the bog, and I was so sick I couldn't even answer him. We walked along the edge of it in the darkness, and every now and then Hawkins would call a halt and begin all over again, as if he was wound up, about our being chums, and I knew that nothing but the sight of the grave would convince him that we had to do it. And all the time I was hoping that something would happen; that they'd run for it or that Noble would take over the responsibility from me. I had the feeling that it was worse on Noble than on me.

STOP

- What has happened now to change the situation of the prisoners?
- From what you have read so far about Hawkins and Belcher, are you surprised at the way they each say their goodbye to the old woman? *Now read on …*

IV

At last we saw the lantern in the distance and made towards it. Noble was carrying it, and Feeney was standing somewhere in the darkness behind him, and the picture of them so still and silent in the bogland brought it home to me that we were in earnest, and banished the last bit of hope I had.

Belcher, on recognising Noble, said: 'Hallo, chum,' in his quiet way, but Hawkins flew at him at once, and the argument began all over again, only this time Noble had nothing to say for himself and stood with his head down, holding the lantern between his legs.

It was Jeremiah Donovan who did the answering. For the twentieth time, as though it was haunting his mind, Hawkins asked if anybody thought he'd shoot Noble.

'Yes, you would,' said Jeremiah Donovan.

'No, I wouldn't, damn you!'

'You would, because you'd know you'd be shot for not doing it.'

'I wouldn't, not if I was to be shot twenty times over. I wouldn't shoot a pal. And Belcher wouldn't – isn't that right, Belcher?'

'That's right, chum,' Belcher said, but more by way of answering the question than of joining in the argument. Belcher sounded as though whatever unforeseen thing he'd always been waiting for had come at last.

'Anyway, who says Noble would be shot if I wasn't ? What do you think I'd do if I was in his place, out in the middle of a blasted bog?'

'What would you do?' asked Donovan.

'I'd go with him wherever he was going, of course. Share my last bob with him and stick by him through thick and thin. No one can ever say of me that I let down a pal.'

'We've had enough of this,' said Jeremiah Donovan, cocking his revolver. 'Is there any message you want to send?'

'No, there isn't. '

'Do you want to say your prayers?'

Hawkins came out with a cold-blooded remark that even shocked me and turned on Noble again.

'Listen to me, Noble,' he said. 'You and me are chums. You can't come over to my side, so I'll come over to your side. That show you I mean what I say? Give me a rifle and I'll go along with you and the other lads.'

Nobody answered him. We knew that was no way out.

'Hear what I'm saying?' he said. 'I'm through with it. I'm a deserter or anything else you like. I don't believe in your stuff, but it's no worse than mine. That satisfy you?'

Noble raised his head, but Donovan began to speak and he lowered it again without replying.

'For the last time, have you any messages to send?' said Donovan in a cold, excited sort of voice.

'Shut up, Donovan! You don't understand me, but these lads do. They're not the sort to make a pal and kill a pal. They're not the tools of any capitalist.'

I alone of the crowd saw Donovan raise his Webley to the back of Hawkins's neck, and as he did so I shut my eyes and tried to pray. Hawkins had begun to say something else when Donovan fired, and as I opened my eyes at the bang, I saw Hawkins stagger at the knees and lie out flat at Noble's feet, slowly and as quiet as a kid falling asleep, with the lantern-light on his lean legs and bright farmer's boots. We all stood very still, watching him settle out in the last agony.

Then Belcher took out a handkerchief and began to tie it about his own eyes (in our excitement we'd forgotten to do the same for Hawkins), and, seeing it wasn't big enough, turned and asked for the loan of mine. I gave it to him and he knotted the two together and pointed with his foot at Hawkins.

'He's not quite dead,' he said. 'Better give him another.' Sure enough, Hawkins's left knee was beginning to rise. I bent down and put my gun to his head; then, recollecting myself, I got up again. Belcher understood what was in my mind.

'Give him his first,' he said, 'I don't mind. Poor bastard, we don't know what's happening to him now.'

I knelt and fired. By this time I didn't seem to know what I was doing. Belcher, who was fumbling a bit awkwardly with the handkerchiefs, came out with a laugh as he heard the shot. It was the first time I had heard him laugh and it sent a shudder down my back; it sounded so unnatural.

'Poor bugger!' he said quietly. 'And last night he was so curious about it all. It's very queer, chums, I always think. Now he knows as much about it as they'll ever let him know, and last night he was all in the dark.'

Donovan helped him to tie the handkerchiefs about his eyes.

'Thanks, chum,' he said. Donovan asked if there were any messages he wanted sent.

'No, chum,' he said. 'Not for me. If any of you would like to write to Hawkins's mother, you'll find a letter from her in his pocket. He and his mother were great chums. But my missus left me eight years ago. Went away with another fellow and took the kid with her. I like the feeling of a home, as you may have noticed, but I couldn't start another again after that.'

It was an extraordinary thing, but in those few minutes Belcher said more than in all the weeks before. It was just as if the sound of the shot had started a flood of talk in him and he could go on the whole night like that, quite happily, talking about himself. We stood around like fools now that he couldn't see us any longer. Donovan looked at Noble, and Noble shook his head. Then Donovan raised his Webley, and at that moment Belcher gave his queer laugh again, He may have thought we were talking about him, or perhaps he noticed the same thing I'd noticed and couldn't understand it.

'Excuse me, chums,' he said. 'I feel I'm talking a hell of a lot, and so silly, about my being so handy about a house and things like that. But this thing came on me suddenly. You'll forgive me, I'm sure.'

'You don't want to say a prayer?' asked Donovan.

'No, chum,' he said. 'I don't think it would help. I'm ready, and you boys want to get it over.'

'You understand that we're only doing our duty?' said Donovan.

Belcher's head was raised like a blind man's, so that you could only see his chin and the top of his nose in the lantern-light.

'I never could make out what duty was myself,' he said. 'I think you're all good lads, if that's what you mean. I'm not complaining.'

Noble, just as if he couldn't bear any more of it, raised his fist at Donovan, and in a flash Donovan raised his gun and fired. The big man went over like a sack of meal, and this time there was no need of a second shot.

I don't remember much about the burying, but that it was worse than all the rest because we had to carry them to the grave. It was all mad lonely with nothing but a patch of lantern-light between ourselves and the dark, and birds hooting and screeching all round, disturbed by the guns. Noble went through Hawkins's belongings to find the letter from his mother, and then joined his hands together. He did the same with Belcher. Then, when we'd filled in the grave, we separated from Jeremiah Donovan and Feeney and took our tools back to the shed. All the way we didn't speak a word. The kitchen was dark and as we'd left it, and the old woman was sitting over the hearth, saying her beads. We walked past her into the room, and Noble struck a match to light the lamp. She rose quietly and came to the doorway with all her cantankerousness gone.

'What did ye do with them?' she asked in a whisper, and Noble started so that the match went out in his hand.

'What's that?' he asked without turning round.

'I heard ye,' she said.

'What did you hear?' asked Noble.

'I heard ye. Do ye think I didn't hear ye, putting the spade back in the houseen?'

Noble struck another match and this time the lamp lit for him.

'Was that what ye did to them?' she asked.

Then, by God, in the very doorway, she fell on her knees and began praying, and after looking at her for a minute or two Noble did the same by the fireplace. I pushed my way out past her and left them at it. I stood at the door, watching the stars and listening to the shrieking of the birds dying out over the bogs. It is so strange what you feel at times like that that you can't describe it. Noble says he saw everything ten times the size, as though there were nothing in the whole world but that little patch of bog with the two Englishmen stiffening into it, but with me it was as if the patch of bog where the Englishmen were was a million miles away, and even Noble and the old woman, mumbling behind me, and the birds and the bloody stars were all far away, and I was somehow very small and very lost and lonely like a child astray in the snow. And anything that happened to me afterwards, I never felt the same about again.

Four-Part Story Planner

Opening: Introduces the setting (the time, the place, the atmosphere) and the characters

Start the action and create a point of conflict

Build up to a dramatic climax: tension mounts to its highest point (a moment of great emotion/excitement

Ending/ Resolution – the outcome: strong ending, either positive or negative. Often a moment of realisation, reflection or truth

EXPLORE

1. Bonaparte • Jeremiah • Donovan • Noble • Belcher • Hawkins

Imagine each one of these characters is a plant, a tree or a flower. Decide what each man would be and explain your decision.

2. Bonaparte makes various statements about Jeremiah Donovan, scattered throughout the story. Quote two of them. What picture of Jeremiah builds up? What sides of his personality show in the killing of Hawkins and Belcher?

3. In the final paragraph, Bonaparte says that he felt 'like a child astray in the snow'. To go astray means to take the wrong path or to be lost. Do you understand why he compares himself with a child who has taken the wrong path and is lost in the snow? Why a child? Why lost in the snow?

4. This story is based on a true incident that happened in Cork during the War of Independence. It is regarded as one of the world's great anti-war stories. What do you think the story says about war in general?

5. Do you think that people involved in violent conflict in their young days might see things differently or have regrets when they grow older? What experiences in their lives might change them?

Beginnings and Endings

A reads the first paragraph of the story aloud and then **B** reads the last paragraph.

Take time to read your paragraph silently to yourself first. Prepare the tone of voice that you think is appropriate for the piece you have to read.

Then you each do your reading in turn. As you listen to your partner reading the opening or the closing paragraph, imagine the place, the time and the people that are being described as if it was a film showing the people and the place.

Then each answer the following questions.

1. Name the characters in the paragraph you listened to.

2. Say where the paragraph is happening.

3. Write a few sentences simply stating what was happening in the paragraph your partner read.

4. Between you, discuss what happened in the story as a whole and how life changed for the people in the story between the first and last paragraph.

CREATE

Opening Paragraph

In his opening paragraph, this storyteller gives you a time (dusk) and place (the fireside) and introduces five characters; big Belcher, little Hawkins, Noble, Jeremiah Donovan and the narrator. He also gives you some dialogue that reveals something about Donovan.

> At dusk the big Englishman, Belcher, would shift his long legs out of the ashes and say, 'Well, chums, what about it?' and Noble and myself would say, 'All right, chum' (for we had picked up some of their curious expressions), and the little Englishman, Hawkins, would light the lamp and bring out the cards. Sometimes Jeremiah Donovan would come up and supervise the game, and get excited over Hawkins's cards, which he always played badly, and shout at him as if he was one of our own, 'Ah, you divil, why didn't you play the tray?'

Now write the opening sentences of your own war story, giving a time and place, introducing several characters and adding a little snippet of dialogue.

Here is an example from a student.

> As light snowflakes began to fall, Sergeant McLeman led the platoon through the moonlit fields, his weary soldiers crouching low to avoid the sharp eyes of enemy snipers. Private Dillon dragged his wounded left foot through the snow, supported by Lance Corporal Grabowski, who carried Dillon's pack. Luca Buzzone, the Italian paramedic, whispered to the sergeant, 'Dillon can't go much further without a shot of painkiller.'

Closing Paragraph

Now try writing a closing paragraph for your story, imagining that things have happened to change the lives of your soldiers.

SHOW WHAT YOU KNOW

 You have learned many writing and speaking skills in this collection of texts. Now it's time to *Show What You Know!*

My Writing Task

Write a news broadcast about a missile attack on a city.
Your two concerns in this kind of writing are **content** and **style**.
Content is the *information* which you must give. **Style** is *how* you present the story.

SUCCESS CRITERIA

Self-Assessment

Read your news broadcast and check what you have written against the success criteria. What do you think you did especially well? Is there anything you could do better?

Redrafting

When you are happy with it, you may decide that your news broadcast is good enough to be included in your Collection of Texts. You could then do a little more research to improve the information, read your piece aloud to check how it sounds and proof-read it until you are happy that all the details are correct.

I should

- Use as many words as possible from the war vocabulary I learned in this chapter
- Communicate the panic and terror in the city
- Give details of buildings or areas of the city that have been destroyed
- Include a quote from an eyewitness in the city

I must

- Begin with a formal phrase, such as, 'Good evening and welcome to the 9 o'clock news'
- Write a clear opening sentence telling listeners *what* has happened and *where* it has happened
- Tell them *when* it has happened
- Use the formal language of a news report
- Present my information in short paragraphs
- Punctuate carefully

I could

- Give details of official government and military responses to the incident
- Listen to or read some war reports to see how good journalists present this kind of news story, perhaps modelling my report on the best one I find
- End with a formal phrase, such as, 'Join us at 11.30 for the final round-up of today's news'

Reflection Note

If you choose to place this news broadcast into your **Collection of Texts**, complete your reflection note.
Hint: See the success criteria above to help you.

Oral Communication

Speak your news broadcast to your class.

Engage your audience by:

- Looking forward at the 'camera' so you are making eye contact with the viewers
- Speaking clearly
- Pausing at commas and full stops
- Pronouncing place names correctly
- Varying your tone of voice

Remember, if *you* sound interested in what you are saying, *others* will be interested too.

Peer Assessment Sheet with Success Criteria for a News Broadcast

The quality of	Excellent	Very good	Good	My suggestion for improvement
Information				
Correct, well-used vocabulary				
Tone of voice to hold the listeners' attention				
Clear pronunciation				
Correct pacing, neither too slow nor too fast				
Any other point				

Feedback from Listeners

In this news broadcast	Comment
I liked	
I was surprised by	
I thought the best part was	
I think there could be some improvement in	

Peer Assessment

Based on the feedback you got from your classmates, you may wish to speak your news broadcast again, taking their comments on board to improve your tone of voice, the pace at which you speak, the pauses you insert, your eye contact, etc.

Reflection Note

Now complete the **Oral Communication Template for Student Reflection.**

Young and Old

As I explore this collection I will learn about:

- Blog entries
- Exclamation marks
- Perspective
- Vlogging
- Statistics, anecdotes, rhetorical questions and quotes
- Question marks
- Pitch and pace
- Monologues
- Giving my opinion clearly
- Humorous and serious tones
- Informal writing
- Setting
- Speaking confidently and persuasively
- Emotive language
- Plot twists
- Atmosphere

SHOW WHAT YOU KNOW

The skills you learn in this collection will enable you to **show what you know** in your final tasks at the end of this collection.

For my writing task I will:
Write a blog entry

For oral communication I will:
Deliver a speech

Learning Outcomes
OL5, OL7, OL9, R8, R12, W3, W4, W13

Exploring the Theme – Young and Old

Young and **old**: two words representing the ends of the age spectrum. When you are young, it can be hard to imagine getting to a stage in your life where you might consider yourself as 'old'. Walt Disney once said: 'Laughter is timeless. Imagination has no age and dreams are forever.' So, are young and old people really that different or do they share common goals?

 In pairs, write down some of the positive points about being both young and old.

 Being young/old is great because …

Now write down some of the negative points about being both young and old.

I would hate to be young/old because …

Blog Entry

> **What I will learn:**

to explore and practise blog entries; to give my opinion clearly; to explore the effectiveness of humorous and serious tones

The term 'blogging' comes from the 1990s' term 'weblog', meaning a regularly updated website or web page, typically run by an individual or small group and usually written in an informal or conversational style.

'Weblog' became 'blog' and people who wrote blogs became known as 'bloggers'.

Blogging is often associated with young people as it is considered new and involves technology, but over the years blogging has become a way for both young and old to express themselves, as you will read in 'The Cranky Old Man' blog and Konni Kim's blog.

PREPARE

1. Write down the date of your sixtieth birthday.

2. What type of activities do you expect to be involved in when you are sixty?

The Cranky Old Man

Thursday 9th June 2016

How to Stay Young

I hope to never move to a 'Senior Community' or even worse an assisted living home. There is a lot to be said for a Senior/Retirement community, and if need be, assisted living beats the heck out of being left alone and vulnerable.

My objection to both these living arrangements is there are too many old people in these venues. Mind you, I love old people. I am an 'old people' myself; it is just that hanging with old people makes you … well … old!

The way to stay young is to hang around young people.

I became a father for the fourth time when I was fifty-two. When I was with my son, and other young fathers, I felt younger than fifty-two. Because I had a young child, the actual young people treated me as if I was also young. It helps to feel young if people treat you as if you actually are young.

As my young son grew, I was forced to do young things. Throw a ball, catch a ball, coach youth teams, and even run from time to time.

When I was sixty, I associated not with other sixty year olds, but with other parents of eight-year-olds. Occasionally I may have been referred to as 'The Old Fart,' but I was still mostly one of the younger crowd. Talk was of little league, fractions, grade school, teacher conferences, you know … young stuff. I felt young and almost spry.

When my oldest brother was ill, I paid a visit to him in North Carolina. I went to his granddaughter's music recital and a party afterwards. I found myself mingling with parents of young children, parents the same age as my crowd back in Jersey, only now I was introduced as Grandpa's brother. I was treated by these young people like a grandpa, like an old person.

I immediately felt old.

By the time I went back to Jersey, I had arthritis in my hip, I had gained ten pounds, and what hair I had was greying around the edges.

I recovered a little, but when my son was taken off to Massachusetts because Jersey judges suck, I lost my youth attachment. When he does visit, he is a teenager now and teens will always make you age.

Old people and teenagers are the fountain of elderly.

The only thing that could make me feel older is if on my next birthday I am told patronisingly that I am seventy years YOUNG. Nothing says they just dropped the landing gear on your airplane of life than to be told you are xx years YOUNG!

Anyway, the youth thing was a good run while it lasted. I gotta stop writing now; it's time for my nap.

---

at 3.58pm   3 comments

View my profile

Search this Blog

Search

 Check out the entertaining poem about old age by Roger McGough, 'Let Me Die a Younger Man's Death', on YouTube.

EXPLORE

1. Make a list of what makes the author feel young and what makes him feel old.

2. List some of the negative words used by the author in paragraph one and two, e.g. 'never'.

3. Write down three things you notice about how this piece was written, for example: 'The paragraphs are different lengths.'

4. Do you think the author likes being old?

5. Do you think the title of the blog 'The Cranky Old Man' is witty?

6. If you were writing a blog for teenagers, what title would you give it?

7. 'This author uses a humorous tone in his writing.' Would you agree or disagree?

Sample P I E for Question 7

I agree that this piece could be considered as having a humorous tone, though one which many adolescents would regard as 'old people humour'. The author achieves this through contradiction where he states two things that do not agree with each other. **'My objection to both these living arrangements is there are too many old people in these venues. Mind you, I love old people.'** The author makes a bold statement, which would more than likely upset some people but it is directly followed by a contradictory statement. 'Mind you, I love old people.'

To me, this shows that the author has a humorous style, which shocks his audience for dramatic effect. This is often used by comedians to try and deliver a more sarcastic and effective performance.

The author also directly mocks himself, ridiculing his own age. **'I gotta stop writing now; it's time for my nap.'** He finishes his piece by sharing a personal joke with his readers. He is suggesting he is too old to write for this long without a nap. I believe he makes the reader focus on the stereotyping of old people and makes fun of himself!

TOP TIP

When you write your explanation, you should try to give your own personal response. **Elaborate** with as much detail and opinion as possible. Your explanation should always be the longest part of the answer.

FUN FACT

Wordpress and Blogspot are two of the most popular platforms for bloggers.

The author of this blog doesn't hold back on giving his opinion. This is a huge part of writing a successful blog. Make a list of three things that make you 'cranky'. Pick one point and write a paragraph about why it bothers you. Try to use some of the negative language you identified from the blog entry. The following phrases are helpful in giving your opinion:

- I believe that …
- I have no doubt that/I'm certain that …
- To be honest …
- As far as I know …
- I'm absolutely certain that …
- It is a complicated issue but for me …
- I have come to the conclusion …
- I think it is fair/reasonable to say …
- This may be controversial but …
- In my limited experience …

TOP TIP

Blogs are mostly written in an informal style. Writers have more freedom to experiment with layout, language and grammar. It is important that you are aware that not every piece will be grammatically accurate nor that spelling will be correct because bloggers don't have editors to check their work.

What do you like about being the age you are right now? Are there things you are looking forward to doing when you turn eighteen?

This next author is a young South Korean girl who, at the age of fifteen, created a fashion blog that is now hugely popular. In this particular entry, she talks about her fear of growing up and moving into adulthood.

KONNI KIM

A tribute to our generation

HEY, I'M KONNI.

Hey, I'm Konni. I'm 18, Korean. I love writing, music, fashion, art and Harry Potter. I blog (obviously) and am currently working as an editor for Korea Style Week.

FOLLOW KONNI KIM

FOLLOW US VIA EMAIL

Brighten up your inbox, enter your email address to follow this blog and receive notifications of new posts by email. You know you want to. We promise we won't send you useless spam.

Join 2,140 other followers

Enter your email address

I Don't Want to Grow Up Because

January 20, 2016 • by Konni Kim

Lots of changes are being made in my life these days. At school, aside from the usual schoolwork, I now have to start writing college applications for next year and I must also take several exams, again, for college. And then outside of school I have this whole other world of blogging and fashion business and social media frenzy, where things are starting to become really exciting – keep an eye out for new collaboration projects which are gonna be here soon guys. I can't dish out much info now but you'll find out in a bit! You'll be surprised 🙂 And THEN we're left with my personal life – relationships, family, and all that jazz. Obviously I can't reveal too much about THAT either, but for now, all I can say is that I feel that I'm becoming much more mature in terms of relationships with people. I think it's because I'm growing to be more accepting.

With so much around me and inside me transitioning, I'm excited yet anxious, as any growing teenager my age would be. Soon I'm going to be of legal age. (Do you hear that? LEGAL. AGE. My goodness, time flies.) Every day I'm feeling new emotions, I'm experiencing new things, and through all this newness I can feel myself getting older. I've always held a fear of growing old. **It's not necessarily a fear of seeing the numbers of my age get bigger. It's a fundamental fear of 'change'. I can't imagine myself mentally, emotionally, or physically being different from how I am now.** It's almost like I can't believe that someday I'll have to hand in my youthful skin and dreaming mind for a set of wrinkles and a careful, serious attitude attributed to a lifetime of experience. Of course, not all cases of aging go like this, and I do acknowledge that wrinkles and old age have their own beauty. However, right now I just feel like THIS – the way I am at this moment – is me.

I'm only 17 and a half and already I'm noticing that I've changed so much – from a mischievous yet smart little girl in London to a quiet, reserved pre-teen after suddenly moving to Korea (I knew little Korean back then), and finally to who I am now, a confused yet pretty self-actualised and excited teenager with so many problems and so little time. And looking back, I miss my old self sometimes. I think, *'Maybe I'd have become a more positive person if I hadn't so suddenly moved here, maybe I needed more time'*, and *'What if the little girl inside me is gone forever?'* These thoughts usually creep up on me when I'm feeling sentimental in a sad way. And then these thoughts move on to scare me about how much I'll change in the future. *'Look how much you've changed in just 17 years. Imagine how much more you'll change as you become an adult and get thrown into the reality of society, with money and real relationships and all the other hazards of the adult world that you're being protected from right now!'* says the voice in the back of my head.

I don't want to grow up because I love myself the way I am now, all the flaws too. I do want to improve, and don't get me wrong – I am truly *exhilarated* just thinking of the future and all my dreams and ambitions – but I don't want myself to radically change. It may sound cowardly and oh-so-typical-teenager-like, but it's something I've been thinking about for a long time now. **I. don't. want. to. grow. up.**

But I guess the best I can do at present is to just work harder toward my goals and hope for the best; hope that I won't become too materialized, hope that I'll stay passionate, hope that I'll grow stronger, hope that all the scars will heal and shape a better 'me' for the future.

Thanks for taking the time to read this, guys.

? EXPLORE

1. State whether each of the following sentences are **true** or **false** based on your reading of this blog entry. In each case, write down a sentence that supports your answer.

- The author is at a stressful but exciting time in her life.
- The author is very open about her personal life.
- Growing old is totally normal for this teenager.
- The author hates all her negative qualities and can't wait until she grows up and gets rid of them.
- The author will bide her time and hope for better things in the future.

2. Konni uses informal and colloquial (everyday) language. Write down a list of words and phrases from this piece that you consider to be colloquial.

3. What kind of audience is this piece aimed at?

4. The layout of this blog entry looks very unusual and different to the other texts you have read in this book. For example, the author uses smiley faces. What other elements of informality do you notice about the layout?

P I E

5. This blog is written in the first person narrative. Look for two examples of this. Why is this important in blogs?

6. The tone of this piece could be described as serious and reflective. For example, the author remarks, *'All I can say is that I feel that I'm becoming much more mature in terms of relationships with people. I think it's because I'm growing to be more accepting.'* This is an example of a reflective tone. Can you find two further examples that highlight the serious and reflective tone of this article?

REMEMBER
Tone is the general attitude of a piece of writing (or a way of speaking). It expresses a particular feeling or mood.

Tips for Writing a Blog

✱ Create an eye-catching **headline** to attract your audience, for example, 'Eating Crickets in Plaza Hildago' or 'Stripes and Monochrome – This Season's Must Haves'.

✱ Use popular **search queries** when deciding on a heading for a blog entry, for example, 'How to …', 'How to get more …'

✱ Keep your headline **short** and simple.

* Give your **opinion**: this is the core element of blog-writing.

* Use strong **verbs**, e.g. 'build', 'overcome', 'maintain', or strong adjectives, e.g. 'sleek', 'tasty' 'unbelievable'.

* Insert an appropriate **picture** or **image** to catch the audience's attention or curiosity.

* Give your **name** and the **date** at the top of the entry.

* Enlarge the first letter of the blog piece and/or highlight it in a bold colour so that it looks interesting visually (this is known as a **drop cap**).

TOP TIP

Don't post anything unless you are happy for the world to see it. Remember, once something goes up on the internet, it is there for life (or at the very least, it is incredibly difficult to get rid of), even if you delete it.

 CREATE

 W3.2

Write a blog entry where you imagine the moment you turn either eighteen or fifty. Think about the following questions to help you:

* Why is this moment so significant?
* How does it make you feel?
* What plans do you have for your future?
* How do you feel about your age?

✓ Blog Writing Checklist

☐ Heading
☐ Image
☐ Author and date
☐ Drop cap
☐ Your opinion
☐ First person narrative
☐ Informal tone and language
☐ Accurate spelling and grammar

A Poem

What I will learn:

to identify and understand the speaker's perspective

One aspect of growing older can be the loss of imagination. As teenagers and adults, we become more aware of ourselves and in some cases lose our sense of creativity and freedom. In the next poem, the speaker worries about losing his imagination.

FUN FACT

Albert Einstein is known as an inventor and scientist, so it might surprise you to know that he placed a big emphasis on imagination. 'I am enough of an artist to draw freely upon my imagination. Imagination is more important than knowledge. Knowledge is limited. Imagination encircles the world.'

Think back to when you were a little girl or boy. What kind of creative games did you play? What characters did you pretend to be?

 On Turning Ten

by Billy Collins

The whole idea of it makes me feel
like I'm coming down with something,
something worse than any stomach ache
or the headaches I get from reading in bad light –
a kind of measles of the spirit,
a mumps of the psyche,
a disfiguring chicken pox of the soul.

You tell me it is too early to be looking back,
but that is because you have forgotten
the perfect simplicity of being one
and the beautiful complexity introduced by two.
But I can lie on my bed and remember every digit.
At four I was an Arabian wizard.
I could make myself invisible
by drinking a glass of milk a certain way.
At seven I was a soldier, at nine a prince.

But now I am mostly at the window
watching the late afternoon light.
Back then it never fell so solemnly
against the side of my tree house,
and my bicycle never leaned against the garage
as it does today,
all the dark blue speed drained out of it.

This is the beginning of sadness, I say to myself,
as I walk through the universe in my sneakers.
It is time to say good-bye to my imaginary friends,
time to turn the first big number.

It seems only yesterday I used to believe
there was nothing under my skin but light.
If you cut me I could shine.
But now when I fall upon the sidewalks of life,
I skin my knees. I bleed.

EXPLORE

1. Who is the speaker of the poem? What age and gender are they?

2. Name two imaginative things the speaker liked to do when they were younger.

3. Pick the word you think best describes one of the possible themes of this poem. Defend your choice to your partner using the starter sentences below to help you.

   In my opinion one of the possible themes of this poem is:
   loss • new beginnings • imagination • youth • innocence
   I believe this because …

4. The speaker refers to 'measles of the spirit, mumps of the psyche, a chicken pox of the soul'. What do you think the poet means by this? Read the whole poem first, and then read the lines together to gain a better understanding of their meaning.

5. Why does the speaker now 'bleed' at the end of the poem? In no more than twenty words, explain the speaker's perspective (point of view/way of looking at things).

A **theme** is an important idea that runs through a text.

REMEMBER

Thinking back again on what characters you pretended to be when you were younger, pick one of these characters and imagine yourself in their shoes, e.g. a doctor, a witch, a gymnast. Write a poem as this very same character. You must have at least **three stanzas** and a **strong theme**.

OR

Write two separate diary entries from the perspective of your character.

Radio Play

What I will learn:

to use an informal writing style

We all find it difficult to remember the earliest years of our lives. You will listen to an excerpt from a radio play written by the well-known and much-loved Irish author, Maeve Binchy, entitled 'Infancy'. In the play, baby Fintan is very aware of the actions that unfold around him, though he can't communicate with his family. This piece demonstrates the difficulties in communication between the young and the old.

Make a list of your earliest memories. Share these with your partner. Do you have any common or similar earliest memories?

REMEMBER

Synonyms are words that have the same meaning.

You can use the following vocabulary to help you discuss your memory:

Synonyms for 'to remember':	reminisce	recall	recollect	remind	recount
Positive adjectives to describe feelings:	excited	ecstatic	overjoyed	delighted	comforted
Negative adjectives to describe feelings:	scared	apprehensive (nervous)	worried	hesitant	anxious
Describe how clear the memory is:	vivid	muddled (mixed up)	incomplete	concrete (specific)	tangible (touchable)
Describe the importance of the memory:	special	favourite	precious (valuable)	abiding (long lasting)	significant

Excerpt from 'Infancy' by Maeve Binchy

You will now listen to the excerpt from 'Infancy' twice.

?
EXPLORE

W3.4

1. Indicate whether the following statements are true or false in the left-hand column based on what you remember of the radio play after your first listening. Then, listening to the excerpt again, tick the correct answer in the right-hand column.

Answer here from memory **after your first listening**			Answer these questions again **after your second listening**	
True	**False**	**Statement**	**True**	**False**
		The baby's name is Fintan		
		Fintan's mother works at home and at the office		
		Fintan's mother never buys new clothes		
		Michael studies history at university		
		Barbara is going to college after her Leaving Cert		
		Satellite is missing a paw		
		Michael was the cause of Satellite's accident		
		Fintan's father works in the bank		
		Fintan's parents fight a lot		
		Sean and Francesca are enjoying being parents again		
		Fintan's mother is finding work difficult		
		Nobody cares about Fintan's first words		
		Sean's bank is corrupt		
		Francesca will be back in the office in two years		
		Fintan thinks adults get less intelligent the older they get		
		Barbara's friends are dizzy		

2. Do you think that Fintan is a believable character? **P I E**

3. Suggest a different name for this play and justify your choice. **P I E**

 **RESEARCH ZONE** Create an author profile for Maeve Binchy.

 WRITE

Write a letter from Fintan to both his parents, Francesca and Sean, that he will send to them on his 21st birthday. Consider the following questions when planning your letter.

- What will the family situation be like when Fintan is twenty-one years of age?
- What do you imagine Fintan will be like when he is twenty-one?

SUCCESS CRITERIA

You must
- Have a chatty, friendly style
- Write in the first person narrative
- Put your address in the top right-hand corner
- Include the date under your address
- Open your letter with 'Dear'/'Hello'/'Hi'
- Use paragraphs
- End your letter with 'Bye for now'/'See you soon'/'Lots of love'

You should
- Refer to all the family members at least once
- Create a clear picture of family life since Fintan was a baby

You could
- Experiment with vocabulary and phrasing

Article

What I will learn:

to speak clearly and confidently; understand, evaluate and create a vlog

 PREPARE

- Do you know what 'vlogging' is?
- If not, can you guess based on what you have learned so far in this collection?
- Do you know of any vloggers?
- Can you explain who their target audience is?
- What makes them appealing?

Read the following article on vlogging.

'Blogging? No, I Said Vlogging!'

Vlogging: all the 'cool' kids are doing it these days! A video blog, or 'vlog', is a blog that contains video content. It's another type of blogging that allows people to share their opinions on just about everything.

Many bloggers will embed videos into their blogs because it allows them a different approach to attracting followers. Let's face it, watching a 'How to Make an Oreo Cheesecake' baking demonstration is much more exciting than reading about it. It also makes you hungry so you will probably want to jump up and make that delicious cheesecake by the end of it! Video blogs allow communication with people on a whole new level, but you don't need to be a blogger to be a vlogger.

Platforms like YouTube and Vimeo have allowed people to reach millions of viewers worldwide, with some very basic bedroom video diaries becoming global internet hits. As long as you are talking about something people want to listen to, then you're off to a great start.

You don't need to be a tech genius to start vlogging. Smart phones allow people to record and post in seconds. In some cases the material shouldn't get posted at all, with some videos being too embarrassing to watch! However, applications like Vidtrim and Magisto allow you to edit video content. If you want better camera work, then you need to arm yourself with a camera and tripod or use a webcam. Software like Window's Movie Maker or Lightworks allow you to edit on your PC or Mac.

If you are interested in vlogging, take your time and figure out what works best for you. You should ensure your lighting and audio are of good quality and you might like to have a script to guide you. Most popular vloggers are funny and charismatic. They have opinions and are not afraid to share them.

Can you believe some people are able to make a living just by posting videos on YouTube? If you manage to create a popular vlog or channel, the commercial possibilities are incredible. Just ask Shay Carl Butler and his family, whose YouTube channel, 'The Shaytards', became a worldwide sensation. How about Zoe 'Zoella' Sugg, whose popular fashion vlog 'Zoella' has seen her gain unprecedented fame? She has been awarded Best Beauty Vlogger, Best British Vlogger and has even written her own novel, *Girl Online*.

All this considered, if a person thinks they have the charm, wit and subject matter to entertain the masses, they could become the next big vlogger.

Watch a vlog from Donal Skehan's YouTube channel and analyse (examine) both the language and format he uses. Use the following headings to rate Donal's vlog:

Easy Analysis			
VLOG ELEMENT	😊	😐	☹
Content			
Easy to understand			
Enjoyable			
Charisma (force of personality)			
Camera work			
Audio			
Music			

Pick one vlog element from the table and explain why you think it was successful or unsuccessful.

 Your job is to create a vlog using the tips from the article you read. Pick a subject you would like to speak about, e.g. fashion, music, art, food or sport.

Check out the YouTube vlogs of John Green (the author of *The Fault in Our Stars* and *Paper Towns*).

TOP TIP

When you are using PIE, 'illustrate' doesn't always require you to quote, it may just require you to give an example, like in the case of the vlog.

Drama

What I will learn:

to investigate the importance of setting; to identify the correct use of exclamation marks and question marks; to explore emotive language and speak persuasively

Often life is not about age but rather about how much freedom you have to enjoy it. Unlike the narrator in Maeve Binchy's drama, who didn't enjoy much freedom, the next drama piece is about a group of schoolboys who find themselves alone and fending for themselves.

PREPARE Imagine teenagers and adults swapped places in the world. Brainstorm some of the rules you would change if you and your friends were in charge of running the country.

READ This drama piece is adapted from the novel, *Lord of the Flies*, written by William Golding in 1954.

Characters

Ralph	Piggy	Jack	Sam
Simon	Eric	Choir	

Lord of the Flies by William Golding, adapted by Nigel Williams

Enter Piggy. Ralph sees him after a short while …

Ralph: It's amazing!

Piggy: What's amazin'?

Ralph: The sun.

Piggy: Don't see what's so amazin'.

Ralph: It's like a huge eye looking down at you.

Piggy: It's hot. That's what it is. Hot.

Ralph: That's a funny T-shirt.

Piggy: My auntie give it me … It's thermal you see.

Ralph: So? (*Stands facing the sun.*) It's amazing … That's a lagoon. Great for swimming.

Piggy: I can't swim. I sink.

Ralph: You don't you know.

Piggy: I do. I know I do.

Ralph: Blubber …

Piggy: Leave off. (*Piggy sits on the wing … it is hot.*) What's your name?

Ralph:	Ralph. What's yours?
Piggy:	Not telling.
Ralph:	Is it a secret?
Piggy:	It's a stupid name.
Ralph:	What is it?
Piggy:	Look, are they all dead do you think?
Ralph:	What?
Piggy:	The plane broke up. It's in bits.
Ralph:	They can't be.
Piggy:	Why not? … If they weren't they'd be here. Organisin'. And worse things happen. My auntie says …
Ralph:	What does your auntie say?
Piggy:	A lot … head really hurts. (*Uses inhaler.*)
Ralph:	I'm sorry.
Piggy:	That's why I can't swim.
Ralph:	Why?
Piggy:	Assma.
Ralph:	'Assma'?
Piggy:	Asthma. I get it … Quite badly in fact.
Ralph:	Do you?
Piggy:	Quite badly. Maybe they're all dead anyway.
Ralph:	What?
Piggy:	Here. There. Everywere. All over.
Ralph:	Don't be stupid.
Piggy:	Could be. They got those bombs now … could …
Ralph:	They're not all dead, stupid. Not everyone in England, stupid. Not the whole of the British Isles. Not our parents. (*He moves centre stage and does a handstand.*)
Piggy:	Could be … That's good!
Ralph:	It's easy. You try!
Piggy:	Can't.
Ralph:	Come on. If you know so much …
Piggy:	Can't.
Ralph:	Give us your feet. I'll pull you …
Piggy:	Oh blimey.
Ralph:	What's your name?
Piggy:	What?

Ralph:	What's your name?
Piggy:	Piggy. (*He lets go.*)
Ralph:	Piggy!
Piggy:	Piggy … But you're not to tell anyone. Not anyone.
Ralph:	I won't. Piggee! Piggee!
Piggy:	Don't.
Ralph:	Sorry … I won't then … I'm Ralph. Look!
Piggy:	Look where?
Ralph:	Look at this!
Piggy:	What is it?
Ralph:	It's a shell. A conch. That's what they call it. A conch.
Piggy:	I seen one. At my auntie's friend's house. I –
Ralph:	You blow in them, don't you?
Piggy:	I don't. My assma …
Ralph:	From down here. It's like the flute. I'm in the orchestra.
Piggy:	You what?
Ralph:	The flute. You know. Not the flute. The saxophone. Or the clarinet.
Piggy:	Uh?
Ralph:	Don't you know anything? It makes a … (*A farting sound.*)
Piggy:	Oh what? Do it again then. Since you're in the orchestra … Some orchestra.
Ralph:	You can, though! You can make a really good noise. If you get it right.
Piggy:	Yeah?
Ralph:	I bet there are people. I bet there are some others here. And I bet if I blow I'll call them. They'll come. I bet. And …
Piggy:	And what?
Ralph:	I don't know what …
Piggy:	Call 'em then. If they're there let's call 'em. Eh? Blow. And let 'em all come … Look! Over there.

(*A note is picked up by the soundtrack and the choir who enter. Jack followed by Simon, Maurice and Sam and Eric … Roger enters and breaks away from the group and dives into a key sunbathing spot.*)

Jack:	Guide me
Choir:	Guide me!
Jack:	I am mighty
Choir:	You are mighty!

Jack:	You are weak
Choir:	We are weak
Jack:	Aaaa …
Choir:	Men!
Jack:	Where's the man with the trumpet? In a line! Come on! In a line! You have to keep in a line otherwise …
Simon:	Otherwise what, Merridew?
Jack:	Otherwise … You have to keep line. That's all.
Simon:	I'm hot.
Jack:	Who was blowing the trumpet?
Ralph:	Me … You're the choir?
Jack:	Yes.
Ralph:	You're good.
Jack:	I thought it was a grown-up. I got them to sing.
Ralph:	You're good.
Jack:	I'm a choir prefect. The others are slacking. And so are you. Come on!
Ralph:	I'm Ralph
Jack:	Merridew. That's Cambourne. That's Walsh. That's –
Sam:	Sam
Eric:	'N Eric
Sam/Eric:	Samaneric
Jack:	They're all slack. Are we going to have proper names or what? Like school?
Piggy:	I'll take 'em down.
Jack:	Who's he!?
Ralph:	He's … I don't know who he is.
Piggy:	I'll take names. What was yours?
Jack:	We have to have some system you see. Come on then!
Ralph:	Look! Over there! By those trees! There are some little kids. D'you see?
Jack:	But no grown-ups!
Ralph:	They were in the front of the plane. They –
Jack:	Come on you! You too! Whoever you are! Come on! Why is he just lying on the beach?
Ralph:	Well …
Jack:	Well what?
Ralph:	I s'pose he can …
Jack:	Can what?
Ralph:	Well … He's got all day.

Jack:	All day to do what? That's the question! Come on then! Why can't you keep in line?
Maurice:	It's hot, Merridew.
Jack:	I'm choir prefect. What are you?
Ralph:	I'm … I'm Ralph. I dunno.
Piggy:	We should have a meetin'.
Jack:	Should we? Who did you say he was?
Ralph:	Ask him.
Piggy:	All I said was – we should 'ave a meetin'.
Jack:	Who are you?
Piggy:	Never mind who I am. We should 'ave a meetin'. An' we should take all the names and get organised.
Jack:	Well, we'll start with your name shall we?
Piggy:	All I'm saying is –
Ralph:	He's got quite a funny name in fact …
Piggy:	Ralph!
Ralph:	What?
Piggy:	You promised.
Ralph:	Promised what?
Piggy:	You know what.
Ralph:	I don't know what you're on about. His name's Piggy, in fact. Jack, Piggy.
Piggy:	You promised!
Ralph:	Piggy!
Jack:	Oh! Brilliant!
Piggy:	You did! You promised!
Ralph:	Well, you were being stupid!
Maurice:	Why do we want a meeting? What do we want a meeting for?
Ralph:	Because …
Piggy:	To see about being rescued. An' we have to have a meetin'. To decide –
Jack:	First of all we have to decide who's in charge. And I should be in charge because I'm a prefect. Are you a prefect in your school?
Ralph:	I will be. Probably.
Jack:	Where are you?
Ralph:	Upton.
Jack:	I don't know that. Is that a good school?
Ralph:	It's OK I suppose.
Piggy:	I go to Barnabas High. Anyone know it?

Jack:	No, 'Piggy', in fact we don't, 'Piggy', and if that's its uniform I don't think we do want to know it do we.
Simon:	He's right though. We should. We should have a meeting.
Jack:	Cambourne has spoken! We have to have a meeting! Well done, Cambourne.
Ralph:	What did you say your name was?
Simon:	Simon.
Jack:	Cambourne.
Simon:	Simon Cambourne.
Jack:	It has to be names like at school doesn't it? Otherwise we'll all end up like a lot of savages. Come on you lot! Come on!
Ralph:	He's right really.
Jack:	Who is?
Ralph:	Him.
Piggy:	He's right really. We have to have a meeting.
Jack:	Meetings are jolly useful of course.
Ralph:	Where do you say you were at …?
Jack:	Godstone.
Ralph:	Oh yes.
Jack:	Have you heard of it?
Ralph:	I think so.
Maurice:	We thrashed Audley Grange at rugby.
Roger:	Completely annihilated them.
Simon:	They did. It was quite horrible.
Ralph:	My dad says if you can run with the ball …
Jack:	Where do you play? Are you useful?
Ralph:	I'm a forward. I can run with the ball. I … (*Jack is running for him.*) Hey!

(*With Jack chasing, the boys pass the conch like a rugby ball among them until eventually Jack tackles Ralph to the ground, forcing him to pass the conch to Piggy.*)

Jack:	Not bad! You're not bad!
Ralph:	Well … you know … only a genius …
Piggy:	When you've all finished runnin' all over the place, maybe we can start doin' things prop'ly because if all the grown-ups aren't here, I mean, if there aren't any, I mean, if the bombs have …
Jack:	Shut up, can't you? You stupid little boy!
Ralph:	Who's going to be in charge? Will it be one person or –
Simon:	You have to have a vote.
Piggy:	You do. You have to have a vote.

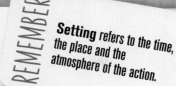

REMEMBER

Setting refers to the time, the place and the atmosphere of the action.

EXPLORE

1. Setting is a very important element to be familiar with when trying to understand a piece of writing fully. Where do you think this play is set? Why do you think this? Why do you think setting is so important to this story?

2. Are any of the characters friends?

3. Why do you think such a diverse (different or distinct from each other) group of children were on the same plane?

4. Is there any evidence to indicate why their plane has crash-landed?

5. Write down the similarities and differences between the characters of Piggy and Ralph.

6. Who do you think will be elected leader of the group of boys? Give reasons for your answer.

Persuasive Writing and Emotive Language

The art of **persuasive writing** involves convincing people of a particular point of view. Often writers and speakers focus on emotive language.

Emotive language is a way of speaking that appeals to our emotions. Ideas can be expressed in a non-emotive manner:

The woman died in the fire.

or they can be expressed in an emotive manner, making the audience really sympathise with your point of view.

The woman suffered <u>horrific</u> third degree burns leading to an <u>agonising</u> death.

Emotive language

WRITE

Rewrite these non-emotive sentences as emotive statements.

● The tourist was attacked on Shop Street.

● The student was bullied for five months.

● The building was torn down after flood damage.

Your class has crash-landed on an island like the boys in *Lord of the Flies*. Write and then present to your class a persuasive one-minute speech as to why you or your friend should be elected leader of your class group.

- Explain five positive things you/your friend will do for your group and what your/their best qualities are.

The following persuasive and emotive words may help you create your statement:

worthwhile (*adj.*)	prove (*v.*)	tremendous (*adj.*)
safe (*adj.*)	proven (*adj.*)	implore (*v.*)
popular (*adj.*)	bravely (*adj.*)	leader (*n.*)
urge (*v.*)	hero (*n.*)	guarantee (*v.*)
best (*adj.*)	suggest (*v.*)	magnificent (*adj.*)
confident (*adj.*)	honest (*adj.*)	remarkable (*adj.*)
beseech (*v.*)	effective (*adj.*)	expect (*v.*)
entreat (*v.*)	extremely (*adj.*)	superior (*adj.*)

QUESTION MARKS AND EXCLAMATION MARKS

This short piece, taken from another part of the play, is missing **five question marks** and **four exclamation marks**. Can you insert them in the correct places?

Ralph: We might you know.

Maurice: Might what

Ralph: Might have to have rules. If what Piggy … if what he says is right then … maybe there is, you know … just us

Jack: Is that so bad

Simon: Depends on us.

Jack: So what So what if they're all dead. Eh Look. Look over there. There's fruit on those trees. And there's fish in the sea. And it'll be like … it doesn't matter. We can do whatever we like can't we

Roger: Ye-eaahh

Maurice: Smash the place up …

Roger: Ye-eeaah

Maurice: Midnight feasts

Roger: Murder unlimited

Exclamation mark *n.*

Definition: Used to indicate a strong emotion. Looks like this !

Question mark *n.*

Definition: Used to indicate where a question is being asked. Looks like this ?

Based on what the boys suggest they might do with their freedom, what do you think happens next in the story? Continue the script, bringing their story to a conclusion.

OR

Imagine you are a reporter who discovers the boys on the island. Write a tabloid newspaper report on the incident. Make sure the language you use throughout, as well as what you use as your headline, is dramatic and emotive.

A Short Story

Cliché *n*.
Definition: A phrase that is overused and unoriginal. Some examples are 'Fit as a fiddle', 'Cat got your tongue' and 'All's well that ends well'.

What I will learn:

to explore and practise pitch and pace; to understand and discuss plot twists

Age is nothing but a number, or so the old cliché goes. Often in writing, age is how we identify a character's opportunities but also their restrictions. Good writers will often allow their characters to break the boundaries of the reader's expectations, as this young author has done in his short story, 'A Twist in the Tail'. The protagonist (main character) is an elderly lady but she is not your stereotypical pensioner.

In this exercise, you will need to play the part of an elderly person. In groups of four, practise the following performance elements:

1. Movement and pace – are you active and fit or arthritic and slow? How will you move about? Practise different types of walks or getting up out of a chair.

2. Pitch and tone – how does an old person speak? Are they clear and loud or croaky and soft in their voice? Practise saying the phrase 'cheese sandwich' at different pitch levels – high, medium and low.

3. Next, each person in the group will say 'cheese sandwich' using different emotions: happy, sad, excited, anxious, bored and stressed.

Using the dramatic techniques you have just practised, imagine yourself to be an eighty-year-old woman/man discussing their plans for the weekend. You must really get into the character of someone who is that age.

'A Twist in the Tail' was written by first year student Michael Somers (*pictured*), from Newbridge College. He won the Cecil Day Lewis Literary Award for it in 2015.

'A Twist in the Tail' by Michael Somers

Penny Johnson woke from a light sleep when the alarm on her iPhone went off. She got up, put her feet into cold slippers and looked at the reflection in the mirror. Her curly, grey hair was a mess and her face looked more wrinkled than last night. Shuffling over to the kitchen, she put the kettle on for breakfast. 'Come on Tinkerbell,' she said, opening the balcony door. Tinkerbell jumped quietly across the threshold of the door and sat beside the dish. The cat's tail was dancing in the air, and her voice was purring a song for breakfast. Living on the 4th floor of an apartment block was not easy for a young curious cat, but somehow Tinkerbell had learned how to survive. While the porridge was cooling down, Penny went to her room and dressed. She had no time to spare, especially if she wanted to be first in the queue at the post office.

As the bus screeched to a stop, Penny huffed and puffed up the steps. Her hip was giving trouble since the operation last year. 'Morning Tom,' she said, out of breath. 'Hello my dear Penny,' came the usual reply. The short journey to the village normally lasted only a few minutes. Today the trip took longer. Past the school and the old chapel, left at the roundabout and through the cross roads. Looking out the window Penny could see the post office in the distance. Road works were causing a traffic jam. 'Oh fiddlesticks,' she thought. 'I'm going to be late in the queue.' At ten minutes past nine she arrived at the post office. The queue had already begun.

With her pension safely tucked away she left the post office and crossed the road to the grocery shop. 'Apples, oranges, bananas and spuds. Is that all, Miss Johnson?' said the young man in the brown coat. 'Yes, that's all,' she replied. She carefully placed the fruit and veg in two red plastic shopping bags and left the smelly shop with a sly grin on her face. Nobody had noticed the peaches and grapes in the bottom of her handbag.

When Penny left the grocery store she looked at her watch: she was behind schedule. 'Oh no, I'll miss the bus home if I don't get to the bank on time,' she muttered to herself. Reaching the bank she took a ticket and sat herself on the sofa close to the counter. She had to wait ten minutes for the local businessmen to finish their lodgements. At last, counter number four was free and her ticket was called.

She heaved herself up off of the sofa and shuffled over to the counter with her bags. Mr Lawrence Pritchard greeted her with a smile. 'Good morning, Larry,' she said. 'I'd like to lodge a cheque please.' 'Of course, Miss Johnson. Would you like me to lodge it to your savings account or to your regular account?' Before she could answer, she heard a loud BANG.

Right behind her were two masked men, one tall and thin and the other small and round. They had arrived at the bank moments before in a black car which pulled up at the front of the building. 'GET ON THE FLOOR,' the two men screamed, firing their guns in the air. In seconds everyone was horizontal. Penny noticed the tall one pulling two red shopping bags out of his pocket. He walked up to counter number four and placed them in front of Lawrence Pritchard. 'FILL THE BAGS,' he shouted in a horrifying tone. 'If you don't fill the bags, I'll shoot you in the head!' 'Ok Ok,' Larry cried. Just as the bags were filled, the sound of the alarm caught everyone by surprise. The man pulled the bags off the counter, dropped them on the ground and ran over to the window to see if the police were there. He waved at the driver in the car outside, ran back to the counter and quickly picked up the bags. He shouted at the thin robber and they both ran out the door.

The whole thing was over in a few minutes. When everybody calmed down, Penny quietly got to her feet, picked up her shopping bags and left the bank with a sly grin on her face. 'Sorry I can't wait, Larry,' she said. 'I really have to catch a bus.' When the robbers returned to their lair, they were very surprised to find the two red bags filled with apples, oranges and bananas and spuds instead of cash, cash, cash.

EXPLORE

1. Pick two memorable sentences used in the first paragraph.

2. Pick an interesting verb from the first paragraph. Think about why the author chose that particular verb.

3. How does the reader know Penny is elderly? **P I E**

4. Examine paragraph two closely and extract the clue for the twist at the end of the story.

5. What does the author use to indicate loud sounds?

6. From reading this story, what impression do you get of Penny? **P I E**

Writing a Short Story

This story works because of the choice of **character** and the readers' **expectations** of what an elderly woman is capable of. She is capable of stealing the money, but no one really expects it of her.

It is a great idea to challenge yourself when creating your main character for your short stories. Use your imagination and pick someone who is far from your writing 'comfort zone', for example, a thirty-year-old nurse, or a seven-year-old boy living in Bangladesh. You might need to do a little research to build your character.

REMEMBER How to write a short story, p. 72.

Four-Part Story Planner

Opening: Introduces the setting (the time, the place, the atmosphere) and the characters

Start the action and create a point of conflict

Build up to a dramatic climax: tension mounts to its highest point (a moment of great emotion/excitement

Ending/Resolution – the outcome: strong ending, either positive or negative. Often a moment of realisation, reflection or truth

Plot Twists

Another element that really worked in the short story you read was the **plot twist**.

Plot twist n.

Definition: A completely unexpected outcome at the end of a narrative

There are a number of different ways to build up to a plot twist.

* Leave extremely subtle (present but difficult to spot) hints for the reader. The reader should not think about these clues until the very end when they realise they have been duped (tricked).

* Point the finger at someone else. Mislead your audience by arousing suspicion with another character.

* Reveal a character reversal. Does your hero become a villain or vice versa?

* Open endings can be used as a gesture towards plot twists but writers need to be careful. There is a difference between leaving a surprising open end to a story and just leaving the reader unsatisfied.

CREATE

Create a short story which includes a character that does something unexpected.

You **must:**
- Create a brainstorm of your ideas and plan the structure for your story
- Have a unique or entertaining character
- Use paragraphs
- Have accurate grammar and spelling

You **should:**
- Include strong verbs and adjectives
- Choose a character which challenges you
- Use the RAFT structure

You **could:**
- Include a successful plot twist

A Speech

What I will learn:

to understand and effectively use statistics, anecdotes, rhetorical questions and quotes

The next author and speaker is certainly not limited by her age. Emma Watson, one of the stars of the *Harry Potter* films, has received many accolades (awards) at a very young age. At the UN Convention on Gender Rights, she made a powerful and articulate speech as the Global Goodwill Ambassador for UN Women.

The following vocabulary appears in Emma Watson's speech. Read through the words and definitions, which do not match. Before you listen to the speech, try and match the words with the correct definition. During or after watching the speech, you can review your answers and change any incorrect guesses.

Word	Definition	Before Listening	During/After Listening
advocate	making something unrecognisable		
humanitarian	separate something to keep it on its own		
distinguished	not being treated equally		
inequality	giving in to the demands of someone else		
galvanise	to support something		
tangible	involving support or helping improve human lives		
isolating	able to be touched or felt		
distort	shock someone into taking action	*galvanise*	
submissive	unsafe or unstable		
precarious	being recognised for success or achievements, standing out	*distinguished*	

You Tube Emma Watson's Speech for the UN Convention on Gender Rights

 Now look up 'Emma Watson at the HeForShe Campaign 2014 – Official UN video' on YouTube.

1. From listening to her speech, what does Emma Watson think about gender roles?

2. Do you think this speech is inspiring? PIE

3. Regarding the final part of the speech, do you think it was an effective way for Emma Watson to end? Explain your view, referring to the words she uses.

In response to Emma Watson's speech, write two paragraphs of a speech you would give regarding gender inequality. You can refer to her speech or use some of her statistics/anecdotes/rhetorical questions/quotes to help you communicate your opinion about the issue.

* You might include a **greeting** to introduce both yourself and your speech. Emma Watson's greeting is: 'Your Excellencies, UN Secretary General, President of the General Assembly, Executive Director of UN Women and distinguished guests.'

* **Statistics** are a collection of numerical data usually given as a percentage or by use of the phrase 'x in every x', e.g. '1 in every 4 Irish teenagers has been cyberbullied more than once.' Emma's example is: 'Less than 30% of the audience was male.'

* **Anecdotes** are short accounts of an episode or event in your own life. Emma's example is: 'When I was eight, I was confused with being called "bossy" because I wanted to direct the plays which we would put on for our parents, but the boys were not.'

* **Rhetorical questions** are questions that do not expect an answer, either because they don't have an answer or because they were asked to introduce or emphasise a point. Emma's example is: 'If not me, who? If not now, when?'

* **Quotes** are when you refer to someone else's words. Emma's example is: 'Statesman Edmund Burke said, "All that is needed for the forces of evil to triumph is for good men and women to do nothing."'

Write the first two paragraphs for a speech on the topic: 'Young people don't have the ability to make a difference.' You must carry out some research to find **two statistics** and **one quote** that you can use in your speech. You must also include an **anecdote** from your own life and a **rhetorical question**.

A Poem

What I will learn:

to write a monologue; to identify the atmosphere of a piece

Just as the authors of short stories do, poets often write about things that we do not expect, or talk about events in an unusual way. In the next poem, Seamus Heaney recalls a life-changing family event when he was a young student.

Are you the youngest or eldest in your family? Do you have siblings? If not, do you wish you had? Discuss the positives and negatives of being part of a family.

Mid-Term Break

by Seamus Heaney

I sat all morning in the college sick bay
Counting bells knelling classes to a close.
At two o'clock our neighbours drove me home.

In the porch I met my father crying–
He had always taken funerals in his stride–
And Big Jim Evans saying it was a hard blow.

The baby cooed and laughed and rocked the pram
When I came in, and I was embarrassed
By old men standing up to shake my hand

And tell me they were 'sorry for my trouble'.
Whispers informed strangers I was the eldest,
Away at school, as my mother held my hand

In hers and coughed out angry tearless sighs.
At ten o'clock the ambulance arrived
With the corpse, stanched and bandaged by the nurses.

Next morning I went up into the room. Snowdrops
And candles soothed the bedside; I saw him
For the first time in six weeks. Paler now,

Wearing a poppy bruise on his left temple,
He lay in the four-foot box as in his cot.
No gaudy scars, the bumper knocked him clear.

A four-foot box, a foot for every year.

 Look up Seamus Heaney reading this poem on YouTube.

EXPLORE

1. Match up the following words/phrases used in the poem with their correct meaning.

coo	very obvious marking or decoration that stands out
knell	murmur softly
soothe	area of a school where ill students can wait for attention
stanch	to calm or comfort
gaudy	the sound made by a bell being rung slowly, usually to mark someone's death
sick bay	stop the flow of a liquid, e.g. blood

2. Tell the story of this poem in no more than thirty words.

3. Who are the people affected by the death described in this poem?

4. Draw two images that represent what you think are key moments in the poem. Show them to your class and describe why you feel these are key moments. Attach quotes to the images.

5. Create three questions you would like to ask the poet about this poem.

6. How did this poem make you feel? Give a reason for your answer.

7. Put yourself in the poet's shoes. Vocalise your thoughts by writing a monologue in which you explain the thoughts running through your head when you arrive home.

8. How would you describe the atmosphere or mood of this poem? Choose three words or phrases to support your answer.

9. Heaney uses examples of the following poetic techniques in his poem. Find an example of one of them:

- Simile
- Alliteration
- Onomatopoeia
- Repetition
- Assonance

TOP TIP

You could use websites such as Voki or GoAnimate to create a character for question 7 and make them talk.

Monologue n.
Definition: A long, uninterrupted speech by one actor or character. It usually explains the inner feelings and thoughts of this character that they might not want to share with anyone else.

Atmosphere n.
Definition: The dominant mood of a piece of written work

CREATE

Write a dialogue between the mourners at the funeral where they discuss how members of the family will deal with the death of the poet's brother. You **should**:

- Draw attention to the different ways the poet describes people reacting to the death.

- Suggest (through the dialogue) how the poet himself has dealt with the death of his brother.

Dialogue *n*.
Definition: A conversation between two or more people (usually as featured in a book, play or film). An improvised dialogue is one which is spontaneous and unscripted – you just make it up on the spot.

Blog Entry

What I will learn:

to write a formal blog entry

As you will have noticed from the poem 'Mid-Term Break', young people are often forced to deal with problems or tragedies that, in an ideal world, no young person would have to deal with.

PREPARE

Think about the hardest thing you have had to deal with. This answer may be quite different from person to person, as it might be a minor problem like not winning the County Final, not getting to see Ed Sheeran with your friends, losing your phone; or it could be something more serious, like losing a parent, fighting with a friend, dealing with an illness or bullying. Do not discuss it with anyone but spend a minute thinking about how you dealt with that hardship.
Ask yourself:

- Did you deal with it well?

- Are you still trying to come to terms with it?

- Can you do something to help yourself or make a positive change for yourself?

TOP TIP

If you are experiencing something you find difficult to deal with, don't do it alone. Talk to a family member, a friend, a teacher or a guidance counsellor. It really helps to talk about your problems – you don't have to face them alone.

In this next blog entry, the youth of today are again showing their incredible resilience in the face of hardship. This blog entry is more formal and quite similar in style to an article.

'Give Peace a Chance – Run With Youth' by Ettie Higgins

One year after fighting broke out in the world's newest nation, its youth are gunning for peace.

Rambang 'Raymond' Tot Deng was eighteen and attending his final year of school when fighting erupted in South Sudan's capital Juba, one year ago. In the ensuing violence, as Raymond's school books burned, thousands of South Sudanese were killed, including two of his cousins. Many fled to UN bases for protection or to neighbouring countries. 'I saw children killed and women killed and everybody was crying,' Raymond recalls.

It was never meant to be this way. The bells of celebration that rang around South Sudan just two years ago, are today emergency sirens. And while South Sudan is a crisis for children and young people, sparse global attention has been paid to them. This must change.

The well of pain runs deep in many parts of Africa, and yet it is young people who offer the best chance for true conflict resolution and lasting peace. Conflict-affected youth are often the most ambitious, the hardest workers. They want back what was taken from them: opportunity. They want an education and they want to earn a liveable wage.

Since conflict began, an estimated 1.8 million South Sudanese have fled their homes. Many remain on the move, while tens of thousands are living in camps in South Sudan, such as the UN Protection of Civilian Camp 1 on the outskirts of southern Juba. Here Raymond lives alongside 10,000 other youth. Whilst ever grateful for the protection the camp offers, Raymond says: 'Life in the camp is difficult. You can see people just lying, sitting down, there's nowhere people can go, nothing for them to do.'

Raymond's experience of war, violence and suffering has been shared by hundreds of thousands across the region. But during the past two to three decades, it has consistently been young people who have been most affected by the conflicts that have raged.

erupted: burst out

ensuing: as a result

sparse: little

estimated: roughly calculated

This early experience of conflict leaves young people in a kind of no man's land. Education interrupted, opportunities crushed. In South Sudan, 400,000 young people have lost the chance to have an education in this year alone. Hundreds of thousands more are jaded, frustrated and disconnected, putting them at a critical crossroads, do they fight or fight for peace? 'Some of the youth with whom I was together outside [the camp] joined the rebellion,' says Raymond. 'They would say, "If I could be in this dire situation we are now in, why should I be here?"' And yet Raymond offers an important caveat: 'Fighting cannot take everybody everywhere. Only peace can unite people as one.'

How then to do this? Unicef believes one answer is through providing essential services, and in particular education. Basic education and vocational-skills training can lift people out of poverty by providing opportunity. But an education can be so much more, teaching war-torn children things many of us take for granted. At school children learn about the environment, about sanitation, and the importance of good nutrition. In turn, they become agents of change, conveying good practices to their families. Importantly, children who go to school are less likely to be recruited by armed groups. UNICEF, through Learning for Peace, our Peace-building, Education and Advocacy Programme, is helping to rebuild and improve schools in both conflict and former conflict zones in South Sudan, providing materials and psychosocial support to help children cope with the traumas they have suffered.

UNICEF believes a key strategy for governments, the African Union, IGAD and development agencies is to counter insecurity through harnessing and connecting with youth. On this, Raymond should be a poster child. Despite the horror he experienced a year ago, the boredom of the camp and the frustrations of having his education suspended, he is a born peacemaker. Now part of a youth forum in the Juba camp, he leads discussions on the root causes of conflict and reconciliation. Raymond deserves to have his voice heard. 'Let all youth in the world facing the same thing we are, know that forgiveness is the first priority,' he says. 'Give us the tools, and we will create peace.'

UNICEF: United Nations International Children's Emergency Fund

IGAD: Intergovernmental Authority on Development

EXPLORE

1. Where is South Sudan?

2. What was Raymond doing just before the fighting broke out?

3. According to paragraph three, how has violence changed the young people of South Sudan?

4. According to paragraph four, what is one problem for the youth in the camp?

5. Explain why people would want to join the rebellion, in your opinion. What is going through their minds?

6. Do you agree that Raymond is a mature person considering his age? What makes you agree or disagree?

7. What do the following phrases mean?

   - 'Conflict resolution'

   - 'No man's land'

   - 'Critical crossroads'

CREATE

Write a formal blog entry in which you talk about one of the following topics:

- Injustice experienced by young people

- The youth of today are changing the world

- Young people are forced to make mature decisions today

Formal writing demands that you are much more careful with your word choice and sentence structure. There is less room for conversational language and informal phrases. However, you are still writing a blog so you have a lot of freedom. Ensure your opinions are backed up with evidence.

There are many other examples of young people in conflict situations. Find another story where a young person has to deal with a very adult situation. Bring it into class and share the story with your classmates.

The following websites might be useful:

www.unicef.ie

www.concern.ie

www.savethechildren.net

www.barnardos.ie

Learn more about Raymond Tot Deng's story in a short video on YouTube, 'Displaced in South Sudan, Raymond, 18, shares his hopes for peace'.

SHOW WHAT YOU KNOW

You have learned many writing and speaking skills in this collection of texts. Now it's time to *Show What You Know!*

My Writing Task

Write a humorous or serious blog entry where you explore the differences between old and young people.

Self-Assessment

Re-read what you have written and then write down two things you think you did well and one thing you could improve on.

Redrafting

Reviewing the success criteria again to make sure you have met all the requirements, and taking into account your own self-assessment notes, revise your blog to create a second draft. When you are happy with your blog, you can put it in your Collection of Texts.

I must

- Include a headline
- Give my opinion
- Write in the first person narrative
- Use paragraphs
- Provide an image
- Use accurate spelling and grammar

I should

- Include drop caps
- Experiment with different vocabulary
- Do some research for my topic
- Use the RAFT structure

I could

- Design the blog page
- Write multiple entries to complement the piece
- Publish it online (with my guardian's permission)

Reflection Note

If you choose to place this task into your **Collection of Texts**, complete a reflection note.
Hint: See the success criteria above to help you.

Oral Communication

Deliver a speech based on the following topic:
'The young and old are the most vulnerable groups in society.'

SUCCESS CRITERIA

I should

- Experiment with different vocabulary
- Use statistics, anecdotes, rhetorical questions and quotes
- Use the **RAFT** structure

I must

- Brainstorm ideas
- Include a greeting and conclusion
- Use emotive language
- Use the correct tone of voice
- Speak slowly and clearly
- Use eye contact
- Use body language and gestures correctly (not too much)

I could

- Give a more passionate and dramatic performance
- Use pitch and pace effectively

Peer Assessment

Reflect on your classmate's oral communication and then write down two things you think they did well and one thing they could improve on.

Redrafting

After you have practised your speech in front of someone, make a list of how you can improve it. You should also review the success criteria again to ensure you have met all the requirements. At this point, make any necessary changes to your speech. When you are happy with it, you can present it orally or record and then present/submit it to your teacher.

Reflection Note

Now complete the
**Oral Communication
Template for
Student Reflection.**

Journeys

Journeys

in the news → in history → in stories

Punctuation marks

Newspaper editorial

Capital letters for authors' names, correct spelling for book titles

As I explore this collection I will learn about:

Rhyme scheme

Imagery in poetry

Modelling my paragraphs on a paragraph by a famous writer

Mind-mapping poems

foreshadowing ← Storytelling skills → twist-in-the-tail

suspense ← → character creation

SHOW WHAT YOU KNOW
The skills you learn in this collection will enable you to **show what you know** in your final tasks at the end of this collection.

For my writing task I will:
Write *either* a newspaper editorial about something I have an opinion on *or* a story about a character who sets out alone on a journey

For oral communication I will:
Speak either my editorial or my short story

Learning Outcomes
OL5, OL8, OL9, OL10, R1, R4, R6, R9, R12, W3, W5, W11

Exploring the Theme – Journeys

Twenty years from now you will be more disappointed by the things you didn't do than by the ones you did do. So sail away from the safe harbour. Explore. Dream. Discover.
Mark Twain

Two roads diverged in a wood and I – I took the one less travelled by.
Robert Frost

List the journeys of your life so far. What was the first journey of your life? Who took you/carried you on that journey? What was the first journey you made on your own? Have you made any memorable or unusual journeys?

Complete two of the following sentences.

1. The best journey of my life was …

2. One journey that I would love to make is …

3. The most interesting journey I ever heard of was …

Compare and **contrast** what you wrote with the person beside you.

Famous Journeys in Fact and in Fiction

Going on a journey is the theme of many stories.

 In pairs, link the **famous fictional character** with the journey.

_____ went to the ball.

_____ stepped through the looking glass.

_____ travelled to Hogwarts.

_____ was swept by a tornado to the Land of Oz.

_____ swam to a desert island.

_____ sailed down the Mississippi.

_____ searched for the Lost Ark.

_____ went to Mount Doom to destroy a dangerous ring, forged by the Dark Lord Sauron.

_____ boldly went where no man has gone before.

Add a sentence of your own about another character who went on a journey.
Put a line in place of the character's name so that you do not reveal it yet.

Indiana Jones	**Robinson Crusoe**	**Huckleberry Finn**
Harry Potter	**Dorothy**	**Alice**
The Starship Enterprise	**Cinderella**	**Frodo**

Ask the person beside you to try to name the missing character in the sentence you added above. Then add that character's name to the list.

There have been many famous journeys in **history**.

Link the **historical character** with the journey below.

_____ crossed the Atlantic.

_____ travelled to the Crimea to nurse wounded soldiers.

_____ travelled the Silk Road to China.

_____ was the first person to fly solo from Honolulu to California.

_____ orbited the earth.

_____ stepped on to the moon.

Add a sentence of your own about another famous person who went on a journey. Put a line in place of the person's name so that you do not reveal it yet.

Yuri Gagarin   **Amelia Earhart**   **Neil Armstrong**

Marco Polo   **Florence Nightingale**   **Columbus**

Ask the person beside you to try to name the famous person in the sentence you added above. Then add that person's name to the list.

The Journey of Migration

In this 21st century of '**global migration**', millions of people are making long journeys to new countries, seeking work, peace or new lives.

Look at the map of the world.

Give an example of migration that you have heard about in the news. Who are the people? Where are they coming from? Where are they going to?

The UNHCR (find out what these initials stand for) is an agency of the United Nations that works on behalf of migrants and refugees fleeing war, persecution and poverty. It was established after World War II to help Europeans displaced by the conflict. It is as crucial today as it was then.

PUNCTUATION

- Titles of stories and poems are written in **capitals** and placed between **inverted commas** ('/').

- Prepositions in a book title are written in **lowercase**.

- Authors' names get capital letters. Initials are followed by a **full stop**, e.g. J. K. Rowling.

- A question is marked by a **question mark** (?).

- An **exclamation mark** is used to show surprise (!).

- A brief pause is marked by a **comma** (,).

'Pride and Prejudice' **'To Kill a Mockingbird'** **'Lord of the Flies'**

'Of Mice and Men' **'The Shadow of a Gunman'** **'The Merchant of Venice'**

Have you read 'The Wizard of Oz', written by L. Frank Baum? It's fantastic!

1. Now write these sentences correctly, inserting capital letters, inverted commas, full stops or question marks.

    i.   alice's adventures in wonderland was written by lewis carroll

    ii. robinson crusoe was written by daniel defoe

    iii. have you read huckleberry finn written by mark twain

    iv. did you know that the field was written by john b keane

    v.   romeo and juliet was written by william shakespeare

    vi. is s e hinton the author of the outsiders

    vii. the lake isle of innisfree was written by w b yeats

    viii. a rare handwritten edition of the tales of beedle the bard the storybook mentioned in harry potter and the deathly hallows sold at auction for a record 2.7 million euro

2. Write down the titles and authors of the novels, plays and films that you are studying for this course. Include the title of one poem. Each sentence will read as follows:

    '..' was written by ....

    Pay strict attention to capital letters and inverted commas.

Crossword

Complete this crossword by using the correct words to describe different kinds of journeys.

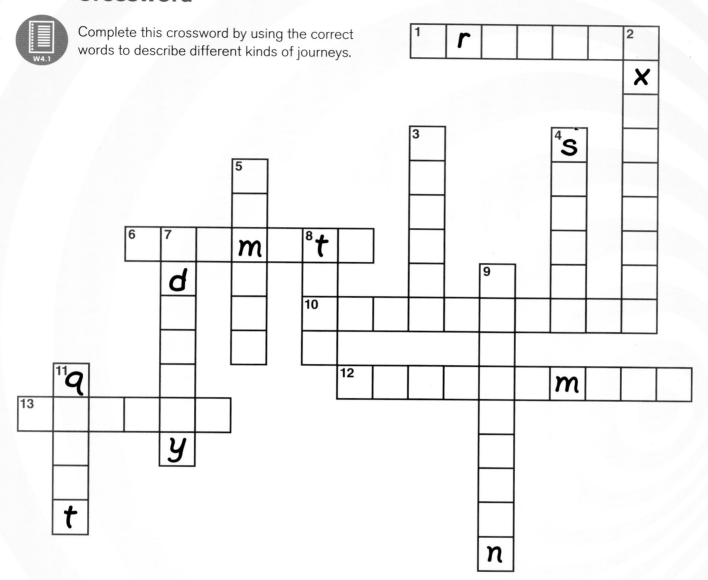

Across

1. Medieval journey to fight religious war [7]
6. Journey to and from work [7]
10. Journey for a specific purpose, e.g. science [10]
12. Religious journey to a holy place [10]
13. Official trip, supposedly serious, but actually for pleasure [6]

Down

2. Pleasure trip made by a group of people [9]
3. Sea journey [6]
4. Overland expedition observing animals [6]
5. Leisurely walk in the country [6]
7. Epic long journey of adventure [7]
8. Long, tough walk [4]
9. Large group of people or animals moving from one country to another [9]
11. Determined search to find something lost or solve a mystery [5]

CREATE

You've seen an advertisement for a competition called 'Tell Us about *Your* Journey'.

Choose a journey you have made that you think people would like to read about. In a series of separate paragraphs, write about the anticipation, the experiences on the journey and the arrival at your destination.

The winning entry will be published in a national newspaper, so remember to answer the questions WHO? WHAT? WHEN? WHERE? WHY? **and** HOW?

You could illustrate your writing with pictures or photographs.

The 5 Ws are very important, but it is also important to consider 'how'; in this case, how the journey was accomplished.

A Newspaper Editorial

What I will learn:

how to write an editorial in a newspaper, following six key points

An editorial in a newspaper or magazine presents that publication's opinion on an issue in the news. It lays out facts, lists points that it disagrees with and gives evidence for its own point of view. It tries to persuade readers that its point of view is the correct one.

READ

In the following newspaper editorial about global migration, the editor aims to inspire compassion for migrants who set out on dangerous journeys hoping to reach safety.

Paragraphs 1 and 2 lay out the facts; paragraph three states the opposing point of view. Evidence and statistics are given to persuade readers to be sympathetic to the plight of migrants. The final paragraph makes the point that fortunate people should be willing to welcome those less fortunate than themselves.

Six Key Points in Writing an Editorial

1. Choose a topic in the news.
2. Give your editorial a title.
3. Write a strong starter sentence and short opening paragraph that briefly states the facts.
4. State an opposing point of view with which you disagree.
5. Find supporting evidence, recent events, examples and statistics from respected sources that back up your point of view. Your aim is to persuade readers that you have taken the correct stance on this topic.
6. Write a persuasive closing paragraph stating your conclusions.

Aim for 350–400 words.

Dangerous Journeys

by Ian Fredice

The numbers of people crossing borders in search of a better life are greater than ever before in the history of the planet. UN and Red Cross reports tell us that since 2000, through persecution, war, poverty, famine, violence and lack of human rights, over 60 million people have left their homes in search of peace or simply to survive.

Human suffering in the Middle East, Afghanistan, Pakistan, the Congo, Somalia, Syria, Central America, South Sudan, Ukraine, Burma and Iraq, among others, have caused people to flee their homes. One in every 122 humans on the planet is a refugee.

Many people living in wealthy countries believe that this challenge must be met by more border patrols, only the most basic provisions in camps for displaced persons, a complete ban on being able to work in the new country, and the penalty of being sent back 'home' at any point.

In spite of the risk of death on dangerous journeys and the lack of welcome on arrival, people continue to flee from misery. Whether it's an overcrowded leaking boat, a suffocating container on a truck or a ship, or a climb over razor wire fences, a recent UN report tells us that people are willing to set out in terrible circumstances to try to find a new life abroad.

For example, up to half a million Central American migrants jump on to freight trains heading to the US every year. Many die from heat or thirst or become the victims of violent robbery. They are likely to be the poorest citizens, who cannot afford to pay a smuggler to organise their journey. These trains, known as 'La Bestia', or the beast, carry cargo northwards. These would-be migrants lie on the roof of the moving train, with nothing to hold on to, facing loss of limb or life if they fall.

We who live in peace, free from hunger, making journeys only in the comfort of a car or a plane, do not know what it is like to leave everything we know and hold dear and travel without money, passport or prospects. Do you know how it feels to stand with your children at a barbed wire fence with nothing in your pockets and a border patrol between you and a decent life? We should be pressing our governments to provide asylum, shelter and decent lives for those unfortunate enough to be born in the wrong place at the wrong time.

(395 words)

Find these countries on the map of the world on page 117. Which of these countries is also known by another name?

TOP TIP

A newspaper *article* gives the facts about a topic. A newspaper *editorial* gives the **facts** as well as the newspaper's **opinion** on the topic.

EXPLORE

W 4.2

The title of this editorial is 'Dangerous Journeys'. Write another suitable title for it.

1. The editorial states that there are different points of view on this issue. In paragraph three, what negative point of view does it present?

2. What is the purpose of this editorial? What does the author want to achieve?

3. Mention two examples of dangerous journeys, facts or statistics that are offered in the editorial to back up the case that is being made.

4. In your opinion, what is the strongest sentence in the editorial? Explain your choice.

RESEARCH ZONE

Choose one of the countries mentioned in the editorial and find an online article, a newspaper article or a news broadcast about that country. Read or show your item to the class.

Remember to use reliable newspapers or websites in your research.

MIND YOUR LANGUAGE

REVISING CAPITAL LETTERS AND PUNCTUATION

1. Without looking back at the editorial, rewrite this passage correctly:

    for example up to half a million central american migrants jump on to freight trains heading to the us every year many die from heat or thirst or become the victims of violent robbery they are likely to be the poorest citizens who cannot afford to pay a smuggler to organise their journey these trains known as la bestia or the beast carry cargo northwards these would be migrants lie on the roof of the moving train with nothing to hold on to facing loss of limb or life if they fall

2. Using this passage as an example, write at least three bullet points on the importance of capital letters and punctuation. Some points are started for you here.

    *   A sentence must begin with a _____ _____.

    *   Names of countries get a _____ _____.

    *   A short pause in a sentence is marked by a _____.

    *   A sentence should end with a _____ _____.

    *   _____ _____ s are placed around the titles of things.

Poetry

What I will learn:

rhyme scheme; imagery; alliteration

PREPARE

The first poem you will read in this lesson is by Robert Frost. It was written when he was living in the White Mountains in the north-east of the USA. It tells the story of a man with a horse and cart who stops to look into the woods as he travels home one snowy night in late December.

The poem has an interesting rhyme scheme. As you read, make a note of the end word of the third line of each stanza. Then note the end word of the first line in the next stanza. You will see (and hear!) that a very musical repetition of rhyming sounds is created.

Fill in the gaps in the rhyme scheme.

 ## Stopping by Woods on a Snowy Evening
by Robert Frost

Whose woods these are I think I know.	*a*
His house is in the village though;	__
He will not see me stopping here	*b*
To watch his woods fill up with snow.	__
My little horse must think it queer	*b*
To stop without a farmhouse near	__
Between the woods and frozen lake	__
The darkest evening of the year.	*b*
He gives his harness bells a shake	__
To ask if there is some mistake.	*c*
The only other sound's the sweep	*d*
Of easy wind and downy flake.	__
The woods are lovely, dark and deep,	*d*
But I have promises to keep,	__
And miles to go before I sleep,	__
And miles to go before I sleep.	__

FUN FACT

Robert Frost was the first poet to be invited to speak at the inauguration of a US President (that of J. F. Kennedy in January 1963). Since then, four more poets have read their poems at inaugurations.

Write about the poem, explaining its story, its imagery, sounds and any alliteration you picked up on. Describe its pace, tone and rhyme scheme. Say what you enjoyed about it. Use the mind map below to guide you.

EXPLORE

Mind Map for 'Stopping by Woods on a Snowy Evening'

The words you write in each box can then be used to develop a series of short paragraphs about the poem.

Who is in the poem? **Where** and **when** is it happening?

Image(s): What pictures form in your mind as you read the poem? You can imagine the snow, the trees and the lake. You can hear the little sounds of the rising wind, the harness bells and the soft swish and fall of snowflakes.

Describe the **pace** and **tone** of voice, in the first four lines and the last four lines, e.g. Which words or phrases should be spoken slowly? quickly? My tone of voice would be thoughtful, anxious, happy, sad, angry, puzzled, contented, relaxed, mysterious, etc.

My **two favourite lines** are …

'Stopping by Woods on a Snowy Evening' by Robert Frost

In this poem, **I enjoyed** …

What are the **sounds** in the poem? Can you point out examples of **alliteration**?

Describe the **rhyme scheme**. Try to catch its lilting **rhythm** as you read it aloud. Notice how it imitates the sound of a horse's hooves falling clip-clop as it pulls the cart. There are eight beats in every line. One light beat is immediately followed by the next heavy beat, as in, 'Whose **woods** these **are** I **think** I **know**'.

When the poet says, 'But I have promises to keep,/And miles to go before I sleep', *I think he means …*

PREPARE

The next poem is 'The Listeners' by Walter de la Mare. One night, a man arrives on horseback to a house in a forest that has a link with his past life. He has something important to say, but it seems there is no one there to hear him. He knocks and shouts out that he has been honourable, that he has kept his word or his side of the bargain. He senses that someone is listening, but no one replies.

 # Crossword

Check that you understand the poem's vocabulary by completing this crossword.

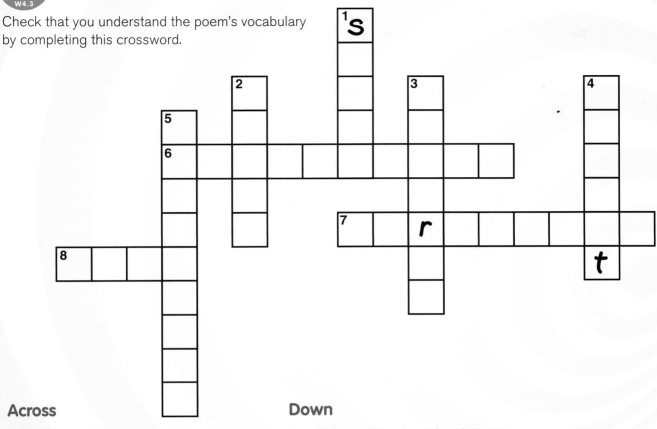

Across

6. Old word for listening [10]
7. Bewildered, confused, puzzled [9]
8. Flowerless soft green plant [4]

Down

1. Old word for struck hard [5]
2. Old word for spoke [5]
3. Metal object in which you place your foot [7]
4. Small tower on a house or castle [6]
5. Crowding, filling a space [9]

 ## The Listeners
by Walter de la Mare

'Is there anybody there?' said the Traveller
Knocking on the moonlit door;
And his horse in the silence champed the grasses
Of the forest's ferny floor;
And a bird flew up out of the turret,

Above the Traveller's head:
And he smote upon the door again a second time;
'Is there anybody there?' he said.
But no one descended to the Traveller;
No head from the leaf-fringed sill
Leaned over and looked into his grey eyes,
Where he stood perplexed and still.
But only a host of phantom listeners
That dwelt in the lone house then
Stood listening in the quiet of the moonlight
To that voice from the world of men:
Stood thronging the faint moonbeams on the dark stair,
That goes down to the empty hall,
Hearkening in an air stirred and shaken
By the lonely Traveller's call.
And he felt in his heart their strangeness,
Their stillness answering his cry,
While his horse moved, cropping the dark turf,
'Neath the starred and leafy sky;
For he suddenly smote on the door, even ⎯⎯⎯
Louder, and lifted his head:–
'Tell them I came, and no one answered,
That I kept my word,' he said.
Never the least stir made the listeners,
Though every word he spake
Fell echoing through the shadowiness of the still house
From the one man left awake:
Ay, they heard his foot upon the stirrup,
And the sound of iron on stone,
And how the silence surged softly backward,
When the plunging hoofs were gone.

> Notice the use of enjambment here, i.e. the meaning runs on to the next line

1. Imagine you're making a short film of this poem. Agree or disagree with the following suggestions, and give a reason for your answer.

Statements	I agree	I disagree	My comment/suggestion
The bird that flies out of the turret should be a robin or a cuckoo			
The 'phantom listeners' should look like the ghosts of the dead			
The Traveller should speed away looking angry			
The horse should be a little white pony			

2. Suggest a piece of music or a song that you would play in the closing shot.

3. Write a commentary about the poem, using the mind map below to guide you.

Mind Map for 'The Listeners'

Each box becomes a short paragraph in your answer.

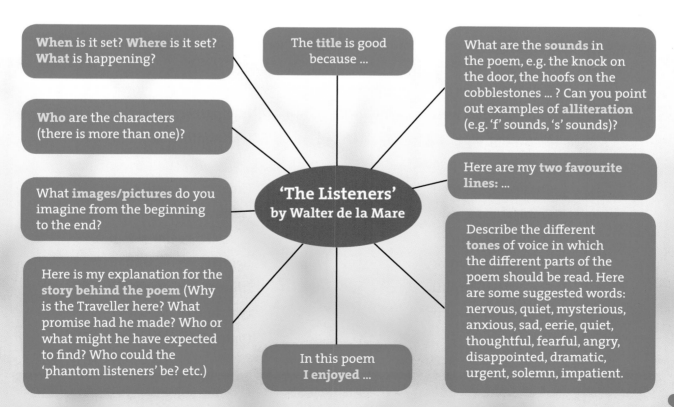

When is it set? **Where** is it set? **What** is happening?

The **title** is good because ...

What are the **sounds** in the poem, e.g. the knock on the door, the hoofs on the cobblestones ... ? Can you point out examples of **alliteration** (e.g. 'f' sounds, 's' sounds)?

Who are the characters (there is more than one)?

'The Listeners' by Walter de la Mare

Here are my **two favourite lines:** ...

What **images/pictures** do you imagine from the beginning to the end?

Describe the different **tones** of voice in which the different parts of the poem should be read. Here are some suggested words: nervous, quiet, mysterious, anxious, sad, eerie, quiet, thoughtful, fearful, angry, disappointed, dramatic, urgent, solemn, impatient.

Here is my explanation for the **story behind the poem** (Why is the Traveller here? What promise had he made? Who or what might he have expected to find? Who could the 'phantom listeners' be? etc.)

In this poem **I enjoyed ...**

A Classic Piece of Storytelling

storytelling techniques, e.g. how to create fear; dramatic verbs and adjectives to show a character in a state of panic; to use a repeated phrase to create a dramatic effect

The following passage is taken from the famous children's classic, *The Wind in the Willows.*

This children's book is so popular, it has never been out of print since it was first published in 1908. It has been made into countless films, TV series, musicals, ballets and plays. Many famous actors have done the voices in cartoon versions. Ricky Gervais is the latest star to play the voice of Mole in the most recent movie version.

You can learn a lot of storytelling skills from this short extract. You will see how a writer communicates the panic felt by a character who is lost and terrified. From reading it you will learn how to write excellent descriptions.

In this extract, as Mole goes deeper into the 'Wild Wood', the light fades and he fears that he is being watched by hidden weasels and stoats.

VOCABULARY

Although this book was written as a story to be read to children, its vocabulary is quite advanced and sophisticated. See if you can unscramble the following words that appear in the story.

Try doing them on your own first, and then checking those you can't unscramble by reading the extract.

Determined decision to do something	(iontulores) *begins with r*
Old-**fashioned** word for a little sitting room	(roulpar) *begins with p*
Menacing, promising danger or harm	(earthgninte) *begins with t*
Made a cracking sound	(edcarkcl) *begins with c*
Chain of rocks on the sea surface	(free) *begins with r*
Comical, exaggerated likenesses	(serracutiac) *begins with c*
Own, belong to	(osspess) *begins with p*
Spite, evil intention	(lcimae) *begins with m*
Opposite of breadth	(thgnel) *begins with l*
Regular repeated pattern of sound	(yhtrhm) *begins with r*
Vanished	(ppreadsiead) *begins with d*

Extract from *The Wind in the Willows* by Kenneth Grahame

The Wild Wood

Mole had a good deal of spare time on his hands, and so one afternoon, he formed the resolution to go out by himself and explore the Wild Wood.

It was a cold still afternoon with a hard steely sky overhead, when he slipped out of the warm parlour into the open air. He pushed on towards the Wild Wood, which lay before him low and threatening, like a black reef in some still southern sea.

There was nothing to alarm him at first entry. Twigs crackled under his feet, logs tripped him, funguses on stumps resembled caricatures, and startled him for the moment by their likeness to something familiar and far away; but that was all fun, and exciting. It led him on, and he penetrated to where the light was less, and trees crouched nearer and nearer, and holes made ugly mouths at him on either side.

Everything was very still now. The dusk advanced on him steadily, rapidly, gathering in behind and before; and the light seemed to be draining away like flood-water.

Then the faces began.

It was over his shoulder, and indistinctly, that he first thought he saw a face; a little evil wedge-shaped face, looking out at him from a hole. When he turned and confronted it, the thing had vanished.

He quickened his pace, telling himself cheerfully not to begin imagining things, or there would be simply no end to it. He passed another hole, and another, and another; and then – yes! – no! – yes! certainly a little narrow face, with hard eyes, had flashed up for an instant from a hole, and was gone. He hesitated – braced himself up for an effort and strode on. Then suddenly, and as if it had been so all the time, every hole, far and near, and there were hundreds of them, seemed to possess its face, coming and going rapidly, all fixing on him glances of malice and hatred: all hard-eyed and evil and sharp.

If he could only get away from the holes in the banks, he thought, there would be no more faces. He swung off the path and plunged into the untrodden places of the wood.

Then the whistling began.

Very faint and shrill it was, and far behind him, when first he heard it; but somehow it made him hurry forward. Then, still very faint and shrill, it sounded far ahead of him, and made him hesitate and want to go back. As he halted in indecision it broke out on either side, and seemed to be caught up and passed on throughout the whole length of the wood to its farthest limit. They were up and alert and ready, evidently, whoever they were! And he – he was alone, and unarmed, and far from any help; and the night was closing in.

Then the pattering began.

He thought it was only falling leaves at first, so slight and delicate was the sound of it. Then as it grew it took a regular rhythm, and he knew it for nothing else but the pat-pat-pat of little feet still a very long way off. Was it in front or behind? It seemed to be first one, and then the other, then both. It grew and it multiplied, till from every quarter as he listened anxiously, leaning this way and that, it seemed to be closing in on him. As he stood still to hearken, a rabbit came running hard towards him through the trees. He waited, expecting it to slacken pace, or to swerve from him into a different course. Instead, the animal almost brushed him as it dashed past, his face set and hard, his eyes staring. 'Get out of this, you fool, get out!' the Mole heard him mutter as he swung round a stump and disappeared down a friendly burrow.

The pattering increased till it sounded like sudden hail on the dry leaf-carpet spread around him. The whole wood seemed running now, running hard, hunting, chasing, closing in round something or – somebody? In panic, he began to run too, aimlessly. He ran up against things, he fell over things and into things, he darted under things and dodged round things. At last he took refuge in the deep dark hollow of an old beech tree, which offered shelter, concealment – perhaps even safety, but who could tell?

EXPLORE

1. What frightens Mole as he goes deeper and deeper into the dark wood?

2. What words would you use to describe his state of mind?

3. How many sounds does he hear? Describe them.

4. In the closing paragraph, the author uses verbs that give movement, drama and suspense to the writing. Write down at least four of these verbs. (Remember to include them if you choose to write the scary story at the end of this collection.)

5. Quote what you think are the two best written sentences or phrases in the passage. What do you like about each of them?

FUN FACT

William Golding's *Lord of the Flies* was rejected by twenty publishers before it was accepted.

FUN FACT

Harry Potter was rejected by twelve publishers. J. K. Rowling remembers being especially upset when one of them kept her folder: 'I really minded about the folder, because I had almost no money and had to buy another one.'

FUN FACT

Kenneth Grahame wrote *The Wind in the Willows* to read to his son, first as bedtime stories and then in letters to him while he was at boarding school. It was rejected by many publishers, but when President Theodore Roosevelt read it, he insisted that it be published in the US. It went on to sell millions.

Modelling

You can learn to write by **modelling**. For example, if you model a paragraph on one from *The Wind in the Willows*, you change the character, the weather and/or the place, but keep the basic sentences. You might, for example, change the place and the character but keep some of the adjectives, e.g. warm, low, threatening, black.

It was a cold still afternoon with a hard steely sky overhead, when he slipped out of the warm parlour into the open air. He pushed on towards the Wild Wood, which lay before him low and threatening, like a black reef in some still southern sea.

Here is one student's example of modelling on the above paragraph.

It was a miserable windy morning with a low black sky overhead, when Danny peeped out of the warm tent into the cold, damp air. He looked across the dark field towards the massive grey waves, which lay before him crashing loudly on the sand like a threatening storm in the freezing Arctic Ocean.

Now you try!

It was a ...

Continue to imitate other paragraphs, changing little details.

He quickened his pace, telling himself cheerfully not to begin imagining things, or there would be simply no end to it. He passed another hole, and another, and another; and then – yes! – no! – yes! certainly a little narrow face, with hard eyes, had flashed up for an instant from a hole, and was gone.

Here is another student's example.

Emily slowed her footsteps, telling herself fearfully not to start panicking, or she would never find her auntie's house. She passed another gate on the dark, private road, and another, and another; and then – yes! – no! – yes! savage, growling noises roared from every gate she passed. There were angry guard dogs ready to pounce all along the way.

A Classic Short Story

how a storyteller creates suspense by foreshadowing; creating character through dialogue, gestures, clever little details; twist-in-the-tail endings

PREPARE

Match the following words from the next story with their definitions.

trilby	a mark, an imperfection that spoils the appearance
dragon	person studying for a university degree
façade	dog with long, low body and drooping ears
chrysanthemums	brightly coloured flowers that bloom in winter
dachshund	strong feeling, making you do something
compulsion	large, ferocious, fire-breathing creature
frisky	soft hat with a crease on the top and a narrow brim
sigh	front wall or face of a building
undergraduate	lively, jumpy, playful, cheerful
blemish	absolutely still and without movement
motionless	a little intake of breath, expressing sadness or tiredness

READ

You will now read a famous short story by Roald Dahl, entitled 'The Landlady'. You can read this story as a drama, which will require casting the roles of the characters listed.

Characters

Billy, the Landlady, a railway porter, Mr Greenslade, a narrator

'The Landlady'
by Roald Dahl

Billy Weaver had travelled down from London on the slow afternoon train, with a change at Reading on the way, and by the time he got to Bath, it was about nine o'clock in the evening, and the moon was coming up out of a clear starry sky over the houses opposite the station entrance. But the air was deadly cold and the wind was like a flat blade of ice on his cheeks.

'Excuse me,' he said, 'but is there a fairly cheap hotel not too far away from here?'

'Try The Bell and Dragon,' the porter answered, pointing down the road. 'They might take you in. It's about a quarter of a mile along on the other side.'

Billy thanked him and picked up his suitcase and set out to walk the quarter-mile to The Bell and Dragon. He had never been to Bath before. He didn't know anyone who lived there. But Mr. Greenslade at the head office in London had told him it was a splendid town. 'Find your own lodgings,' he had said, 'and then go along and report to the branch manager as soon as you've got yourself settled.'

Billy was seventeen years old. He was wearing a new navy-blue overcoat, a new brown trilby hat, and a new brown suit, and he was feeling fine. He walked briskly down the street. He was trying to do everything briskly these days. Briskness, he had decided, was *the* one common characteristic of all successful businessmen. The big shots up at the head office were absolutely fantastically brisk all the time. They were amazing.

There were no shops on this wide street that he was walking along, only a line of tall houses on each side, all of them identical. They had porches and pillars and four or five steps going up to their front doors, and it was obvious that once upon a time they had been very swanky residences. But now, even in the darkness, he could see that the paint was peeling from the woodwork on their doors and windows and that the handsome white façades were cracked and blotchy from neglect.

Suddenly, in a downstairs window that was brilliantly illuminated by a street lamp not six yards away, Billy caught sight of a printed notice propped up against the glass in one of the upper panes. It said BED AND BREAKFAST. There was a vase of yellow chrysanthemums, tall and beautiful, standing just underneath the notice.

He stopped walking. He moved a bit closer. Green curtains (some sort of velvety material) were hanging down on either side of the window. The chrysanthemums looked wonderful beside them. He went right up and peered through the glass into the room, and the first thing he saw was a bright fire burning in the hearth. On the carpet in front of the fire, a pretty little dachshund was curled up asleep with its nose tucked into its belly. The room itself, so far as he could see in the half darkness, was filled with pleasant furniture. There was a baby grand piano and a big sofa and several plump armchairs, and in one corner he spotted a large parrot in a cage. Animals were usually a good sign in a place like this, Billy told himself; and all in all, it looked to him as though it would be a pretty decent house to stay in. Certainly it would be more comfortable than The Bell and Dragon.

On the other hand, a pub would be more congenial than a boarding house. There would be beer and darts in the evenings, and lots of people to talk to, and it would probably be a good bit cheaper, too. He had stayed a couple of nights in a pub once before and he had liked it. He had never stayed in any boarding houses, and, to be perfectly honest, he was a tiny bit frightened of them. The name itself conjured up images of watery cabbage, rapacious landladies, and a powerful smell of kippers in the living room.

After dithering about like this in the cold for two or three minutes, Billy decided that he would walk on and take a look at The Bell and Dragon before making up his mind. He turned to go.

And now a queer thing happened to him. He was in the act of stepping back and turning away from the window when all at once his eye was caught and held in the most peculiar manner by the small notice that was there. BED AND BREAKFAST, it said. BED AND BREAKFAST, BED AND BREAKFAST, BED AND BREAKFAST. Each word was like a large black eye staring at him through the glass, holding him, compelling him, forcing him to stay where he was and not to walk away from that house, and the next thing he knew, he was actually moving across from the window to the front door of the house, climbing the steps that led up to it, and reaching for the bell.

He pressed the bell. Far away in a back room he heard it ringing, and then at once – it must have been at once because he hadn't even had time to take his finger from the bell button – the door swung open and a woman was standing there.

Normally you ring the bell and you have at least a half-minute's wait before the door opens. But this dame was like a jack-in-the-box. He pressed the bell – and out she popped! It made him jump.

She was about forty-five or fifty years old, and the moment she saw him, she gave him a warm, welcoming smile.

'Please come in,' she said pleasantly. She stepped aside, holding the door wide open, and Billy found himself automatically starting forward. The compulsion or, more accurately, the desire to follow after her into that house was extraordinarily strong.

'I saw the notice in the window,' he said, holding himself back.

'Yes, I know.'

'I was wondering about a room.'

'It's all ready for you, my dear,' she said. She had a round pink face and very gentle blue eyes.

'I was on my way to The Bell and Dragon,' Billy told her. 'But the notice in your window just happened to catch my eye.'

'My dear boy,' she said, 'why don't you come in out of the cold?'

'How much do you charge?'

'Five and sixpence a night, including breakfast.'

It was fantastically cheap. It was less than half of what he had been willing to pay.

'If that is too much,' she added, 'then perhaps I can reduce it just a tiny bit. Do you desire an egg for breakfast? Eggs are expensive at the moment. It would be sixpence less without the egg.'

'Five and sixpence is fine,' he answered. 'I should like very much to stay here.'

'I knew you would. Do come in.'

She seemed terribly nice. She looked exactly like the mother of one's best school friend welcoming one into the house to stay for the Christmas holidays. Billy took off his hat and stepped over the threshold.

'Just hang it there,' she said, 'and let me help you with your coat.'

There were no other hats or coats in the hall. There were no umbrellas, no walking sticks – nothing.

'We have it all to ourselves,' she said, smiling at him over her shoulder as she led the way upstairs. 'You see, it isn't very often I have the pleasure of taking a visitor into my little nest.'

* STOP * You Tube

Stop reading and **listen** to the first three minutes of a radio play adaptation of this story. You will find it on YouTube: 'The Landlady (by Roald Dahl) – Radioplay Adaptation'. In the radio play, Billy is telling the story as 'I', i.e. first person narration. Listen as far as the moment when the landlady says, 'You see, it isn't very often I have the pleasure of taking a visitor into my little nest.'
Speculate: Quietly write what you think will happen in the rest of the story. Don't show anyone what you have written at this point. *Now read on …*

The old girl is slightly dotty, Billy told himself. But at five and sixpence a night, who cares about that? 'I should've thought you'd be simply swamped with applicants,' he said politely.

'Oh, I am, my dear, I am, of course I am. But the trouble is that I'm inclined to be just a teeny-weeny bit choosy and particular – if you see what I mean.'

'Ah, yes.'

'But I'm always ready. Everything is always ready day and night in this house just on the off chance that an acceptable young gentleman will come along. And it is such a pleasure, my dear, such a very great pleasure when now and again I open the door and I see someone standing there who is just exactly right.' She was halfway up the stairs, and she paused with one hand on the stair rail, turning her head and smiling down at him with pale lips. 'Like you,' she added, and her blue eyes travelled slowly all the way down the length of Billy's body, to his feet, and then up again.

On the second-floor landing she said to him, 'This floor is mine.'

They climbed up another flight. 'And this one is all yours,' she said. 'Here's your room. I do

hope you'll like it.' She took him into a small but charming front bedroom, switching on the light as she went in.

'The morning sun comes right in the window, Mr. Perkins. It is Mr. Perkins, isn't it?'

'No,' he said. 'It's Weaver.'

'Mr. Weaver. How nice. I've put a water bottle between the sheets to air them out, Mr. Weaver. It's such a comfort to have a hot-water bottle in a strange bed with clean sheets, don't you agree? And you may light the gas fire at any time if you feel chilly.'

'Thank you,' Billy said. 'Thank you ever so much.' He noticed that the bedspread had been taken off the bed and that the bedclothes had been neatly turned back on one side, all ready for someone to get in.

'I'm so glad you appeared,' she said, looking earnestly into his face. 'I was beginning to get worried.'

'That's all right,' Billy answered brightly. 'You mustn't worry about me.' He put his suitcase on the chair and started to open it.

'And what about supper, my dear? Did you manage to get anything to eat before you came here?'

'I'm not a bit hungry, thank you,' he said. 'I think I'll just go to bed as soon as possible because tomorrow I've got to get up rather early and report to the office.'

'Very well, then. I'll leave you now so that you can unpack. But before you go to bed, would you be kind enough to pop into the sitting room on the ground floor and sign the book? Everyone has to do that because it's the law of the land, and we don't want to go breaking any laws at this stage in the proceedings, do we?' She gave him a little wave of the hand and went quickly out of the room and closed the door.

Now, the fact that his landlady appeared to be slightly off her rocker didn't worry Billy in the least. After all, she not only was harmless – there was no question about that – but she was also quite obviously a kind and generous soul. He guessed that she had probably lost a son in the war, or something like that, and had never gotten over it.

So a few minutes later, after unpacking his suitcase and washing his hands, he trotted downstairs to the ground floor and entered the living room. His landlady wasn't there, but the fire was glowing in the hearth, and the little dachshund was still sleeping soundly in front of it. The room was wonderfully warm and cosy. I'm a lucky fellow, he thought, rubbing his hands. This is a bit of all right.

He found the guest book lying open on the piano, so he took out his pen and wrote down his name and address. There were only two other entries above his on the page, and as one always does with guest books, he started to read them. One was a Christopher Mulholland from Cardiff. The other was Gregory W. Temple from Bristol.

That's funny, he thought suddenly. Christopher Mulholland. It rings a bell.

Now where on earth had he heard that rather unusual name before?

Was it a boy at school? No. Was it one of his sister's numerous young men, perhaps, or a friend of his father's? No, no, it wasn't any of those. He glanced down again at the book.

Christopher Mulholland

231 Cathedral Road, Cardiff

Gregory W. Temple

27 Sycamore Drive, Bristol

As a matter of fact, now he came to think of it, he wasn't at all sure that the second name didn't have almost as much of a familiar ring about it as the first.

'Gregory Temple?' he said aloud, searching his memory. 'Christopher Mulholland?…'

'Such charming boys,' a voice behind him answered, and he turned and saw his landlady sailing into the room with a large silver tea tray in her hands. She was holding it well out in front of her, and rather high up, as though the tray were a pair of reins on a frisky horse.

'They sound somehow familiar,' he said.

'They do? How interesting.'

'I'm almost positive I've heard those names before somewhere. Isn't that odd? Maybe it was in the newspapers. They weren't famous in any way, were they? I mean famous cricketers or footballers or something like that?'

'Famous,' she said, setting the tea tray down on the low table in front of the sofa. 'Oh no, I don't think they were famous. But they were incredibly handsome, both of them, I can promise you that. They were tall and young and handsome, my dear, just exactly like you.'

Once more, Billy glanced down at the book. 'Look here,' he said, noticing the dates. 'This last entry is over two years old.'

'It is?'

'Yes, indeed. And Christopher Mulholland's is nearly a year before that – more than three years ago.'

'Dear me,' she said, shaking her head and heaving a dainty little sigh. 'I would never have thought it. How time does fly away from us all, doesn't it, Mr. Wilkins?'

'It's Weaver,' Billy said. 'W-e-a-v-e-r.'

'Oh, of course it is!' she cried, sitting down on the sofa. 'How silly of me. I do apologise. In one ear and out the other, that's me, Mr. Weaver.'

'You know something?' Billy said. 'Something that's really quite extraordinary about all this?'

'No, dear, I don't.'

'Well, you see, both of these names – Mulholland and Temple – I not only seem to remember each one of them separately, so to speak, but somehow or other, in some peculiar way, they both appear to be sort of connected together as well. As though they were both famous for the same sort of thing, if you see what I mean – like… well … like Dempsey and Tunney, for example, or Churchill and Roosevelt.'

'How amusing,' she said. 'But come over here now, dear, and sit down beside me on the sofa and I'll give you a nice cup of tea and a ginger biscuit before you go to bed.'

'You really shouldn't bother,' Billy said. 'I didn't mean you to do anything like that.' He stood by the piano, watching her as she fussed about with the cups and saucers. He noticed that she had small, white, quickly moving hands and red fingernails.

'I'm almost positive it was in the newspapers I saw them,' Billy said. 'I'll think of it in a second. I'm sure I will.'

There is nothing more tantalising than a thing like this that lingers just outside the borders of one's memory. He hated to give up.

'Now wait a minute,' he said. 'Wait just a minute. Mulholland … Christopher Mulholland … wasn't that the name of the Eton schoolboy who was on a walking tour through the West Country, and then all of a sudden ….'

'Milk?' she said. 'And sugar?'

'Yes, please. And then all of a sudden …'

'Eton schoolboy?' she said. 'Oh no, my dear, that can't possibly be right, because my Mr. Mulholland was certainly not an Eton schoolboy when he came to me. He was a Cambridge undergraduate. Come over here now and sit next to me and warm yourself in front of this lovely fire. Come on. Your tea's all ready for you.' She patted the empty place beside her on the sofa, and she sat there smiling at Billy and waiting for him to come over.

He crossed the room slowly and sat down on the edge of the sofa. She placed his teacup on the table in front of him.

'*There* we are,' she said. 'How nice and cosy this is, isn't it?'

Billy started sipping his tea. She did the same. For half a minute or so, neither of them spoke. But Billy knew that she was looking at him. Her body was half turned toward him, and he could

feel her eyes resting on his face, watching him over the rim of her teacup. Now and again, he caught a whiff of a peculiar smell that seemed to emanate directly from her person. It was not in the least unpleasant, and it reminded him – well, he wasn't quite sure what it reminded him of. Pickled walnuts? New leather? Or was it the corridors of a hospital?

At length, she said, 'Mr. Mulholland was a great one for his tea. Never in my life have I seen anyone drink as much tea as dear, sweet Mr. Mulholland.'

'I suppose he left fairly recently,' Billy said. He was still puzzling his head about the two names. He was positive now that he had seen them in the newspapers – in the headlines.

'Left?' she said, arching her brows. 'But my dear boy, he never left. He's still here. Mr. Temple is also here. They're on the fourth floor, both of them together.'

Billy set his cup down slowly on the table and stared at his landlady. She smiled back at him, and then she put out one of her white hands and patted him comfortingly on the knee. 'How old are you, my dear?' she asked.

'Seventeen.'

'Seventeen!' she cried. 'Oh, it's the perfect age! Mr. Mulholland was also seventeen. But I think he was a trifle shorter than you are; in fact I'm sure he was, and his teeth weren't quite so white. You have the most beautiful teeth, Mr. Weaver, did you know that?'

'They're not as good as they look,' Billy said. 'They've got simply masses of fillings in them at the back.'

'Mr. Temple, of course, was a little older,' she said, ignoring his remark. 'He was actually twenty-eight. And yet I never would have guessed it if he hadn't told me, never in my whole life. There wasn't a blemish on his body.'

'A what?' Billy said.

'His skin was *just* like a baby's.'

There was a pause. Billy picked up his teacup and took another sip of his tea; then he set it down again gently in its saucer. He waited for her to say something else, but she seemed to have lapsed into another of her silences. He sat there staring straight ahead of him into the far corner of the room, biting his lower lip.

'That parrot,' he said at last. 'You know something? It had me completely fooled when I first saw it through the window. I could have sworn it was alive.'

'Alas, no longer.'

'It's most terribly clever the way it's been done,' he said. 'It doesn't look in the least bit dead. Who did it?'

'I did.'

'*You* did?'

'Of course,' she said. 'And have you met my little Basil as well?' She nodded toward the dachshund curled up so comfortably in front of the fire. Billy looked at it. And suddenly, he realised that this animal had all the time been just as silent and motionless as the parrot. He put out a hand and touched it gently on the top of its back. The back was hard and cold, and when he pushed the hair to one side with his fingers, he could see the skin underneath, greyish black and dry and perfectly preserved.

'Good gracious me,' he said. 'How absolutely fascinating.' He turned away from the dog and stared with deep admiration at the little woman beside him on the sofa. 'It must be most awfully difficult to do a thing like that.'

'Not in the least,' she said. 'I stuff *all* my little pets myself when they pass away. Will you have another cup of tea?'

'No, thank you,' Billy said. The tea tasted faintly of bitter almonds, and he didn't much care for it.

'You did sign the book, didn't you?'

'Oh, yes.'

'That's good. Because later on, if I happen to forget what you were called, then I could always come down here and look it up. I still do that almost every day with Mr. Mulholland and Mr. … Mr. …'

'Temple,' Billy said, 'Gregory Temple. Excuse my asking, but haven't there been *any* other guests here except them in the last two or three years?'

Holding her teacup high in one hand, inclining her head slightly to the left, she looked up at him out of the corners of her eyes and gave him another gentle little smile.

'No, my dear,' she said. 'Only you.'

> Now read back on what you wrote when you stopped to speculate on what would happen next.

Foreshadowing is a technique used by storytellers in tales of suspense. The writer gives the reader little clues all through the story. You only really notice them and realise their importance when you read the story a second time. The following questions will help you to look for examples of foreshadowing in this story. You may add others that you noticed yourself.

1. At a distance, the houses look rich and impressive, but when you look closer you notice other things. What do you notice?

2. Draw a picture of the sign and what stands beneath it. Might this drawing remind you of something else?

3. Mention some of the things that Billy likes when he looks in the window.

4. What does each word on the sign look strangely like to him?

5. What does the peculiar smell remind him of?

6. What does the landlady say they don't want to do at this stage in the proceedings?

Roald Dahl wrote only by hand, in pencil, and always on yellow paper.

Building Up Suspense

Read back over the story for the answers to these questions

PART 1 – Approaching the house

1. What is the weather like when Billy steps out of the station on to the street?

2. Write the first five words of the paragraph that tells you that Billy is young and innocent and anxious to impress if he can.

PART 2 – The first conversation

1. What surprises Billy about his entrance into the hall?

2. 'She seemed terribly nice.' What does she say or do that makes her seem so 'terribly nice' to Billy?

3. What adjectives does Billy use to describe the landlady's face, eyes and lips?

4. What does the landlady call her house when she talks about the pleasure of welcoming a visitor?

5. Are there any moments when you suspect that something sinister may be going on or that the landlady may not be the 'kind and generous soul' that Billy supposes?

6. What does she say about signing the book?

141

PART 3 – Billy alone with the guest book

1. What does Billy think when he reads the two names in the guest book?

2. Why does he not have time to remember?

PART 4 – The final conversation

1. With what strange thing does Billy compare the way in which the landlady holds the silver tea tray?

2. What adjectives does he use to describe her hands and her fingernails?

3. Where does the landlady say that Mr Mulholland and Mr Temple are now?

4. At a certain moment, Billy begins to see the room differently from when he looked through the window. Where exactly would you place that moment? Mention two differences that he now notices.

This story is a masterclass in creating a strange **atmosphere**. Each time you read it, you notice more delicate hints: the stuffed animals, the landlady's eyes examining Billy, her 'small, white, quickly moving hands', the whiff of 'bitter almonds' in the tea …(In murder mysteries, cyanide poisoning is often revealed as the cause of death by the smell of bitter almonds from the corpse.)

REWRITING IN YOUR OWN WORDS

Rewrite these phrases and sentences from the story in your own words.

1. The wind was like a flat blade of ice on his cheeks.

2. The big shots up at head office.

3. Once upon a time they had been very swanky residences.

4. A downstairs window that was brilliantly illuminated by a street lamp.

5. Do you desire an egg for breakfast?

6. Billy stepped over the threshold.

7. The old girl is slightly dotty.

8. And we don't want to go breaking any laws at this stage in the proceedings.

9. This landlady appeared to be slightly off her rocker.

10. That's funny, he thought suddenly, that name rings a bell.

> **Suspense *n.***
> *Definition*: An atmosphere of uncertainty, an excited or anxious feeling that something unexpected may be about to happen.

Billy Weaver has gone missing.

Write two paragraphs for the news, announcing Billy as a missing person; where he was last seen; the last person to whom he spoke; what is known about his final movements; his age, height, hair colour, eye colour; the clothes he was wearing; his parents' appeal to the public for help in tracing him, etc.

Read your written piece aloud as if you were the television newsreader. You could begin and end with these words:

Police are appealing for information about a young man who was last seen …

Anyone who thinks they may have seen this young man or who has information about him is asked to contact …

 Listen to the remaining six minutes of the radio play on YouTube.

Dialogue

Some days after Billy's disappearance, a witness tells a detective that he saw a young man answering Billy Weaver's description going into a bed and breakfast in Bath. The detective decides to visit this B&B and question the owner.

Write the conversation that takes place between the detective and the landlady. **A** writes the detective's questions. **B** writes the landlady's replies.

Begin with the landlady answering the doorbell. The conversation starts at the door and moves inside to the warm and cosy sitting room with the big armchairs, the baby grand piano, the stuffed dachshund at the fire and the parrot in the cage. An example is given on the next page.

Detective: Good morning Madame, I am Detective … I'm investigating the disappearance of the young man in this photograph. He was last seen on this road on Monday evening. May I come in?

The landlady might want time to think, so she doesn't answer the questions immediately. Instead, she simply says the exact words that she spoke to Billy:

Landlady: Why don't you come in out of the cold?

When you have written the dialogue in full, act it out, speaking the parts you have written.

①

'The Landlady' on Stage and Screen

The first photograph is from a stage play adaptation of 'The Landlady. The second is from a film. In each case, the actress playing the landlady has entered into the part in her facial expressions and her movements. Her character has been created in costume, in make-up and in hairdressing.

Taking each photograph in turn:

a. Give a mark out of 10 to each actress according to how successfully you think she is acting the role of the landlady. Your answer should mention facial expression, gesture, eyes and anything else you notice.

b. Give a mark out of 10 for costume, hair and make-up in each case.

Then answer both questions in relation to the actor playing Billy in the first photograph.

②

TOP TIP

A **twist** is a sudden, unexpected turn; **in the tail** means it happens at the end. Roald Dahl's stories often end with an unexpected moment that takes you by surprise and reveals something shocking. It is only at the end that you understand that something has been hinted at throughout the story.

SHOW WHAT YOU KNOW

 You have learned many writing and speaking skills in this collection of texts. Now it's time to *Show What You Know!*

My Writing Task

Write **EITHER**

1. **A newspaper editorial.**

Newspaper Editorial Success Criteria

You will achieve success if you remember the **Six Key Points** in writing an editorial, and aim for 350–400 words.

1. Choose a topic in the news, something that you have opinions about.
2. Give your editorial a title.
3. Write a strong starter sentence and short opening paragraph that briefly states the facts.
4. Make at least two good points for your side of the argument, but also state an opposing point of view.
5. Give evidence, examples and statistics from respected sources to back up your points.
6. Write a persuasive closing paragraph stating your conclusions. You could include a powerful question that challenges your audience. You should end with a strong persuasive punchline that convinces your readers that you are right.

OR

2. **A story about a character who sets out alone on a journey in which s/he faces fear or danger.**

STORY SUCCESS CRITERIA

I should

- Think about books, films, songs and poems I know where a character goes on a journey
- Think about current news stories regarding people who are making journeys

I must

- Write a suitable title
- Divide my writing into paragraphs
- Re-read what I have written to check for correct punctuation, spelling, capital letters or any words left out

I could

- Use the excellent choices of descriptive words and phrases, especially verbs and adjectives, that I read in stories such as 'The Wild Wood' from *The Wind in the Willows* and 'The Landlady', and poems such as 'The Listeners' and 'Stopping by Woods on a Snowy Evening'.
- Create a mysterious atmosphere, as all the writers in this collection did. I will read my paragraphs aloud to myself or to someone else to check how they sound and to see if I have achieved a scary atmosphere.

If you chose the editorial

Self-Assessment

Read it as if you had just bought the newspaper and were interested to hear the editor's views.

Check what you have written against the list of success criteria. What do you think you did especially well? Is there anything you neglected?

Redrafting

Add anything that might improve your writing. Perhaps you need to change some wording that doesn't sound right. When you are happy with it, you may decide that it is good enough to include in your Collection of Texts.

Reflection Note

If you choose to place this task into your **Collection of Texts** now, complete a **reflection note**.
Hint: See the success criteria on the previous page to help you.

If you chose the story

Self-Assessment

Read it dramatically as if you were making a recording of the story or you are the guest reader in a bookshop or a library.

You can list some success criteria for this task by listening again to the first two minutes of the radio play of 'The Landlady.' Listen as far as, 'She was like a jack-in-the box. It made me jump.'

As you listen, these bullet points may help you to make notes on what makes this a good story:

- The **title**. How does the actor read this title and the author's name? Is it important to read the title in a way that makes you expect a good story?
- **Clarity**. Is the pronunciation of each word clear? Are any words emphasised?
- **Engagement** with the audience. Does the voice catch and hold your attention? How?
- **Pace**. Is this a slow or a fast reading? Can you hear little pauses at commas and full stops? Do these pauses help you to imagine the scene and enjoy the story?
- **Tone**. How would you describe the storyteller's tone of voice? Does it change at certain words?
- **Volume**. Does the volume change at certain moments? Why?
- **Sound effects**. Are sound effects used? What are they? Can you add sound effects to make your story extract more realistic and enjoyable?

Redrafting

After you have written your story, re-read the success criteria to check that you have done the best you can. Make any necessary changes. When you are happy with it, you can include it in your Collection of Texts. Be sure to revise and polish for accuracy in punctuation, spelling, capital letters, etc.

Reflection Note

If you choose to place this task into your **Collection of Texts**, complete a **reflection note**.
Hint: See the success criteria on the previous page to help you.

Oral Communication

If you chose to write the editorial

If you chose to write the editorial, read either your editorial or the editorial on page 121. You are speaking to a live audience who have assembled in a public place to hear different people express their views on a topic. Carefully follow these instructions.

Success Criteria for Speaking to a Live Audience

- Begin with the words, 'Ladies and gentlemen …' Speak with confidence and conviction (the feeling of being absolutely convinced about what you are saying).
- You could just take the keywords from the editorial and either highlight them or put them on flashcards. As you glance at the words, you will cover all your points, but perhaps not use the exact sentences written in the editorial.
- If you decide to have the full script, learn as much as you can beforehand so that you can look up regularly and make eye contact with your audience. (You don't have to look directly at anyone – you can just pick a spot at the back of the room and look at that.)
- Do not go too fast! Listeners need time to take in what you are saying. Pause at full stops and ends of paragraphs.
- Vary the tone and the volume of your voice both to hold the attention of your listeners and to convince them of your point of view. Put conviction in your voice when you ask a question.
- Pause briefly before the final paragraph and look at your audience. Say, 'And finally …' so they know that you are about to deliver your final points.
- Stop again for a moment before the final sentence and look directly at the audience as if you are about to say the most important thing of all and you want them to be ready to hear this crucial sentence.
- At the end, thank your audience and invite questions from them. 'And now I invite you to ask me any questions that you think are important …'

Reflection Note

Now complete the **Oral Communication Template for Student Reflection.**

Peer Assessment

After you have read your editorial aloud, invite your listener/s to tell you two things that you did well and one thing you might do better. This will help you to redraft your work.

Redrafting

After you have practised aloud, review the success criteria to check that you have met all the requirements. Make any necessary changes, and when you are happy with it you can read it aloud again, taking on board the suggestions for improvement that were made to you.

If you chose to write the story, read it aloud to a group of listeners as an audio story.

Success Criteria

- Read dramatically, changing your voice for different characters. You might even like to appoint other readers for different characters. They would need to see your story and rehearse their parts in advance.
- Pause when you want to create suspense.
- Vary your tone of voice to engage your listeners and hold their attention.
- Be sure to read slowly enough for your listeners to imagine the people and places you are describing.
- Pause briefly before the final paragraph so your listeners know that the story is about to come to an end.

Peer Assessment

After you have read your story aloud, invite your listeners to tell you two things that you did well and one thing you might do better. This will help you to redraft your work.

Redrafting

After you have practised aloud, review the success criteria to check that you have met all the requirements. Make any necessary changes, and when you are happy with it you can read it aloud again, taking on board the suggestions for improvement that were made to you.

Reflection Note

Now complete the **Oral Communication Template for Student Reflection.**

Triumph Over Adversity

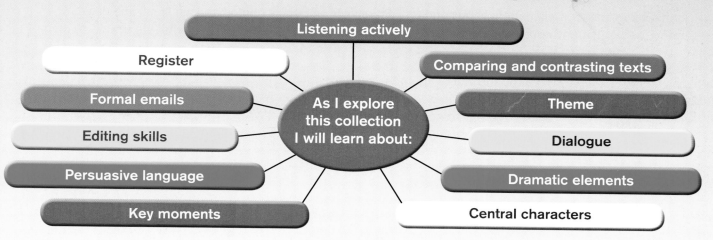

- Listening actively
- Register
- Comparing and contrasting texts
- Formal emails
- Theme
- Editing skills
- Dialogue
- Persuasive language
- Dramatic elements
- Key moments
- Central characters

As I explore this collection I will learn about:

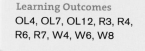

Learning Outcomes
OL4, OL7, OL12, R3, R4, R6, R7, W4, W6, W8

SHOW WHAT YOU KNOW

The skills you learn in this collection will enable you to **show what you know** in your final tasks at the end of this collection.

For my writing task I will:
Write a formal email to a local business asking for a donation for a charitable organisation that is important to me

For oral communication I will:
Make an oral presentation or do an interview about a charitable organisation of my choice that helps people to overcome adversities

Exploring the Theme – Triumph Over Adversity

Sometimes life isn't easy. Bad things happen to good people, and good things happen to bad people. At some point in all our lives, we have faced or will face challenging times. The key is how we cope with these struggles, and what we do to survive and hopefully triumph against the odds.

In this collection you will meet fictitious and real characters who have battled against small and great challenges. In the end some will triumph, others won't, while the rest will cope with what life throws at them.

 PREPARE **1 MIN** What do the words 'triumph' and 'adversity' mean? In pairs, use a dictionary to find a definition for these words. Then share your definitions with the rest of the class, and as a group, come to agreed definitions.

GOAL SETTING WITH **REALISTIC** expectations
3 1 2

SELF ESTEEM

LEARNING from their **MISTAKES**

problem SOLVING **SKILLS**

Understanding and **ACCEPTANCE** OF THEIR OWN strengths and weaknesses

 **RESILIENCE**

Ability **TO RECOGNISE** their own EMOTIONS **and those of others**

SELF-CONTROL

SOCIAL SKILLS AND ABILITY **TO SEEK** ASSISTANCE FROM **OTHERS**

OPTIMISTIC thinking PATTERNS

 **WILLINGNESS** to OVERCOME DIFFICULTIES rather than **AVOID PROBLEMS**

www.beyondblue.org.au

As you will remember from Collection 2, an **infographic** is an image that presents information or data clearly. One of the main characteristics that successful people demonstrate when they face challenging times is resilience. This infographic (left) illustrates ten personal qualities of people who have resilience.

1. Choose one of the characteristics of resilience that you think you could work on in your own life and write a short paragraph about how you intend to do this. Put this into an envelope, seal it and give it to your teacher. On an agreed date in the future, you can open your envelopes and reflect on whether you achieved your aims.

2. Working in groups, come up with one more tip for resilience that you could add to the infographic.

3. Now, in your groups, do this crossword. The words are taken from or are a variation of words in the infographic, but see how many you can work out before looking back at it.

Crossword
W5.1

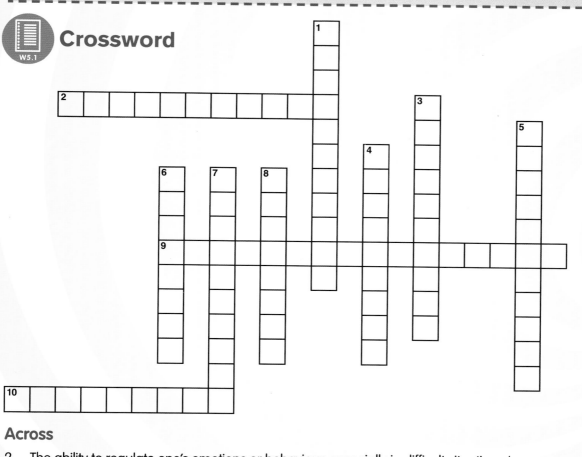

Across

2. The ability to regulate one's emotions or behaviour, especially in difficult situations (s _ _ _ c _ _ _ _ _ _) [4/7]

9. Manner of thinking (t _ _ _ _ _ _ _ p _ _ _ _ _ _ _) [8/8]

10. Representing things in a way that is accurate and true to life (r _ _ _ _ _ _ _ _) [9]

Down

1. Thinking about your ideal future and motivating yourself to turn it into reality (g _ _ _ s _ _ _ _ _ _) [4/7]

3. Confidence in one's own worth and abilities (s _ _ _ e _ _ _ _ _) [4/6]

4. Consenting or agreeing to something (a _ _ _ _ _ _ _ _) [9]

5. The state of being prepared to do something (w _ _ _ _ _ _ _ _ _ _) [11]

6. Strong feelings (e _ _ _ _ _ _ _) [8]

7. Hopeful and confident about the future (o _ _ _ _ _ _ _ _ _) [10]

8. The state or condition of being weak (w _ _ _ _ _ _ _) [8]

CREATE

Think about any real people or imaginary characters you know of who have faced a challenge in their lives and have come out on top. Profile them using a grid. An example has been done for you.

Name	Ellen Keane
Who are they	Irish Paralympic swimmer
Challenge	Amputee since birth (left arm)
Resilience	Double world bronze medalist in the Paralympics

A Radio Documentary

What I will learn:

to listen actively and carefully to an aural text in order to understand and remember details; to understand and appreciate a variety of registers and their use in the spoken word

PREPARE

Add fifteen years to today's date. What would the date be?
In groups, discuss the following questions, thinking about what life might be like in fifteen years' time:

- How much do you think a bar of chocolate/pair of jeans will cost?
- How will students of your age communicate with each other?
- What new inventions will be in use?

LISTEN

W5.2

'Small Lives and Great Reputations' (RTÉ Radio 1, *Documentary on One*)

This radio documentary is about Irishman, Paddy Armstrong, who was wrongfully imprisoned for fifteen years at the age of twenty-four for the bombing of pubs in England in 1974. Paddy and three others (known as the Guildford Four) were finally cleared of this crime when it was found that police officers had lied and forced them to confess. They were released in 1989.

The section you will read and listen to is a conversation between Paddy, his wife, Caroline (whom he met when he came out of prison), his solicitor, Alastair, and Alastair's wife, Pat. On the 25th anniversary of Paddy's release, they are all talking about how Paddy adjusted to life 'on the outside' after fifteen years in prison.

FIRST LISTENING

Listen carefully to the entire clip to get the gist of the story – it lasts for just two and a half minutes.

SECOND LISTENING

Now listen to the clip again and this time, while you listen, fill in the blanks.

Narrator: _____ years after it was taken from him, Paddy was given his old Afghan coat and a _____ ticket and sent on his way.

Paddy: I came out to a different world entirely (*laughs*).

Narrator: Alastair took Paddy to Guildford to live with him while he adjusted to life on the outside.

Pat: He didn't even know how to cross the road properly. He didn't know what _____ was 'cos he hadn't done it for such a long time – he'd just been given what he was going to have to eat … Paddy, how long did you live with Alastair when you came out?

Paddy (*to Alastair*): About _____ months, nine months or something wasn't it, when I first came out and stayed with you?

Alastair: About six months. It took us that long to train you to walk in the street without getting _____ (*laughing*).

Paddy: I know … and stop me buying all bars of _____ and everything.

Alastair: With ten _____ notes.

Paddy: Yeah, I know (*laughs*).

Caroline: Paddy lost his father when he was quite young, I don't know what age but he died young … so Alastair really is his _____ figure.

Paddy: We got money from Yorkshire TV for doing a programme for them and we then got a down-payment from the _____ – fifty thousand I think it was.

Pat: He went up to Scotland and he was just conned by everybody … buying drinks. He spent his money and what little bit of compensation he got was _____ very quickly and he'd come back down to see Alastair and say, 'I've got no money. What do I do, what do I do?' And they got given it in gradual tranches …

Narrator: (_____ *in background*) Twenty-five years after his release, Paddy and his wife Caroline are back in Guildford for a celebration lunch with old friends, Alastair and Pat.

Alastair: To our _____ (*clink of glasses and sounds of cutlery in background*).

Pat: Twenty-five years, well done mate, you've done well.

Paddy: Thank you (*clink of glasses*).

Pat: Bless him … and Caroline.

Alastair: One of the best clients I ever had.

Paddy: You have to learn to start living with it and just doing your normal life.

Narrator: It was hard to be normal. Paddy and Gerry found themselves in the spotlight. Rock stars and _____ all wanted to hang out with them and share in their newfound freedom.

Paddy: I think when we came out, the best time we had was when me and Gerry drove across America with a couple of friends. It was _____. Me and Gerry had great times together.

Pat: And then he went back to Ireland (*pause*) and that's when he met Caroline, *thank goodness*. It was just heaven for us because we just felt as though somebody really cares, somebody really loves him. And it was just divine, you know, because I'm not old enough to quite be his mother but you do feel as _____ they're your child.

EXPLORE

W5.3

Now spend five minutes reading through the background summary and the transcript carefully and try to remember as many details as possible.

1. Read the statements below and decide whether they are true or false, based on what you remember. Do not go back and check – this is a test of your memory. Tick the boxes on the left-hand side to indicate if the statement is true or false.

2. Re-read the text above, and check the answers, this time ticking the boxes on the right-hand side.

Answer here from memory **after your first reading** of the transcript			Answer these questions again **after re-reading** the transcript	
True	**False**	**Statement**	**True**	**False**
		Paddy spent six years in prison		
		Paddy lived in London after he was released		
		It has been twenty-five years since Paddy was released from prison		
		Paddy bought a lot of crisps when he left prison		
		Paddy lived with Alastair, his solicitor, for around six months		
		The released men received money from the BBC for a programme		
		The currency when Paddy came out of prison was pounds		
		Paddy, Caroline, Alastair and his wife are eating in one scene		
		Paddy's solicitor's wife is called Pam		

REGISTER

Register is about the words we use, how formal we are and even how careful we are in pronouncing our words. For example, you speak to your friends in a different way than you would speak to your teacher. Register can range from very formal to very informal, or somewhere in between.

Imagine you are Paddy: you have just come out of prison and you are looking for the local shop. Using the scale below, imagine what kind of register you would use to ask the following people for directions (1 is extremely formal while 10 is extremely informal).

* Alastair, your solicitor who you live with and have known for fifteen years

* **A police officer**

* A teenager

* An elderly lady

Extremely formal	Quite formal	Quite informal	Extremely informal
1 2 3	4 5	6 7	8 9 10

There are five different voices in the documentary. List the voices you heard and decide whether the language they use is formal or informal, giving some examples. You may need to refer back to the script to help you.

Name of the person speaking	Is the register they use formal or informal?	Pick out some words/phrases they use to illustrate that they're using a formal/informal register

Working in small groups, script the scene when Paddy tries to cross the road for the first time since being released from prison. Show clearly who is talking at each point in the conversation (as it is in the extract). You might also like to indicate any scenery, props or sound effects. There are a number of possible characters in this drama such as Paddy, Paddy's solicitor (Alastair), a friend who helps him, a driver who is driving along the road at the time, passers-by, policemen, etc.

In the documentary, Paddy describes some of the challenges he faced adjusting to life in 1989 after being imprisoned for fifteen years. Using the internet or books, and by interviewing people who lived during that time, research other changes that took place during the late 1980s/early 1990s, e.g. wars, inventions, music, etc. Share your findings with a classmate and then present your combined knowledge with another pair of students.

Formal Email

What I will learn:

to write a formal email competently using appropriate vocabulary, tone and style;
to appreciate the purpose of formal register

In today's world, a formal letter is often replaced by a formal email. Many businesses now choose to do their internal (within the company) and external (outside the company) communications via email.

Now you will learn how to write a formal email.

Read the correspondence from a woman who sends an email to Salthill Buses to complain about an experience she had on a bus in Galway.

The sender's email, which comes up automatically

The date and time, which comes up automatically

A formal greeting when you don't know who you're writing to

The person you are sending the email to; you need to type this in

You need to give a 'subject' to your email – what your email is about

Summarise the reason for the email

Explain the circumstances

Go into detail

Sign off. For emails, 'Regards' or 'Kind regards' are sometimes used in place of 'Yours faithfully' or 'Yours sincerely'

From:	Tracey O'Hara51988@gmail.com
Date:	16 July 2016 16:34:56
To:	customercomment@salthillbuses.com
Subject:	Complaint

To whom it may concern,

I am writing to complain about a problem I had while trying to board one of your buses yesterday.

As I attempted to board the number 100 bus, with two children and another in a buggy, I almost slipped. This was because there was too much of a gap between the pavement and the bus. Your driver kindly got out and helped me lift the buggy and I am extremely grateful for his help.

I wish to complain because I think this is very dangerous and could result in an accident on another occasion. In other cities, buses have an electric step which can be lowered to accommodate people with buggies or indeed wheelchairs.

Could you kindly investigate this situation and let me know whether you have any plans to update your buses. If not, I will be forced to drive into the city with my children, something I'm sure nobody wants if we are trying to free our cities of congestion and pollution.

I would appreciate your response and thank you for taking the time to address this issue.

Yours faithfully,

Tracey O'Hara

Now read the reply from Salthill Transport in relation to the complaint.

Case reference number, which can be quoted in further correspondence

Explains the purpose of the email

Explains the policy of the company with regard to complaints

Addresses the complaint specifically and how it will be dealt with

Name of person in the company dealing with the complaint

Apologises and thanks the customer for contacting them

Job title
Name of company
Email address
Facebook page/ Twitter handle
Website

From:	customercomment@salthillbuses.com
Date:	17 July 2016 10:34:56 IST
To:	tracey.ohara51988@gmail.com
Subject:	Case Reference 9525845

Dear Ms. O'Hara,

I refer to your correspondence regarding the facilities on route 100.

We always endeavour to satisfy our customers but occasionally there are deviations from the required standard. We take a very serious view of such incidents, which reflect poorly on the organisation.

I can confirm that all reports are taken very seriously and investigated thoroughly. We have obtained the CCTV footage from the bus and the Depot Manager will be going out to look at this bus. I can assure you that our buses are modern and safe. We will respond to you again once our investigations have been completed.

On behalf of Salthill Buses, please accept our apologies and thank you for bringing this matter to our attention.

Regards,

_____

Martin James
Customer Service Manager
Galway Transport
E: enquiries@salthillbuses.com
FB: SalthillBuses Twitter: @BusesSalthill
WWW: www.salthillbuses.com

Using a Venn Diagram

Compare a formal letter and a formal email. Think about the features they have in common and where they differ. Present these similarities and differences in a Venn diagram.

VENN DIAGRAM

Formal Letter

Formal Email

Features in common

Tips for Writing a Formal Email

Do

- Write as though you are writing a formal letter
- State the problem first and then what you hope will happen
- Be polite – as the saying goes, you attract more bees with honey!

Don't

- Use overly casual or familiar language
- Ever use text language – 'tnx 4 ur email'
- Use emoticons
- Write anything you might later regret. The old idiom 'Marry in haste, repent at leisure' applies here also!

It's not what you say, it's the way that you say it …

When you are writing a formal letter or email, it is a good idea to ask questions indirectly as it sounds more polite and respectful.

For example, instead of saying:
'How much does it cost to stay in your hotel?'

You might say:
'Could you please inform me about the cost of staying in your hotel?'

Practise this by rewriting the following sentences:

1. Where is your shop?
2. When does the concert start?
3. Do you have a student discount?
4. Are there any jobs going?

Here are some useful ways to start sentences or sign off a formal letter.

Making a request	Could you please	I would be grateful if	Kindly	I would appreciate
Explaining the context	In relation to	With regards to	Further to	Concerning
Finishing off	Yours sincerely (if you know their name)	Yours faithfully (if you don't know their name)	Regards	Kind regards (a little less formal than 'Regards' but still very polite)

Draft a formal email to enquire about a course that you and your brother want to do during the Hallowe'en break. In your email, ask about the price, activities involved, location and whether there will be a discount if more than one family member attends.

Before submitting this to your teacher, ask another student to read your email and suggest two things they like about it and one thing you could change. Redraft your work as necessary, and when you are happy with it, submit it to your teacher. If you are happy with this work, you could complete the Student Reflection note and include it in your **Collection of Texts**.

A Radio Drama

What I will learn:

to listen actively to get the gist and main purpose of an aural text; to use editing skills to correct punctuation and spelling; to identify the effects of dramatic elements

Sometimes, in the face of adversity, we find comfort in the most unexpected places: a friend we didn't know we had; an unexpected piece of good luck; or perhaps something a little bit more magical and inexplicable takes place …

Take one of these scenarios and imagine how a **peculiar twist** could bring a **happy outcome**.

* A boy loses his dog while out walking in the forest.

* Two friends miss the plane for the holiday they have been saving up for.

* An old woman misplaces a winning lottery ticket.

* A farmer is hit by floods and his crops have been destroyed.

LISTEN

'Yardstick' by Joe O'Byrne
(RTÉ Radio 1, *Drama on One*)

'Yardstick' is a radio drama by Joe O'Byrne. In it, a young girl is being bullied by her classmates. What she doesn't yet realise is that she has an unusual ally (friend): her phone, Moby. This unusual **characterisation** adds to the uniqueness of the story. The dramatist has also used **personification**. This is when personal qualities are given to a non-human object, animals or ideas. For example 'the angry wind'; 'the trees danced lightly in the wind'.

Laura has fallen out with her friend, Katy, because they both like a guy called Conor. Laura has been receiving threatening text messages, so she has stayed away from Conor, even though they both like each other. With her parents having just announced that they are separating, Laura is isolated and lonely.

The play contains an unusual twist: the character of Moby. Moby is Laura's new mobile phone, who is trying to help her. In the previous scene, Moby intervened and forwarded Conor one of the threatening texts from Katy, resulting in Laura and Conor finally meeting again to talk.

Test your memory

Listen carefully to the excerpt. Afterwards you will answer the ten multiple choice questions below.

? EXPLORE

1. Answer these multiple choice questions.

a) Conor tells Laura that things are bad for him because

  • His dad lost his job   • His mum lost her job   • His parents are fighting

b) Conor reveals that he is moving to

  • Austria   • Australia   • America

c) Conor tells Laura that he is moving

  • Next week   • In two weeks' time   • Next month

d) Conor explains to Laura that he realised he fancied her when

  • She avoided him   • He saw her today   • His dad told him they were moving

e) According to Laura, since she started avoiding Conor, the bullying

  • Got worse   • Got better   • Stayed the same

f) While talking to Conor, Laura gets a text message with an image of a girl with

  • A bruise   • Spit in her hair   • A mobile phone

g) Moby compares the image to what in her memory?

- A knife
- A dagger
- A blade

h) Moby wants Laura to

- Ignore Conor
- Write a letter to Conor
- Show Conor the message

i) Katy's full name is

- Katy Molloy
- Katy Malone
- Katy Mooney

j) Conor wishes they had

- Stood up to Katy
- Bullied Katy back
- Ignored Katy

Give yourself one point for each correct answer.

2. Listen to the extract again, and this time record short comments on the following dramatic elements and their effect on you.

Element	What I noticed	The effect on me
Atmosphere		
Sound effects		
Characters		
Use of suspense		

3. Choose **two** of the following statements with which you agree with and write a paragraph explaining why. Use your notes on the dramatic elements you noticed to help you construct your answer.

* 'Yardstick' uses very clever dramatic techniques to address the issue of bullying.

* 'Yardstick' is a play that a lot of students can identify with.

* 'Yardstick' is very difficult to understand.

* 'Yardstick' includes both realistic and unrealistic characters.

MIND YOUR LANGUAGE

PUNCTUATION

Ellipses (…) are three dots in a row that are used to show words that have been removed as they are unnecessary. They can also be used to indicate a dramatic pause in a conversation.

Commas (,) are used for many reasons including: for lists, in direct speech, to separate clauses in a sentence, to indicate a brief pause that would occur if the sentence were spoken aloud.

Exclamation marks (!) are used to end sentences that express an exclamation: 'Ouch! That was painful!' or to indicate something that was shouted: "Watch out!' she cried.' It may also be used to show the writer's surprise or amusement.

Apostrophes (') are used to show possession (John's brother; the dog's tail). They are also used for contractions, i.e. to shorten phrases (you might shorten 'It is cold' to 'It's cold').

Below is an extract from 'Yardstick'. Rewrite it, **correcting the spelling** and **inserting relevant punctuation** (capital letters, commas, full stops, question marks, exclamation marks, ellipses, etc.).

Voice/Moby: a digtal image like a blaid into my memory a girl with spit in her hair doing the rounds

Conor: what is it

Voice/Moby: Show him

Laura: oh nothing nothing you need to know about

Voice/Moby: he does just show him show him

Laura: so how soon is soon

Conor: a week

Laura: so this is goodby

Conor: we can see each other again

Laura: no this is goodbye

Conor: oh thats a pity its so stupid isnt it why did Katy Malone have to fancy me

Laura: she did thats the thing

Conor: we should have ignored her shouldnt we

Laura: Yeah

A Promotional Film

What I will learn:

to identify persuasive language and other persuasive techniques

 PREPARE

In this section you will watch a short informative film about an NGO (non-governmental organisation) school in Tanzania that educates some of the country's poorest children.

 1 MIN

Before watching, with a classmate, brainstorm a list of any charities you know that help children in Ireland or overseas.

TOP TIP

When you're making notes, only write down the key words and phrases to help you remember the most important information.

 WATCH

Watch the film 'Join Our Family', about the School of St Jude in Tanzania. While you watch, make notes on **five** of the aspects listed.

1. Life/living conditions in Tanzania.

2. Education in Tanzania.

3. The people who work for the School of St Jude.

4. Facilities in the school.

5. How the school is helping Tanzanian children/families.

6. Lopoi (5th form student) and his family.

7. How the school is helping the Tanzanian economy.

8. How the school changes students' lives.

9. Ways that people can support the school.

10. The school's founder (Gemma Sisia) and her beliefs.

Now share your answers with another student and combine them. Then join up with another pair of students to form a group of four and combine all your answers.

EXPLORE

Examine this image on the right, which is of one of the final frames in the video, then answer the following questions:

a) What is the main message of the video?

b) What is the school's website address?

c) Which two objects appear in the school's logo? Why do you think they chose these two objects?

(*Hint:* One refers to a very important geographical feature close to the school in Tanzania.)

Join us in fighting poverty through education

www.schoolofstjude.org

EXPLORE

W5.8

1. This video is persuasive for a number of reasons. Using at least **three** of the following headings, write a paragraph explaining why you think it is persuasive and give an example for each heading you select.

Rhetorical questions	Tension
Repetition	Statistics
Emotive language/music/imagery	'Feel good'
A 'call to action'	Testimonials

To revise persuasive language, see page 97.

2. What, for you, was the most memorable moment?

3. What is the main message of the video, in your opinion?

CREATE

You have been asked to include an extra scene in the video. Make a list of the people you would interview, where you would record the scene, what props you would use and the music you would include. Share your ideas with another student and combine the best ideas.

WEBSITES AND DIGITAL ELEMENTS

Now that you have learned how charities can use videos to tell people about their work, you will learn about one of the most important marketing tools that charities and businesses have – websites.

Like newspapers and magazines, no two websites are identical. However, they all have some **digital elements** in common, such as scroll bars, search tools, etc. You will probably recognise most of these digital elements but you may not know the names for them.

PREPARE

Looking at the screenshot from the Temple Street Foundation website below, notice the different digital elements. Study this for one minute and try to memorise as many of the eight different digital elements as possible. When you are ready, close your book and, working in pairs, test each other to see how many of the eight elements you can remember. You get one mark for every one you get right.

READ

Read this article, from an interview conducted with Siobhan Lavery, Managing Director of ICAN, Ireland's leading digital marketing agency. ICAN designed the Temple Street Foundation website.

'Digital elements' refers to any aspect of digital content.

"The Importance of Websites and How to Build a Successful Website

Websites are hugely important to every business. They are a convenient and fast way for customers to get the information they need, such as food menus, opening times, product instructions, etc., and they are usually people's first experience of that business. Websites let you do so much more than traditional forms of advertising, such as:

- Giving people interactive product demonstrations

- Allowing them to buy products and services on the spot
- Talking with customers through online chat and forums.

Websites can also work hand in hand with traditional advertising. Advertising can let potential customers know where to find more information or to buy their product or service online.

A good website should include:

A clear message: People make the decision to stay or leave a website within a few seconds, so it should be clear what benefit your business can provide them.

Content written for the audience: If your customers aren't technical, then you shouldn't use technical language. It should be easy for everyone to understand.

Easy navigation: Your main navigation should have seven or less links so it is easy to scan and find the content you need.

Search functionality: Customers should be able to find the products or information they are looking for quickly; it shouldn't be a case of having to click into page after page to find what it is they're looking for.

Adjustment to mobile devices: More than 30% of website traffic will be from mobile phones and tablets. If your website doesn't adjust to fit those screen sizes, it will be difficult for customers to do anything on your website.

Charity websites in particular should:

Visualise the problem that needs to be solved so people will feel drawn to help. Powerful imagery and urgent language should be used to achieve this.

Have the ability to accept donations quickly: The longer it takes, the more likely it is that donors won't complete the process.

Include fundraising information and support: People also want to donate their time, so let them know how they can participate by listing your upcoming fundraising events.

Make donors feel valued: It's very important to thank your donors and tell them that their contribution has made a difference.

After we redesigned the Temple Street Foundation website, we noticed a significant improvement in the number of people visiting their website but, more importantly, the number of people donating online increased.

Overall, my best piece of advice to students who want to design a website is to think of the audience first and the brand or business second. The audience will decide who they want to interact with and why. Think about what you want them to think, feel and do, and then make it easy for them to carry out that task. Think of it like a shop – invite them in, show off your products or services, and lead them along the aisle to the checkout … 99

Siobhan Lavery, ICAN

EXPLORE

1. After reading this article, imagine that you are working as a website expert for students. Pick out five pieces of advice that you would give to a student who was thinking of designing a website to sell original hand-painted t-shirts. Choose two images that you would advise them to include on their website.

2. Using the information from the article and the screenshot from the UNICEF website on the right, answer the following questions:

a) What is its motto?

b) Mention one way that, according to the website, you can help children.

c) Identify three digital elements on the website. How do each of these elements help to improve communication between the charity and the public?

d) Mention one thing that you like about this website and one thing that you would change if you were the web designer or copywriter.

Draw or design the front page of a website for a charity that you like or support. Do this without looking at the charity's website as it will influence your ideas.

Remember to include persuasive techniques, digital elements and text, like those on the two websites you have seen and any others you like. Use the advice from the article on pages 165/166.

Show it to another student when you have finished and ask them to pick out two things that you did well and one thing that you could improve on. You could also look at the actual site and add in some of their ideas. You can then redraft this work, and if you are happy with it, you can write a Student Reflection Note and include it in your **Collection of Texts**.

TOP TIP

You might like to use Weebly for Education to mock up your website: www.education.weebly.com

A Short Story

What I will learn:

to understand and appreciate character, setting, story and action in a text; to identify a key moment and to write about it

The short story you will read next is called 'Reunion'. Before you read it, working in pairs, imagine a reunion that might take place, e.g. a school reunion. Next, imagine how the reunion might go wrong. Now finish the story by finding a resolution to the problem. Finally, act out your scene in pairs. You can write a quick plan or do an improvisation.

Planning versus Improvising

When you are acting out a scene, you can **plan** it in advance (by writing a script or just jotting down some bullet points for the main things you want to say). Alternatively, you can **improvise**, which means that you agree on a starting point and then make it up as you go along, taking the lead from each other.

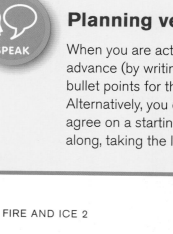

Planned Drama

You know how it will end

You have agreed what will happen

You may have a script

It isn't as scary as improvising

There isn't room for creativity

Features in Common

You know how it will start

You are acting

You can have many actors

You are performing live

Improvised Drama

You don't know how it will end

You can surprise the other actors

It will be unscripted

It can be intimidating

You can be as creative as you like

Try to memorise as many points as possible from this diagram and then test yourself by filling in a blank Venn diagram.

'Reunion' was written by John Cheever, an American writer who was most famous for his short stories and novels. Just six weeks before his death in 1982, he was awarded the National Medal for Literature by the American Academy of Arts and Letters. 'Reunion' was first published in 1962 in *The New Yorker*, a weekly American magazine which features a range of writing including articles, cartoons, short stories and poetry. This story is about a father and son who meet for lunch for the first time in three years.

'Reunion' by John Cheever

The last time I saw my father was in Grand Central Station. I was going from my grandmother's in the Adirondacks to a cottage on the Cape that my mother had rented, and I wrote my father that I would be in New York between trains for an hour and a half, and asked if we could have lunch together.

His secretary wrote to say that he would meet me at the information booth at noon, and at twelve o'clock sharp I saw him coming through the crowd. He was a stranger to me – my mother divorced him three years ago and I hadn't seen him since – but as soon as I saw him I felt that he was my father, my flesh and blood, my future and my doom. I knew that when I was grown I would be something like him; I would have to plan my campaigns within his limitations.

He was a big, good-looking man, and I was terribly happy to see him again. He struck me on

the back and shook my hand. 'Hi, Charlie,' he said. 'Hi, boy. I'd like to take you up to my club, but it's in the Sixties, and if you have to catch an early train I guess we'd better get something to eat around here.' He put his arm around me, and I smelled my father the way my mother sniffs a rose. It was a rich compound of whiskey, after-shave lotion, shoe polish, woolens, and the rankness of the mature male. I hoped that someone would see us together. I wished that we could be photographed. I wanted some record of our having been together.

We went out of the station and up a side street to a restaurant. It was still early, and the place was empty. The bartender was quarrelling with a delivery boy, and there was one very old waiter in a red coat down by the kitchen door. We sat down, and my father hailed the waiter in a loud voice. '*Kellner!*' he shouted. '*Garçon! Cameriere! You!*' His boisterousness in the empty restaurant seemed out of place. 'Could we have a little service here!' he shouted. 'Chop-chop.' Then he clapped his hands. This caught the waiter's attention, and he shuffled over to our table.

'Were you clapping your hands at me?' he asked.

'Calm down, calm down, *sommelier*,' my father said. 'If it isn't too much to ask of you – if it wouldn't be above and beyond the call of duty – we would like a couple of Beefeater Gibsons.'

'I don't like to be clapped at,' the waiter said.

'I should have brought my whistle,' my father said. 'I have a whistle that is audible only to the ears of old waiters. Now, take out your little pad and your little pencil and see if you can get this straight: two Beefeater Gibsons. Repeat after me: two Beefeater Gibsons.'

'I think you'd better go somewhere else,' the waiter said quietly.

'That,' said my father, 'is one of the most brilliant suggestions I have ever heard. Come on, Charlie, let's get the hell out of here.'

I followed my father out of that restaurant into another. He was not so boisterous this time. Our drinks came, and he cross-questioned me about the baseball season. He then struck the edge of his empty glass with his knife and began shouting again. '*Garcon! Kellner! Cameriere! You!* Could we trouble you to bring us two more of the same.'

'How old is the boy?' the waiter asked.

'That,' my father said, 'is none of your God-damned business.'

'I'm sorry, sir,' the waiter said, 'but I won't serve the boy another drink.'

'Well, I have some news for you,' my father said. 'I have some very interesting news for you. This doesn't happen to be the only restaurant in New York. They've opened another on the corner. Come on, Charlie.'

He paid the bill, and I followed him out of the restaurant into another. Here the waiters wore pink jackets like hunting coats, and there was a lot of horse tack on the walls. We sat down, and my father began to shout again. 'Master of the hounds! Tallyhoo and all that sort of thing. We'd like a little something in the way of a stirrup cup. Namely, two Bibson Geefeaters.'

'Two Bibson Geefeaters?' the waiter asked, smiling.

'You know damned well what I want,' my father said angrily. 'I want two Beefeater Gibsons, and make it snappy. Things have changed in jolly old England. So my friend the duke tells me. Let's see what England can produce in the way of a cocktail.'

'This isn't England,' the waiter said.

'Don't argue with me,' my father said. 'Just do as you're told.'

'I just thought you might like to know where you are,' the waiter said.

'If there is one thing I cannot tolerate,' my father said, 'it is an impudent domestic. Come on, Charlie.'

The fourth place we went to was Italian. '*Buon giorno,*' my father said. '*Per favore, possiamo avere due cocktail americani, forti, forti. Molto gin, poco vermut.*'

'I don't understand Italian,' the waiter said.

'Oh, come off it,' my father said. 'You understand Italian, and you know damned well you do. *Vogliamo due cocktail Americani. Subito.*'

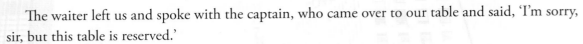

The waiter left us and spoke with the captain, who came over to our table and said, 'I'm sorry, sir, but this table is reserved.'

'All right,' my father said. 'Get us another table.'

'All the tables are reserved,' the captain said.

'I get it,' my father said. 'You don't desire our patronage. Is that it? Well, the hell with you. *Vada all'inferno.* Let's go, Charlie.'

'I have to get my train,' I said.

'I'm sorry, sonny,' my father said. 'I'm terribly sorry,' He put his arm around me and pressed me against him. 'I'll walk you back to the station. If there had only been time to go up to my club.'

'That's all right, Daddy,' I said.

'I'll get you a paper,' he said. 'I'll get you a paper to read on the train.'

Then he went up to a news stand and said, 'Kind sir, will you be good enough to favour me with one of your God-damned, no-good, ten-cent afternoon papers?'

The clerk turned away from him and stared at a magazine cover. 'Is it asking too much, kind sir,' my father said, 'is it asking too much for you to sell me one of your disgusting specimens of yellow journalism?'

'I have to go, Daddy,' I said. 'It's late.'

'Now, just wait a second, sonny,' he said. 'Just wait a second. I want to get a rise out of this chap.'

'Goodbye, Daddy,' I said, and I went down the stairs and got my train, and that was the last time I saw my father.

?
EXPLORE

1. At the beginning of the story, we get the impression that the boy is proud to be with his father. How do we know this? **P I E**

2. By the end of the story, the boy's feelings toward his father have changed. How have his feelings changed, in your opinion, and how is this illustrated (shown) in the story?

3. Choose a key moment in the story (there is often more than one). What does this key moment tell us about one of the central characters? To revise key moments, go back to page 37.

REMEMBER

A key scene or key moment is a turning point, a situation which demands a response.

4. Choose two adjectives to describe each of the two main characters (protagonists) in the story. For each adjective, give an example from the text of where it is displayed by the characters. **P I E**

5. Choose a character you have studied from another text (novel, short story or film). Compare and contrast them with one character from the short story, 'Reunion'. In your answer, write two paragraphs in which you mention one main similarity and one main difference between them. When you are writing you might like to use some of these sentence starters to help you structure your answer.

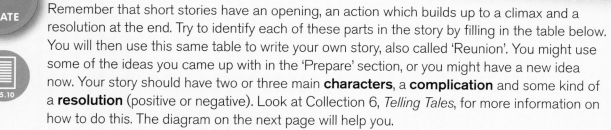

The first text I am writing about is ... by ...

The character I'm discussing is ...

They are ... (*explain who they are*)

I will be comparing this character to the character (*name*) in (*author/director's name*)'s film/novel/play (*text 2*).

One thing that the two characters have in common is ...

We see this in (*text 1*) when ...

Similarly, in (*text 2*) this is evident when ...

One of the main differences between the two characters is ...

For example (*character name*) in (*text 1*) ...

This is not the case in (*text 2*) because ...

Now it's time to plan a story.

Remember that short stories have an opening, an action which builds up to a climax and a resolution at the end. Try to identify each of these parts in the story by filling in the table below. You will then use this same table to write your own story, also called 'Reunion'. You might use some of the ideas you came up with in the 'Prepare' section, or you might have a new idea now. Your story should have two or three main **characters**, a **complication** and some kind of a **resolution** (positive or negative). Look at Collection 6, *Telling Tales*, for more information on how to do this. The diagram on the next page will help you.

Part of the story	What happens in Cheever's story 'Reunion'	Your story 'Reunion'
Opening (time, place, characters)		
Start the action		
Build-up to climax		
Ending/Resolution		

Structuring Your Story

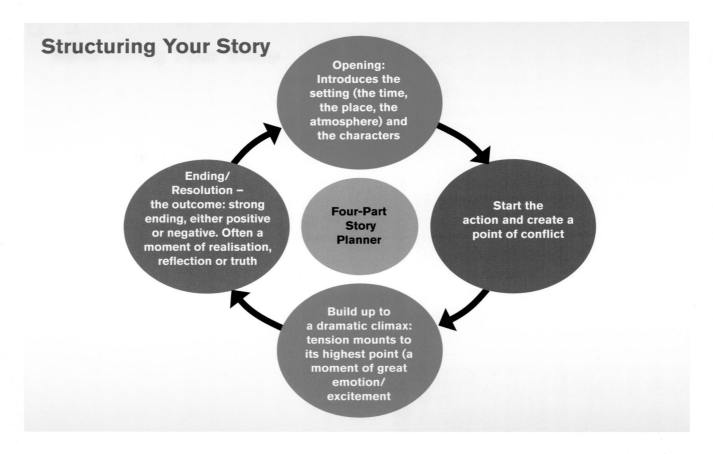

Four-Part Story Planner

Opening: Introduces the setting (the time, the place, the atmosphere) and the characters

Start the action and create a point of conflict

Build up to a dramatic climax: tension mounts to its highest point (a moment of great emotion/excitement

Ending/Resolution – the outcome: strong ending, either positive or negative. Often a moment of realisation, reflection or truth

A Short Film

What I will learn:

to compare two texts and explain why I prefer one over the other; to consider the theme of a text

For some students, moving to a new school is a smooth and easy transition. For others it is difficult to fit in and a real challenge to make new friends and get used to all the changes. Think back to when you started secondary school or if you ever had to move school. Now, working in groups, make a list of all the words you associate with starting/moving school.

New Boy (Steph Green, dir.)

This film is about a young boy's experience as he moves from a small rural school in Africa to Ireland: a new country, a different school system and whole new set of customs.
Having watched the film, answer the questions on the next page.

EXPLORE

1. What is the title and who is the director of this film?

2. Who is your favourite character in the film? Explain your answer.

3. Choose a key moment and explain why it is important.

4. How is this film related to the theme 'Triumph Over Adversity'?

5. Choosing any other film or story you have studied, write a paragraph comparing it with this film, explaining which you preferred and giving reasons for your answer.

What is the central message of the story (the theme) in your opinion? Discuss your thoughts with a classmate. Revise **theme** on page 2.

CREATE

(a) In the *Friendship* collection, you learned how to write a review. Write a review of *New Boy* for your school yearbook. Make sure to refer back to the section on writing a review when you are planning your own (p. 22).

OR

(b) Design the back of the DVD cover of this film. Give your work a main heading that will draw in potential viewers. You **must** include a short 'blurb' (synopsis) of the film, without giving too much away. It's helpful to include some quotes from newspapers or famous people that praise the film and recommend people watch it. You **should** also include an image (you can draw this or find it online).

After you have completed one of these tasks, think back on the work you did and complete the following sentences:

● The title of my work was …

● What I learned from creating this text was …

● What I would do differently next time is …

Blurb *n.*

Definition: A short piece of text on the back of a book/DVD cover/game cover, giving an idea of what the product is about and promoting it to the consumer.

Drama

to study and analyse central characters using critical vocabulary; to appreciate the importance of word choice in dialogue; to think about the setting/physical location of a play

The following extract is taken from the play, *The Cripple of Inishmaan*, written by Martin McDonagh. Nominated for a Tony Award (one of the most prestigious awards a playwright can receive), the play has been staged all around the world. In 2014 the main character was played by Daniel Radcliffe in the West End (London) and on Broadway (New York).

The play is set around 1934 on Inishmaan, a fictitious island off the west coast of Ireland. It centres around a small community whose lives are turned upside down when a film crew arrives on the neighbouring island, Inishmore. One of the main characters is Billy (known to locals as 'Cripple Billy'), a young man with a physical disability who lives with his aunts.

The scene you will read takes place in Billy's aunts' shop on Inishmaan as they anxiously await Billy's return from the neighbouring island after auditioning for a part in the film. In this scene, they are joined by Johnny Patteenmike, a local man who tells the news in return for items he needs, like food. Eileen and Kate are very keen to speak to him, to find out if he has heard any news about Billy. Read/listen carefully as you will be given a memory test at the end.

Scene Five of *The Cripple of Inishmaan* by Martin McDonagh

The shop. A few dozen eggs stacked on the counter.

Johnny enters, strutting.

Eileen: Johnnypateenmike.

Kate: Johnnypateenmike.

Johnny: Johnnypateen does have three pieces of news to be telling ye this day.

Kate: Only tell us if it's happy news Johnnypat, because we're a biteen depressed today, we are.

Johnny: I have a piece of news concerning the Inishmore trippers, but I will be saving that piece of news for me third piece of news.

Kate: Is Billy okay, Johnnypateen? Oh tell us that piece of news first.

Eileen: Tell us that piece of news first, aye, Johnnypateen.

Johnny: Well if ye're going arranging what order I tell me pieces of news in, I think I will turn on me heels and be off with me!

Kate: Don't go, Johnnypat! Don't go!

Johnny: Hah?

Eileen: Tell us your news in whatever order you like, Johnnypateen. Sure, aren't you the man who knows best about news-ordering?

Johnny: I am the man who knows best. I know I'm the man who knows best. That's no news. I see you have plenty of eggs in.

Eileen: We do, Johnnypateen.

Johnny: Uh-huh. Me first piece of news, there is a sheep out in Kerry with no ears at all on him.

Eileen: (*Pause*) That's a great piece of news.

Johnny: Don't ask me how he hears because I don't know and I don't care. Me second piece of news, Patty Brennan's cat was found dead and Jack Ellery's goose was found dead and nobody in town is said to've seen anything, but we can all put two and two together, although not out loud because Jack Ellery's an awful tough.

Kate: That's a sad piece of news because now it sounds like a feud is starting.

Johnny: A feud is starting and won't be stopped 'til the one or the two of them finish up slaughtered. Good. I will take six eggs, Mrs., for the omelette I promised me mammy a fortnight ago.

Eileen: What was the third piece of news, Johnnypateen?

Johnny: I mention me mammy and nobody even asks as to how she is. Oh it's the height of politeness in this quarter.

Kate: How is your mammy, Johnnypateen?

Johnny: Me mammy's fine, so she is, despite me best efforts.

Eileen: Are you still trying to kill your mammy with the drink, Johnnypateen?

Johnny: I am but it's no use. A fortune in booze that b_____ has cost me over the years. She'll never go. (*Pause*) Well now, I have me eggs, I've told you me two pieces of news. I suppose that's me business finished here for the day.

Kate: The … the third piece of news, Johnnypateen?

Johnny: Oh, the third piece of news. Wasn't I almost forgetting? (*Pause*) The third piece of news is Babbybobby's just pulled his boat up on the sands, at the headland there, and let the young adventurers off. Or, let two of the young adventurers off anyways, Helen and Bartley. There was no hide nor hair of Cripple Billy in that boat. (*Pause*) I'm off to have Babbybobby arrested for throwing stones at me head. I thank you for the eggs.

Johnny exits. Pause. Kate sadly caresses the old sack hanging on the wall, then sits at the table.

After reading the extract from *The Cripple of Inishmaan*, answer these questions.

1. Use your **Show-Me Boards** to answer these **True** or **False** statements.

a) This scene takes place in Johnnypateen's home.

b) Johnny has four pieces of news.

c) Billy's aunts are called Kate and Ellen.

d) Bobby has an unusual relationship with his mother.

e) Johnnypateen wants ten eggs.

f) According to Johnnypateen, a cow in Kerry has no ears.

g) A cat and goose were found dead.

h) Babbybobby has returned and Billy is with him.

2. In this scene we meet three characters, Eileen, Kate and Johnnypateen. Note down at least two adjectives to describe each of them and back it up with an appropriate quote.

Here is a list of adjectives to help you.

self-satisfied	innocent	disrespectful
mean-spirited	lonely	**greedy**
comic	acerbic	funny
naïve	manipulative	arrogant
wise	**malicious**	bitter
sarcastic	violent	**maternal**

Character's name	Adjective	Quote
Eileen		
Kate		
Johnnypateen		

3. Now choose one of these characters and expand your description by writing a short paragraph about them using the PIE method.

P I E
Johnnypateen is a very unusual character. This is best illustrated when he calmly refers to trying to kill his mother and complains that it's costing him a 'fortune in booze'. This is a very strange thing to say as most people would never admit to doing this, and certainly not so calmly. I thought this was a very amusing line and I really like this character.

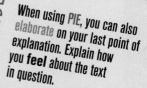

REMEMBER When using PIE, you can also elaborate on your last point of explanation. Explain how you **feel** about the text in question.

4. In the play, Billy is often referred to as 'Cripple Billy'. What does this tell you about the culture of the time when the play was set. How have things changed since then?

5. This play has been described as a 'dark comedy'. What evidence can you find of this?

TOP TIP

Dark comedy (also known as 'black humour') is a comic work that uses farce and morbid humour to mock serious subjects like death and religion. It is often controversial for that reason.

 Choose a **play** or **film** (a short film is fine) you have studied where the setting/physical location is important. Write a paragraph about the setting/physical location and why it is important, including:

- The title of the play/film
- The name of the playwright/director
- Details about the setting and why it is important in your chosen play/film.

 Watch the clip of an interview with Daniel Radcliffe where he discusses the role of Billy in *The Cripple of Inishmaan*.

Part 1: The Characters and Plot

1. What do we learn abut black humour?

2. What do we learn about the central character, Cripple Billy?

3. What is his 'ticket' off the island and why?

Part 2: The Acting Challenge

1. What challenges does Daniel Radcliffe mention?

2. Detail one of these challenges fully.

3. What do we learn about how Daniel approached learning the local accent.

1. Imagine you were going to direct an actor in the stage version of your favourite text. Choose one character and one actor to play them, and make a list of the important considerations they would have to think about:
   - Accent
   - Gestures
   - Costumes

2. Imagine an interview between your favourite presenter and the actor you selected to play the character. Write five questions and possible responses about the challenges they encountered.

EDITING

'Kill your darlings' – **Stephen King**

'So the writer who breeds more words than he needs, is making a chore for the reader who reads' – **Dr Seuss**

'Rereading reveals rubbish and redundancy' – **Duane Alan Hahn**

'What is written without effort is in general read without pleasure' – **Samuel Johnson**

Editing is one of the most difficult tasks a writer must do. Good writers will often spend more time rewriting than they do writing. Irish children's author Sarah Webb has this to say:

'I was asked recently how long it took me to write a book. A quarter of my time is spent writing, three-quarters rewriting is the honest answer. I do several rewrites before it goes to my editor and several more after that. Six/seven/eight rewrites in total or sometimes more, depending on the book.'

Practise writing short, concise sentences by limiting the number of words or characters you can use. A great way to do this is to use the Twitter model (currently 140 characters or less).

A 'character' in Twitter includes punctuation and spaces!

REMEMBER

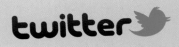

Home Profile Find People

WRITE

Pick one of the pieces you read in this collection (a poem, novel extract, drama, film, documentary, etc.) and write a short paragraph explaining how you would edit it to make it better/more enjoyable for a reader.

SHOW WHAT YOU KNOW

You have learned many writing and speaking skills in this collection of texts. Now it's time to *Show What You Know!*

My Writing Task

You are fundraising for a charitable organisation that is important to you. The organisation needs to raise at least €10,000 as soon as possible to help them purchase essential materials. Your teacher has suggested that you email a number of local businesses to request their assistance.

Draft an email to one local business telling them about the cause and outlining exactly what you need.

SUCCESS CRITERIA

I must

- Use the appropriate layout for a formal email
- Use formal, polite language
- Include a relevant sentence in the subject line to explain the purpose of the email
- Outline the reason for the email in the opening paragraph
- Provide information about the organisation you are fundraising for
- Conclude by outlining the desired outcome of your email (what I wish to happen)

I should

- Use the RAFT structure
- Use persuasive language
- Include my contact details
- Provide an outline of how the money will be spent
- Explain the charity/organisation's mission statement

I could

- Suggest a meeting with the company if they would like more information
- Offer to include the company logo if they donate money
- Mention other people or companies in the community who are supporting the organisation
- Include a quote or testimonial from someone who has benefited from the organisation

Self-Assessment

Re-read what you have written and then write down two things you think you did well and one thing you could improve on.

Redrafting

Reviewing the success criteria again to make sure you have met all the requirements, and taking into account your own self-assessment notes, you can now revise your email to create a second draft. When you are happy with your email, you can put it in your Collection of Texts.

Reflection Note

If you choose to place this task into your **Collection of Texts** now, complete a reflection note.
Hint: See the success criteria above to help you.

Oral Communication

You have been asked to speak to your class about a charity or organisation that helps people to overcome an adversity in their lives. Your **aim** is to convince the class to fundraise for this particular cause.
Prepare and deliver an oral presentation or interview about this worthy cause.
This could be presented as a talk with accompanying photos, as a PowerPoint/Prezi presentation or as an interview with someone who volunteers for or benefits from the organisation.

SUCCESS CRITERIA

I must

- Research the presentation properly (consult the website or flyers from the cause)
- Plan and practise my presentation
- Show an early draft to another classmate or my teacher
- Consider the audience (classmates) when planning and speaking
- Be persuasive: try to convince classmates about the importance of this cause
- Speak slowly and clearly when I am presenting

I should

- Include some statistics about the issue (e.g. if you were trying to raise money for guide dogs, you might mention that the lifetime cost of a guide dog is €38,000 and 80% of the organisation's costs are obtained through fundraising)
- Use real facts where possible
- Incorporate images into the presentation
- Try to speak without reading when I present (flash cards are useful)
- Show enthusiasm and passion for the cause

I could

- Mention possible fundraising ideas (make them fun and appealing for the audience)
- Use music in the presentation, where appropriate
- Interview people who work for or who have been helped by the charity and include quotes from/photos of them.

Peer Assessment

Reflect on your classmate's oral communication and then write down two things you think they did well and one thing they could improve on.

Redrafting

After you have practised your speech in front of someone, make a list of how you can improve it. You should also review the success criteria again to ensure you have met all the requirements. At this point, make any necessary changes to your speech. When you are happy with it, you can present it orally or record and then present/submit it to your teacher.

Presentation Websites

Here are some great websites for making presentations:

Prezi
Animoto
Biteslide
Slideshare
Present.me
Popcorn maker

Reflection Note

Now complete the **Oral Communication Template for Student Reflection.**

Telling Tales

Reading short stories for pleasure

Openings

Key moments

Narration

First point of conflict

Suspense

Climax

Varying sentence length

Ending/Resolution

As I explore this collection I will learn about:

Prequel and sequel

Themes

Prepositions

Verbs

Creating a character

Dialogue

Direct and indirect speech

'Show Don't Tell'

SHOW WHAT YOU KNOW

The skills you learn in this collection will enable you to **show what you know** in your final task at the end of this collection.

For my writing task I will:
Write a short story

Learning Outcomes
R1, R2, R6, W4, W10, W11, W12

What do you know about . . . Short Stories?

W6.1

To help you revise what short stories are all about, rewrite the following by inserting the correct words from the list.

Short stories are smaller than a _____. A short story should be long enough to grab your attention and short enough to be read in one sitting. Most short stories have a clear structure: the _____, the first point of co_____, the _____ and the _____.

With a short story the _____ is developed in a much shorter space of time. There are fewer _____ and they are not as well developed as the characters in a novel. The s_____ is much less detailed and complex and might only consist of one location.

If a short story has a good _____, we will want to know what happens next, but more importantly why something has happened. Some stories can have a p_____ t_____, which adds to the reader's excitement. Su_____ can also be used to build the tension of a story, making it more entertaining. A story can be written in any _____, for example comedy, horror, tragedy or romance.

In preparation for a short story an author must b_____. A good story will have an important central idea or _____. It will have a mix of n_____ and d_____ s_____, which allows us to keep track of the author's p_____ o___ v_____ while learning about the characters.

The _____ is the main character in the story. It is common to have an _____, a character who is in conflict with the hero.

climax	narration	novel
plot *(x 2)*	setting	brainstorm
theme	point of view	conflict
characters	genre	resolution
suspense	protagonist	opening
direct speech	antagonist	plot twist

W6.2

If you look up http://www.britannica.com/art/short-story, you will find a great video giving advice on writing short stories.

FUN FACT

It is claimed that famous American author, Ernest Hemingway (*pictured*), is responsible for writing the shortest ever short story, although many have attempted to write the shortest short story since. It had six words and was written to win a bet. The story was:

For sale: Baby shoes. Never worn.

Catching the Reader's Attention – Good Openings

What I will learn:

to understand a key element in creating a good plot (openings)

The openings of short stories are just like a game of chess: your first move can influence how the game will go. Unlike novels, the opening line and paragraph of a short story needs to establish setting, tone and characters quickly and deftly (skillfully).

This mind map details some of the classic **techniques** for writing an opening.

Focus on your **character** and describe them. **Show Don't Tell.** *'He walked with a limp and a scowl, glaring at anyone who crossed his path.'*

Arouse **interest** or **tension** by creating a sense of mystery. *'What do you mean, he's not coming back? He has the only key.'*

Writing an Opening

Make a bold/unusual **statement** to **hook** your reader. *'The sun had not risen in five days.'*

Skip to the **first point of conflict** and tell your audience what the problem is straight away. *'Scurrying wildlife screamed in fear as the forest fire engulfed their precious homes.'*

Bring the **setting** to life with expressive nouns, adjectives, verbs and adverbs. *'The sheer rock face towered silently above me and the valley below was now only a blur of greens, yellows and browns.'*

Now read the following short story openers and state which classic opening techniques are being used. (There could be more than one.) Give a reason for your answer.

Opening	Technique	I think this because …
'All the trouble began when my grandfather died and my grandmother – my father's mother – came to live with us.' From 'First Confession' by Frank O'Connor		
'Whoever has made a voyage up the Hudson must remember the Kaatskill mountains … When the weather is fair and settled, they are clothed in blue and purple, and print their bold outlines on the clear evening sky; but, sometimes, when the rest of the landscape is cloudless, they will gather a hood of gray vapors about their summits, which, in the last rays of the setting sun, will glow and light up like a crown of glory.' From 'Rip Van Winkle' by Washington Irving		
'When Janey Mary turned the corner into Nicholas Street that morning, she leaned wearily against a shop-front to rest. Her small head was bowed and the hair which was so nondescript and unclean covered her face.' From 'Janey Mary' by James Plunkett		
'She was a large woman with a large purse that had everything in it but a hammer and nails. It had a long strap, and she carried it slung across her shoulder. It was about eleven o'clock at night, dark, and she was walking alone, when a boy ran up behind her and tried to snatch her purse.' From 'Thank You, M'am' by Langston Hughes		
'Ready?' 'Ready.' 'Now?' 'Soon.' 'Do the scientists really know? Will it happen today, will it?' From 'All Summer in a Day' by Ray Bradbury		

Choose one of these stories and read it in full. Write a short paragraph explaining if you felt it lived up to what you expected from reading the opening lines.

Short Story [1]

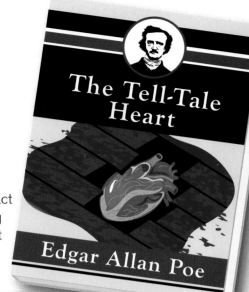

What I will learn:

to recognise different styles of narration

Edgar Allan Poe is one of America's greatest storytellers. He wrote stories of imagination and mystery. He claimed a short story should have a 'compact unified effect' and he was convinced that a tale should be capable of being read completely in one sitting. His opening paragraph from one of his most famous short stories, 'The Tell-Tale Heart', is a wonderful example of his ability to 'hook' his readers.

PREPARE

1. What's a 'tell-tale'? In your opinion, is being a 'tell-tale' a positive or negative thing?

2. Examine the book cover for 'The Tell-Tale Heart' above, and read the opening paragraph of the story below. Then discuss with your partner what you think this story is going to be about.

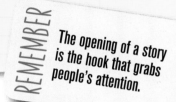

REMEMBER

The opening of a story is the hook that grabs people's attention.

'The Tell-Tale Heart' by Edgar Allan Poe

TRUE! – nervous – very, very dreadfully nervous I had been and am; but why *will* you say that I am mad? The disease had sharpened my senses – not destroyed – not dulled them. Above all was the sense of hearing **acute**. I heard all things in the heaven and in the earth. I heard many things in hell. How, then, am I mad? **Hearken**! and observe how healthily – how calmly I can tell you the whole story.

STOP

1. List three words or phrases that have immediately caught your attention.

2.. Explain why this opening would encourage you to keep reading.

3. The writer uses punctuation very effectively in this opening paragraph. For example, exclamation marks and dashes are used. How does the writer's use of punctuation make the story exciting to read? *Now read on …*

TOP TIP

A dash indicates a separation, not of words, but of thoughts or phrases. It is used to heighten drama and when something stronger than a comma is needed, and instead of more formal punctuation like a colon or semi-colon. The dash is used more commonly in informal writing, and should be used sparingly.

It is impossible to say how first the idea entered my brain; but once **conceived**, it haunted me day and night. Object there was none. Passion there was none. I loved the old man. He had never wronged me. He had never given me insult. For his gold I had no desire. I think it was his eye! yes, it was this! He had the eye of a vulture – a pale blue eye, with a film over it. Whenever it fell upon *me*, my blood ran cold; and so by degrees – very gradually – I made up my mind to take the life of the old man, and thus rid myself of the eye forever.

Now this is the point. You fancy me mad. Madmen know nothing. But you should have seen me. You should have seen how wisely I proceeded – with what caution– with what **foresight** – with what **dissimulation** I went to work! I was never kinder to the old man than during the whole week before I killed him. And every night, about midnight, I turned the latch of his door and opened it – oh so gently! And then, when I had made an opening sufficient for my head, I put in a dark lantern, all closed, closed, that no light shone out, and then I thrust in my head. Oh, you would have laughed to see how **cunningly** I thrust it in! I moved it slowly – very, very slowly, so that I might not disturb the old man's sleep. It took me an hour to place my whole head within the opening so far that I could see him as he lay upon his bed. Ha! would a madman have been so wise as this? And then, when my head was well in the room, I undid the lantern cautiously – oh, so cautiously – cautiously (for the hinges creaked) – I undid it just so much that a single thin ray fell upon the vulture eye. And this I did for seven long nights – every night just at midnight – but I found the eye always closed; and so it was impossible to do the work; for it was not the old man who **vexed** me, but his Evil Eye. And every morning, when the day broke, I went boldly into the chamber, and spoke courageously to him, calling him by name in a hearty tone, and inquiring how he has passed the night. So you see he would have been a very **profound** old man, indeed, to suspect that every night, just at twelve, I looked in upon him while he slept.

Upon the eighth night I was more than usually cautious in opening the door. A watch's minute hand moves more quickly than did mine. Never before that night, had I *felt* the extent of my own powers – of my **sagacity**. I could scarcely contain my feelings of triumph. To think that there I was, opening the door, little by little, and he not even to dream of my secret deeds or thoughts. I fairly chuckled at the idea; and perhaps he heard me; for he moved on the bed suddenly, as if startled. Now you may think that I drew back – but no. His room was as black as pitch with the thick darkness, (for the shutters were close fastened, through fear of robbers,) and so I knew that he could not see the opening of the door, and I kept pushing it on steadily, steadily.

I had my head in, and was about to open the lantern, when my thumb slipped upon the tin fastening, and the old man sprang up in bed, crying out – 'Who's there?'

I kept quite still and said nothing. For a whole hour I did not move a muscle, and in the meantime I did not hear him lie down. He was still sitting up in the bed listening; – just as I have done, night after night, hearkening to the death watches in the wall.

Presently I heard a slight groan, and I knew it was the groan of mortal terror. It was not a groan of pain or of grief – oh, no! – it was the low stifled sound that arises from the bottom of the soul when overcharged with awe. I knew the sound well. Many a night, just at midnight, when all the world slept, it has welled up from my own bosom, deepening, with its dreadful echo, the terrors that distracted me. I say I knew it well. I knew what the old man felt, and pitied him, although I chuckled at heart. I knew that he had been lying awake ever since the first slight noise, when he had turned in the bed. His fears had been ever since growing upon him. He had been trying to fancy them causeless, but could not. He had been saying to himself – 'It is nothing but the wind in the chimney – it is only a mouse crossing the floor,' or 'It is merely a cricket which has made a single chirp.' Yes, he had been trying to comfort himself with these **suppositions**: but he had found all in vain. *All in vain*; because Death, in approaching him had stalked with his black shadow before him, and enveloped the victim. And it was the mournful influence of the unperceived shadow that caused him to feel – although he neither saw nor heard – to *feel* the presence of my head within the room.

When I had waited a long time, very patiently, without hearing him lie down, I resolved to open a little – a very, very little crevice in the lantern. So I opened it – you cannot imagine how **stealthily**, stealthily – until, at length a simple dim ray, like the thread of the spider, shot from out the crevice and fell full upon the vulture eye.

It was open – wide, wide open – and I grew furious as I gazed upon it. I saw it with perfect distinctness – all a dull blue, with a hideous veil over it that chilled the very **marrow** in my bones; but I could see nothing else of the old man's face or person: for I had directed the ray as if by instinct, precisely upon the damned spot.

And have I not told you that what you mistake for madness is but over-acuteness of the senses? – now, I say, there came to my ears a low, dull, quick sound, such as a watch makes when enveloped in cotton. I knew *that* sound well, too. It was the beating of the old man's heart. It increased my fury, as the beating of a drum **stimulates** the soldier into courage.

But even yet I refrained and kept still. I scarcely breathed. I held the lantern motionless. I tried how steadily I could to maintain the ray upon the eye. Meantime the hellish tattoo of the heart increased. It grew quicker and quicker, and louder and louder every instant. The old man's terror *must* have been extreme! It grew louder, I say, louder every moment! – do you mark me well? I have told you that I am nervous: so I am. And now at the dead hour of the night, amid the dreadful silence of that old house, so strange a noise as this excited me to uncontrollable terror. Yet, for some minutes longer I refrained and stood still. But the beating grew louder, louder! I thought the heart must burst. And now a new anxiety seized me – the sound would be heard by a neighbour! The old man's hour had come! With a loud yell, I threw open the lantern and leaped into the room. He shrieked once – once only. In an instant I dragged him to the floor, and pulled the heavy bed over him. I then smiled gaily, to find the deed so far done. But, for many minutes, the heart beat on with a muffled sound. This, however, did not vex me; it would not be heard through the wall. At length it ceased. The old man was dead. I removed the bed and examined the corpse. Yes, he was stone, stone dead. I placed my hand upon the heart and held it there many minutes. There was no pulsation. He was stone dead. His eye would trouble me no more.

If still you think me mad, you will think so no longer when I describe the wise precautions I took for the concealment of the body. The night waned; and I worked hastily, but in silence. First of all I **dismembered** the corpse. I cut off the head and the arms and the legs.

I then took up three planks from the flooring of the chamber, and deposited all between the **scantlings**. I then replaced the boards so cleverly, so cunningly, that no human eye – not even *his* – could have detected anything wrong. There was nothing to wash out – no stain of any kind – no blood-spot whatever. I had been too wary for that. A tub had caught all – ha! ha!

When I had made an end of these labours, it was four o'clock – still dark as midnight. As the bell sounded the hour, there came a knocking at the street door. I went down to open it with a light heart, – for what had I *now* to fear? There entered three men, who introduced themselves, with perfect **suavity**, as officers of the police. A shriek had been heard by a neighbour during the night; suspicion of foul play had been aroused; information had been lodged at the police office, and they (the officers) had been **deputed** to search the premises.

I smiled, – for *what* had I to fear? I bade the gentlemen welcome. The shriek, I said, was my own in a dream. The old man, I mentioned, was absent in the country. I took my visitors all over the house. I bade them search – search *well*. I led them, at length, to his chamber. I showed them his treasures, secure, undisturbed. In the enthusiasm of my confidence, I brought chairs into the room, and desired them *here* to rest from their fatigues, while I myself, in the wild **audacity** of my perfect triumph, placed my own seat upon the very spot beneath which **reposed** the corpse of the victim.

The officers were satisfied. My *manner* had convinced them. I was singularly at ease. They sat, and while I answered cheerily, they chatted of familiar things. But, ere long, I felt myself getting pale and wished them gone. My head ached, and I fancied a ringing in my ears: but still they sat and still chatted. The ringing became more distinct: – it continued and became more distinct: I talked more freely to get rid of the feeling: but it continued and gained definiteness – until, at length, I found that the noise was *not* within my ears.

No doubt I now grew *very* pale; – but I talked more fluently, and with a heightened voice. Yet the sound increased – and what could I do? It was a *low, dull, quick sound – much such a sound as a watch makes when* **enveloped** *in cotton*. I gasped for breath – and yet the officers heard it not. I talked more quickly – more **vehemently**; but the noise steadily increased. I arose and argued about trifles, in a high key and with violent **gesticulations**; but the noise steadily increased. Why *would* they not be gone? I paced the floor to and fro with heavy strides, as if excited to fury by the observations of the men – but the noise steadily increased. Oh God! what *could* I do? I foamed – I raved – I swore! I swung the chair upon which I had been sitting, and grated it upon the boards, but the noise arose over all and continually increased. It grew louder – louder – *louder*! And still the men chatted pleasantly, and smiled. Was it possible they heard not? Almighty God! – no, no! They heard! – they suspected! – they *knew*! – they were making a mockery of my horror! – this I thought, and this I think. But anything was better than this agony! Anything was more tolerable than this derision! I could bear those hypocritical smiles no longer! I felt that I must scream or die! and now – again! – hark! louder! louder! louder! *louder*!

'Villains!' I shrieked, 'dissemble no more! I admit the deed! – tear up the planks! here, here! – it is the beating of his hideous heart!'

GLOSSARY

acute – powerful and sharp
hearken – listen
conceived – think or imagine something
foresight – ability to think ahead
dissimulation – disguise of feelings or intentions
cunningly – clever/able to get away with things
vexed – frustrated or angered by something
profound – serious
sagacity – wisdom
suppositions – suggestions
stealthily – trying to avoid being noticed
marrow – soft tissue
stimulates – encourages or builds excitement about something
dismembered – cut a limb from the body
scantlings – thin piece of timber
suavity – politeness or charm
deputed – given duties/responsibilities
audacity – daring
reposed – in a state of rest
enveloped – to completely enclose or cover something
vehemently – to act or speak with great force
gesticulations – movements of the arms and hands when speaking

 You can watch a great animated production of 'The Tell-Tale Heart' by Annette Jung on YouTube.

Imagine you are working for a theatre company that is staging a production of this story. Create a poster where the central image represents a **key moment**. You will present this to your class explaining why you have chosen this significant moment.

REMEMBER Key moments, p. 37.

Guide to Choosing Your Narrator

You will notice that Edgar Allan Poe uses a wicked and eccentric (strange) narrator, which makes this short story absolutely gripping. Ask yourself the following questions:

- Is the narrator and protagonist the same person?
- Is the narrator a hero or a villain?
- Is he a reliable narrator? Can we trust what he is saying?

You should also bear these questions in mind when you decide to create your own narrator.

FIRST PERSON NARRATIVES

- Are written from one (or more) character's **point of view**
- Have narrators who **speak directly** to the reader about themselves but they are not always the main character
- Are identified by **personal pronouns** such as 'I' 'my' 'I'd', etc.
- Have narrators who share their **emotions** but can be unreliable

E.g. Katniss Everdeen narrates *The Hunger Games* from her point of view.

REMEMBER Pronouns are words that substitute for nouns, for example 'me', 'your' or 'it'.

SECOND PERSON NARRATIVES

- Make the **reader the protagonist** of the story
- Can be identified by the pronouns '**you**' or '**we**'

E.g. Nathanial Hawthorne's story 'The Haunted Mind' invites the reader to become the character.

THIRD PERSON NARRATIVES

- **Don't directly involve** the writer in the action
- Are identified by pronouns such as '**he**', '**she**' and '**they**', etc.
- Are useful in describing **various characters'** actions and feelings

E.g. Sometimes third person narrators can be omniscient: they can go anywhere at any time in the story. The narrator of *The Lord of the Rings* can jump from Sam and Frodo in Mordor to Gandalf and Aragorn in Rohan. This narrator knows everything!

Exam Focus

1 All of the lines below describe the exact same moment in a story. Decide whether they are first, second or third person narrators.

- You crawled along the slimy pipeline, beyond the room you used to sleep in, until finally, you saw the gap which would give you your freedom from Alcatraz.

- 'What is this rotten substance under me?' I mouthed. I dared not make a sound, for that was the bed I used to sleep in. Jerry's there now – he is a light sleeper and I can almost see the gap. Goodbye Alcatraz, hello freedom!

- George crawled along the pipe line; he was not impressed by the oily substance underneath him. He was careful not to wake anyone up; after all, he was near to his escape route from Alcatraz. 'Hmmm, what was that?' Jerry wondered. Ever since he had moved to George's new cell, he wasn't sleeping very well and he could definitely hear something above him.

2 Take a key moment from 'The Tell-Tale Heart' and write it in either the second or third person narrative.

3 If you were adapting 'The Tell-Tale Heart' to be made into a film, what actor would you get to play the protagonist? Justify your answer to your partner.

4 Imagine you were the old man with the 'Evil Eye'. Create a short monologue where you explain your experience of living with the wicked narrator. Act it out for your class. Try to create the atmosphere of the situation as well as the emotion and movement of the man. You could use a prop or piece of costume to make your character really come alive.

REMEMBER Monologue, p. 107.

Short Story [2]

What I will learn:

to understand a key element in creating a good plot (first point of conflict); to investigate the creation of suspense and tension in a text

The next short story, 'The Sniper' by Liam O'Flaherty, deals with the themes of war, family and death. It was written in 1923 at a time of severe political tension in Ireland. O'Flaherty's story brilliantly builds tension and suspense. He writes the story in the **third person narrative**. Like all great storytellers, O'Flaherty gains the reader's attention with his **opening** and then quickly **introduces the problem**.

Brainstorm vocabulary you would associate with the main themes of this story: war, family and death. Share your ideas with your partner. When you have finished reading the story, review your list and see if Liam O'Flaherty used any of the same ideas or vocabulary you came up with.

W6.5

'The Sniper'
by Liam O'Flaherty

The long June twilight faded into night. Dublin lay enveloped in darkness but for the dim light of the moon that shone through fleecy clouds, casting a pale light as of approaching dawn over the streets and the dark waters of the Liffey. Around the beleaguered Four Courts the heavy guns roared. Here and there through the city, machine guns and rifles broke the silence of the night, **spasmodically**, like dogs barking on lone farms. Republicans and Free Staters were waging civil war.

> **spasmodi-cally:** sudden but brief

On a rooftop near O'Connell Bridge, a Republican sniper lay watching. Beside him lay his rifle and over his shoulders was slung a pair of field glasses. His face was the face of a student, thin and **ascetic**, but his eyes had the cold gleam of the fanatic. They were deep and thoughtful, the eyes of a man who is used to looking at death.

> **ascetic:** serious, severe

He was eating a sandwich hungrily. He had eaten nothing since morning. He had been too excited to eat. He finished the sandwich, and, taking a flask of whiskey from his pocket, he took a short draught. Then he returned the flask to his pocket. He paused for a moment, considering whether he should risk a smoke. It was dangerous. The flash might be seen in the darkness, and there were enemies watching.

He decided to take the risk. Placing a cigarette between his lips, he struck a match, inhaled the smoke hurriedly and put out the light. Almost immediately, a bullet flattened itself against the parapet of the roof. The sniper took another whiff and put out the cigarette. Then he swore softly and crawled away to the left.

Cautiously he raised himself and peered over the parapet. There was a flash and a bullet whizzed over his head. He dropped immediately. He had seen the flash. It came from the opposite side of the street. He rolled over the roof to a chimney stack in the rear, and slowly drew himself up behind it, until his eyes were level with the top of the parapet. There was nothing to be seen – just the dim outline of the opposite housetop against the blue sky. His enemy was under cover.

Just then an armoured car came across the bridge and advanced slowly up the street. It stopped on the opposite side of the street, fifty yards ahead. The sniper could hear the dull panting of the motor. His heart beat faster. It was an enemy car. He wanted to fire, but he knew it was useless. His bullets would never pierce the steel that covered the grey monster.

STOP

What is the problem that arises for the sniper in paragraphs four and five?

Introducing the Problem

The author has introduced a vivid setting (paragraph one) and a central character (paragraph two) during his opening. In paragraphs four and five, the author has introduced the problem. This is where the reader experiences the first point of conflict in the story. *Now read on …*

Then round the corner of a side street came an old woman, her head covered by a tattered shawl. She began to talk to the man in the turret of the car. She was pointing to the roof where the sniper lay. An informer.

The turret opened. A man's head and shoulders appeared, looking toward the sniper. The sniper raised his rifle and fired. The head fell heavily on the turret wall. The woman darted toward the side street. The sniper fired again. The woman whirled round and fell with a shriek into the gutter.

Suddenly from the opposite roof a shot rang out and the sniper dropped his rifle with a curse. The rifle clattered to the roof. The sniper thought the noise would wake the dead. He stooped to pick the rifle up. He couldn't lift it. His forearm was dead. 'I'm hit,' he muttered.

Dropping flat onto the roof, he crawled back to the parapet. With his left hand he felt the injured right forearm. The blood was oozing through the sleeve of his coat. There was no pain – just a deadened sensation, as if the arm had been cut off.

Quickly he drew his knife from his pocket, opened it on the breastwork of the parapet, and ripped open the sleeve. There was a small hole where the bullet had entered. On the other side there was no hole. The bullet had lodged in the bone. It must have fractured it. He bent the arm below the wound. The arm bent back easily. He ground his teeth to overcome the pain.

Then taking out his field dressing, he ripped open the packet with his knife. He broke the neck of the iodine bottle and let the bitter fluid drip into the wound. A **paroxysm** of pain swept through him. He placed the cotton wadding over the wound and wrapped the dressing over it. He tied the ends with his teeth.

Then he lay still against the parapet, and, closing his eyes, he made an effort of will to overcome the pain.

In the street beneath all was still. The armoured car had retired speedily over the bridge, with the machine gunner's head hanging lifeless over the turret. The woman's corpse lay still in the gutter.

The sniper lay still for a long time nursing his wounded arm and planning escape. Morning must not find him wounded on

paroxysm: a sudden attack/ outburst

the roof. The enemy on the opposite roof covered his escape. He must kill that enemy and he could not use his rifle. He had only a revolver to do it. Then he thought of a plan.

Taking off his cap, he placed it over the muzzle of his rifle. Then he pushed the rifle slowly upward over the parapet, until the cap was visible from the opposite side of the street. Almost immediately there was a report, and a bullet pierced the centre of the cap. The sniper slanted the rifle forward. The cap clipped down into the street. Then catching the rifle in the middle, the sniper dropped his left hand over the roof and let it hang, lifelessly. After a few moments he let the rifle drop to the street. Then he sank to the roof, dragging his hand with him.

ruse: trick

Crawling quickly to his feet, he peered up at the corner of the roof. His **ruse** had succeeded. The other sniper, seeing the cap and rifle fall, thought that he had killed his man. He was now standing before a row of chimney pots, looking across, with his head clearly silhouetted against the western sky.

The Republican sniper smiled and lifted his revolver above the edge of the parapet. The distance was about fifty yards – a hard shot in the dim light, and his right arm was paining him like a thousand devils. He took a steady aim. His hand trembled with eagerness. Pressing his lips together, he took a deep breath through his nostrils and fired.

He was almost deafened with the report and his arm shook with the recoil.

When the smoke cleared, he peered across and uttered a cry of joy. His enemy had been hit. He was reeling over the parapet in his death agony. He struggled to keep his feet, but he was slowly falling forward as if in a dream. The rifle fell from his grasp, hit the parapet, fell over, bounded off the pole of a barber's shop beneath and then clattered on the pavement.

Then the dying man on the roof crumpled up and fell forward. The body turned over and over in space and hit the ground with a dull thud. Then it lay still.

The sniper looked at his enemy falling and he shuddered. The lust of battle died in him. He became bitten by remorse. The sweat stood out in beads on his forehead. Weakened by his wound and the long summer day of fasting and watching on the roof, he revolted from the sight of the shattered mass of his dead enemy. His teeth chattered, he began to gibber to himself, cursing the war, cursing himself, cursing everybody.

He looked at the smoking revolver in his hand, and with an oath he hurled it to the roof at his feet. The revolver went off with a concussion and the bullet whizzed past the sniper's head. He was frightened back to his senses by the shock. His nerves steadied. The cloud of fear scattered from his mind and he laughed.

Taking the whiskey flask from his pocket, he emptied it at a draught. He felt reckless under the influence of the spirit. He decided to leave the roof now and look for his company commander, to report. Everywhere around was quiet. There was not much danger in going through the streets. He picked up his revolver and put it in his pocket. Then he crawled down through the skylight to the house underneath.

When the sniper reached the laneway on the street level, he felt a sudden curiosity as to the identity of the enemy sniper whom he had killed. He decided that he was a good shot, whoever he was. He wondered did he know him. Perhaps he had been in his own company before the split in the army. He decided to risk going over to have a look at him. He peered around the corner into O'Connell Street. In the upper part of the street there was heavy firing, but around here all was quiet.

The sniper darted across the street. A machine gun tore up the ground around him with a hail of bullets, but he escaped. He threw himself face downward beside the corpse. The machine gun stopped.

Then the sniper turned over the dead body and looked into his brother's face.

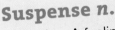

Suspense *n.*

Definition: A feeling of excitement or anxiety about what may happen next
Synonyms: anxiety, tension, uncertainty, doubt

EXPLORE

This story is notable for building suspense and tension from the early stages right until the end.

1. How does the first point of conflict come about for the protagonist?

2. What words or phrases does the author use to show that this is a point of conflict?

3. Choose three moments in the story where you felt suspense building.

4. Identify any words or phrases that make you feel tense in one of these moments.

5. Why do you think suspense is important in a story? P I E

Guide to Building Suspense

- Liam O'Flaherty creates a **DRAMATIC SETTING** for the action to unfold.
    - *'The long June twilight faded into night. Dublin lay <u>enveloped in darkness</u> but for the <u>dim light of the moon</u> that <u>shone through fleecy clouds</u>, casting a pale light as of approaching dawn over the streets and the dark waters of the Liffey.'*

- He puts the main character in **DANGER**. There are things about the main character that we may not like but the author also develops sympathy for him. He is cold and hungry and is clearly fighting for a cause he believes in. Once he is placed in danger, it raises the tension and suspense.
    - *'He was eating a sandwich hungrily. He had eaten nothing since morning ...'*

- He creates **DRAMATIC ACTION** that panics the reader.
    - *'<u>Almost immediately</u>, a <u>bullet flattened</u> itself against the parapet of the roof.'*
    - *'The <u>blood was oozing</u> through the sleeve of his coat. There was no pain — just a deadened sensation, as if the arm had been cut off.'*
    - *'The revolver went off with a concussion and the <u>bullet whizzed</u> past the sniper's head.'*

- He uses **SHORT, SNAPPY SENTENCES** to build towards a dramatic moment.
    - *'He took a steady aim. His hand trembled with eagerness. Pressing his lips together, he took a deep breath through his nostrils and fired.'*

- He follows through on the building of suspense and tension with **SHOCKING MOMENTS** for the reader.
    - The killing of the vulnerable old woman.
    - The sniper's brush with death.
    - The sniper's discovery of his brother.

> Think of another poem, short story, novel or film that built suspense successfully. Map out how this is done.

REMEMBER — Interviewers should have a mix of open questions (a question that allows the interviewee to provide more information) and closed questions (questions that require only one-word answers).

1. Imagine you have been given the opportunity to interview the sniper several years after the events described in the story. Compile **at least ten questions** that you would ask him.

2 Choose one theme that you think best describes the central idea in this story. Write an email to a friend explaining how this story is about the theme you have picked.

3 Using the graphic organiser, compare 'The Sniper' to another short story, poem, film or novel you have read.

Exam Focus

Short Story [3]

What I will learn:

to understand a key element in creating a good plot (climax); to discuss the effectiveness of varying sentence length in story-writing

The author of this short story is best known for his novels in the *Skulduggery Pleasant* series. In this short story, 'The Hero of Drumree', Derek Landy creates a witty and unique character in Fleece, whose adventures bring him to a rather startling **climax**. Fleece's experiences bring up the themes of courage, loyalty and war.

 Describe your idea of a hero/heroine. List his/her qualities or traits. Give examples from books or films you have studied.

TOP TIP
The opposite of a hero is a villain or antihero.

'The Hero of Drumree'
by Derek Landy

'There may come a day,' roared General Tua, 'when the legacy of Man falls! When his shields splinter under Fomorian sword! But it will not be this day!'

A roar sounded among the troops, and Tua's horse reared back on two legs, before the general kicked in his heels and galloped up the line.

'When they speak of this day, they will speak of loyalty! Of duty! Of …'

The last word was lost to Corporal Fleece as Tua sped further way, but he was relatively sure it was 'honour'. Tua was big on honour.

Men **jostled** him from all sides, and despite the cold winter wind, Fleece felt uncomfortably hot. It stank here too. Bathing was not high on the list of requirements for the foot soldiers of the Hibernian Army. Being big, brutish and ugly, however, seemingly *were*, and as such Fleece reckoned himself to be a soldier lacking. He couldn't even see the valley where they were going to be fighting – couldn't even see the Formorian Army amassed on the other side. Although this was probably a good thing.

General Tua rode back into range.

> **jostled:** knocked or bumped

spawned: the source of something

encroach: trespass

antagonise: cause someone to become hostile/angry

'Here, on the fields and in the valleys of Drumree, we will send these demons back to the seas where they were **spawned**! Then they will learn what it means to **encroach** on the lands of Man! They will …' And off he went again. Up the line in the other direction.

Fleece turned his head, got a blast of foul breath and wrinkled his nose. He saw Iron Guts, his best friend in the whole of Hibernia, and tried to squeeze through the throng of men towards him. Failing miserably, he resorted to waving and shouting over the soldiers' heads.

'Iron Guts! Iron Guts! I missed that last bit! What did he say? What did he say after "encroaching on our lands"?'

Iron Guts looked back, and scowled. 'Shut,' he said, 'up'. Then he paused a moment before adding, 'You idiot.'

Fleece smiled weakly, and did as he was told. He didn't want to **antagonise** his only friend, the only man in the army who had not yet threatened to kill him. He was sweating beneath his chain mail and his shoulders ached from its weight.

He sighed; he was already exhausted and it wasn't mid-morning yet – the battle hadn't even *started* and he needed a lie-down. This did not bode well for any heroics he might later be required to perform. Not that he was *ever* required to perform any heroics, unlike the men around him with their glorious names. Ranfield the Raging. Wolftooth the Cruel. Iron Guts the Bloody. If anyone would ever be suitably motivated to come up with a name for Fleece, it would probably be something along the lines of Fleece the Thoroughly Unsuited to Battle, or Fleece the Far Too Pretty to Be Hit, or, the most likely option, Fleece the Where the Hell Has He Run Off to Now?

Bravery was not one of his strong points. It wasn't even one of his weak points. The fact of the matter was that bravery just wasn't one of his points. During armed conflict, Fleece liked to pick a little section of the battlefield, somewhere along the edge, and pretend to be dead. He kept some fresh cow's blood in a pouch inside his tunic, and he'd give himself a healthy splatter when he got comfortable. Then, when all the fuss was over, he would miraculously recover, and hurry back to camp with all the other survivors. It was a tricky business, and once or twice he had come close to actually encountering a living enemy, but his luck had held. So far.

He didn't like the turn this day was taking, however. He was jammed right in the middle of ten thousand Hibernian soldiers. When Tua gave the order to advance, he'd have to slip sideways to the edge, which wasn't going to be easy. He looked up, trying to peek over the brutish, ugly, stinking men in front of him, and saw the top of Tua's head as he rode back towards them.

winced: make a expression of pain

bellowed: shout loudly

'For freedom!' Tua roared, and Fleece **winced** as the troops **bellowed**, 'For Hibernia!' and then, in another bellow, even more animalistic than the first, 'For the King!'

Swords were drawn and held aloft and the roaring went on and on. Fleece didn't know how anyone could have drawn their swords when they were this tightly packed in.

Leaving his in the sheath by his leg, he instead waved his little knife and shouted a bit. It was all fairly ridiculous. Getting worked up about freedom and Hibernia was one thing, but the king? The king was a fat slug who'd had his golden throne shipped over so he could sit back in the camp and eat and drink while his loyal subjects fought and died for him. Naturally, Fleece didn't count himself among their number.

'Advance!' General Tua roared, and troops surged ahead violently.

Fleece was thrown forward, his face squashed against the man in front. Trying to regain his balance, his feet were clipped by the man behind so he had to take tiny quick steps. He got an elbow in the face and howled as he reached out to steady himself. His knife nicked someone as he did so and they cursed at him.

'Sorry!' he called. He could feel his face already starting to swell. He tried to slip sideways, to the edge of the throng, but there were no gaps between the hulking, shouting, grunting soldiers.

Suddenly they were moving faster, jogging, but Fleece's feet were no longer touching the snow-covered ground. He was being carried along with them, held aloft by the huge shoulders squashing in on either side. Now he could see over the heads of the men in front. Now he could see the Fomorians, their green skins covered in armour and leathers and furs, as they sprinted towards them. He started shrieking.

The front line of Hibernian soldiers clashed with the Fomorians and Fleece jerked to a painful halt. He watched as swords cleaved skulls in two. Axes hacked at necks and arms and legs. Spears **skewered**. Arrows pierced. Knives sliced.

'Let me down!' Fleece screamed, but nobody heard him above the roar of their own insanity.

He struck out in desperation, heaved himself higher. Somehow he managed to clamber over the heads of his comrades-in-arms, terrified, trembling like a leaf on the surface of a fast-flowing and ill-tempered stream. Hands reached up, redirecting him, sending him straight to the front line.

'Wrong way!' he screamed. 'Wrong way!'

A spear was pressed into the chest of the man beneath him and Fleece tumbled down. He was kicked and kneed and thrown about by soldiers bizarrely eager to get at the enemy. Through the gaps he could see the Fomorians – one in particular, the biggest he'd ever seen, stood out, his green skin slimy beneath burnished-red armour that was already splattered with human blood. His left foot was missing but that didn't seem to slow him, and his headpiece was magnificent, a helmet carved into horns, a devil's face on the head of a demon. Only one Fomorian wore such a headpiece, Fleece knew. This was Cichol Gricenchos, the Fomorian king.

A Hibernian soldier charged. Gricenchos's sword was a massive thing of shining steel. It knocked the Hibernian's blade from his hand and separated his head from his body in one lazy swipe, cutting through armour and chain mail like it was nothing. Two more Hibernian soldiers went at Gricenchos, and two more were dispatched with similar ease.

A circle of sorts had formed in the midst of the battle, an arena where the Fomorian king took on all comers. Fleece wondered what it felt like for the other demons to know that their leader was with them at all times like these. It was probably inspiring. Not like for him and the other Hibernians with

skewered: pierce something with a sharp rod

their fat slug of a leader back at camp. The only threat he'd pose to an enemy would be if he rolled over them on his way to the chicken.

A heavy wave rippled through the ranks, knocking Fleece to his knees, and then General Tua charged through the crowd on his horse, heading straight at Gricenchos.

The Fomorians screeched, maybe warning their king, maybe protesting at the unfairness of it all, but Gricenchos didn't turn and run. Instead he stepped to one side and brought his sword round with both hands. The horse's head flew, and General Tua was thrown from its saddle, the horse flipping over and landing on top of him. Gricenchos didn't even do him the honour of killing the general himself. He left Tua to the stabbing of the Fomorians, and turned back to the Hibernian soldiers, awaiting his next challenger.

Fleece was sent stumbling out of the crowd. The Formorian king looked down at him. Beneath the horned headpiece his nose was long and his mouth was wide, filled with sharp black teeth. He was not, even as far as Fomorians went, particularly handsome. Fleece clasped his hands in front of him.

'Please don't kill me,' he whimpered.

'Coward!' Iron Guts roared, breaking away from the Hibernian men, swinging his sword for Gricenchos's head.

The Fomorian king moved faster than Fleece would have thought possible for someone his size. Steel clashed and Gricenchos sent Iron Guts stumbling away. He brought his great sword down but this time it was Iron Guts who moved, deflecting the blade with his shield and shifting sideways, as nimble as a dancer, although Fleece would never have said that aloud. He watched the man and the demon go at it, snarling and spitting at each other, swinging savage cuts, feinting and parrying and doing all the things that Fleece had once been shown by his father, but which he had never paid that much attention to. Pity. Such a skill set would have come in very useful today.

Gricenchos battered the shield on Iron Guts's arm, driving him to his knees, showing his back to Fleece and letting him, from his low vantage point, look right up between the scales of his attacker's armour to the green skin beneath.

Something strange and foreign seized Fleece's heart. Courage? Was that what he was feeling? He highly doubted it, but couldn't think what else it could be. This was his chance to turn his life round, to do something heroic and brave and noble. Only on the battlefield, he despaired, would plunging your sword into someone's back be considered noble.

The Fomorian king splintered the shield and Iron Guts, the only friend Fleece had in the whole of Hibernia, fell back. Fleece narrowed his eyes, focused in on the gap in Gricenchos's armour. His hand went for his sword, and clutched stupidly at air. It wasn't in his sheath! Why wasn't it in his sheath? His eyes widened as he remembered. He'd left his sword in his tent.

Gricenchos split Iron Guts's head wide open, roaring as he did so, and kicked the corpse away from him. He turned back to Fleece, who only had his little knife.

Fleece had had that knife since he was a boy. His father had done his best to teach him how to throw it. His younger brothers had learned well enough, but Fleece himself had grown bored of practice after a few weeks and never returned to it. It was fairly basic, though, from what he remembered: hold the tip of the blade, get the balance right, throw with the arm and flick with the wrist, and the blade embeds in the target with a solid *thunk*, he thought. Simple. Basic. The only chance he had left.

Fleece flipped the knife so he was holding the tip, and hurled it at the Fomorian king. It spun through the air between them, miraculously on target, catching Gricenchos just inside the curve of the headpiece. What a throw! It would have been a legendary throw, a throw talked about thought the ages, sung

about in songs, celebrated as the throw that pushed back the demon hordes, if only it had been the *blade* that had hit Grichenchos between the eyes, and not the handle. As it was, the knife bounced off the demon's face, dropping into the slush and the mud and the snow, and Gricenchos growled.

Fleece scrambled to his feet as Gricenchos stalked

forward, his massive hand closing round Fleece's slender neck. He lifted Fleece off the ground. Fleece gasped for air, legs kicking and body twisting. It felt like his head was going to pop off and float away into the air. Bright lights were exploding across his vision and the battle raged all around him but all he could see was Gricenchos's snarling face.

He dug a hand inside his tunic, grabbing the small pouch he kept in there. He pushed out the stopper with his thumb and flung the cow's blood into the Fomorian king's face. Gricenchos snarled and snapped, but finally had to drop Fleece in order to wipe the blood from his eyes.

As Fleece tried to crawl away, his own side swarmed the area. Someone kicked him as they ran by and he sprawled on to his back, gazing up at the grey sky with the grey clouds drifting across it, bringing the promise of more snow. Then someone else stepped on his face and he gladly sank into unconsciousness.

STOP

You have just read the **climax** of the story.

Climax is usually the highest point of drama or intensity in a story. In this case it is where Fleece is knocked out and we don't know if he is dead or alive.

From this point onwards the conflict or problem begins to be resolved. It is the 'turning point' where things change for Fleece in a positive or negative way.

What do you think happens next? *Now read on …*

When he woke, it was snowing and there were hands on him. He kept his eyes closed. The battle still raged, but it sounded further away. In the distance. The hands rifled through his pockets. The breath was foul. The touch was cold. Demon or human, he couldn't tell. He cracked open one eye, then immediately closed it. A Fomorian. One of perhaps dozens who were combing the area. A small, scrawny thing. Not soldiers but scavengers, picking through the dead and dying in search of valuables. He'd let them. He never carried anything of value on to a battlefield anyway. He didn't *own* anything of value.

The Fomorian whispered curses in that strange language of theirs, and abruptly knelt on Fleece's groin. Fleece shot up, howling, and the Fomorian leapt off him with a scream. Like frightened birds, the scavengers took off, leaving Fleece along with the dead.

Soldiers, both human and demon, lay like freshly cut wheat around him, covered in a light frosting of snow. To the north, the fighting continued. Fleece didn't much care. Such was the cynicism of the battle-hardened warrior, he supposed. For that was what he was now, and no mistake. No more Fleece the Thoroughly Unsuited to Battle – instead, he would be Fleece the Cowardly, Fleece the Craven, or Fleece the One Who Drops to His Knees and Begs His Enemies Not to Kill Him. A proud name to have, to be sure.

He checked his face to see if he had any scars to showcase his deeds, maybe one along his cheekbone to emphasise how sharp they were. But while there was some swelling and bruising, there didn't appear to be anything too dramatic. Well, maybe next time.

He was sore, though. All that pushing and jostling had taken its toll. Still, he'd picked a nice place to lie down. He settled back in the mud, arranged his arms in a suitably splayed pose, turned his head to the side and opened his mouth in a silent, frozen scream. The only good thing about battles in winter was the lack of flies on the bodies. When he'd played dead at battles in the summer, those lazy, bloated flies would buzz at his nose and ears and crawl into his mouth and he'd have to lie there and take it. He didn't miss the flies. He missed the heat, of course. By the gods, it was freezing. If he continued to lie out in the snow like this, he'd catch his death.

He sat up, shivering, and saw a hand raised in the middle of a clump of bodies, its fingers curled. It was a familiar hand. He crawled over to it, grabbed the remains of a Hibernian soldier and grunted as he shoved it away. Beneath, still trapped under the bodies of more of Fleece's countrymen, was the corpse of the Fomorian king.

Fleece looked around, wondering what the procedure was at a time like this. Surely if a king falls, that side automatically loses? But maybe word simply hadn't spread. Maybe the demons were still fighting because no one had told them to stop.

Maybe no one knew that Gricenchos was dead.

A name entered Fleece's mind, and it was not Fleece the Cowardly, or Fleece the Craven, or Fleece the One Who Drops to His Knees and Begs His Enemies Not to Kill Him. It was a new name. It was Fleece the Hero. And then it was Fleece the Demon Killer.

He seized the demon king's headpiece, hands wrapping round the twin horns, and hissed with the effort of removing it. Finally it came free, and Gricenchos's head rolled back. He didn't look so tough now, being dead. Fleece briefly wondered if he should cut off the head, but decided against it. It would take too long, be too much trouble, and be much too disgusting. So he made do with the helmet, dropping it into a sack that had been used to carry arrows, before making his way back to the Hibernian camp. No more skulking around the edges of the battlefield for him, oh no. No more pretending to be dead, stinking of cow's blood and trying not to snore. Corporal Fleece? Try *Captain* Fleece. *Major* Fleece. He grinned. *General* Fleece.

He kept his grin to himself as he reached the camp. He was ignored by everyone, as they rushed around tending to the multitudes of injured men. Messengers scuttled between tents, leapt on to horses or leapt off them. There was a lot of shouting, a lot of screaming, a lot of crying.

Fleece found the biggest tent, its entrance flanked by Royal Guards.

'What do you want?' one of the guards said, barely looking at him.

'They want me in there,' Fleece said, smiling with confidence.

His weapons had never been swords and spears, after all. His weapons had always been words. He could cut a man down with insults and build him up with flattery. With words, he could block, **parry** and **riposte**, reducing each and every opponent to a quivering, shivering wreck.

'I have important information for the high generals and the king. They said I should just walk in.'

Now the guard looked at him, frowning. 'Who are you?'

'I'm the Hero of Drumree.'

'We're *in* Drumree,' said the guard.

'I know,' said Fleece. 'And that's what they're going to call me. Stand aside.'

The guard frowned and did as he was ordered.

Fleece entered the tent. It was a magnificent place, bigger than his own house and infinitely more luxurious. At its centre was a large table, at which crowded the high generals, stabbing their fingers at a map and arguing loudly among themselves.

Fleece took a moment, absorbing the energy, figuring out the best way to approach. With all the sharp words and bluster, with all the blame being hurled back and forth, he realised the only way was his favourite way – using huge amounts of baseless confidence. He strode to the table, gripped the sack by its underside and emptied the headpiece on to the map. It rolled to a stop, and the voices died down. The high generals stared at it, then at Fleece.

High General Cairbre was the first to speak. 'That's …'

Fleece nodded. 'I took it from the Fomorian king's head myself, after I killed him.'

Another high general slapped his hands flat on the table, like he needed support to keep from falling. 'He's dead? Gricenchos is *dead*?'

'Indeed he is, sir.'

'That's … That's … Who are you?'

'Corporal Mordha Fleece, of General Tua's Infantry, at your service.'

'Where is Tua?'

'Sadly cut down. He died a hero, a shining beacon of light to those who served under him. It was thanks to his inspiring leadership that I summoned the courage to do what I did. I'd like to recommend him for a medal of some description.'

'The Fomorian king is dead,' Cairbre muttered, and smiled. 'He's dead. We've won!'

'Not yet,' a thin-faced high general said. 'The Fomorian Army still fights, and we continue to suffer heavy losses. We need something to inspire the troops.'

'Something …' Cairbre said, nodding. 'Or some*one*.'

He looked directly at Fleece, who felt his smile fading.

'The troops need a leader,' Cairbre continued, 'fighting alongside them. Now that Tua's dead, they need a man to look up to. A man of courage, of fighting spirit. They need a hero.'

All the high generals were looking at Fleece now, and he was feeling quite nauseous.

'I'm no hero,' he croaked.

Cairbre smiled. 'They need their king.'

Fleece almost collapsed with relief. 'Yes. Yes, I agree. Their king. They need their king fighting alongside them.'

Such was the weight of his relief that it took him a moment to wonder about the feasibility of the fat slug engaging in any kind of physical activity that didn't involve eating. And then he realised that the golden throne at the back of the tent was empty, and there was something behind it, lying beneath a gigantic sheet.

Cairbre came over, wrapped an arm round Fleece's shoulders, started to walk him away from the others. 'Our brave king died before the battle began,' he said in his ear. 'Choked to death on a chicken bone. The royal physician tried to force it from his throat, but he could not reach round his royal girth to do so. The king is without heir. We need a hero, someone of noble virtue, to take his place and begin a new legacy.'

'You want to make *me* king?'

'Corporal Mordha Fleece, you said your name was? No. How about His Royal Majesty, *King* Mordha?'

Fleece was turned, and Cairbre placed both hands on his shoulders and pushed him down into the throne. A man in priestly vestments hurried over, mumbling words. He put the crown on Fleece's head. It was too big, but nobody seemed to care. And then, like something out of a bad dream, it was over, and everyone was bowing down to him.

'Uh,' Fleece said.

Cairbre pulled him from the throne, led him from the tent. There were people fussing all around him, throwing a **garb** of fresh chain mail over him that was so bright and polished and golden he near blinded everyone he passed. A belt was tied round his waist, and a magnificent sword the length of his leg was hung from it, the tip dragging behind him like an anchor. Cairbre was telling him something about the battle, about tactics, about leading from the front, and the next thing Fleece knew he was stepping on someone's specially stooped back and swinging his leg over a gigantic white horse, fit for a king.

garb: clothing, especially of a distinctive kind

His royal guard went with him, close in on all sides, making it impossible to break away. Together they thundered away from the camp, into the swirling snow, across the fields, down to the north end of the valley, to where the demons were, and still-raging battle, and the axes and the swords and the dying.

The guard on his right turned to him as they rode and shouted, 'Orders, Your Majesty?'

Fleece stared at him, eyes wide, mouth hanging open. His vaunted words weren't doing him much good here. His tongue, no matter how sharp, would scarcely nick the oily hides of the Fomorians they were charging towards. He tried remembering anything that the high general had said, but his mind remained stubbornly empty. Fleece the Hero, Fleece the King. Fleece the Forgotten. Fleece Who?

'Charge!' he finally shouted, even though they were already charging. It was something to say, he supposed.

The other men took out their swords, held them high and roared. Fleece grabbed his own sword, struggled with it, having to shift in his saddle to get it out of the sheath it was so damned long. He tried holding it aloft but by the gods it was heavy, and it dipped and stabbed the side of the horse next to him, making the horse go down and the guard who had spoken to him flip over and disappear from sight.

'Sorry!' Fleece yelled but he could see the horse wasn't fatally wounded and at least now there was a gap. He yanked on the reins, veering right. 'The rest of you continue on!' he screeched. 'I'm going to **outflank** them!'

He put his head down against the snow and dug in his heels, letting the ridiculous sword fall in order to hold on with both hands. Behind him, the royal guards smashed into the demon horde. He galloped for the trail between the trees.

Fleece the **Abdicator**. Fleece the Deserter. Sod it. Sod it all. They could call him whatever the hell they liked. He was Fleece the Living, and he was going to stay that way for as long as he bloody well could.

outflank: move around the side of an enemy to out-manoeuvre them

abdicator: someone who resigns their position

Use your **Show-Me-Boards** to answer these **True** or **False** statements. Explain your answers.

Statements

- Fleece is shy but courageous.
- The Formorians are another species of the human race.
- Iron Guts is brave but he is also patient.
- The most important values for the soldiers to have are freedom and patriotism towards the king.
- Fleece has high regard for his king.
- Fleece lived by a routine of dodging battle.
- Gricenchos was easily defeated and cowardly.
- Fleece had planned all along to kill Gricenchos.
- It was a relief to Fleece to see the Formorian scavengers.
- Fleece showed great cunning in acquiring the head of Gricenchos.
- It had always been Fleece's ambition to become a royal figure.
- Fleece showed remorse when he deserted the troop of soldiers.

Guide to Writing the Climax

If you were on a rollercoaster and you got to the very top of the ride, chances are that just before you'd go down the big drop, your nerves would be all over the place. This analogy is similar to the climax of a story.

The **CLIMAX OF A STORY** can happen halfway through a story or very near the end. There is no set time when it should occur, but it should be an action/event that leaves your readers with a sense of excitement or tension.

Answer these questions to help you revise the climax in 'The Hero of Drumree'.

1. Who is the protagonist?
2. What is his problem?
3. How does this problem get worse for the character?
4. What is the most exciting part of the story, in your opinion?
5. What happens after the exciting moment you have picked? Do things change for the protagonist?

1. Rearrange these sentences to complete the plot structure of 'The Three Little Pigs'.

   a)   The pigs live happily ever after.

   b)   The pigs leave their mother's home to go and build a new life for themselves, and new houses of course.

   c)   The wolf gets frustrated with the pigs, decides to climb down the hot chimney, falls into a pot of hot water and dies.

   d)   The wolf begins to threaten the three little pigs.

Plot element	Sentence
Opening	
First point of conflict	
Climax	
Resolution	

2. Pick a story you have studied that has an exemplary (excellent) plot climax. Map out the plot structure using the rollercoaster analogy. Sometimes you might have dips before you get to the big climax. If you feel there are moments of high or low action/tension, make sure you mark them as well.

3. One of the dominant themes in 'The Hero of Drumree' is courage, or a lack thereof. Write a speech around the following statement: 'Young people must have courage in their lives today.'

Sample Question & Answer

Explain how Derek Landy uses varied sentence length effectively in 'The Hero of Drumree'.

Sample Answer Using

P Derek Landy uses varied sentence length competently throughout his story from start to finish.

I 'It was fairly basic, though, from what he remembered: hold the tip of the blade, get the balance right, throw with the arm and flick with the wrist, and the blade embeds in the target with a solid thunk, he thought. Simple. Basic. The only chance he had left.'

E Landy uses a very long sentence at the start of this quote. He breaks it up by using commas, a colon and a conjunction: 'and'. This long sentence mimics the great action of the climax, where there is no room for a long pause as it is the most intense part of the story. The action is followed by two one-worded sentences: 'Simple' and 'Basic'. It was Fleece's only opportunity and he knew it, and the short sentences reflect this realisation. The length of the last sentence is again different to make the reader focus on Fleece's life or death decision.

I believe this sentence combination works extremely well because it doesn't allow the reader to lose focus on this important part of the story. The mixing of sentence length also reveals Fleece's thought process; it is a much more realistic way to show how we think.

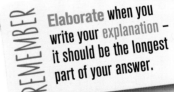
Elaborate when you write your explanation – it should be the longest part of your answer.

Short Story [4]

What I will learn:

to understand a key element in creating a good plot (ending/resolution); to understand and use 'Show Don't Tell' in your writing; to identify direct speech, indirect speech and dialogue

Make a list of verbs you could use to express the five senses: sight, hearing, smell, touch and taste. You could challenge yourself to make them *expressive verbs* by having an accompanying adverb.

An adverb tells you *how* an action is being carried out. For example: 'She roared **angrily**'. But adverbs can also describe adjectives (the describing words), e.g. 'Oliver was **extremely sinister**'. Two examples have been completed for you.

Sight	Hearing	Smell	Touch	Taste
See clearly			**Brush** gently	

'Humming Through My Fingers'
by Malorie Blackman

My hands slowed down, then stilled on my book as I listened. I turned my head and sniffed at the wind. Mum always said I had ears like a bat, but if it wasn't for the wind blowing in my direction, I doubt if even I would have heard this particular conversation.

I listened for a few moments until I'd heard enough, then returned to my book – which was far more interesting. Nine pages on and I was interrupted. He stood directly in front of me, blocking the sunlight, making my arms and face feel instantly cooler. I'd thought I'd get at least twelve pages on before he plucked up the nerve to come over.

'Hi, Amber. It's me. Ethan. Ethan Bennett.'

I sniffed the air in the direction of his voice. He didn't have to tell me his name. I recognised his voice. Ethan Bennett – the new boy in my brother Joshua's class. Well, when I say new, I mean he'd joined Josh's class last September and been to our house four or five times when I was there, but this was the first time he'd said anything other than 'Hi' to me.

The last time he left our house, I had tried less than subtly to ask Joshua about him. 'Josh, what's Ethan like?'

'Why?' asked my brother, suspicion lacing his tone.

'I like his voice,' I replied.

'He looks like Quasimodo and he's constantly farting,' Josh replied. 'He's lactose intolerant so God help you if you're around him without a gas mask after he's had a pizza or a glass of milk.'

So much for trying to get a straight answer out of my brother.

'Hello, Ethan.'

'Can I sit down?'

'I don't know.' I shrugged. 'Can you?'

'Huh?'

I smiled. A teeny-tiny smile for a teeny-tiny joke.

'No, I … er … meant, d'you mind if I sit down?' Ethan's voice was anxious, eager for me to understand.

'Help yourself.' Why ask me if he could sit down? Did I own the field or the grass in it? I carried on reading my book while he parked.

'What're you reading? Is it any good?'

'It's *Misery* by Stephen King. I've read it before, and yes, it is good,'

'If you've read it before, why're you reading it again?' asked Ethan.

'It's one of my favourite books.' As I spoke I carried on reading, my fingers skimming

over the page. But then my fingers unexpectedly touched Ethan's and an electric shock like summer lightening stung through my fingers and up my arm.

'Ouch!' Ethan exclaimed.

With his touch still humming through my fingers, I drew my hand away. 'What happened?'

'I just got a shock.' Ethan dismissed it easily. I could hear that he was still shaking his sore fingers. He mused, 'I don't see how we could've been shocked sitting on grass.'

I said nothing. There'd been something unexpected in his touch, something more interesting than the obvious, but harder to read. It was this that stopped me from telling him to get lost.

'Sorry about that,' said Ethan. 'I just wanted to see what Braille was like.'

'Why?'

I could smell his surprise at my question. 'I've never seen a Braille book before. How does it work?'

Here we go again. I sighed inwardly. Another explanation. Another embarrassed pause followed by a murmur of sympathy and, if the usual pattern was followed, a sudden mumbled excuse to leave.

'Each of the series of raised dots represents a letter or a number. I use my fingers to read the dots rather than my eyes to read the words on a page, that's all.'

'Can I have a try?'

'Go ahead.'

I picked up the book and held it in Ethan's direction. He took it from me, careful not to touch my fingers this time.

'It must take ages to learn all this lot. It would take me years.' Ethan whistled appreciatively. 'How long did it take you?'

'Quite a few months, actually, and I'm still learning.' OK, I admit it, I was surprised. No pity, no sympathy, just two people talking.

'Were you born blind?'

Another surprise. No one over the age of ten ever asked me about my eyesight – not directly, at any rate. It was a taboo subject, conspicuous by its absence. How come Ethan had never got round to asking my brother or one of his other friends? Too afraid they'd mistake his questions for interest? I wondered who else was present, who else was listening. I sniffed the air. I couldn't smell anyone else nearby. Just Ethan – and his lie. Not lies plural. Just one lie.

'No.' I was going to say more, but the words didn't seem to want to come out of my mouth.

'Here's your book back.' I reached out my hand. Ethan placed it in my upturned palm.

'So how did you become blind, then?' he asked.

Wow! Direct much? Truth to tell, I kind of liked it. It was refreshing.

'I'm a diabetic and I'm one of the unlucky few who developed diabetic retinopathy.' I faked a nonchalant shrug. 'I played fast and loose with taking my insulin and watching my diet. My vision started going fuzzy and I didn't put two and two together until it was too late. So here I am.'

'What d'you miss most?'

'People's faces – and colours.' Silence stretched between us as I listened to Ethan search for something else to say. 'What would *you* miss most?'

'Pardon?'

I repeated the question and smiled inwardly as I felt Ethan frown. 'I don't know,' he answered at last. My question had disturbed him. 'Josh told me that you see things with your other senses, though.'

I didn't reply. Slowly, I closed my book and waited.

'He said that you can hear colours and sense certain things that most people can't.'

Hearing colours – was that why I'd been singled out by Ethan? Was that all there was to it? Check out the weird girl and have a laugh while doing it?

'Is that true?' Ethan persisted.

I shrugged. I'd have to have a serious word with Josh when I caught up with him. He wasn't meant to tell anyone about that. It wasn't even his secret to tell, it was my secret. Who else had my brother blabbed to?

'I hope you don't mind me mentioning it. Josh swore me to secrecy and he hasn't told anyone else – at least, that's what he said.'

'Why did he tell you?'

'I don't know. Maybe he thought he could trust me.' Pause. 'He could see that I wanted to know more about you.'

Hhmm! I shrugged noncommittally, careful to keep my expression neutral.

'I've never heard of anything like that before,' Ethan stated.

'It's called synaesthesia. I've always had it but it became heightened when I lost my sight. About ten people in every million have it, so don't go thinking I'm a fruit loop or something.' An edge crept into my voice.

'I didn't think anything of the kind,' Ethan laughed. 'What's it like?'

'What's it like to see using your eyes?'

It's … well, it's … it's a bit difficult to explain. Ah! OK!'

And I knew then that he'd got the point. 'Exactly.' Wanting to change the subject, I asked, 'So what d'you think of Belling Oak, then?'

'It's not bad, actually. It's a lot better than my old school. How come you didn't come here with your brother?'

Whoosh! Instantly my face flamed, in spite of myself. I turned away, listening to the distant cheers and the shouting as the 100 metres sprint race started.

'I was here for four years, but … there were problems,' I said, still half listening to the race.

'What sort of problems?'

I sighed inwardly. I'd say one thing for Ethan: he was persistent. 'The teachers spouted on and on about how it would be too dangerous for me, too hazardous, too nerve-racking, how I'd be teased and bullied – stuff like that. The head insisted that Belling just wasn't set up for students who were visually challenged. He couldn't even say the word – blind.'

'Sounds like excuses to me.' Ethan sniffed.

I turned to face him again. 'It was. I already had friends here, I'd already been here for four years since junior school and after the first year I could've found my way around blindfolded. Mum, Dad

and I kept telling him that I was willing to put up with the rest, but he wouldn't have it. Then he started quoting health and safety regulations at us and they said it would cost too much to have the school converted so that I could find my way around without help. So it didn't happen.'

'You must've been disappointed.'

'Of course. I'd set my heart on staying at Belling.' I looked around, seeing it with my memory. All around me were acres of grounds, divided by a trickling stream known as 'The Giggler' because of the sound it made. I remembered the intensity of the green of the grass in spring, how in spring and early summer it was always covered in daisies and buttercups. From the upper classroom window the daisies made the ground look like it was covered in summer snow, they were that thick on the ground. And then there were the tall, sprawling oaks fringing the stream on both sides. The oaks had always been my favourite. They whispered amongst themselves, using the wind for cover. At one end of the upper field was the red-brick school building and way across on the other side, past the lower fields, were the tennis and netball courts which doubled as basketball courts. And the whole thing had been so beautiful. I only started to appreciate its beauty when I started to lose my sight. Precious little time left to drink in the sights and sounds of the place before I got bounced out.

'So where d'you go now?' asked Ethan.

'Arenden Hall. We've already broken up for the summer, though.'

'Never heard of it.'

'It's a college for the blind, about ten kilometres from here.'

'D'you like it?'

I shrugged. 'Yes, I do. They treat me like I'm more than my eyesight there. They know that my blindness isn't the one and only thing to define me.'

I turned back towards the sports field. I was seated near the stream, under the arms of one of the huge oak trees that gave Belling its name. Every sports day, I always sat in the same spot. Far enough away from everyone else so that I wouldn't have to worry about being knocked over or swept aside by the enthusiastic crowds, but close enough to hear what was going on. Some of my Belling friends thought it strange that I would want to sit by myself for most of the afternoon, but they were used to me by now. To be honest, I liked my own company. That and the fact that my friends made me remember ... different times. I forced my mind away from the past to concentrate on the here and now.

Joshua, my twin brother, was due to run in the Upper Sixth 200 metres later on. He'd come last, or close to it. He always did, but he didn't mind, and neither did anyone else. It would've been good to see him run, although my friends said he didn't so much run as saunter. Josh always said he was built for endurance, not speed. In cross-country runs, he invariably crossed the finish line first and fresh as a daisy while his friends collapsed all around him several minutes later.

'I'm sorry if I asked too many questions,' said Ethan. 'I didn't mean to upset you.'

'It's OK,' but I didn't deny that he'd upset me. 'May I ask you something?'

I heard him nod, then catch himself and say, 'Yeah! Sure!'

'Why are you over here? I mean, why aren't you with everyone else watching the races?

Please tell me the truth. Please.

'I saw you over here and I just wanted to say hello. We've never really had the chance to have a proper conversation before.'

'I see.' The heat from his lie swept over me like volcanic ash, tasting bitter and acrid against my tongue.

Ethan cleared his throat. 'Actually, I wanted to ask you something. Would you … er … I'm going for a pizza after all the events are over. I don't suppose you'd like to come with me?'

Silence stretched between us like a rubber band.

'You're inviting me to go for a meal with you, my brother and your friends?'

'Well, I thought if you agreed to have pizza with me, we could go by ourselves?' Ethan cleared his throat again at the end of his rushed sentence. He obviously did that when he was nervous. Useful to know.

'OK,' I said, at last.

'Really? Great!'

The obvious relief in his voice made me stifle a smile. It meant that much to him?

'Aren't you lactose intolerant, though?' I said. 'Is a pizza wise?'

'What did Josh say about me?' Ethan sounded mortified.

'Is it true?'

'I have a mild case and it's cumulative. I'm OK with just one pizza.'

'You will keep away from the ice cream with your dessert though, right?' I teased.

Ethan didn't reply but I could've been on Mars and still felt his embarrassment.

'Are you in any of the races?' I took pity on him and changed the subject.

'No, athletics isn't really my thing.'

'What is?'

'Rugby. And tennis sometimes.'

'Oh, I see. Are you heading back to your friends to watch the races now?' I asked.

'No, I thought I'd stay here with you, if that's all right?'

Whoa! So he was going for it, was he? Two could play that game.

'Sure. Tell you what, let's go for a walk,' I said.

'A walk?'

'Around the grounds. Away from everyone else.'

'Can you …? I mean, do you want …?'

I laughed. 'It's my eyes that don't work, my legs are fine.'

'Yeah, of course. Sorry.' I heard Ethan get to his feet. I stood up, ignoring the hand he put out to help me.

'Let's walk downstream towards the car park, then cross the stream and walk round behind the tennis courts,' I suggested.

'Fine with me.'

We started walking. Ethan stuffed his hands in his pockets until I placed my hand on his bare forearm. And there it was again, that strange humming through my fingers. Ethan's arm started to flap about like a fish out of water. He didn't know what to do with it, where to put it so I could rest my hand on it. I stopped, withdrawing my hand as I waited for him to figure it out. After a moment or two, he took my hand and placed it on his forearm, which was now steady. We carried on walking in a strangely amiable silence.

'So tell me what you can see,' I said.

'Huh?'

'Describe what you can see.' I smiled at Ethan. Unless, of course, you'd rather not.'

'No, I don't mind. I just … Ok …well, we're walking beside the stream now and there are oak trees on either side of the stream and over there is the car park and over there is the school and –'

My hand gently squeezed his arm. 'That's not what I meant. Tell me what you can *see*.'

'But I just did.'

I gave him a hard look. 'Ethan, are you wearing your school tie?'

'Yes. Why?'

'Could you take it off and put it around your eyes?'

'Come again?'

I smiled. 'You heard me right the first time.'

'Why d'you want me to do that?' Ethan asked.

'I'm going to take you around the school grounds.'

'With my eyes blindfolded?' Ethan asked, aghast.

I laughed at the panic in his voice. 'That's right. You're going to have to trust me.'

'But you … you can't see.'

'Oh my God! Thanks for telling me. I hadn't noticed!' I teased. 'So are you going to do it, or are you too much of a chicken?'

Slowly, Ethan removed the tie from around his neck and tied it around his eyes.

'You've got to do it so you can't see anything,' I told him.

'I have.'

'No, you haven't.'

'How d'you know?' The amazement in his voice was very gratifying. 'OK! OK! My eyes are totally covered now.'

'Let me touch your face.'

I felt him lean forward. I raised my hands to run my fingers lightly over his face. My fingers began to hum again as I touched his skin. He had a large forehead (lots of brains!), a strong nose and a firm chin, and his lips were full and soft. I couldn't tell about his eyes because they were covered with his tie. His tie smelled of sweet green and sharp, tangy gold. Belling Oak colours. I would've been able to tell the colours even if I didn't already know what they were. Satisfied that his eyes were indeed completely covered, I linked his arm with my own. He instinctively stiffened at that.

'Don't worry, your friends won't be able to see us over here.'

'It's not that,' he denied. 'But suppose we end up in the stream or something?'

'Then we'll get wet!'

There was a pause, then Ethan laughed. His body relaxing, he said, 'All right then. D'you know where you're going?'

'I know this school like the back of my hand. Don't worry. Now … which way are we facing again?'

A sharp intake of breath from Ethan had me cracking up.

'You're not funny,' he grumbled.

We walked for a minute, listening to the distant cheers and the occasional birdsong.

'What d'you think of this tree?' I asked.

'What tree?'

'The one right in front of us. It's my favourite of all of them here,' I said, adding, 'No, don't,' when I felt his other hand move upwards to remove the tie from around his eyes.

'But I can't see it. I can't see anything.'

'See it without using your eyes.'

'How do I do that?' Frustration began to creep into Ethan's voice.

I took Ethan's hand and stretched it out in front of him until it touched the tree trunk.

'What does it feel like?' I asked, my hand resting lightly over his so I could feel what he was doing.

'Rough.'

'What else?'

His fingers began to move slowly across the tree bark. 'Cool. Sharp in places. Here's a smooth bit.'

'And what does it smell like?'

Ethan looked over towards me.

'Go on!' I encouraged. 'It's international hug-a-tree day! Tell me what it smells like and feels like. Don't be shy.'

Reluctantly, Ethan moved closer to the tree. He stretched out his arms to hold it. Waves of 'what-the-hell-am-I-doing?' rippled out from his entire body.

'It feels … strong. Like it could be here for ever if it was left alone.' Ethan's voice grew more quiet but more confident. 'And it's got secrets. It's seen a lot of things and knows a lot of things, but it's not telling. And it smells like … like rain and soil and a mixture of things.'

'Come on,' I said, taking his arm again.

'Where're we going?'

'To our next stop.'

I led Ethan further down the stream before I turned us to our left and walked a few steps.

'Now you have to do exactly what I say,' I told him, leading him down a gentle slope.

'Are we going to cross the stream, here?' he asked, a frown in his voice.

'That's right,' I smiled. 'We're going to jump across.'

'But … but I can't see where I'm going,' said Ethan horrified.

'Then use your other senses. I'll help you.'

'Why can't we use one of the bridges?'

'Because everyone does that. We're going to be more adventurous. I want you to jump from here. It's less than half a metre to the other side at this point. Just jump, then let your weight fall forward and grab hold of one of the tree roots sticking out of the ground. OK?'

No answer.

'OK, Ethan?'

'D'you really think this is a good idea?'

'Trust me. And once you've grabbed the tree root, haul yourself up out of the way 'cause I'll be right behind you.'

'All right,' Ethan said dubiously.

I placed my hands on his shoulders and turned him slightly to straighten him up so he wouldn't be jumping at an angle. 'Don't worry, Ethan. My nan can jump half a metre and she's got bad knees – always assuming I've led us to the right bit of the stream, of course.'

'You mean, you're not sure?' Ethan was appalled.

'I'm only winding you up,' I told him gleefully.

'You're enjoying this, aren't you?'

'You'd better believe it! Now then. After three. One … two …'

'Three!' Ethan shouted. And he jumped.

To be honest, I was impressed. I thought he'd need a lot more coaxing. I heard an 'Ooof!' followed by the mad scramble of his hands as he sought and found a tree root. The ground here was covered in exposed tree roots so I knew he'd have no problem. He hauled himself up the bank to the level ground beyond.

'Here I come!' And I jumped. In a way, I'm sorry Ethan didn't see me. A sighted person couldn't have done it better. I landed cleanly, then stepped up the bank, pushing against the roots beneath my feet. No need to get my hands dirty.

'Are you OK?' I asked.

'I think so.'

'How did it feel to jump?'

'I don't know,' said Ethan.

'Yes, you do.'

His sharp intake of breath told me that I was right. 'I was a bit nervous. I know the water is only a few centimetres deep but it suddenly felt like it was kilometres deep and kilometres down.'

'And how did you feel when you landed on the other side?'

'Relieved!'

'Anything else?'

'Yeah. Kind of proud of myself.'

'Being blind is like jumping off a cliff – except you jump never knowing what's on the other side. Everything is an adventure for me. Walking along the street, going into a shop, meeting new people, even reading a book. I see things I never saw before. D'you know how much I hate reading the phrase, "How could I have been so blind?" when the author is using it to mean stupid? That really pisses me off, but I never even noticed it before losing my sight. I travel through life never knowing what I'll come across or what I'll find, whether I'll be delighted or disappointed, hurt or happy. Everyone else travels that way but most take it for granted. I don't. Not anymore. Does that make sense?'

'I think so.' Ethan didn't sound sure at all. But it was enough.

I reached out to link arms with him again. 'Have you still got the tie around your eyes?'

'Yes.'

'Then it's time for our next stop.' I led the way along the fence and past the car park.

'I have no idea where we are,' Ethan said, perplexed.

'That's OK. I do.'

We walked on for another few minutes before I stopped.

'Where are we now?' asked Ethan.

'By the tennis courts. What can you hear?'

Ethan was still for a moment. 'Birds and a faint droning sound.'

'That drone is the traffic on the other side of the school building.'

Ethan turned his head slightly. 'I can hear some cheering now from the sports field but it's very faint.'

'Anything else?'

'I don't think so.'

'OK. Kneel down.'

'Why?'

'Trust me!'

Ethan shook his head but he still knelt down. I smelled what I was looking for. The scent was overwhelming. I took Ethan's hand and put it out to touch the thing I could smell.

'Just use your index finger and thumb to touch this,' I said. 'Rub it gently between your fingers but don't touch anything else except this bit.'

When Ethan's fingers were on the object, I let go of his hand.

'What is it?' he asked.

'What d'you think it is?'

'I don't know …' Ethan said slowly. 'It feels like a bit of velvet but there wouldn't be velvet around the tennis courts.'

I reached out and touched the object, my fingers next to Ethan's. 'A deep yellow velvet.'

'How can you tell what colour it is?'

'Yellow has got quite a high voice. This yellow's voice is slightly lower, which means the shade is deeper, but it's definitely yellow.'

'Do you know what it is I'm touching?'

'Yes, I do.' And all at once I didn't want to do this anymore. I felt wistful and sad.

'Take off your tie now. Have a look at what you're touching.'

Ethan removed his tie at once and gasped. 'It's … a flower …' he said shocked.

'Beautiful, isn't it?'

'A deep yellow flower,' Ethan whispered.

'There's more to seeing than just looking, Ethan,' I told him. 'Your eyes work. Never forget what a gift that is. I can feel colours and I'm grateful. But to see …'

'A flower.' Ethan's voice was awestruck. I didn't have his full attention. I wondered if he'd even heard me.

'Ethan, touching that flower and seeing it with your fingers – that's what seeing with my other senses is a tiny bit like. I see things in ways that you can't or won't because you don't have to. I'm grateful for that as well, because I can still appreciate the things around me. Maybe even more than a lot of sighted people do.'

I sensed Ethan looking at me then. Really looking – for the first time. I wondered how he saw me now. I smiled at him.

'I … look, I have to tell you something,' Ethan began uneasily.

'Forget it.'

'No it's important. I –'

'Harry and Jacob bet you that you couldn't get me to go out for a pizza with you and get a kiss out of me. But for your information, they've both asked me out and I've always turned them down flat, so they reckoned you had no chance.'

Silence.

STOP

You are about to read the ending/resolution: this is the outcome of a story. The resolution can be either positive or negative but it must not leave the reader unsatisfied. Note that is often a moment of realisation, or reflection, or truth.

What do you think happens next? *Now read on …*

'Stop it. You're staring!' I laughed.

'How did you know that?'

'What? About the bet or that you were staring?'

'Both.'

'I could tell you, but then I'd have to kill you,' I teased. 'And by the way, I wouldn't tell my brother about the bet if I were you. He's massively over-protective where I'm concerned and he'd probably want to punch your face into next week.'

'I'm sorry, Amber. I … I suppose you don't want anything more to do with me.'

'I knew about the bet before you'd even said one word to me – remember?'

'I still don't understand how.'

'I heard you.'

'You couldn't have. We were practically across the field,' Ethan protested.

'Exaggerate much? You were only a few metres away and the wind was blowing in my direction.' When Ethan didn't answer, I said, 'I have ears like a bat. Always have done. And I've always had a sixth sense when it comes to spotting when people are lying to me.'

A profound silence followed my words. How I wished I could see Ethan's face at that moment.

'We'd better get back,' Ethan said at last, his tone strange.

Now it was my turn to be bemused. 'What's the matter?'

Ethan took my arm and rested it on his arm. His touch lingered a little longer than was necessary on the back of my hand. We started back towards the sports field, my hand lightly resting on his arm. I knew the way back without any problem but I wanted to sense what he was feeling. From the way his muscles were bunched and tense beneath my fingers I could guess what was going on in his head. He wasn't happy.

'Ethan?'

'I'm really sorry, Amber. You must think I'm a real d…. And I don't blame you.' His words came out in a rush of genuine embarrassment. And there was something else, something more behind them.

'Why would I think your wits are d…?' I smiled.

Ethan looked at me then. And his gaze hadn't changed back – I could tell. He was still looking at me with the eyes of someone who could see *me*. Not a blind girl and nothing else. Not someone to be pitied or patronised or mocked. Not someone who was less than him. But a girl who could see without using her eyes.

'Can I … can I touch your face?' said Ethan.

Surprised, I nodded. He moved to stand in front of me. A moment later his fingers were exploring my face, starting from my forehead and working their way down, skimming my eyebrows, my closed eyes, my nose, my cheeks, my lips, my jaw, my chin. He leaned in closer. I could feel his warm breath on my face. He smelled of mints and chocolate. Was he going to kiss me? Ethan's hands dropped to his side as he straightened up.

'Why did you do that?' I asked, wondering why I felt so disappointed.

'I … I don't know.' He took my arm in his and we carried on walking.

'What about Jacob and Harry? Didn't you have to kiss me to win your bet?' I asked.

'Those two can go …' Ethan swallowed the next word, '… themselves. If I kiss you it won't be to win some stupid bet.'

I smiled. 'So where are we going for this pizza, then?'

Stunned, Ethan stopped walking and turned to look at me. 'You still want to go out with me?'

'Course I do. I'm starving.'

The sigh of relief that came from Ethan made me giggle.

'D'you know something?' Ethan looked around.

'I never noticed it before, but everything around me is so … so …'

He shut up then. I raised my hand to touch his radiating cheek.

'I could fry an egg on your face,' I grinned. 'A couple of rashers of bacon too.'

'Shut up!' said Ethan.

I burst out laughing. 'Come on,' I said. 'Let's go and watch my brother come last in the four-by-one-hundred relay.'

And we walked over the bridge together to join the others.

EXPLORE

W6.9

1. Compose a tweet to summarise this story.

2. Identify the five Ws of this story: Who, What, Where, When, Why.

Guide to Writing Your Ending

Once a story arrives at its climax, the action usually lessens and the story moves towards a conclusion. If there has been a major complication or conflict, it is usually resolved. **RESOLUTIONS** are a crucial factor as to whether or not a reader enjoys a story. Readers invest their emotions in a story and usually care for the protagonist. A weak ending will certainly annoy your reader.

1. Characters should have an **ANSWER TO THE CONFLICT**. For example:

   * Superman defeats Lex Luther but realises he can't have a normal relationship with Lois.

   * In the film *Rocky*, the main character is a boxer determined to prove his worth. At the end, we think he is going to beat his opponent but he doesn't. However, he has gained the respect of his fellow boxers by putting up a great fight. ← **SPOILER ALERT!**

2. **DO NOT** use the following resolutions 'I woke up and realised it was all a dream' or 'Then I died'. These endings have been overused and readers don't appreciate having invested their time and emotions in a story only for it to end like this.

3. Often resolutions feature a moment of **REALISATION** or an **EPIPHANY**. This means that the main character begins to think differently based on their experiences.

   * James Joyce is known for his use of the epiphany technique in his short story, 'Araby': 'Gazing up into the darkness I saw myself as a creature driven and derided by vanity; and my eyes burned with anguish and anger.' The protagonist realises he has been selfish, thinking only of his own importance, and he finally realises how his behaviour was wrong.

4. A character can also experience a **CHANGE IN CHARACTER**. They may believe one thing at the beginning of the story but will experience something that changes their way of thinking.

  * In *Jurassic World*, one of the main characters, Claire, is a career-driven and self-obsessed operations manager for the dinosaur theme park, Jurassic World. At the beginning of the film, she ignores her family and possible love interest to focus on her job and her success. At the end of the film, she has experienced a change as she and her family are almost killed when the dinosaurs break free. She realises family and friends are more important.

Write an alternative ending for 'Humming Through My Fingers'. Bear in mind the tips you have been given.

SHOW DON'T TELL

Malorie Blackman doesn't tell us Amber is blind but *she shows us*.

● *'My hands slowed down, then stilled on my book as I listened.'*

This is the first line of the story and already there is an emphasis on Amber's other senses: hearing and touch. We get to know that Amber is blind, but the author does not state it explicitly at the start; rather she leads up to it and gives us hints along the way.

● *'He stood directly in front of me, blocking the sunlight, making my arms and face feel instantly cooler.'*

Again, the author focuses on how the figure affects Amber's senses. She 'sees' him not through her eyes, but through her awareness of something blocking the light and warmth of the sun.

Direct Speech, Dialogue and Indirect Speech

Direct speech is where the actual words spoken appear in text, as they would have been spoken in real time. Direct speech is an excellent way to reveal a character's emotion and reaction.

● Direct speech is enclosed between quotation marks when written. *'I like his voice,' I replied.*

● Sometimes direct speech stands on its own, for example: *'I've never seen a Braille book before. How does it work?'*

● More often, direct speech is accompanied by a verb and sometimes an adverb that indicate how it is spoken. *'It must take ages to learn all this lot. It would take me years.'* Ethan **whistled appreciatively**.

When direct speech becomes a conversation between two or more people, we call it **dialogue**.

'What're you reading? Is it any good?'
'It's Misery *by Stephen King. I've read it before, and yes, it is good,'*
'If you've read it before, why're you reading it again?' asked Ethan.
'It's one of my favourite books.'

Indirect speech, also known as reported speech, is where the words someone has said are reported (orally or in text). A reporting verb is used and there are no quotation marks.

REPORTING VERB   REPORTING VERB

'Then **he started** quoting health and safety regulations at us and **they said** it would cost too much to have the school converted so that I could find my way around without help.'

EXPLORE

1. The author unveils a range of emotions throughout this story. Make a list of these emotions and find corresponding pieces of dialogue to show these feelings. What does it tell us about the characters?

2. Write down three examples of direct speech from the story that you liked. Give reasons for your choice.

Exam Focus

W6.10

(1) **SHOW DON'T TELL.** Write a paragraph about a character that is homeless. Don't tell the reader that he/she is homeless, but rather try and show them.

(2) Describe the general atmosphere of the closing stages of 'Humming Through My Fingers', showing how the writer uses sounds and images to create the atmosphere. Use quotes from the short story to support your opinion.

(3) Choose an ending from a story you have studied and explain how you think the audience would react to it.

Short Story [5]

What I will learn:

to create a unique character; to use verbs effectively in writing

PREPARE

Create a list of frightening thrills that people sometimes undertake; a parachute jump, for example. Rate them 1–10 based on their level of 'scariness' (with 1 being, 'Well, that wasn't so bad!' and 10 being, 'Oh my god, why am I doing this?')

'Fall'
by Emma Donoghue

Harnessed and pillowed in her pod as tight as an unborn, Annie waits. Gives herself up, gives herself over. Too late to uncurl, scramble out, escape this watery fate. Knees to double chin, she can't straighten an elbow; there's nothing in the world she can do now. Beyond all hope of an easy way out. Her lid is nailed down and it was she who paid the young boatman to do it, that's the joke.

Her weighted barrel hangs upright in the water, bobbing on its rope. Is she animal, vegetable or mineral, now, stuffed in her crate? The wicked hag at the end of the fairytale gets packed in a barrel for her just desserts. This one is narrower at the bottom, like a coffin. The mummy clears her throat, adjusts her grip on the handles, twitches in her bindings. Her stomach is empty, in case she might vomit. It's black in here, and her feet are wet already.

Outside, she knows, the afternoon sun is glittering on the crowds that clog both shorelines. The motion picture company will have set their camera rolling. She's heard the touts are offering a thousand to one on her coming through alive. Her manager has a letter from her in his pocket, fully exonerating him.

What age would you be, ma'am, if you don't mind, the boy at the oars mumbled, *the reporters will want to know*. Annie didn't know what to say. Her hair is grey, her throat is wattled; the only thing she dreads is ending up in the poorhouse. The body creaks but the spirit flares. Seven, when she'd first been knocked speechless by the sight of the Horseshoe Falls at Niagara. Nineteen, when she'd lost husband and baby. *I'm forty-three and I don't mind your asking*, she told the boatman, hiding a grin at her own lie. At forty-three she'd still been clinging on to gentility; still thought she could earn her crust by teaching children elocution or piano, acrobatics or languages or whatever was a la mode. These days Annie has less to lose; her face is gone already, and all she owns are her debts. Yes, forty-three, a good age; she can be forty-three again because time is loose and sparkles like water, and she's turning, she's turning, diving back into her life like a salmon, thrashing upstream to the unforgotten home.

The other thing the boatman asked Annie as he was rowing her out to the island was whether she was a strong swimmer. She almost laughed, turning to wave to the mobs of sightseers. *I've never got around to learning*, she murmured. Which made the young man grimace. *But swimming won't help*, she told him, *if my barrel gets smashed.*

Under his breath: *if you ask me, ma'am, this is just suicide by a genteel name.*

A hissing, a sizzling; the man's compressing her oxygen with a foot pump now, like she told him to. She fits her lips around the mouthpiece. Breathing tightens. *Abandon hope, all you who enter here.* Her mind speeds up. *Cowards die many times before their death.* Knock knock on the roof, and who's there? Not that there's any way to knock back; her fists are curled like ferns. *All ready*, she calls hoarsely. Knife grinds through the rope. Her cord is cut.

And she's away, loosed on the current, though all she knows is a giddiness. Terror in her skirts; the scalding wet comes from her. A rocking, a slurring from side to side, a roll below, a heave as the water yanks at her, she can't tell which way she's going but what way but one is there to go? A catch, a lurch, she's upsidedown. The rocks spit her out sideways. Too close to the Canadian shore, now? No use fretting. The barrel rights itself and plunges on. An inch and a half of oiled oak between her and her death. Sss, sss, she breathes as slowly as she can, pictures her craft's crazy passage as if with the indifferent eye of a passing heron. Half a mile north to the rapids, but it won't take more than a few minutes. This is a one-track suck to the brink of the Horseshoe Falls, the most inevitable place Annie's ever been.

Thrown, slammed, now, shaken like a baby's rattle. What kind of a pure lunatic would – but there is no her any more, only a tube of wood with a secret inside and what does the water care? The almighty river's seen stranger sights than this one, smashed greater crafts, accepted finer sacrifices. She knows the statistics: a 158-foot drop from the cataract's brim, four dead sightseers a year.

Smooth water. A terrible pause. Here goes what falls what what who'd a thought what such a why whee save me save the water water everywhere and not a whit not a jot not a wherever in the world whirling falling falling like hail like a stone flung down a well a spear a bird a jesus jesus

Her brains are kedgeree, her eyes are pickles, bruised in their own brine.

Annie thinks she's alive, just about. Her barrel is swirling in the whirlpool, or it it? She doesn't know where or what or how she is. She's soaked, as cold as fish, but the water hasn't reached her mouth quite. She had air enough for an hour and she reckons she's used it all up. Funny, that, if a woman were to stifle, sandmouthed in the middle of all this flood. She gasps, she yawns, she hasn't an inch to stretch and catch a breath.

For a lifetime she feels herself dangle, spun from rock to rock.

Then the clang of metal on oak makes her jump. Again, again. Has she been hooked? A scraping, a dragging. Shore! *Oh my Niagara, my new found land.*

Some difficulty with the lid. She waits while a saw chews the wood a few inches from her head.

Then light like an elbow in the eye.

Strangers drag her out onto the rocks as dizzy as a faun. Her vision adjusts; she's on a reef below the Falls. Her hands are greenish blue. The decks of the *Maid of the Mist* are thick with faces; when she staggers to her feet and brushes down her wet trunks, a long cheer goes up. Her barrel's iron hoops are stoved in; the thing looks like flotsam. Despite her bruises Annie manages a curtsey, wipes water off her face that turns out to be blood. Her manager runs forward with a red carnation, and an overcoat to make her decent. She's staring past the sightseers, up up up, telling herself that she came through all that white tumult, but she can't comprehend it. And she certainly can't remember why.

A photograph flashes silver.

Is Annie changed? What does she know now? Why, nothing; nothing more than when the first hands wrenched her into the world sixty-three years ago: ignorant, fierce, hungry for the air.

Note

'Fall' is inspired by Annie Edson Taylor (1838–1921), a teacher and traveller from Auburn, New York, who on 24 October 1901 was the first person to go over Niagara Falls. She hoped to make her fortune on speaking tours, but she was abandoned by her managers, impersonated by more photogenic actresses and had her barrel stolen. She eked out a living selling pamphlets about herself and working as a clairvoyant, and died destitute in the Niagara County Infirmary twenty years after her fall.

EXPLORE

Imagine you are the protagonist of this story and you are being interviewed for the weekly magazine, *Niagara News*. Give your answers to the following questions the interviewer asks you.

In this week's edition, we interview a woman who is no stranger to us. She has just achieved one of the most unusual and daring feats. Annie has survived the great drop at Horseshoe Falls, Niagara.

Reporter: *So Annie, did you decide to do this yourself or did your agent propose the idea?*

Annie: _____

Reporter: *How did you feel before the barrel was nailed shut?*

Annie: _____

Reporter: *Why did you decide to do this?*

Annie: _____

Reporter: *Tell me some of the things going through your head when you were bobbing along in the barrel.*

Annie: _____

Reporter: *My last and final question. Do you feel this event has changed you in any way?*

Annie: _____

Guide to Creating Your Character

INDIANA JONES, HUCKLEBERRY FINN, CAT IN THE HAT, ALICE IN WONDERLAND, EDWARD CULLEN ...

These names might be familiar to you. They are some of the most-loved characters from books and films.

Creating your character is just like making a curry. You have to throw in some spice so that it isn't bland!

Become the character! Think like the character! Adopt their voice! →

Planning is essential. Use the grid below to help you create your character.

Physical appearance	Personality	Occupation
Hair	Emotions	Career
Eyes	Likes and dislikes	Education
Build (posture)	Introverted or extroverted?	Ambition
Clothes	Strong or vulnerable?	Skills
Movement (is it restricted?)		Location
Voice/accent		Interesting or boring?
Strange mannerisms		
Annoying habits		
Relationships	**Role in the story**	**Social background**
Family	Protagonist	Religion
Friends	Antagonist	Beliefs
Work or school?	Narrator	Growing up
Dependent or independent?		Location
Complex or straightforward?		Wealthy, poor or in-between?

W6.11

Look at these three photos. Pick one character and write a character profile for them.

CREATE

Annie Edson Taylor had hopes of becoming famous from her stunt, but she was replaced by more 'photogenic actresses'. Actors and actresses can often have fascinating lives as they experience many unusual things. Choose a film star and write a number of diary entries describing 'your' daily experiences on set.

VERBS ARE VITAL!

Emma Donoghue's style of writing in this piece includes the use of **powerful verbs**. Verbs represent the energy of the story but they can also display emotion and drama in a more intense manner.

- Use **active verbs** rather than passive: for example, 'her lid is *nailed* down' (active), rather than 'they *put a nail* in her lid' (passive).

- **Concise verbs** are stronger than verbs ending in 'ing': for example, 'grinds' rather than 'grinding', 'spit' rather than 'spitting'.

- Use verbs that **appeal to the senses**: for example, verbs such as 'roar' and 'thump' appeal to our sense of hearing.

- Use verbs to create **verbal music**. This is when verbs are used to create a pattern or rhythm: 'dangle, spun from rock to rock …'.

Read these two excerpts. The first is from 'My Oedipus Complex' by Frank O'Connor, and the second is from 'Superman and Paula Brown's New Snowsuit' by Sylvia Plath, both of which are amazing short stories and well worth a read in your own time. Identify all the verbs in the two extracts. Then put each verb into the following categories:

Active   Passive   **Past Participle ('ing' verbs)**   **Sensual Verbs (appealing to the senses)**

1. 'I shrieked and shrieked, and danced in my bare feet, and Father, looking awkward and hairy in nothing but a short, grey army shirt, glared down at me like a mountain out for murder.'
(From 'My Oedipus Complex' by Frank O'Connor)

2. 'These nightly adventures in space began when Superman started invading my dreams and teaching me how to fly. He used to come roaring by in his shining blue suit with his cape whistling in the wind, looking remarkably like my Uncle Frank who was living with Mother and me.' *(From 'Superman and Paula Brown's New Snowsuit' by Sylvia Plath)*

Exam Focus

(1) Identify the plot structure in the story 'Fall'. Use the grid and headings to help you.

Plot element	Sentence
Opening	
First point of conflict	
Climax	
Resolution	

(2) Find this simile used in the story and fill in the blanks

H_____ and p_____ in her p_____ as t_____ as an u_____ …

(3) The author uses many examples of similes. Find three more.

(4) The words 'hissing' and 'sizzling' are examples of:

a. personification   b. onomatopoeia   c. cliché

(5) 'grind and grind' is an example of:

a. onomatopoeia   b. allegory   c. repetition

(6) 'oily oak' is an example of:

a. alliteration   b. assonance   c. cliché

(7) 'crowds that clog' is an example of:

a. alliteration   b. assonance   c. hyperbole

(8) Explain the following phrases in your own words:

'The body creaks but the spirit flares'

'… she could earn her crust by …'

(9) What do the words 'kedgeree', 'pickles' and 'brine' have in common?

(10) Write two paragraphs about a character who has 'an unexpected adventure'. Pick four powerful verbs used by Emma Donoghue in her short story and use them in your two paragraphs.

Short Story [6]

What I will learn:

to explore various themes; to identify prepositions

True or False

PREPARE

Use your **Show-Me-Boards** to answer these **True** or **False** statements about women and girls during World War I.

Statements

- When World War I broke out and men went off to fight, women took up their jobs.

- Women were allowed to fight on the 'front line' (group of troops closest to the enemy).

- Women began wearing trousers due to work demands.

- Women already had the right to vote so they were allowed to work.

- The British Army recruited women solely for cooking for the army personnel and cleaning the army barracks.

- Farm work, driving buses and working on the railway are just some of the positions women held during the war.

- Women were paid the same wage as men to do their jobs.

- Female workers often worked for thirteen days without a break.

- When men returned from the war, women held on to their jobs working alongside the men.

'Mother and Mrs Everington' by Melvin Burgess

Mother was busy knitting. I think that she must have knitted over a mile of scarves and enough socks to clothe the feet of nations. She had the maid and the cook doing the same and tried to get me at it too, but I told her I'd rather stab my eyes out than sit still knitting all day when our young men were dying for their country.

'What are the troops going to do with all these scarves, Mother, strangle the Bosch to death with them?' I asked.

'It's all about morale, Effie,' she said. 'It shows the men that the women are behind them.'

Behind them, indeed! What Mother doesn't realise is that this War, dreadful though it is, is a wonderful opportunity for us women to show the men what we're made of. Women of her generation may be used to being things of ornament, painting their lives out in a whalebone cage, but that's not for me. I want to be an inspiration. And if I can't be that, I'll damned well be useful at least!

Sorry for the language. As you can see, I feel strongly about it.

So, while Mother and her dear fat friend Mrs Everington were producing scarves by the mile, I was learning how to drive. I commandeered my brother Robbie's little car and drove it round and round the padlock behind the house, churning up the mud and scaring the pony half to death. I got Jimmy, the milkman's boy, to teach me the basics. He was scared to come with me at first, but within a few hours I could drive better than him. That's what he said, anyway, although as soon as he was out of the car he claimed it was just an excuse to escape.

'You're a wet blanket,' I told him. 'If you're scared of me driving you around a field, how are you going to cope in the trenches? Or is that why you haven't joined up yet?'

Jimmy said he'd rather face the Bosch than my driving any day. 'And I'm not eighteen yet, miss,' he said. 'It'll be another year and more before I'm old enough to fight.'

'That didn't stop my brother, did it?' I said. Robbie did the bravest thing and lied about his age in

order to fight for his country. Mother helped him – it's amazing what you can get away with if you're only born a male. She wrote a letter assuring the draft that he was over eighteen and ready to go. Mrs Everington was furious about it and told her she was putting the men at risk, sending a boy out to do a man's job, but we all know she was just jealous. Her son Howard joined up at eighteen and she was livid that Mother had stolen a march on her. You should have seen her face when she heard! If she'd had a genie in a lamp, I swear she'd have got him to conjure her up another son, a month or so younger than Robbie, just to win back the edge.

It's pathetic, really, but Mother is just as bad. They are at it hammer and tongs, desperate to outdo each other in the War effort. Still, it was a triumph for us, no denying it – and you should have seen the party we put on when Robbie left. Mother made a cake iced in the Union flag and I painted a scene in watercolours of the trenches with our brave boys chasing the Hun across Flanders mud, and nursing their noble wounds back in the trenches.

I think I shamed Jimmy in the paddock that day, but he would have been horrified if he'd known what I was planning. It's no use us women crying out for the vote and equality all warm and dry in our cosy sitting rooms while the men are out there sacrificing their very lives for King and country. We have to show them that we are their equals. In fact, we have to do better than them, be braver and more willing to risk everything, even though we're weaker in body, if we're to win back those centuries of lost pride. And Mother and Mrs Everington are content to knit while the menfolk give all!

Not this generation – not this woman! I told Robbie I was going to drive the butcher's van so as to give a fit young man a chance to go to the Front, but that was never my real idea. I wanted to be where the action was. I had set my heart on being an ambulance driver.

I was ready to find my way to the Front that very week but I had to put it off because – great news! – Robbie was on his way back to us! He had been wounded – nothing serious, thank God, just a bullet through the leg, but they'd sent him home to the loving arms of his family, to get better the faster so he can return to fight the Hun.

Of course, we went to town all over again. Mother invited Mrs Everington over to join in the festivities. She came, although she was clearly livid that our family had been the first to shed blood for our country. We were so proud! We got out the bunting and put Union flags out of all the windows, and red, white and blue flowers on every surface. Father took time off from his work in town, which he hardly ever does during these days of National Emergency.

Father and Mother went to pick Robbie up from the station, but I had something else up my sleeve. I wanted to give him a surprise, you see. I was hidden behind the curtains in the sitting room ready to jump out on him, like we used to only a few years ago – gosh, it feels like an age! – when we were still small. The trick was that even though the other might guess you were hiding, you still had to catch them out and make them jump.

If I had only known the unknowable – the unthinkable! What can I say? The whole thing went disastrously wrong.

I waited until they were all gathered in the sitting room. I was certain Robbie must know where I was. It was just a game, that's all. I waited until he was settled in the armchair by the standard lamp, with everyone around him talking admiringly about how smart he looked in his uniform. Then I leaped out with a terrific yell.

It was terrible. I never regretted anything so much in my life. Robbie jumped to his feet with a terrible roar.

'Effie, you stupid bloody cow,' he bawled. His whole face twisted with rage. I swear for a moment he looked like an angry dog. The whole room froze. It was the worst moment of my life.

'Watch your language, sir!' Father snapped at him. And Robbie – God help us, poor Robbie – he sank to his knees and began to cry like a baby.

I burst into tears. Mother rushed across to embrace her poor boy. Mrs Everington gave Robbie a look which I can only describe as utter hatred, mingled no doubt with relief that it wasn't her boy blubbing on the sitting room floor. 'I said it was a bad idea, sending a boy out there!' she screeched.

Father ordered everyone out. I didn't need telling. I fled upstairs to my room and wept and wept. I had ruined everything. I had turned the family pride into shame!

STOP

Why do you think Robbie got upset? Discuss why the author chose to include this moment. *Now read on …*

One thing was dreadfully clear to me – our Robbie was a broken man. What terrible things had happened to him over there? He was always so strong and brave! Surely, I thought, it must be this dreadful War and the horrible machines they use to fight it that has done him in. And if it's happened to Robbie, it could happen – must happen, has happened – to all the other young men too. Because the thought – the thought that Robbie alone …

I won't say it. It can't be true.

* * *

That night, when all was still, I crept into his room to beg forgiveness. He looked so white and useless lying there, I couldn't help but think that if it was men like this we depended on, we were going to be hard-pressed to win. But I pushed such thoughts out of my mind. I had come to comfort him and not to judge, even though – I must be honest – my belief in him was shaken.

'Oh, it's you Effie,' he said, and he blushed – his shame, I'm sure.

'I'm so sorry – I really put my foot in it, didn't I?' I said.

'The fault was mine. I just wasn't expecting … After all that noise at the Front, I was expecting quiet here at home,' he said; but I couldn't meet his eye.

'Weren't you in hospital for a good while?' I asked.

'Yes, but they started shelling positions just in front of us and, you know, Effie, how I always hated loud bangs, ever since I was little. Just before I was wounded we had three weeks of it, three weeks of constant shelling – the bloody things whizzing overhead and blowing up all around us and … and …'

And bless me, poor Robbie started weeping again.

I stayed with him an hour that night and he told me some terrible things, about how men die, and the stink, and the pain, and so on. But I could not answer – I could not! All it did was confirm my worst fears. These things are to be expected in war. They didn't shock me. No, it was Robbie who shocked me. Robbie – my brave, gallant Robbie – was a coward! I would never stop loving him, of course, but I cannot tell you how ashamed I was – for myself, for our family, for our country, but most of all, for him.

'Don't think badly of me, Effie,' he begged. 'Other fellows get their nerves shot to pieces as well. We all need to escape after a time.'

On and on he rattled, but he must have known what I felt. The truth is, if I was him, I would rather be dead, killed a hundred times over, than to come home turned into this yellow creature, this white-feather crybaby.

But – but! If I am to work in the ambulances I shall have to put up with such stuff. There can be no judgement in the medical services, no putting one before the other. All are sick – the brave, the cowardly, the enemy even. So I held his hand and listened while he excused himself. I swore I understood, and he would get better like any other soldier and soon be back in the thick of it, earning medals for his country and his family.

I tried to tell him my own plans – how I was going to make it to the Front to nurse the men and drive an ambulance. Of course, he did everything he could to dissuade me. The Front was no place for a girl, he said – for him of all people to make that claim! – and it was full of bad language – which made me laugh as well, for he had brought that very language into our sitting room! – and he feared I would be dishonoured. 'The girls who go out there often sink very low,' he said. 'It is odd how morals tend to fall away when there is so much death and destruction about.'

I put my chin up and told him there was no fear of that, not while I was alive, unless my honour was taken against my will – and that is a risk every woman must take if she is to fare bravely in this world. He tried to make me promise not to go, but my mind was made up more firmly than ever. There was no getting away from it – Robbie had let us down. It was up to me to make up for his failings.

I had a plan afoot. I had read in the papers about Mrs Huntley, the suffragette, who had put aside her militancy for the War effort and was taking a brand of like-minded women over to the Front to nurse the wounded right on the edges of the battlefields. That was the stuff for me! It was all to be done unofficially, of course, because the authorities were all frowning away desperately on women at the Front, especially suffragettes. But as Mrs Huntley said in the newspapers, if you left it up to the men, they would let the world fall to bits rather than allow a woman to help them. So women were making their own way – taking their own provisions and using their own money – even though the generals and politicians and clergy shrieked hysterically at them to stop.

Mrs Huntley was leaving from Dover on the Thursday evening. That gave me a few days at home to practise my nursing skills on poor Robbie and say goodbye to my family – in my own way, of course; they would only know what I had been doing after I had gone. If they had even the slightest inkling of my plans, they would certainly have locked me in a tower like Rapunzel!

* * *

Of course Mrs Everington was around the very next day after Robbie had disgraced himself, full of understanding. She had an article with her about shell shock, and how even the bravest and most willing soldiers can fall foul to it.

'It is one of the sufferings of modern warfare, like a wound, if not quite so noble,' she explained. It could happen to anyone and she only thanked God that her son Howard hadn't suffered in the same way. She put it down to her grandfather having been such a notable soldier.

Then we all had to listen to her for half an hour, lecturing us in great detail about how aristocratic blood, like her grandfather's for example, had been bred for centuries to cope with the shocks of warfare but that other blood lines couldn't be expected to cope so well. Which inspired me to point out that half the country must have aristocratic blood in their veins, too, because it was well known that aristocrats – like her grandfather, for example – did tend to stray from the marital fold somewhat, didn't they?

Mother sent me out hurriedly on an errand, but not before giving me one of her most arch looks and a little nod of approval. Normally, marital relations are something we never discuss in this house – but when it comes to taking Mrs Everington down a peg or two, exceptions can be made.

When I came back in they were discussing a new military weapon: liquid fire, a kind of blazing fluid that burns the enemy to ashes on the spot. It sounded just the thing! The three of us raised our

teacups and prayed to God that we might gets lots and lots of it, to send those German soldiers back down to where they came from, and where the Devil himself no doubt keeps a good supply of it to keep them entertained for the next few thousand years.

On the day, I was up at dawn. I'd told Mother and Father I was off to visit my cousin Lizzie. They'd given me money for my fare, which made me feel bad, but it was the only way. I only hope they'll understand once they have time to think about it. Every nurse and, especially, every female driver who gets to the Front releases a man to fight. One of our brave Englishmen are worth five Bosch, I heard Father say the other day, so by doing this I am adding five soldiers on our side. Unless of course those soldiers are like poor Robbie, whose nerves are so shot, I wonder if he will ever recover. Every night, I hear him raving in his sleep. It makes me wonder how brave I will be, with the same blood flowing in my veins. But even as a child I was more daring and bold than Robbie. Whenever I have doubts I tell myself to keep faith – in my country, in my family, in myself, and in womankind. I shall prevail!

I caught up with Mrs Huntley at the docks, ready to depart. She was a little doubtful at first, because of my age – even though I'd added a year to make the magic eighteen. But her doubts melted away when I showed her the letter from my mother, blessing me and my enterprise, praising my abilities as a driver, a nurse and a hard worker with a stout heart – and hoping that Mrs Huntley would take me on board!

'And if the boys can fight at eighteen, why cannot I nurse them, Mrs Huntley?' I demanded.

I knew that appealing to her suffragette instincts would pave my way. She held out her hand. 'Welcome aboard, my dear – we have need of more like you,' she said, I jumped up the gangplank and that was it. I was part of the team.

Many months later I told her how I'd forged that letter from my mother, and she forgave me at once. By then, I'd already made myself indispensable.

It took us a little over two months to set up our base, in the face of much lip-curling from both French and English generals, who clearly thought us weak and silly women, unable to cope with the stress of the Front.

'Go home, my dear, and sit still. We'll have no women at the Front,' one said to Mrs Huntley.

She looked him in the eye and hit straight back. 'You will have heard of childbirth before now,' she replied. 'But of course having a life burst out from inside of oneself is something a man would suffer gladly every day if it stopped him havin' any kind of serious competition from women.'

How I adore her! They just stood there like idiots and gaped at her. So we got little help but managed anyway, as women will.

The plan was to set up a Forward Dressing Station, where the wounded would be brought straight from off the battlefield to be tended before being sent on to hospitals further away. We found a little house, literally yards away from the trenches. It had no roof, no windows – the shells had long ago seen to all that. Even the walls were full of cracks. It had been looted bare, but it was enough for us. We set up tarps to keep the wind out and the rain off, and cleaned everything to within an inch of its life. We begged, borrowed, bought and stole mattresses, sheets, blankets, bandages – and set about our work.

* * *

I look back now and wonder that this was just six months ago – six months! What a child I was! Sometimes I wonder if I'm even human any more. I can't dismiss my enthusiasm and desire to help, but how I wish I had been born at a time when such things might have been of use, and not in an age when every human virtue is being blown to pieces on the battlefield.

I've learned a great many things on the Front. How not to faint at the sight of blood. How not to retch at the stink of a man's insides. How to smile and look hopeful when a boy no older than I am asks me if he's going to be all right, when there are already flies crawling on his liver.

Oh, yes – and I have learned not to cry. Not a single tear has fled my eye since the first week, when I truly believed I would drown in them. I realised that if I started again, I would never stop. It worries Mrs Huntley though. She is desperate for me to shed a tear. I told her about Robbie and how I was resolved not to cry, because tears were for babies. She scolded me and said that the tears of the brave were worth more than diamonds. I didn't believe it at the time. I do now.

How will I be able to face Robbie when I see him again? The way I spoke to him – the thoughts I had! How could I? I know better now, but no amount of knowing better will ever erase the memory of how I was unable to meet his eye. I thought bravery consisted of knowing no fear, but I understand now that it is not fear but utter terror that is the lot of every soldier, and that enough shelling will turn any man into a jelly.

And Mother! And Father! And Mrs Everington! What on earth will I say to them when I go home, if I survive? No one can ever understand who has not been here. I would like to curse them to their faces for sending their sons away to Hell, but no one will ever hold them to account, because they don't know better, and the words do not exist that can describe this place. Only the knowledge that I was as bad as them will stop me spitting in their faces.

STOP

Do you believe the character has undergone a change? If so, how? *Now read on …*

Oh, Mother and Mrs Everington – how shameless you would think me now! Did you know that I can clean up a man from head to foot without so much as blushing? Imagine what a hussy I've become. And the language! The words Robbie used in the sitting room that day seem so mild now. I'm only astonished that he managed to contain himself so well.

I wish I could show you around, Mother and Mrs Everington, to see our work here. Tending these young men torn to pieces mentally and physically while the old men at home go to work to earn the money to keep them here, and the woman knit or learn to drive in order that one more boy can be freed up to have his insides blown out of him. You see that chap over there, gasping and coughing, Mother and Mrs Everington? What a mess he makes – scarcely the kind of thing we'd want in the drawing room, I think. Don't worry – we'll keep him here until he stops, so you won't have to see it. There he goes again. You'd think he might put a hand to his mouth, if he had any manners at all. And look at the nasty mess he spits out – green and pink. Disgusting. Have you ever seen the like? What on earth can it be, do you suppose? Some new type of cough breeding here in the trenches, do you suppose?

It's his lungs, Mother. Gas does that – it melts the lungs and while the remaining part of them produces mucus, the rest gets coughed up with the sputum, one piece after another; green and pink. Of course, the Germans get gased too – marvellous isn't it, ladies, that we are doing such dreadful things to another mother's son in the name of our country? Does it make you proud, Mother? How about you, Mrs Everington? How you must have wept when you heard that your poor Howard had died. Gas, was it? You're not sure? Don't worry – you won't be told. It's a question of morale, you see. The boys at the Front won't want you to be worrying about them – it might slow down the production of scarves, mightn't it? And that would never, ever do!

Oh, and look at this boy who has come in! He has no face, Mother. How could he have been so careless as to lose it, I wonder. Oh yes, of course – liquid fire, that's what did it. What a shame – the Germans have it as well. See that featureless stump wagging to and fro on his neck, wondering why he can't see or hear or talk. What is it the Bard says? 'Sans teeth, sans eyes, sans taste.' 'Sans life' very soon too. And I think he will be glad of it. I wonder if I should help him on his way? Oh yes, I've done that too. God's commandments melt before the cruelty of man, and we have to learn a new moral code especially for this place.

I am not sure if the boy is English, French or German. His uniform has been burned off him. Odd how they all look the same when their uniforms and faces are burned away. Either way, we shall treat him just the same. Do you want to know why, Mother? Mrs Everington? It's because I no longer particularly care who wins this bloody war. I no longer care, because whoever is proclaimed the victor, I am sure of only one thing – we will all have lost.

There was the most fearful battle nearby yesterday. I was one of the first to get out there – I usually am, because I'm the best driver we have. We found the wounded in a turnip field and gathered them up, like turnips themselves, I thought. We sent ambulance after ambulance back, all four of them, loaded to the gills, and then back again, all four.

And again. It was right at the end that I found the boy, hidden quietly behind a heap of earth. He'd heard us but kept quiet, scared of what we might do to him. German, you see. Scared as a mouse of what we might do to him – as if it hadn't been done already!

The ambulances were all away so I sat and waited with him for them to come back. I gave him some water and we talked a very little in my poor German and his only slightly better English. But we made sense. Can you imagine – he'd joined up early too, poor boy. It seems the Germans are infected by the same disease we are.

We smoked a cigarette and talked about our countries, and we agreed it was still possible to love one's country without agreeing with it in any shape or form and whilst sincerely despising the donkeys who rule it.

He was quiet for a bit and I started to think about what was waiting for me when I got back to the station. I think that was my mistake. Anyway, this boy, this German, he started to cry. It was the most horrible noise, a dreadful, high-pitched whining. It really got on my nerves for some reason – God knows why, it isn't as though I hadn't heard men weeping and screaming in pain before.

'Now, come on, that won't do,' I told him – which was unfair of me, because how could he help it? I tried to comfort him, but nothing seemed to help. He just lay there, staring off, making this terrible noise.

Then the shells started up again, sweeping across our turnip field, bombing the dead, blowing up the living – who knows why they do it? Just to terrorise each other, I suppose. Down they came, all around us, like some kind of devilish rain. It hurts your nerves, it really does. You can't hear a thing and you never know if one is going to land right by you, you see.

Anyway, the noise of the shells was really getting to this lad, because he screamed louder than ever. It was quite unbearable. I thought, Well I can't just sit here waiting while the poor beggar goes mad, can I? There's only one thing to do. I have to get out of it.

After a lot of huffing and puffing I managed to heave him over my shoulders – he wasn't so big fortunately – and off we went, staggering over the turnip field with the shells going off all around us. I know it sounds crazy, but I thought, Well, if one of them's got my number on, it's going to get me anyway. I didn't see the point of sitting waiting for it. It can bloody well come and find me, I thought!

I staggered along God knows how far before it did – finally. I don't know how far away it landed, but there was a noise like all hell blowing up. It blew both of us up in the air and we came down in a great storm of mud and clay. A great clod of it landed on my face and half stunned me, but other than that, I seemed to be all right.

'Well, if that's all that being hit with a shell does, I don't mind it so much,' I said to myself. I just lay there for a while. I thought the German boy must have died, but then, God help me, he started up again, that dreadful noise worse than ever. You never heard anything like it, I couldn't bear to listen to it. I couldn't work out where he was at first, until I realised it was coming from beneath me. I'd come down right on top of him.

The shelling had stopped by this time, but nothing I could say or do made any difference, he just kept on and on and on until I wanted to just bloody strangle him. I dug him out of the earth – it was a real effort, he was no help at all – and set off again over the turnip field with the screaming boy on my back.

I hadn't gone far when I heard a shout. It was Gillian and Sylvia come back from the station with the ambulance at last. 'You took your time,' I said.

They put me on a stretcher, carted me off to the ambulance and shoved me in. Off we went, with Sylvia sitting next to me, stroking my hair. It annoyed me, to be honest, because all this time the German lad was still making that God-awful noise, and all she could do was sit next to me, when I was pretty well all right except for a swollen face, which, believe me, is nothing.

'Can't you give him something for the pain, Sylve?' I asked her. 'That noise is driving me mad. I've been listening to it for hours now.'

'What noise? Who?' she asked.

'That poor boy, can't you hear him? He must be in the most terrible pain to be making a noise like that.'

'That boy you were with, Effie?' she said. 'That boy was dead. He'd been dead for a couple of days by the look of him. He isn't even in the ambulance with us.'

Well, that was ridiculous. I could hear him as clear as a bell.

'Sylve, what's wrong with you? Can't you hear it, that ruddy awful noise he's making?' I asked her.

She gave me a funny look and said, 'Effie, that's you, darling. That's you crying.'

'It can't be me!' I said, but she insisted it was.

Of course I refused to believe it. We argued about it all the way back to the station where they fetched Mrs Huntley to see if she could convince me. She came at once and gave me a sad old smile. 'Here they are, here they are, your precious tears at last,' she said, wiping my face.

I knew then that it was true.

She gave me a hug and told me that no girl had given as much as I had, and that she was sorry she'd waited so long, but now I was going home for a while. Then she tucked me up in bed and went to make arrangements for me to leave the next day.

EXPLORE

Reorder these sentences to create a summary of the story.

a) When Mrs Huntley reprimands (gives out to) her, she begins to realise that Robbie was right.

b) Effie believes she can make a difference as a girl by learning to drive.

(9) c) She plans to run away and join a suffragette movement, who are setting up nurse stations in France.

(1) d) Effie and her family are living in England during World War I.

e) Effie lies to Mrs Huntley, the leader of the movement, and tells her she is eighteen.

f) Effie believes Robbie has become a coward and vows she will never become like that.

g) Effie's mother and Mrs Everington try to outdo each other with regards to their family's patriotism.

h) Effie is shocked at his tears and how he has been affected by the war.

(17) i) Mrs Huntley realises Effie has been affected by the war and sends her home.

j) She confides in Mrs Huntley about her feelings towards her brother.

k) When her brother is wounded, he returns home, only to be traumatised by Effie's surprise welcome.

l) The trauma of her experiences had led her to believe she hears a dying boy crying beside her.

(2) m) Her older brother, Robbie, is away fighting on the Front Line in France while she and her mother try to do whatever they can for the war effort.

n) She realises that innocent boys are being told there is honour in fighting for their country, but they are only being sent to their death.

o) She talks to her mother and Mrs Everington as if they were there, showing them all the misery.

p) They travel to France where Effie becomes a competent and brave nurse.

(15) q) Effie goes out to rescue troops who have been shelled in a turnip field; she herself is injured.

In groups of five, act out the scene in which you imagine Effie returning home to her family for the first time since she has been away. Your cast will include Effie, Robbie, Mother, Father and Mrs Everington. Remember to try and build the emotions felt on all sides by:

- Creating the tone and pace you would associate with seeing someone for the first time in a long time.

- Movements and gestures when people reunite, for example jumping up and down, or hugging. You might like to include some props, for example, a tea set or a suitcase.

PREPOSITIONS

Prepositions are a vital component of language. There are approximately 150 prepositions in the English language.

A preposition is a word that shows the relationship between a noun or pronoun and other parts of a sentence.

e.g. *The bike was left **against** the wall.*

The bike is not just left anywhere, it has been left **against** the wall.

Here are some other examples.

- John walked **through** the door.

- Jane sleeps **in** her bed every night.

- Shona let her earring fall **out** of her hand and it slipped down **between** the seats **of** the airplane.

The following sentences have been taken from the story. Identify the prepositions in each one. The number in brackets indicates how many prepositions are in each sentence.

1. Behind them, indeed! (1)

2. These things are to be expected in war. (1)

3. We got out the bunting and put Union flags out of all the windows, and red, white and blue flowers on every surface. (3)

4. Mrs Huntley was leaving from Dover on the Thursday evening. (2)

5. We smoked a cigarette and talked about our countries, and we agreed it was still possible to love one's country without agreeing with it in any shape or form and whilst sincerely despising the donkeys who rule it. (2)

Exam Focus

1 'Mother and Mrs Everington' deals with a strong female protagonist. Think of another story you may have studied that features a strong character, male or female. Compare and contrast them with the character of Effie from 'Mother and Mrs Everington'. Answer the following questions to remind you of your chosen character:

- Is your character male or female?

- What do they look like?

- What type of personality do they have?

- What makes them strong?

2 • Are they treated fairly and equally?

Imagine the year is 1916 and you are Mrs Huntley, member of the suffragette movement. Write a letter to Prime Minister David Lloyd George demanding voting rights for females. You can refer to the work of women during the war to support your argument.

3 The opening of this story was strategic. It helped the reader to challenge their thoughts about female stereotypes. Explain how it did this. **P I E**

Short Story [7] – A Graphic Short Story

What I will learn:

to identify a central theme; to understand what a prequel and sequel are

The next text is an illustrated short story, or 'graphic short story'. It was created by A. J. Poyiadgi and is called 'Teapot Therapy'. It has a very obvious theme that is dealt with in a clever and serious way.

Based on the title of this story:

* Write a short paragraph (5–6 lines) outlining what you think the plot will be.

* Suggest two themes that may be dealt with in the story.

REMEMBER

A theme is an idea that is obvious throughout a piece of writing.

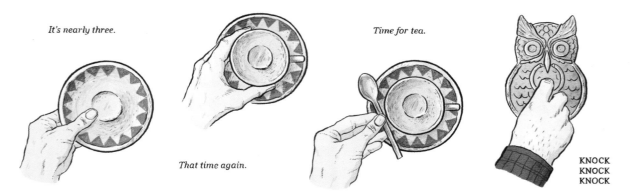

1

The odd factory farmed biccy was fine by you.

Here, try one of these. Mint choc chip.

But I'd insist on homemade.

Still do.

It's like a ritual.

And it certainly beats daytime telly.

Scrumptious.

Right, better see to that boiler.

I still see your face.

All over the place.

"All done."

She's warming up nicely.

I've replaced the missing part, but I won't charge you for it.

That's kind.

Can I at least offer you another cuppa? You've not tried the scones.

Don't tempt me. I've got two more jobs to get to.

Thanks again for the tea.

Pleasure.

3

www.ajpoyiadgi.com

EXPLORE

1. Having read the story, would you change the themes you suggested in the 'Prepare' section?
2. Why has the lady prepared tea?
3. What does the repair man find wrong with the boiler?
4. What do we discover about the problem with the boiler?
5. Is the tea prepared for the repair man unusual in any way?
6. What do we learn about the woman while the repair man is finishing work on the boiler?
7. Explain what you think the phrase 'curtain twitchers' means?
8. Apart from providing her with company, how does daily tea help the woman?
9. How does the writer create sympathy for the woman? **P I E**
10. Do you think the repair man realises what is going on? **P I E**

CREATE

1. Write a dialogue that might take place between the repair man and his work colleagues once he returns to the offices.
2. Create a sequel or prequel to this graphic short story.

A **sequel** is a story that follows on from a previous story. It will almost always be the same genre and explore similar themes. It will retain some of the same characters but will usually have a different plot and ending.

Catching Fire *and* **Mockingjay** *are* sequels *to* **The Hunger Games** *by Suzanne Collins.*

A **prequel** is a story that takes place before the events of a story already told. It gives us background information on characters and plots that we are already familiar with.

Hannibal Rising *was written as a prequel to the three books in the* **Hannibal** *series by Thomas Harris.*

Exam Focus

1. Discuss how the author brings to life the theme of loneliness and loss in the story 'Teapot Therapy'.
2. Track the thoughts of the repair man throughout the story.
3. Graphic short stories rely on images to tell some parts of the story. Choose three images used by the author and explain why they are effective in presenting the story to us.

SHOW WHAT YOU KNOW

You have learned many writing and speaking skills in this collection of texts. Now it's time to *Show What You Know!*

My Writing Task

Write a full short story based on one of the following themes:

- War
- Family
- Loyalty
- Gender Roles
- Death
- Courage
- Mental State

TOP TIP

Remember to edit and redraft your work. Look back to p. 180 for advice.

I must

- Include an opening with an interesting setting, character, narrator and atmosphere
- Create a first point of conflict – the problem
- Have a climax – the highest point of drama
- Reach a resolution – ending where the problem has been resolved
- Explore the theme

I should include

- Suspense
- Dialogue
- Characterisation
- Show Don't Tell
- Expressive verbs
- Powerful verbs

I could include

- Similes
- Alliteration
- Repetition
- Varied sentence length

Self-Assessment

Re-read what you have written and then write down two things you think you did well and one thing you could improve on.

Redrafting

Reviewing the success criteria again to make sure you have met all the requirements, and taking into account your own self-assessment notes, you can now revise your short story to create a second draft. When you are happy with your short story, you can put it in your Collection of Texts.

Reflection Note

If you choose to place this task into your **Collection of Texts**, then complete a reflection note
Hint: Review the success criteria to help you.

Reason in Rhyme: Poetry

Comparing and contrasting poetry

Literary terms

Tone and mood

Imagery

Drafting and re-drafting

Applying PIE to poetry questions

Rhythm and rhyme

Different themes

Writing poetry

As I explore this collection I will learn about:

Sound and music

Performing poetry

Sonnets

Perspective in poetry

Expressing my thoughts and ideas about poetry

Symbolism in poetry

Answering poetry exam questions

SHOW WHAT YOU KNOW

The skills you learn in this collection will enable you to **show what you know** in your final tasks at the end of this collection.

For my writing/oral communication task I will:
Prepare/deliver a three-minute talk about a poem to my classmates and teacher. This will include reading some/all of it aloud and highlighting key images and poetic techniques.

For my exam task I will:
Compare two poems I have studied and select suitable images to accompany them.

Learning Outcomes
OL5, OL8, OL10, R4, R7, R8, R11, W1, W7, W8, W9

POETRY

What do you know about … Poetry?

To help you revise your poetry vocabulary, rewrite the following by inserting the correct words from the list.

According to the great _____ poet Robert Frost, 'a poem begins in delight and ends in wisdom'. The word 'poetry' comes from the ancient Greek for 'I create'. Poetry is a I_____work in which the expression of feelings and _____ is given intensity by the use of style and rhythm. Poems come in a variety of shapes and sizes. Some are just a few words long, while others (such as _____) are very long.

Not all poems follow a p_____ – for example some don't r_____ while others have lines that are all different lengths. This is called _____ verse. There are also poems which adhere to a stricter rhythm and rhyming structure, such as _____ and sonnets.

The key to understanding poetry is to read it slowly around _____ times, looking for clues about the meaning.

The **first reading** should give you the gist of the poem and help you pick out the possible m_____. During this reading, notice one thing – the type of poem it is, its shape, a repeated word, the title, an image, etc. After the first reading you should be able to complete the sentence 'I noticed that …'

When you **read it again** (aloud if possible) you should try to work out what the poem is saying and how the poet _____ about the topic. Try putting plus (+) and minus (-) signs above positive and _____ words (adjectives, verbs and _____).

A **third reading** should help you understand the deeper meaning, and you should notice any significant imagery, as well as the music and rhythm.

If all else fails, try the following techniques:

1. Underline _____ words (not too many).

2. Ask yourself what is the poem about, how the poet communicates the main t_____ and how you feel about the poem.

Don't be disheartened if you can't understand a poem straight away. Share your thoughts with other students and you will often be able to help each other.

limericks	themes	three	feels	key
literary	adverbs	rhyme	free	negative
pattern	ideas	message	epics	American

Now that you've thought about how to read poetry, you'll read, listen to and study some new poems.

When you are exploring a poem, try to answer these **three** questions:

WHAT is the poet saying?

HOW is the poet saying it?

HOW do I feel about the poem?

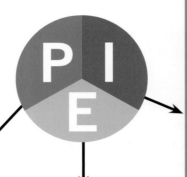

How is the poet saying it? (Illustrate)

Quote using the lines that made a big impression on you – correctly and in inverted commas.

Through language/musical devices

Rhyme – for example …
Rhythm – for example …
Assonance – for example …
Alliteration – for example …
Repetition – for example …
Onomatopoeia – for example …

Through imagery comparisions

Metaphors/similes/personification/symbolism/analogies – for example …

Through the style/shape of the poem

E.g. sonnet/lyric – for example …

What is the poem saying? (Point)

What is the main message of the poem?

What is the central theme?

What is the tone/mood?

How do I feel about the poem/message? (Explain)

What did I enjoy about this poem?

Can I make a connection between the poem and my own life/memories; or the people or places I know?

Literary Devices

Look at the table below and match each of the poetic devices from the list with the correct definition/example.

Simile   Imagery   **Metaphor**   Personification   **Symbolism**

Poetic Device	Definition	Example
	Giving **human qualities** to a non-human (e.g. animal, idea or thing)	'Caustic ticking of the clock'
	Comparing things **without using** the words 'like' or 'as' or 'than'	'A blitz of a boy is Timothy Winters'

Poetic Device	Definition	Example
	The use of **symbols** to suggest a deeper meaning, one that is different from its literal sense	'the girl in <u>scarlet</u> heels'
	Comparing two things **using** the words 'like', 'as' or 'than'	'hold it up to the light <u>like</u> a color slide'
	Descriptions in poems that help to make a picture in the reader's mind, appealing to their senses	'<u>Beetle on its black back, rocking in the lunchtime sun</u>'

Now you will read a poem about one poet's thoughts on studying and teaching poetry. See if you can spot the literary devices as you read.

POET PROFILE

Name: Billy Collins (b. 1941)

Nationality: American

Fact: Poet Laureate of the United States (2001–2003), Collins was labelled 'the most popular poet in America' by the *New York Times*.

Introduction to Poetry
by Billy Collins

I ask them to take a poem
and hold it up to the light
like a color slide

or press an ear against its hive.

I say drop a mouse into a poem
and watch him probe his way out,

or walk inside the poem's room
and feel the walls for a light switch.

I want them to waterski
across the surface of a poem
waving at the author's name on the shore.

But all they want to do
is tie the poem to a chair with rope
and torture a confession out of it.

They begin beating it with a hose
to find out what it really means.

EXPLORE

1. Who do you think are the two characters in the poem, represented by the personal pronouns 'I' and 'they'?

2. What does the 'I' character want and what do 'they' want?

3. The poem has lots of vivid images. Choose your favourite one and explain why you chose it.

4. Many of the images are metaphors. Choose one and explain what the metaphor represents.

5. Do you like this poem? Explain your answer.

CREATE

W7.3

Teaching a Lesson

This poem by Billy Collins represents the difference between how 'they' feel about poetry and how the poet feels. What are your thoughts about poetry? Imagine you had to design an ideal lesson to teach your favourite poem to a group of first year students. How would you teach it? What would you like them to know about the poem? Think about **what** you would teach (the main points and literary devices you would highlight, your favourite lines) and **how** you would teach it (images, music, games or other teaching techniques that have helped you in the past).

This will help you in preparation for your **Oral Communication** task (p. 318).

Poetry in Pictures

Thinking about your favourite image from any poem you have read, present this image on a 'Poetry in Pictures' poster. Mention:

- The title of the poem.
- The name of the poet.
- A quote that contains the image you like best.
- A reason why you like it.

Draw a picture, either on paper or on a computer, or find an illustration or photo (online or in a magazine) that you feel represents the image from the poem.

Poetry in Pictures Poster
The title of the poem is
The name of the poet is
The image I like best is
I like this image because
Here is a picture that I feel best represents this image

Humour

What I will learn:

to identify different types of poems; to do a dramatic reading of a poem; to listen for rhythm and rhyme in poetry; to read narrative poems

POET PROFILE

Name: Edward Lear (1812–88)

Nationality: English

Fact: As well as being a poet and storyteller, Edward Lear also did the illustrations for his poetry, often sketching hilarious images.

The first poem in our *Humour* section is from a famous collection by Edward Lear called *A Book of Nonsense*, originally published in 1846, which included a range of poetry styles, especially limericks. This talented poet made the form of the limerick very popular.

There was an Old Man with a beard
by Edward Lear

There was an Old Man with a beard
Who said, It is just as I feared! –
Two Owls and a Hen, four Larks and a Wren,
Have all built their nests in my beard.

Discuss these three questions with another student.

1. What kind of poem is this?

2. What are the features of this type of poem?

3. Do you know any other poems like this?

If you identified aspects of **rhythm** and **rhyme** as some of the features in the poem, you are on the right track to understanding some techniques that poets use in their work. We will come back to rhythm and rhyme later.

Having identified one type of poem (the limerick), can you think of any others you learned about last year or in primary school? Working in pairs, take one minute to make a list of as many types of poems as possible. If you know of any examples, e.g. 'Humpty Dumpty is a famous nursery rhyme', write them down too.

POET PROFILE

Name: Terry McDonagh (b. 1946)

Nationality: Irish (born in Kiltimagh, Co. Mayo)

Fact: Twelve of Terry McDonagh's poems have been put to music for voice and string quartet. He now works with uilleann piper, Diarmaid Moynihan, as part of a poetry/piper duo.

The next poem in this humour section is about something many people don't like thinking about – head lice! Note how the poet uses humour to address this. Also take a note of how the poem makes you feel.

Head Lice
by Terry McDonagh

I've had head lice
twice …   scratch … scratch.

Nearly went bananas, I did.
Worse than bad breath, it was
Good mates defect to
enemy gangs, take the lice
with them and keep on

scratching.

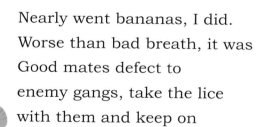

My things were put
in the freezer
to frostbite the life
out of the geezers …   scratch.

I cried for my teddy
in his cold, cold cot …   scratch.

A teacher got lice four times.
The kids went wild and cheered.
The teacher went home ...   ... scratch.

They get into hair
and into clothes
and onto pillows
and onto car seats
and onto toys
and onto teddies
and onto friends.

They get around ...   ... scratch.

louse: one lice (singular)

One kid took
a photo of a louse
and enlarged it.
It looked like a mouse
A small girl fainted
Oh, my God!   Scratch!

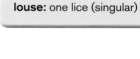

Some say super lice
that can't be killed
are on the way.

Don't let this happen,

please ...   scratch.

My friend said her whole class
had head lice
at her last school
and they scratched
    and scratched
    and scratched

scratch   scratch
scratch

scratch   scratch

scratch

EXPLORE

1. How did you feel while and after reading this poem? Explain your answer.

2. Choose the three most powerful images in the poem and explain how they affected you.

3. The poet repeats certain words in the poem (repetition). Pick out two examples of repetition in the poem and explain its effect on you.

SPEAK

Working with a classmate, do a dramatic reading of the poem together. Take it in turns to read and act; while one person reads, the other can act out the various images from the poem.

CREATE

Write a description of an uncomfortable sensation (a smell, a taste, a feeling, a sound, a sight). Your aim here is to make the people who are reading or listening to your description experience this sensation and to feel uncomfortable.

Now read out your description to another classmate and ask them to rate their discomfort on a scale of one to ten, with ten being the most uncomfortable. Use each other's feedback to redraft and improve your work.

POET PROFILE

Name:	Spike Milligan (1918–2002)
Nationality:	English
Fact:	'Spike' Milligan's real first name was Terence. He started calling himself 'Spike' after hearing a band on the radio called 'Spike Jones and His City Slickers'.

READ

Onomatopoeia is an example of how sound is used to convey meaning. It is used to great effect in this poem by Milligan.

OnaMaTaPia
by Spike Milligan

Onamatapia!
Thud – Wallop – Crash!
Onamatapia!
Snip – Snap – Gnash!

Onamatapia
Whack – Thud – Bash!
Onamatapia!
Bong – Ting – Splash!

SPLASH!

WALLOP!

TOP TIP

'Onomatopoeia' is a tricky word to spell. Breaking it up will help you: On-O-Mat-O–poe-ia. (Notice that 'poe' is in there, which almost makes up the word 'poem'!)

?
EXPLORE

1. Divide this list into two groups: words that you think are good examples of onomatopoeia, and those that are not.

splosh	wink	bang	jam
tap	drop	mushroom	sneeze
beep	drum	boing	squeeze
water	boom	pick	whisper
fire	woof	tinkle	slushy

2. When you have done this, add three more words to each list.

Name: Roald Dahl (1916–90)

Nationality: British (born in Wales)

Fact: Roald Dahl's parents were Norwegian. He wrote poems, novels and short stories for adults and children, many of which were made into films, such as *Charlie and the Chocolate Factory* and *Matilda*.

You will now read a poem that relies heavily on rhythm and rhyme. You will read it again in groups later. This poem – a unique and humorous take on the tale of Little Red Riding Hood – was written by beloved children's author, Roald Dahl. It is taken from his collection, *Revolting Rhymes*. This is a **narrative poem** which means that it tells a story. Wait for the twist at the end!

Little Red Riding Hood
by Roald Dahl

As soon as Wolf began to feel
That he would like a decent meal,
He went and knocked on Grandma's door.
When Grandma opened it, she saw
The sharp white teeth, the horrid grin,
And Wolfie said, 'May I come in?'

Poor Grandmamma was terrified,
'He's going to eat me up!' she cried.
And she was absolutely right.
He ate her up in one big bite.
But Grandmamma was small and tough,
And Wolfie wailed, 'That's not enough!
I haven't yet begun to feel
That I have had a decent meal!'
He ran around the kitchen yelping,
'I've got to have a second helping!'

Then added with a frightful leer,
'I'm therefore going to wait right here
Till Little Miss Red Riding Hood
Comes home from walking in the wood.'

He quickly put on Grandma's clothes,
(Of course he hadn't eaten those).
He dressed himself in coat and hat.
He put on shoes, and after that
He even brushed and curled his hair,
Then sat himself in Grandma's chair.

In came the little girl in red.
She stopped. She stared. And then she said,
'What great big ears you have, Grandma,'
'All the better to hear you with,' the Wolf replied.
'What great big eyes you have, Grandma.'
said Little Red Riding Hood.
'All the better to see you with,' the Wolf replied.

He sat there watching her and smiled.
He thought, I'm going to eat this child.
Compared with her old Grandmamma
She's going to taste like caviar.

Then Little Red Riding Hood said, 'But Grandma,
What a lovely great big furry coat you have on.'

'That's wrong!' cried Wolf. 'Have you forgot
To tell me what BIG TEETH I've got?
Ah well, no matter what you say
I'm going to eat you anyway.'

The small girl smiles. One eyelid flickers.
She whips a pistol from her knickers.
She aims it at the creature's head
And bang bang bang, she shoots him dead.

A few weeks later, in the wood,
I came across Miss Riding Hood.
But what a change! No cloak of red,
No silly hood upon her head.
She said, 'Hello and do please note
My lovely furry wolfskin coat.'

1. Pick out the differences between this poem and the original fairy tale using a Venn diagram.

2. Rhyme is very important in this poem. Re-read the poem silently, paying careful attention to the rhyme. Write out a list of all the words that rhyme, for example: Line 1 = feel; Line 2 = meal.

3. Rhythm is also very important. Count the syllables in each line to work out the rhyming scheme, for example: Line 1 = 8 syllables, Line 2 = 8 syllables, etc. Pick out any parts that are different to the rest of the poem. To remind yourself of rhyming schemes, go to page 123 in the *Journeys* collection.

You can listen to different recordings of this poem on YouTube, such as one by the British actors, Timothy West and Prunella Scales. There are also versions made by students if you search for them. There is a cartoon version too: look up 'Little Red Riding Hood as told by Roald Dahl' by Andrew A. Wilson.

Now, working in groups of four, divide up the parts between yourselves. Take it in turns to read your part aloud.

Characters: The narrator, **Red Riding Hood**, her **grandmother** and **the wolf**.

Speaking Tips

- Adapt your voice to sound like the appropriate character. For example, grandma might have a weaker voice than the wolf, whose voice might be huskier and more intimidating.

- Vary your tone – monotone readings (readings that do not change in pitch or tone) are difficult to listen to.

- Make a note of places you might need to pause, or words you might like to stress (to emphasise them).

- Use good diction (how you pronounce words). Speak clearly even if you imagine your character to have a husky voice – your listeners need to understand you.

- Be aware of what you are doing with your hands. Where appropriate, you may use them to emphasise a line or a word by using a gesture; otherwise keep them down by your side, naturally. Don't wring them together or fiddle.

- For a more polished reading, learn your part off by heart so that you can focus on your presentation (e.g. on eye contact).

- Don't forget to breathe! Often when we are nervous, we rush through our reading or presentation and forget to stop for breath.

You might like to record your presentation and keep it for your Collection of Texts.

Choose a poem that you know or have studied and **prepare a dramatic reading** for a group of students followed by a **two-minute** talk explaining what it is about.

You must:

- **Briefly introduce** the poem (mention the **title**, **poet**, **why** you chose it and at least **two** pieces of information about the poet's life).

- Do a dramatic reading of all/some of the poem.

- Summarise the **main ideas/message** in the poem.

⟶

- Mention at least **two literary devices** employed in the poem.
- Explain how you **personally relate** to the poem and what you **learned** from it.
- Use the tips given for **speaking/presenting**.
- Include a short **conclusion** (you can briefly repeat one or two of the most important points about the poem and/or quote from the poet or poem).

Using the speaking tips, prepare and practise your reading. You can then present it to another student, your class or the teacher.

When you have finished your presentation, think about the experience and write two to three paragraphs using **at least three** of these four pointers:

1 What the most important part of my preparation was.

2 What image(s) I chose to accompany my poem, and why.

3 Two things I did in my performance in order to make the experience engaging for the audience.

4 What I learned from doing this reading and what I would do differently next time.

When you have completed this task, you could complete a **Student Reflection Note** for the **Oral Communication task**. This presentation could be used for your **Oral Communication** or as a practice run for it.

Childhood

What I will learn:

to define and recognise important imagery and symbolism in poetry; to interpret the purpose of images and symbols in a poem; to revise PIE and apply it to questions about poetry

Imagery

According to the poet, Cecil Day Lewis (the father of actor, Daniel Day Lewis), an **image** is 'a picture made out of words'. **Imagery** is the name of those *descriptions* in poems that help to create an image in the mind of the reader and appeal to their senses.

REMEMBER

An **image** appeals to one or many of the reader's senses (sight, hearing, touch, taste and smell). A powerful image should leave the reader (or listener) with a vivid picture in their mind.

We all have memories and images of our childhood. Some people can remember being in a cot while others can recall their first day in school. The next group of poems is about childhood.

Before you read them, think about your own memories of childhood. First, think for a few minutes and pick five of your most vivid childhood memories. Write down a word or phrase to represent each of those memories. Focus on the strongest memory and try to describe it by focusing on the senses – sight, hearing, touch, taste, smell. Try to recreate the experience in your mind and then present this on a spider diagram.

Name:	Adrian Mitchell (1932–2008)
Nationality:	English (born in North London)
Fact:	In a National Poetry Day poll in 2005, Mitchell's poem, 'Human Beings', was voted the one people would most like to see launched into space (so that if aliens were ever to wonder about us, they would be able to read a thought-provoking poem on the matter of 'being human'). You can see him read this poem on YouTube if you look up 'Adrian Mitchell reads Human Beings'.

  Look at the title of the next poem. With a classmate, do a one-minute brainstorm and write down as many words as possible that you associate with the word 'playground'.

Back in the Playground Blues
by Adrian Mitchell

I dreamed I was back in the playground, I was about four feet high
Yes I dreamed I was back in the playground, standing about four feet high
Well the playground was three miles long and the playground was five miles wide

It was broken black tarmac with a high wire fence all around
Broken black dusty tarmac with a high fence running all around
And it had a special name to it, they called it The Killing Ground

Got a mother and a father they're one thousand years away
The rulers of the Killing Ground are coming out to play
Everybody thinking: 'Who they going to play with today?'

Well you get it for being Jewish
And you get it for being black
You get it for being chicken
And you get it for fighting back
You get it for being big and fat
Get it for being small
Oh those who get it get it and get it
For any damn thing at all

Sometimes they take a beetle, tear off its six legs one by one
Beetle on its black back, rocking in the lunchtime sun
But a beetle can't beg for mercy, a beetle's not half the fun

I heard a deep voice talking, it had that iceberg sound
'It prepares them for Life' – but I have never found
Any place in my life worse than The Killing Ground.

1. Write a sentence beginning, 'In this poem, I noticed that ...'. Share your answer with a classmate or your class. Make a note of observations that other students make.

2. Make a list of all the numbers in the poem and what they refer to. What effect does the use of numbers have here?

3. The poem refers to the 'Killing Ground', which makes the playground sound like a war zone. What other war imagery is there in the poem?

4. One of the themes of this poem is bullying. What do you think the poet is saying about bullying?

→

5. Complete the three sentences below by choosing the appropriate words from the list (there may be more than one possible answer, but you can choose the one you prefer). Back up your answer with a quote and brief explanation.

a) The poet still thinks about his school days
- fondly
- with fear
- nostalgically
- with humour

b) The bullies in the poem were
- relentless
- indiscriminate
- harmless
- cruel

c) The young boy in the poem feels
- powerless
- alone
- disgusted
- tiny

You Tube

Listen to the poet reading his poem by looking up 'Back in the Playground Blues by Adrian Mitchell' on YouTube. After you have listened to the poet, work in a group and discuss these questions. Be able to support your answers with reasons.

1. Which experience did you prefer – reading the poem, or listening to it?

2. How did the experience of listening to the poet recite his own poem affect your understanding of it?

In this collection you will be doing several dramatic readings and this will help you to prepare for your **Oral Communication** task, so take a note of things you liked about the poet's reading.

POET PROFILE

Name:	Eavan Boland (b. 1944)
Nationality:	Irish
Fact:	At her inauguration as President of Ireland in 1990, Mary Robinson quoted from Eavan Boland's poetry.

Night Feed
by Eavan Boland

This is dawn.
Believe me
This is your season, little daughter.
The moment daisies open,
The hour mercurial rainwater

> **mercurial:**
> something that contains mercury and is therefore shining

Makes a mirror for sparrows.
It's time we drowned our sorrows.

I tiptoe in.
I lift you up
Wriggling
In your rosy, zipped sleeper.
Yes, this is the hour
For the early bird and me
When finder is keeper.

I crook the bottle.
How you suckle!
This is the best I can be,
Housewife
To this nursery
Where you hold on,
Dear Life.

A silt of milk.

silt: the last bit
at the end of a
bottle

The last suck.
And now your eyes are open,
Birth-coloured and offended.
Earth wakes.
You go back to sleep.
The feed is ended.

Worms turn.
Stars go in.
Even the moon is losing face.
Poplars stilt for dawn
And we begin
The long fall from grace.
I tuck you in.

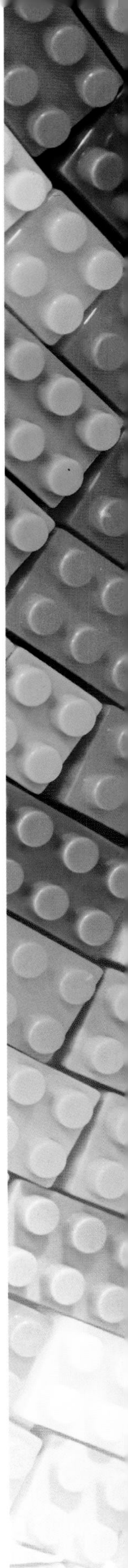

1. There are two settings in the poem – one is inside and one is outside. Choose an image from each setting and draw it. Label the images with an appropriate quote using a 'Poetry in Pictures Poster' like you did on page 259.

2. Write two sentences in answer to each of these questions.

   a) What is the main message of the poem?

   b) Choose three images that highlight what you think is the poet's main message.

   c) How do you feel about the poem and what the poet says?

3. In the poem, Boland personifies natural objects. Choose an example of this from the poem. Compare your example of personification with that of another student or group of students and discuss your choices.

4. One of the final lines of the poem is 'And we begin/ The long fall from grace.' What do you think this means? Discuss this with your partner/ group and then write a short paragraph explaining your answer.

Personification is giving human qualities to non-human objects. If you need to revise this, go back to page 160 in the *Triumph Over Adversity* collection.

REMEMBER

Remember to use PIE when you are discussing poetry.
If you were a solicitor in court, you would have to back up all your points with evidence. Likewise for poetry and literature in general. Also remember to elaborate when you are writing your explanation, and to explain how you feel/what your personal response is to the poem/the text.

Sample Question and Answer using PIE

Question: In the poem, 'Night Feed', the poet uses powerful and simple, natural images. What do these images represent, in your opinion?

Make your POINT

ILLUSTRATE (with an example)

EXPLAIN (the relationship between your point and the example followed by your opinion)

P In my opinion, the powerful and simple, natural images represent the strong, natural connection and bond between a mother and her child.

I We see this in a number of images. I particularly like the stanza when she says: 'I tiptoe in./ I lift you up/ Wriggling/ In your rosy, zipped sleeper./ Yes, this is the hour/ For the early bird and me/ When finder is keeper.'

E In this stanza, the poet uses short, simple lines and monosyllabic language, which allows the reader to easily imagine this moment – a woman lifting her child from its cot in the early hours. I particularly enjoyed the metaphor when the poet compares the baby to a bird because I have often thought that babies are tiny and delicate, just like little birds. I was also impressed by the use of the verb 'wriggling' as this reminds me of a tiny creature trying to feed itself.

POET PROFILE

Name: Charles Causley (1917–2003)

Nationality: English (born in Cornwall)

Fact: Every year in June, the 'Charles Causley Festival' is held in Causley's hometown of Launceston.

READ

The next poem is about a boy called Timothy Winters. When asked whether the boy existed, the poet replied, 'People always ask me whether this was a real boy. My God, he certainly was. Poor old boy. I don't know where he is now. I was thunderstruck when people thought I'd made it up – he was a real bloke. Poor little devil.'

 # Timothy Winters

by Charles Causley

Timothy Winters comes to school
With eyes as wide as a football-pool,
Ears like bombs and teeth like splinters:
A blitz of a boy is Timothy Winters.

His belly is white, his neck is dark,
And his hair is an exclamation mark.
His clothes are enough to scare a crow
And through his britches the blue winds blow.

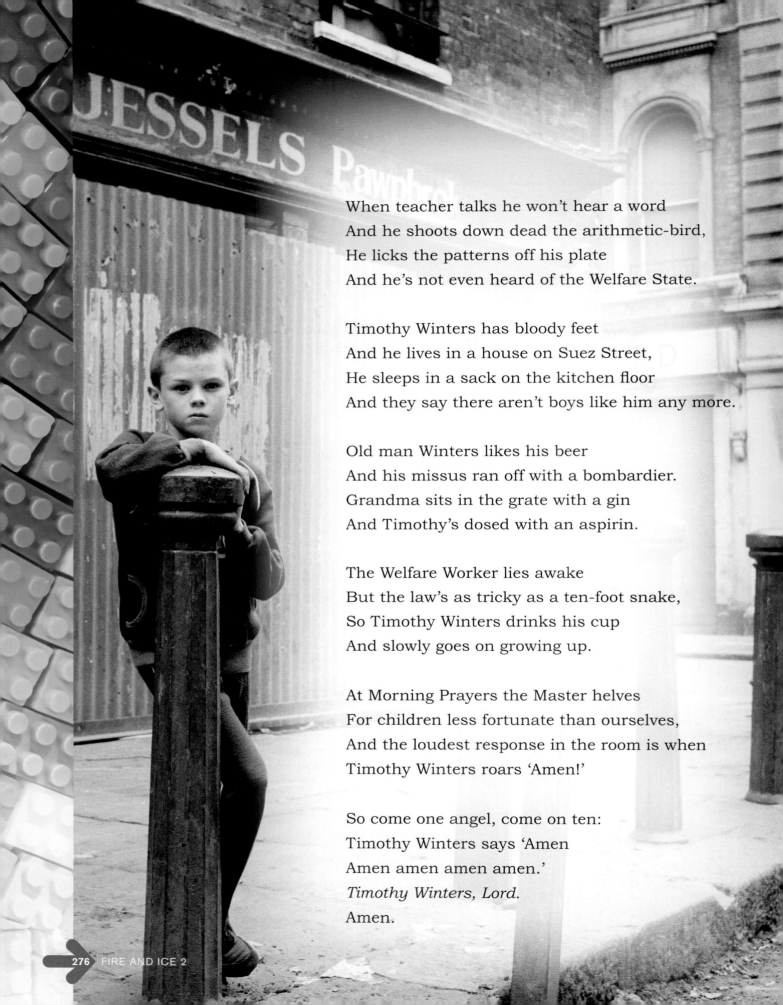

When teacher talks he won't hear a word
And he shoots down dead the arithmetic-bird,
He licks the patterns off his plate
And he's not even heard of the Welfare State.

Timothy Winters has bloody feet
And he lives in a house on Suez Street,
He sleeps in a sack on the kitchen floor
And they say there aren't boys like him any more.

Old man Winters likes his beer
And his missus ran off with a bombardier.
Grandma sits in the grate with a gin
And Timothy's dosed with an aspirin.

The Welfare Worker lies awake
But the law's as tricky as a ten-foot snake,
So Timothy Winters drinks his cup
And slowly goes on growing up.

At Morning Prayers the Master helves
For children less fortunate than ourselves,
And the loudest response in the room is when
Timothy Winters roars 'Amen!'

So come one angel, come on ten:
Timothy Winters says 'Amen
Amen amen amen amen.'
Timothy Winters, Lord.
Amen.

1. What kind of person do you think Timothy Winters is? Choose three adjectives from the list and support your answers with references to the text.

fortunate	pessimistic	serious
unfortunate	neglected	unkempt
optimistic	loved	tidy

2. There are many symbols in this poem. Choose one and explain what it means. For example, the 'cup' that Timothy drinks is a symbol of his pitiful, daily existence.

3. The use of colour in this poem is very powerful. Some colours are obvious while others are implied (suggested). Make a list of all the colours you can imagine. One example has been done for you.

Image	Colour mentioned or implied
Bloody feet	Red

A poem is not just some text in a book to be read passively. Just like a song should be sung, a poem is intended to be read aloud.

Working with another student, make a list of the things you need to think about when preparing a dramatic reading of a poem, e.g. which words you should emphasise, etc.

Now imagine that you are the poet of 'Timothy Winters'. Read through the poem and make a list of the words that you think you would emphasise and where you would pause.

Now listen to the poet read this poem.

FIRST LISTENING

As you listen:

1. Underline any words that the poet emphasises.

2. Draw an **X** when he pauses

Timothy Winters comes to <u>school</u>

With eyes as wide as a football-pool, **X**

Ears like <u>bombs</u> and teeth like <u>splinters</u>:

A <u>blitz</u> of a boy is Timothy Winters. **X** ⟶

SECOND LISTENING

The second time you listen, make a note of the following:

1. If his voice goes up at any point, draw an arrow pointing upward ↑

2. If his voice drops, draw an arrow pointing downward ↓

3. Now compare your answers to your classmates' answers to see if you agree. Discuss how listening to a reading changes your understanding of a poem.

A Poem for Ireland

In September 2014, RTÉ launched a campaign to find Ireland's favourite poem from the last 100 years. More than 130 poems were nominated for 'A Poem for Ireland'. This was then whittled down to ten poems listed below.

The winner of that campaign is the next poem you will read. You can also listen to the poet recite the poem himself too.

A Poem for Ireland

1. 'A Christmas Childhood' by Patrick Kavanagh

2. 'A Disused Shed in Co. Wexford' by Derek Mahon

3. 'Dublin' by Louis MacNeice

4. 'Easter 1916' by W. B. Yeats

5. 'Fill Arís' by Séan Ó Ríordáin

6. 'Filleadh ar an gCathair' by Ailbhe Ní Ghearbhuigh

7. 'Making Love Outside Áras an Uachtaráin' by Paul Durcan

8. 'Quarantine' by Eavan Boland

9. 'The Statue of the Virgin at Granard Speaks' by Paula Meehan

10. From 'Clearances', 3. 'When all the others were away at Mass' by Seamus Heaney

'We all turn to poetry when we can't find the words ourselves to express a sentiment or feeling: at weddings, funerals, and great and small moments in life. This campaign is about celebrating the wonderful canon of Irish poetry of the past 100 years and what it says about us as a people.'

From the RTÉ 'A Poem for Ireland' website

WATCH

You can watch a recitation of the winning poem recorded for 'A Poem for Ireland'.

POET PROFILE

Name:	Seamus Heaney (1939–2013)
Nationality:	Irish (born in Castledawson, Co. Derry)
Fact:	Seamus Heaney won the Nobel Prize for Literature in 1995.

READ

This poem is a section of a longer poem called 'Clearances'. There are eight sections in total in 'Clearances', and every section has fourteen lines, often divided into eight lines grouped together followed by another six lines (like a sonnet, which you will learn about later).

When all the others were away at Mass
by Seamus Heaney

When all the others were away at Mass
I was all hers as we peeled potatoes.
They broke the silence, let fall one by one
Like solder weeping off the soldering iron:
Cold comforts set between us, things to share
Gleaming in a bucket of clean water.
And again let fall. Little pleasant splashes
From each other's work would bring us to our senses.

So while the parish priest at her bedside
Went hammer and tongs at the prayers for the dying
And some were responding and some crying
I remembered her head bent towards my head,
Her breath in mine, our fluent dipping knives–
Never closer the whole rest of our lives.

> **solder:** an alloy used for joining metals

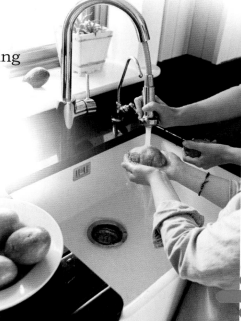

TOP TIP

Symbolism is when a poet or writer uses an object or word to represent something more abstract. For example, colours are often used to represent emotions: black often represents death or evil.

Similarly objects can represent something else – a chain might represent the coming together of two things, while a rock can symbolise something strong and dependable.

EXPLORE

1. In the poem, Heaney uses potatoes as a symbol. What do they represent?

2. Write a short paragraph explaining why you would or would not vote for this poem in the 'Poem for Ireland' campaign.

P I E

CREATE

This poem has cinematic (cinema-like) qualities as it describes two vivid scenes. Imagine you are the stage or film director. Write the stage/screen directions for one of the scenes.

SUCCESS CRITERIA

You must

- Mention what props and costumes will be needed.
- Give instructions about where the characters will stand.
- Use quotes to back up your decisions.
- Include a sketch to accompany your work.

You should

- Note any background music/sound effects required.
- Describe the kind of lighting you think would be appropriate.

You could

- Choose particular actors you wish to play the parts of the different characters.
- Include a little bit of sample dialogue if you wish.

See the *Drama* collection for more on this.

> If you are happy with your work and decide to include it in your **Collection of Texts**, complete a **Student Reflection Note** now.

Exam Focus

W7.3

Write or find an interesting poem about childhood and imagine you had to teach it to a group of your classmates. Design an ideal lesson using the following tips. If you choose to teach an original poem, you could use the one you wrote (p. 275).

Things to consider when teaching a poem to a group of students

- Who is the poet and what is the background to the poem?

- What would you like them to know about the poem?

- How do you plan to teach it?

- Think about **what** you would teach (the main points and literary devices you would highlight, your favourite lines).

- Consider **how** you would teach it (images, music, games or other teaching techniques that have helped you in the past).

- If you decide to teach a published poem, look at some of the poetry websites at the end of this collection (p. 317).

If you are happy with your work and decide to include it in your **Collection of Texts**, complete a **Student Reflection Note** now. This task will also help you to prepare for your **Oral Communication**.

Love

What I will learn:

to consider my thoughts on the theme of 'love'; to consider how sound and music are used in poetry; to understand the structure of a sonnet; to identify perspective in poetry

 Before you start reading what some poets think about love, write five sentences about love by completing these phrases.

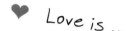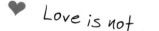

- ♥ Love is ...
- ♥ Love is not ...
- ♥ Love does ...
- ♥ Love does not ...
- ♥ Love should never ...

 Now read this passage, which is from the Bible. It is often used by couples in wedding ceremonies.

Love is Patient
from the Bible, 1 Corinthians 13:4-7

Love is patient, love is kind.
It does not envy, it does not boast,
it is not proud.
It is not rude, it is not self-seeking,

it is not easily angered,
it keeps no record of wrongs.
Love does not delight in evil
but rejoices with the truth.
It always protects, always trusts,
always hopes, always perseveres.
Love never fails.

  Draw a Venn diagram to represent the words you chose to describe love, the words used to describe love in the passage from the Bible, and any words you had in common.

Sounds and Music in Poetry

A lot of poetry has **musical** qualities. Later you will learn about the importance of **rhythm** and **rhyme** in more detail. Now we will think about sounds that are similar in poetry.

In the *Friendship* collection you learned about **assonance** and **alliteration** (p. 5).

Assonance is the repetition of vowel sounds near each other. For example: 'Some say the world will end in fire,/ Some say in ice./ From what I've tasted of desire/ I hold with those who favor fire.' (from 'Fire and Ice' by Robert Frost). Notice the repeated 'I' sound here.

Alliteration is the repetition of consonant sounds near each other. For example: 'Do not go gentle into that good night' (from a poem of the same name by Dylan Thomas). Notice the repeated 'g' sound here.

 Now read this tongue twister and pick out any repeated sounds. Try to work out if they are examples of alliteration or assonance (or both perhaps).

 ## Peter Piper

Peter Piper picked a peck of pickled peppers
A peck of pickled peppers Peter Piper picked.
If Peter Piper picked a peck of pickled peppers
How many pickled peppers did Peter Piper pick?

Do you know any other tongue-twisters with alliteration or assonance?

Name: Patrick Kavanagh (1904–67)

Nationality: Irish (born in Inniskeen, Co. Monaghan)

Fact: In an *Irish Times* survey in 2000 to find 'the nation's favourite poems', ten of Kavanagh's poems were in the first fifty.

This poem has some examples of both assonance and alliteration. Watch out for them as you read and underline them in pencil.

Inniskeen Road: July Evening
by Patrick Kavanagh

The bicycles go by in twos and threes –
There's a dance in Billy Brennan's barn tonight,
And there's the half-talk code of mysteries
And the wink-and-elbow language of delight.
Half-past eight and there is not a spot
Upon a mile of road, no shadow thrown
That might turn out a man or woman, not
A footfall tapping secrecies of stone.

I have what every poet hates in spite
Of all the solemn talk of contemplation.
Oh, Alexander Selkirk knew the plight
Of being king and government and nation.
A road, a mile of kingdom, I am king
Of banks and stones and every blooming thing.

Alexander Selkirk:
A seventeenth-century Scottish sailor who spent more than four years as a castaway on an island. *Robinson Crusoe* is believed to be based on Selkirk's adventure.

?
EXPLORE

1. Which event is the poet describing?

2. What is your favourite image in the poem?

3. Pick out the most powerful examples of assonance and alliteration in the poem.

4. In Stanza 2, the poet compares himself to a king – how does he justify this?

5. The poem is divided into two distinctly different stanzas. Working with a partner, sum up each stanza in thirty words or fewer.

6. How is this poem connected to the theme of love, in your opinion? Can you identify any other possible themes in this poem?

Think about this!

Alliteration and **assonance** can be used to create different **moods** and **effects**. Say the lines of a poem aloud and listen to the words. Think about the sound of the letter that is repeated – is it a soft or harsh sound?

What else are alliteration and assonance used for? Can you think of when it might be useful to use alliteration and assonance?

Business Names

Businesses use alliteration and assonance to make their name memorable, e.g. Mattress Mick, Costa Coffee.

TV Programmes/Songs

Children's programmes and films use assonance and alliteration – 'Peppa Pig' is alliterative, while 'Dora the Explorer' is a great example of assonance. Sam Smith's song 'Writing's on the Wall' is a good example of alliteration, while 'Alone No More' by Philip George is an example of assonance. Don't forget that bands also use alliteration in their names, e.g. Friendly Fires, Fleet Foxes, Stealing Sheep.

Picking <u>one</u> of these categories (idioms, business names, TV programmes or songs), see how many examples you can find where assonance or alliteration is used.

TOP TIP

To remember the difference:

The word **assonance** ends with '**e**', a vowel – assonance is the repetition of vowel sounds.

The word **alliteration** ends with '**n**', a consonant – alliteration is the repetition of consonant sounds.

Name:　　　Sylvia Plath (1932–63)

Nationality:　American

Fact:　　　Plath wrote a novel called *The Bell Jar*, which was published shortly before her death. She was married to another famous poet, Ted Hughes.

The next poem you will read, by Sylvia Plath, is called 'Cinderella', and like the poem 'Little Red Riding Hood' that you read earlier, it is quite different from the original fairy tale.

In her poem, Plath has imagined the moments just before the clock strikes midnight, when Cinderella is dancing with the prince.

Cinderella
by Sylvia Plath

The prince leans to the girl in scarlet heels,
Her green eyes slant, hair flaring in a fan
Of silver as the rondo slows; now reels
Begin on tilted violins to span

> **rondo:** a musical form

The whole revolving tall glass palace hall
Where guests slide gliding into light like wine;
Rose candles flicker on the lilac wall
Reflecting in a million flagons' shine,

> **flagon:** a metal or pottery vessel for wine

And glided couples all in whirling trance
Follow holiday revel begun long since,
Until near twelve the strange girl all at once
Guilt-stricken halts, pales, clings to the prince

As amid the hectic music and cocktail talk
She hears the caustic ticking of the clock.

1. Write a sentence starting with the words, 'In this poem, I noticed that …' and then share your answer with your classmates.

2. Pick out a list of verbs (e.g. sliding) that highlight the movement in the first three stanzas.

3. The poem uses many different colours, and as you learned earlier in this collection (p. 280), colours are often used as symbols. Make a list of all the colours mentioned or implied. Pick three and explain what you think each one means/represents.

4. Using the 'Poetry in Pictures Poster', design a suitable poster to accompany the poem. Pick three quotes from the poem that can be seen in your image and write them beside the image where relevant. For example, if you used an image of a clock (like the image used in the background on page 285), you would point to it and then quote 'the caustic ticking of the clock'.

Sonnets

A sonnet is a poem with a very particular structure and rhyming scheme. There are different types of sonnets – here you will learn about two very important types.

> **FUN FACT**
>
> The word 'sonnet' is from the Italian *sonetto*, which means 'little song'.

Petrarchan Sonnets

The first sonnets were written by Italian poets in the fourteenth century. They were labelled 'Petrarchan' after a famous Italian poet, Petrarch, who was considered to have mastered the form. Many other poets used the Petrarchan sonnet form.

- Petrarchan sonnets are usually love poems addressed to a woman (although the example you will read is written by Christina Rossetti and addressed to a man).

- They consist of fourteen lines.

- They are split into two groups: the **octet** (the first eight lines) and the **sestet** (the following six lines).

- They have a specific rhyming scheme:

  - The octet, which typically introduces the theme or problem, uses a rhyming scheme of *abba abba*.

  - The sestet, which usually provides resolution for the poem, usually follows the scheme of *cdecde* or *cdccdc*.

Shakespearean Sonnets

In the sixteenth century, sonnets became popular in England and were adopted by William Shakespeare. As well as being a famous playwright, Shakespeare wrote many sonnets. They had many things in common with Petrarchan sonnets (for example, both have fourteen lines) but there are also differences between them.

- While sonnets by poets other than Petrarch can be identified as being 'Petrarchan', 'Shakespearean sonnets' only refer to sonnets written by Shakespeare.

- Petrarchan sonnets were first written in the fourteenth century, while Shakespeare wrote his sonnets in the sixteenth century.

- Their rhyming schemes are very different, as you will notice from the next two examples.

- Unlike Petrarchan sonnets, the themes in Shakespearean sonnets are not only about love – Shakespeare also focuses on death, friendship, poetry and other important issues.

Sylvia Plath's 'Cinderella' has a lot in common with a Shakespearean sonnet. Can you work out what it is by looking closely at the rhyming scheme?

POET PROFILE

Name: Christina Rossetti (1830–94)

Nationality: English

Fact: Although Petrarchan sonnets are usually written by a man and addressed to a woman, Rossetti was one of the few prolific (very productive) poets who wrote sonnets from a female perspective (point of view).

Remember

by Christina Rossetti

Remember me when I am gone away,	*a*
Gone far away into the silent land;	*b*
When you can no more hold me by the hand,	*b*
Nor I half turn to go, yet turning stay.	*a*
Remember me when no more day by day	*a*
You tell me of our future that you plann'd:	*b*
Only remember me; you understand	*b*
It will be late to counsel then or pray.	*a*
Yet if you should forget me for a while	*c*
And afterwards remember, do not grieve:	*d*
For if the darkness and corruption leave	*d*
A vestige of the thoughts that once I had,	*e*
Better by far you should forget and smile	*c*
Than that you should remember and be sad.	*e*

counsel: advise

EXPLORE

1. To whom do you think the poet is speaking in this poem?

2. In the first quatrain, where does the poet say that she will go and how will it be different to where she was before?

3. Summarise the main requests the poet makes in each of the three quatrains, e.g. In the first quatrain the poet tells the reader to 'remember' her when she is 'gone away'.

4. What is the final sentiment in the last two lines at the end of the poem?

5. How did this poem make you feel? Explain your answer.

- fearful
- sad
- optimistic
- comforted
- shocked
- *another emotion*

Name:	William Shakespeare (c.1564–1616)
Nationality:	English (born in Stratford Upon Avon)
Fact:	There are no birth records for Shakespeare, only a record of his baptism on 26 April 1564. Scholars celebrate his birthday on 23 April as it is believed that, going by his baptism date, this is when he might have been born.

In this sonnet, the poet compares his lover to a summer's day. As you read the poem, notice which words are positive and which are negative. Use a pencil to draw a **+ sign** above the positive words and a **– sign** above the negative words. Alternatively, draw two columns and write the positive and negative elements into the appropriate columns.

Positive images/words/phrases	Negative images/words/phrases
Summer's day	Rough winds

Shall I compare thee to a summer's day?
by William Shakespeare

Shall I compare thee to a summer's day?
Thou art more lovely and more temperate:
Rough winds do shake the darling buds of May,
And summer's lease hath all too short a date;
Sometime too hot the eye of heaven shines,
And often is his gold complexion dimm'd;
And every fair from fair sometime declines,
By chance or nature's changing course untrimm'd;
But thy eternal summer shall not fade,
Nor lose possession of that fair thou ow'st;
Nor shall Death brag thou wander'st in his shade,
When in eternal lines to time thou grow'st:
    So long as men can breathe or eyes can see,
    So long lives this, and this gives life to thee.

1. As you read through the poem, you noted the positive and negative words. Overall, would you say that this poem is more positive than negative or vice versa?

2. Through the course of the poem, Shakespeare compares the subject of his poem to a summer's day. Make a list of the ways that the poet says the lady is like summer.

3. In the last two lines (a rhyming couplet) of the poem, Shakespeare outlines how he hopes to immortalise his love. How does he intend to do this?

4. Write out the rhyming scheme of the poem, using the example for 'Remember' on page 288.

5. Write a short paragraph discussing the similarities and differences between Christina Rossetti's and Shakespeare's approach to the themes of death and love in the sonnets 'Remember' and 'Shall I Compare Thee?'.

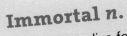

Immortal *n.*

Definition: to live forever

Antonym: mortal

Based on the information above and the two poems you have studied, compare and contrast Petrarchan sonnets and Shakespearean sonnets by drawing a Venn diagram.

VENN DIAGRAM

Petrarchan Sonnet   Elements in common   Shakespearean Sonnet

* First written in fourteenth century

Useful words

* **Octet**   A group of 8 lines
* **Sestet**   A group of 6 lines
* **Quatrain**   A group of 4 lines
* **Rhyming couplet**   A group of 2 lines which rhyme

In the *Places* collection in *Fire and Ice 1*, the poem, 'Composed Upon Westminster Bridge' featured (p. 233). Find this poem and work out what type of sonnet it is, based on its structure.

Name: Macklemore (b. 1983)

Nationality: American

Fact: Macklemore is a stage name – the rapper's real name is Ben William Haggerty.

Next is a song based on the themes of love and equality. It is called 'Same Love'. Read it before you listen to it. If you don't know it, try to imagine how it sounds. Working in pairs, take turns to read it aloud, imagining the rhythm.

Same Love
by Macklemore

When I was in the third grade I thought that I was gay,
'Cause I could draw, my uncle was, and I kept my room straight.
I told my mom, tears rushing down my face
She's like 'Ben you've loved girls since before pre-k, trippin'.'
Yeah, I guess she had a point, didn't she?
Bunch of stereotypes all in my head.
I remember doing the math like, 'Yeah, I'm good at little league.'
A preconceived idea of what it all meant
For those that liked the same sex
Had the characteristics
The right-wing conservatives think it's a decision
And you can be cured with some treatment and religion
Man-made rewiring of a predisposition
Playing God, aw nah here we go
America the brave still fears what we don't know
And 'God loves all his children' is somehow forgotten
But we paraphrase a book written thirty-five-hundred years ago
I don't know

REFRAIN

And I can't change

Even if I tried

Even if I wanted to

And I can't change

Even if I tried

Even if I wanted to

My love

My love

My love

She keeps me warm (*x 4*)

If I was gay, I would think hip-hop hates me

Have you read the YouTube comments lately?

'Man, that's gay' gets dropped on the daily

We become so numb to what we're saying

A culture founded from oppression

Yet we don't have acceptance for 'em

Call each other faggots behind the keys of a message board

A word rooted in hate, yet our genre still ignores it

Gay is synonymous with the lesser

It's the same hate that's caused wars from religion

Gender to skin colour, the complexion of your pigment

The same fight that led people to walk outs and sit ins

It's human rights for everybody, there is no difference!

Live on and be yourself

When I was at church they taught me something else

If you preach hate at the service those words aren't anointed

That holy water that you soak in has been poisoned

When everyone else is more comfortable remaining voiceless

Rather than fighting for humans that have had their rights stolen

I might not be the same, but that's not important

No freedom 'til we're equal, damn right I support it

I don't know

[Refrain]

We press play, don't press pause
Progress, march on
With the veil over our eyes
We turn our back on the cause
'Til the day that my uncles can be united by law
When kids are walking 'round the hallway plagued by pain in their heart
A world so hateful some would rather die than be who they are
And a certificate on paper isn't gonna solve it all
But it's a damn good place to start
No law is gonna change us
We have to change us
Whatever God you believe in
We come from the same one
Strip away the fear
Underneath it's all the same love
About time that we raised up

[Refrain]

Love is patient, love is kind
Love is patient
Love is kind (not crying on Sundays)
Love is patient (not crying on Sundays)
Love is kind (I'm not crying on Sundays)
Love is patient (I'm not crying on Sundays)
Love is kind (I'm not crying on Sundays) (*x 3*)

EXPLORE

1. What does the title of this song mean, in your opinion?

2. Find a synonym for these words or terms from the poem.

   a) Pre-conceived idea

   b) Right-wing

   c) Pre-disposition

   d) Paraphrase

3. Convert these metaphors (figurative language) into literal language:

   a) Doing the math

   b) Man-made rewiring

   c) Playing God

   d) With the veil over our eyes

   e) Strip away the fear

4. In the song there is an example of an allusion (a brief reference to another literary work). Find the example and explain where it comes from (*hint:* you have encountered this literary work already in this section).

5. Though this is a song, it features in this collection of poetry. Explain why, mentioning three poetic features that the song has.

6. To accompany this song, hearts with the rainbow colours of gay pride have been chosen to represent diversity in love. Find or draw another image that could have been used to represent any message/theme in the song and explain your choice.

SPEAK

Learn a poem you have studied in this collection off by heart and recite it for a classmate or your teacher. You might like to look up how it has been read by others, especially if there is a recording by the poet themselves.

Exam Focus

W7.9

Choose **five** key words/phrases from each of the poems featured in this theme of love: 'Love is Patient', 'Inniskeen Road', 'Cinderella', 'Remember', 'Shall I Compare Thee' and 'Same Love'.

1 After inserting the key words/phrases into the Fishbone diagram, draw a + sign beside the positive words/phrases and a − sign beside the negative words/phrases.

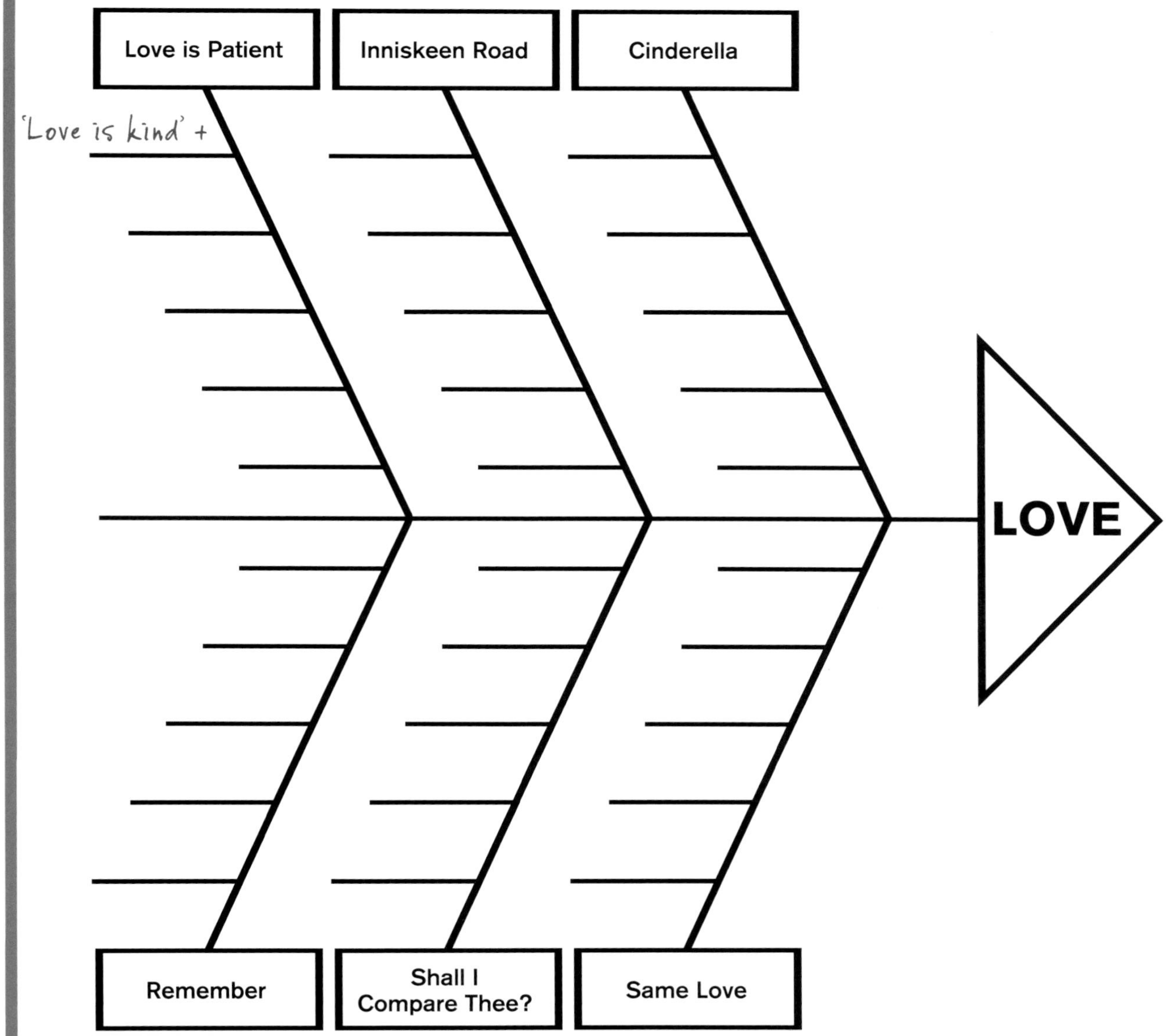

| Love is Patient | Inniskeen Road | Cinderella |

'Love is kind' +

LOVE

| Remember | Shall I Compare Thee? | Same Love |

2 Using the information in your fishbone diagram, complete the following task.

Choose two of the poems and explain which one you think has the most interesting treatment of the theme of love. In your answer you can refer to the imagery, characters, rhyme, rhythm and any other poetic devices used, such as assonance, alliteration, onomatopoeia, personification, etc. You should refer to both poems in your answer.

If you decide to include this answer in your **Collection of Texts**, complete a **Student Reflection Note** now.

Nature

to select important key messages from a poem; to think about the tone and mood of a poem

---

Working in pairs, write a definition for the word 'nature'. Compare your answers with another group, and then share your answer with the class and try to come to an agreed class definition.

POET PROFILE

Name:	W. B. Yeats (1865–1939)
Nationality:	Irish (born in Dublin but grew up in Sligo)
Fact:	Yeats was buried in France. It was only after World War II that his remains were reinterred in Drumcliffe Cemetery, Sligo, with the epitaph, 'Cast a cold eye/ On life, on death./ Horseman pass by'.

The Lake Isle of Innisfree
by W. B. Yeats

I will arise and go now, and go to Innisfree,
And a small cabin build there, of clay and wattles made;
Nine bean-rows will I have there, a hive for the honey bee,
And live alone in the bee-loud glade.

And I shall have some peace there, for peace comes dropping slow,
Dropping from the veils of the morning to where the cricket sings;
There midnight's all a glimmer, and noon a purple glow,
And evening full of the linnet's wings.

linnet: a small bird

I will arise and go now, for always night and day
I hear lake water lapping with low sounds by the shore;
While I stand on the roadway, or on the pavements grey,
I hear it in the deep heart's core.

EXPLORE

1. The poet clearly wants to go back to Innisfree. From your reading of the poem, why does he want to go and what does he intend to do when he gets there?

2. Write a paragraph describing Innisfree using at least three adjectives. Support your answer with quotes from the poem.

3. How would you describe the tone of the poem?

4. A poem often contains more than one key message. Explain one key message from this poem.

5. Do you think that the poet will go to Innisfree?

REMEMBER

The **tone** is the general attitude of the writer or speaker toward the subject, characters or audience. The tone could be formal, intimate, playful, angry, serious, ironic, etc. The **mood** is how the poem makes you, the reader/audience, feel.

Imagine you were giving a reading of the poem, 'The Lake Isle of Innisfree'. Practise saying it aloud with another student, thinking about which words you would emphasise. Try to learn as much of it as possible by testing one another.

 Think about a place that makes you feel calm and at peace. Describe it to another student without telling them what kind of place it is. See if they can guess where it is, based on your description.

POET BIOGRAPHY

Earlier in the collection you read a poem called 'Timothy Winters' (p. 275). This was written by Charles Causley, a British poet who was born in 1917, during World War I. He spent most of his life living in Cornwall with his mother after his father died from injuries sustained in the war.

 This poem by Causley is very different to 'Timothy Winters'.

 # I am the song
by Charles Causley

I am the song that sings the bird.
I am the leaf that grows the land.
I am the tide that moves the moon.
I am the stream that halts the sand.
I am the cloud that drives the storm.
I am the earth that lights the sun.
I am the fire that strikes the stone.
I am the clay that shapes the hand.
I am the word that speaks the man.

EXPLORE

1. As you read or listen to a reading of this poem, make a note of one important thing that you noticed. Now say or write a sentence starting with, 'I noticed that …'

Share your comments with another student or a group in your class. Listen to one another's observations carefully.

When everyone has shared their observations, write down as many as you can remember.

I noticed that …
Other students noticed that …

2. Working in pairs, study the poem and find examples of similes and metaphors and any other literary devices you have learned about. Compare your answer with another student's.

3. Based on the two poems that you have read by Charles Causley, what kind of person do you think the poet was? Use three adjectives to describe him. P I E

CREATE

Make a collage to explain this poem to a group of students who have not read it. You collage should include:

- A copy of the poem
- At least three pictures
- Quotes to accompany the images

The next poem you will read is about choices and decisions. Almost every moment of every day we make choices. Many of them are small and often made unconsciously while others require thought and a deliberate decision: what time to get up, what to wear, what to eat, who to talk to, how to act or react …

1. Make a list of all the decisions you can remember making today, starting from the time you got up.

2. Now choose a decision and imagine what might have happened had you decided to do something differently. Write a paragraph using first person narrative to describe the scene, using these three phrases.

   - Today, instead of …

   - I decided to …

   - As a result …

   It doesn't need to be realistic or even possible – be imaginative and creative.

3. Read your work aloud to another student and listen to theirs. Help each other to make your writing even more imaginative.

4. Join up with another pair of students and share your stories.

POET PROFILE

Name: Robert Frost (1874–1963)

Nationality: American

Fact: Frost won the Pulitzer Prize for Poetry four times for his work, more than any other poet. It is a very big honour to be given this prize once, so winning it four times was very high praise for Frost's work.

This is a section of a letter written by Robert Frost to his friend, Susan Hayes Ward, on 10 February 1912. It is believed that this inspired the famous poem you will read next.

Two lonely cross-roads that themselves cross each other I have walked several times this winter without meeting or overtaking so much as a single person on foot or on runners. The practically unbroken condition of both for several days after a snow or a blow proves that neither is much travelled. Judge then how surprised I was the other evening as I came down one to see a man, who to my own unfamiliar eyes and in the dusk looked for all the world like myself, coming down the other, his approach to the point where our paths must intersect being so timed that unless one of us pulled up we must inevitably collide. I felt as if I was going to meet my own image in a slanting mirror. Or say I felt as we slowly converged on the same point with the same noiseless yet laborious stride as if we were two images about to float together with the uncrossing of someone's eyes. I verily expected to take up or absorb this other self and feel the stronger by the addition for the three-mile journey home. But I didn't go forward to the touch. I stood still in wonderment and let him pass by; and that, too, with the fatal omission of not trying to find out by a comparison of lives and immediate and remote interests what could have brought us by crossing paths to the same point in the wilderness at the same moment of nightfall. Some purpose I doubt not, if we could but have made it out. I like a coincidence almost as well as an incongruity ...

Nonsensically yours,
Robert Frost

You will now read the poem which Frost wrote after this experience.

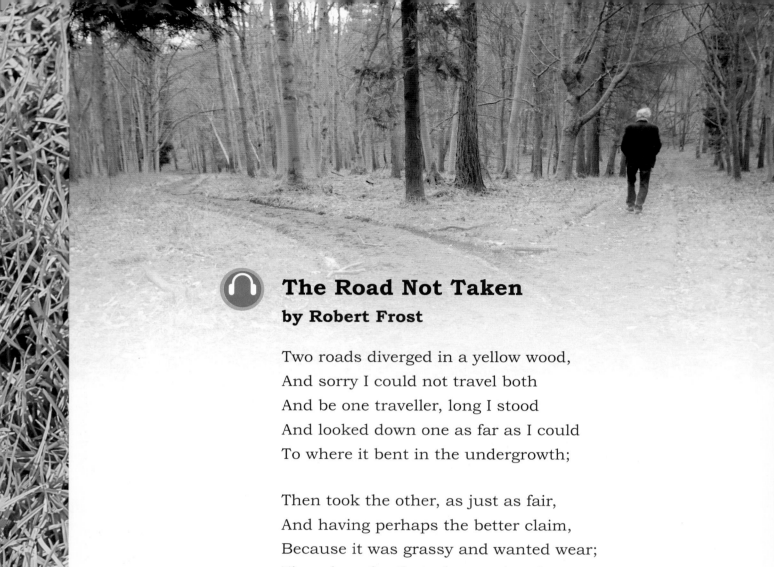

The Road Not Taken
by Robert Frost

Two roads diverged in a yellow wood,
And sorry I could not travel both
And be one traveller, long I stood
And looked down one as far as I could
To where it bent in the undergrowth;

Then took the other, as just as fair,
And having perhaps the better claim,
Because it was grassy and wanted wear;
Though as for that, the passing there
Had worn them really about the same,

And both that morning equally lay
In leaves no step had trodden black.
Oh, I kept the first for another day!
Yet knowing how way leads on to way,
I doubted if I should ever come back.

I shall be telling this with a sigh
Somewhere ages and ages hence:
Two roads diverged in a wood, and I–
I took the one less travelled by,
And that has made all the difference.

EXPLORE

1. Where is the poet standing at the beginning of the poem and who is he with? *(Stanza 1)*

2. What decision does the poet have to make? *(Stanza 2)*

3. The poet is the first person to have arrived at this place in some time. How do we know this? *(Stanza 2/3)*

4. The poet sums up his thoughts in the final two lines. What are his thoughts, in your opinion, and how do they relate to the title of the poem?

5. Did the poet's letter (pp. 296/297) help or hinder your reading of the poem?

Challenge Yourself

1. The poem can be read on two levels – literally and figuratively. Literally this poem is about deciding which road to walk down in a wood. What is the figurative meaning of the poem, in your opinion?

2. Some literary critics have said that the theme of the poem is *carpe diem* (Latin for 'seize the day'). Do you agree with this assessment of the poem?

CREATE
W7.4

Choose your favourite image from the poem and, using the 'Poetry in Pictures Poster', draw it or find an image from a magazine/website to represent how you imagine the scene. You must also include a quote from the poem that explains your image choice.

MIND YOUR LANGUAGE

RHYMING SCHEME

Work out the rhyming scheme of the poem. You can do this by noting the sound of the last word in every line and assigning it a letter: wood = *a*; both = *b*, stood = *a*, etc.).

Learn another poem you have now studied in this collection off by heart and recite it for a classmate or your teacher. You might like to look up how it has been read by others, especially if there is a recording by the poet themselves.

Exam Focus

You have just read three poems that examine the theme of nature. You have been asked to add two other texts to the nature section: two poems about nature or a poem and a song about nature – at least **one** must be a poem..

(1) Name the poem(s)/song you have chosen, and write a short introduction explaining why they belong in a section on nature.

(2) Focus now on one poem and describe what it is about in fewer than thirty words.

(3) Write three questions that could be given to a second or third year class studying your chosen poem. The purpose of the questions is to ensure that the class understands the poem and the poetic devices used. You may find it useful to look at some of the questions that follow poems in this collection.

OR

Choose a poem from the nature section and write a review about it for your student yearbook. Your review will be similar to a book or film review. To recap on how to do this, go to page 22 in the *Friendship* collection. Your review should include:

- The poet and name of the poem

- When and where it was written (if this information is known)

- Some biographical information about the poet, including any other well-known poems they have written

- The main message of the poem

- Any significant poetic techniques used by the poet

- Some important quotes to back up any points you have made

- The reason you chose it

- Anything you didn't like about the poem and would change about it

- A mark out of five (with five being the highest mark)

- Who you think might enjoy this poem

If you decide to include this piece of work in your **Collection of Texts**, complete a **Student Reflection Note** now.

Age and Death

to understand how rhythm and rhyme impact a poem;
to read a poem for meaning; to write poetry in my own
personal voice; planning and redrafting poetry

The PIE strategy will be very useful here to explain and back up your points. State your point, illustrate it with an example, and then explain how the example related to your point.

REMEMBER

'Thou shouldst not have been old till thou hadst been wise.'

The Fool from *King Lear*, Act 1, Scene 5

PREPARE

Before you start reading the poetry in this section, think about your own attitudes to age and death.

1. Draw the diagram you see below into your copy.

2. Read the list of statements below.

3. Depending on whether you agree, disagree or are unsure, write each statement in the relevant part of the diagram.

Statements

- Elderly people are the most important people in our society.
- There is a lack of respect for elderly people in Ireland.
- Elderly people are a burden on the economy.
- I will know everything when I am old.
- Age brings wisdom.
- Death is inevitable.
- Death is too depressing to think about.

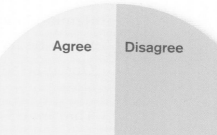

Compare your answers with another student's work. Where there is a difference of opinion, try to convince the other that your opinion is the correct one.

4. Write a paragraph about one of the statements you disagree with or are unsure about.

Rhythm and Rhyme

As you saw in the Humour and Love sections, a lot of poetry has musical qualities. One way that this is created is through **rhythm** and **rhyme**.

Rhythm and rhyme have the same origin – the Greek word *rhuthmos* – because both are related to the pattern of sound.

Rhyme *n.*
Definition: The agreement in final sounds in words or phrases (e.g. face/place)
Synonyms: poem, verse, jingle

Rhythm *n.*
Definition: The beat or movement of something
Synonyms: beat, pace, tempo, metre

Can you spell rhythm and rhyme? Practise writing them down and then check each other's spelling.

Earlier in this collection you read a poem by Patrick Kavanagh. Now you will read another poem by him in which the poet describes a memory of his father.

Memory of My Father
by Patrick Kavanagh

Every old man I see
Reminds me of my father
When he had fallen in love with death
One time when sheaves were gathered.

That man I saw in Gardiner Street
Stumble on the kerb was one,
He stared at me half-eyed,
I might have been his son.

And I remember the musician
Faltering over his fiddle
In Bayswater, London,
He too set me the riddle.

Every old man I see
In October-coloured weather
Seems to say to me:
'I was once your father.'

1. The title of the poem is 'Memory of My Father'. From your reading of the poem, what kind of memories does Kavanagh have of his father?

2. In your opinion, what is the most powerful image in the poem?

3. Choose at least one adjective from the list below to describe the tone of the poem, and explain your answer.

regretful	gloomy	nostalgic	accusatory
sorrowful	bitter	rejoiceful	confused
hopeful	neutral	morose	accepting

RHYME AND MUSICAL LANGUAGE

1. Make a list of all the words that rhyme in the poem (especially end rhymes, i.e. words at the end of a line of poetry as opposed to in the middle of a line). Compare them with another student's list. Are there any words of which you are unsure?

2. There are several examples of musical language in the poem (assonance, alliteration and onomatopoeia). Pick out one such example and explain the impact this has on you, the reader.

Working in groups, discuss the following statement. Think about the poem you just read and your own experiences when you are giving your opinion.

It doesn't matter how happy or healthy somebody is in their lives, how they are at the end is the way we'll remember them.

Present your ideas to the class.

Lyric Poems

Today, the term 'lyric' refers to the words of a song. This is a clue as to what a lyric poem is. It is a poem that could be sung with musical accompaniment. Traditionally, lyric poetry was accompanied by a lyre (an instrument much like a harp).

Lyric poems …

- *always have a musical quality*
- *usually express intense personal emotion*
- *express a specific mood or emotion, often about extremes in life, e.g. love, death*
- *are often written in the first person (the speaker is involved in the poem)*
- *tend to be short*

Name: William Wordsworth (1770–1850)

Nationality: English (born in Cumbria)

Fact: Wordsworth's parents both died when he was young, making orphans of him and his four siblings.

Now read this poem, an example of a lyric poem, written by Wordsworth.

She Dwelt Among the Untrodden Ways
by William Wordsworth

She dwelt among the untrodden ways
Beside the springs of Dove,
A Maid whom there were none to praise
And very few to love:

A violet by a mossy stone
Half hidden from the eye!
—Fair as a star, when only one
 Is shining in the sky.

She lived unknown, and few could know
When Lucy ceased to be;
But she is in her grave, and, oh,
The difference to me!

EXPLORE

1. From your reading of the poem, what did you learn about Lucy, the main subject?

2. How does the poet feel about Lucy?

3. Having read about the features of a lyric poem, which of these features can you find in Wordsworth's poem? Give a quote to support each of the lyric features that you identify.

- A musical quality ☐
- Intense personal emotion ☐
- An emotion about extremes in life ☐
- Written in the first person ☐
- Quite short in length ☐
- Any other feature (specify) ☐

4. What do you think the title of the poem, 'She Dwelt Among the Untrodden Ways', means?

SPEAK

The 'music' in this poem is highlighted through the internal rhyming (assonance). Pick out as many examples of this as possible. *Hint:* It helps to read the poem aloud.

Then, working in pairs, one person reads the poem while the other claps the rhythm. Using this method, work out how many syllables there are in the poem.

POET PROFILE

Name:	Emily Dickinson (1830–86)
Nationality:	American (born in Massachusetts)
Fact:	Dickinson wrote her poems into hand-sewn notebooks (fascicles). When she died, her family members found fascicles containing almost 1,800 poems.

Because I could not stop for Death
by Emily Dickinson

Because I could not stop for Death –
He kindly stopped for me –
The Carriage held but just Ourselves –
And Immortality

We slowly drove – He knew no haste
And I had put away
My labor and my leisure too,
For His Civility –

We passed the School, where Children strove
At Recess – in the Ring –
We passed the Fields of Gazing Grain –
We passed the Setting Sun –

Or rather – He passed Us –
The Dews drew quivering and Chill –
For only Gossamer, my Gown –
My Tippet – only Tulle –

We paused before a House that seemed
A Swelling of the Ground –
The Roof was scarcely visible –
The Cornice – in the Ground –

Since then – 'tis Centuries – and yet
Feels shorter than the Day
I first surmised the Horses' Heads
Were toward Eternity –

EXPLORE

1. Write a sentence about the poem beginning, 'In this poem, I noticed …'. Share your answer with another student/the class and note down everyone else's thoughts.

2. In one paragraph, explain what this poem is about for somebody who has not read it. Include some of the most important quotes and mention the theme and subject.

REMEMBER **Theme** is the central idea or message that runs through a text.

3. Which of the following poetic devices does the poet use in her poem (there may be more than one). For each one, give an example:

- Assonance
- Personification
- Simile
- Alliteration
- Onomatopoeia
- Metaphor

4. In the poem, Death is a character. What kind of character is 'he' portrayed as, and how does this differ from the way death is portrayed in other texts you have read?

CREATE

Imagine you are the character 'Death'. Write a diary entry on the evening before you take the character in the poem to 'Eternity'.

If you enjoyed reading a poem about Death as a central character, you might enjoy reading the novel, *The Book Thief,* by Markus Zusak, which is set in Germany during World War II.

POET PROFILE

Name:	W. H. Auden (1901–73)
Nationality:	British/American
Fact:	W. H. stands for Wystan Hugh. While he was born in Britain, he spent his later years living between America and Austria. He died in Vienna.

The poem you are about to read by W. H. Auden (you may remember reading his poem, 'Epitaph on a Tyrant') was used to great effect in the popular 1990s film, *Four Weddings and a Funeral.* Look it up on YouTube to see the very moving scene in which it is used.

Funeral Blues
by W. H. Auden

Stop all the clocks, cut off the telephone,
Prevent the dog from barking with a juicy bone,
Silence the pianos and with muffled drum
Bring out the coffin, let the mourners come.

Let aeroplanes circle moaning overhead
Scribbling on the sky the message He is Dead.
Put crêpe bows round the white necks of the public doves,
Let the traffic policemen wear black cotton gloves.

He was my North, my South, my East and West,
My working week and my Sunday rest,
My noon, my midnight, my talk, my song;
I thought that love would last forever: I was wrong.

The stars are not wanted now; put out every one,
Pack up the moon and dismantle the sun,
Pour away the ocean and sweep up the wood;
For nothing now can ever come to any good.

? EXPLORE

1. In the poem, the speaker makes a number of requests. Write out as many of them as you can find.

2. Why does the poet make these requests and who do you think he is talking to?

3. The poet uses some very powerful verbs in the poem (e.g. 'muffled'). Make a list of any other powerful verbs he uses.

4. What does the poet mean when he says, 'He was my North, my South, my East and West'?

5. 'Many of the images in the poem are metaphors that the poet uses to try to convey his sense of grief.' Explain this statement, choosing quotes to support your answer.

6. Describe the tone of the poem and explain how the rhyming scheme and rhythm contribute to the tone. (See pages 282 and 297 to revise rhyme, rhythm, tone and mood.)

7. How do you think the poet felt while writing this poem? Imagine that he was your friend and he had just texted you this poem. Write a text message in response.

REMEMBER A verb is a **doing** or **action** word. Using powerful verbs is a very effective way of expressing yourself in fewer words, which is how many poets fit in so much meaning in a short space. For example, instead of saying, 'She ran quickly', you might say, 'She sprinted'.

Exam Focus

W7.3

Of the poetry you have studied so far in this collection, choose a poem with musical qualities that you could teach to your classmates. Plan a three-minute presentation on this poem in which you refer to rhythm, rhyme and any other musical qualities such as assonance, alliteration and onomatopoeia. To prepare for this, go back and listen to professional readings of poems referred to in this collection. You might also like to refer to page 282 for 'Sounds and Music in Poetry' and look at a sample paragraph about music in poetry on page 320.

OR

Write a poem of your own, choosing an image that best represents your poem's message. Consider the following when you are planning and drafting your poem:

- The format and shape you will use (limerick, sonnet, lyrics, etc.)
- What your message is (what you want to say)
- Create interesting images to help you convey your message
- The use of colour and symbolism, etc.
- Which musical qualities you will use (e.g. assonance, alliteration, etc.)
- The rhythm and the rhyming scheme
- The punctuation (or lack of) you will use to control how it is read
- The use of powerful verbs, e.g. instead of saying someone 'cried', you could say they 'snivelled'.

If you choose to include a copy of this presentation in your **Collection of Texts**, complete a **Student Reflection Note** now.

REMEMBER

Just as you would plan, draft and redraft a story, review or any other piece of writing, you should plan, draft and redraft a poem. A lot of poets do many, many drafts of a poem before they are happy – every word, every piece of punctuation, every poetic technique is chosen very carefully.

POET PROFILE

Name: Benjamin Zephaniah (b. 1958)

Nationality: English

Fact: British-Jamaican writer Zephaniah describes himself as 'a poet, writer, lyricist, musician and trouble maker' on his website www.benjaminzephaniah.com.
According to himself, when he left school he was 'virtually illiterate'. He has taught in prisons and schools, and met Nelson Mandela.

For Word

by Benjamin Zephaniah

Thank you for the *words* I read
    Thank you for the **words** I need
    Thank you for the **WORDS** so great
    Thanks for **words** that raise debate,
    Thanks for the **words** on my bookshelf
    Thanx for the **words** I make myself
    Thank you for **words** that make me cry
    And words that leave me feeling dry.

Thanks for **WORDS** that do inspire
    And those words that burn like fire
    Thanks for all the ***words*** I note
    Thank you for all the *words* I quote,
    I thank you for the **words** like me
    Thanks for *WORDS* that set me free
    And I thank you for *words* like you
    I always need a word or two.

Thanks for **words** that make things plain
    And words that help me to explain
    Thanks for **words** that make life fun
    And ***words***, that help me overcome,
    Thanks for **words** that make me rap
    Thanks for *words* that make me clap
    Thanks for **WORDS** that make me smile
    Thanks for WORDS with grace and style.

Thanks for all those **words** that sing
    Thanks for **words** are everything
    Thanks for all the **WORDS** like this
    And little sloppy *words* like kiss,
    Thanks for **words** like hip-hooray
    And those cool **words** I like to say
    Thanks for ***words*** that read and touch
    Thank you very, very much.

Read this poem aloud with another student, one stanza each at a time.

Practise in advance. Make sure that you know how to pronounce all the words, then decide which words/phrases you will place the emphasis on and where you will pause.

You can listen to the poet reading some of his poetry at:

http://poetrystation.org.uk/search/poets/benjamin-zephaniah

SPEAK

TOP TIP

Use the glossary on page 317 for any terms you forget or are unsure about.

REVISION

Working in groups, do this revision quiz. See who can do the quiz most accurately in the time your teacher allocates.

From this collection, find a poem:

1. That includes the words 'heaven' or 'heavenly'.
2. That is a sonnet.
3. That is by an American poet.
4. That is by an Irish female poet.
5. That is a limerick.
6. That does not rhyme (*quote two lines to show this*).
7. That does not include the word 'I'.
8. That is written by a living poet.
9. That repeats a word or phrase more than three times.
10. That has a sad ending (*quote the line/s to show this*).
11. That has a hopeful tone. **P I E**
12. That has examples of alliteration and assonance (*give an example of each*).
13. In which the poet uses personification (*give an example*).
14. In which there are no similes.
15. In which there are metaphors (*give an example*).
16. That has powerful adjectives *and* verbs (*give an example of each*).
17. That has an image referring to a smell (*quote*).
18. That has animal imagery (*give an example*).
19. That was written by a poet who received a literary award (*name the poem, the poet and the award*).
20. That was written by a poet who was born in the nineteenth century (*mention the year of their birth*).
21. That has a rhyming couplet (*give an example*).
22. That has religious imagery (*give an example*).

On your own ...

Answer three of these five questions. Each answer should consist of one paragraph and you should support your answer by referring back to the poems. **P I E**

From this collection, find a poem that ...

1. You really enjoyed.

2. You did not understand.

3. Made you feel sad.

4. Changed the way you thought about something.

5. You could identify with.

Types of Poetry

Below is a list of twelve types of poems.

1. Match each type with a poem you have read from this collection and with other poetry you have studied. For any types you aren't familiar with, research their meaning and find an example.

   Add three other types of poems to the list and give an example of each type.

   * ★ Acrostic
   * ★ Ballad
   * ★ Epic
   * ★ Epigram
   * ★ Epitaph
   * ★ Free verse
   * ★ Haiku
   * ★ Limerick
   * ★ Lyric
   * ★ Ode
   * ★ Riddle
   * ★ Sonnet

Poetry Glossary

Allusion	A figure of speech that refers to a well-known story, phrase, person or event to make a comparison in people's minds.
Alliteration	The repetition of consonant sounds (often at the beginning of words).
Assonance	The repetition of vowel sounds (usually in the middle of words).
Contrast	When a poet highlights differences between two or more things (the opposite of a simile).
Conceits	Extended metaphor between seemingly dissimilar objects.
Enjambment	When a line in a poem has no punctuation at the end so the meaning runs onto the next line; also known as 'run-on line'.
Figurative language	Language that uses words to express a meaning that is different from the literal meaning.
Hyperbole	Exaggeration of ideas in order to create emphasis and gain the reader's attention.
Metaphors	Comparing things without using the words 'like', 'as' or 'than'.
Onomatopoeia	When the sound of the word reflects the meaning.
Rhyme	The agreement in final sounds in words or phrases.
Rhythm	The beat or movement of something.
Similes	Comparing two or more things using the words 'like', 'as' or 'than'.
Symbolism	The use of symbols to give a meaning that is different from its literal sense.

Useful Poetry Websites

http://apoemforireland.rte.ie	Website for *A Poem for Ireland*
www.poetrystation.org.uk	Collections of poetry
www.allpoetry.com	Collections of poetry
www.poetryfoundation.org	Collections of poetry
www.poemhunter.com	Collections of poetry
www.poetryloverspage.com	Collections of poetry
www.favoritepoem.org	Readings of famous poems
www.warpoetry.co.uk	World War I and other war poetry
www.poewar.com/poetry-writing-tips	Poetry writing tips
http://teacher.scholastic.com/writewit/poetry/	Approaches to writing poetry
www.writers-network.com	An online poetry and writing community
www.youtube.com	Enter a poem or poet's name and you never know what you might find!

Also search 'Irish Poetry Reading Archive' on YouTube, where you'll find readings of Irish poems by their authors.

SHOW WHAT YOU KNOW

In this collection you learned how to study and appreciate poetry. While you may not always understand a poem at first, you now know how to recognise many of the techniques that poets use in their work. All of this will help you to *Show What You Know!*

My Writing/Oral Comunication Task

Choose a poem from this collection and prepare a three-minute talk about it that you could deliver to your classmates and teacher. This will include reading all or some of the poem aloud and mentioning the theme, key images and poetic techniques.

SUCCESS CRITERIA

I must

- Make a list of key questions about the poem to guide my research
- Research the poet's life, influences and other works
- Listen to readings of other poems from this section and other sources
- Plan to speak for three minutes
- Draft my work first, practise it (have a friend or teacher listen) and then edit it
- Include an introductory statement with some background on the poet
- Mention the theme, at least two key images and two poetic techniques used
- Include a reading of all/some of the poem in my talk
- Use the speaking tips on page 268 when practising
- Reflect back on my work when I have finished

I should

- Use varied and reputable sources for my research
- Refer to the music in the poem
- Use the PIE technique to back up my points
- Know the poem off by heart, or at least learn the important quotes
- Explain why I chose the poem

I could

- Briefly compare or contrast it with another work by the same poet
- Mention a poem with the same theme that I have already studied
- Use flash cards with key points on them, to which I can refer while I speak
- Use images or audio to accompany the presentation

Peer Assessment

Read your partner's work and then write down two things you think he/she did well and one thing he/she could improve on.

Final Exam Focus

(1) Select two poems that you have studied and compare and contrast them using two of the following headings:

- Theme
- Imagery
- Tone
- Comparisons (similes, metaphors, etc.)
- Sounds and musical qualities (alliteration, assonance, onomatopoeia, rhythm, rhyme, etc.)
- Symbolism
- Colour

(2) Choose a suitable image or piece of music/song to accompany each poem, explaining and justifying your choice.

SUCCESS CRITERIA

I should

- Refer to literary techniques/devices used
- Include only one point in each paragraph to make my argument clear
- Draft my work first, then re-read it and edit it before I submit a final draft
- Be able to justify all my choices (image/song, etc.)

I must

- Mention the titles of each poem and the names of the poets
- Briefly introduce each poem with a sentence to explain its meaning
- Address two points from the list in detail
- For each point, find similarities and differences regarding how it is addressed in each poem **P I E**
- Back up all my points
- Include a suitable image or piece of music/song to accompany it

I could

- Make my own illustrations (hand-drawn or digital)
- Include a Venn diagram to illustrate the similarities and differences between the two poems

TOP TIP

To compare and contrast poems, some of the following phrases may be useful:

- On one hand
- On the other hand
- First
- In addition
- Conversely
- In the same way
- Furthermore
- However
- By contrast
- Similarly

Self Assessment

Reflect on your exam task and write down two things that you think you did well and one thing that could be improved on.

For example, you might compare the music in Yeats's 'Lake Isle of Innisfree' and 'When You Are Old' as follows.

In W. B. Yeats's poem 'The Lake Isle of Innisfree', the peaceful atmosphere is conveyed through the soft, gentle, natural images like 'water lapping with low sounds by the shore'. The use of the soft alliterative 'o' sound here in 'low', 'sounds' and 'shore' has a very gentle and calming effect on the reader, just like the lapping water in the peaceful, lakeside scene that Yeats describes would have.

Similarly, in Yeats's poem 'When You Are Old', the soft alliterative 'o' sounds in the first stanza create a quiet, gentle and accepting tone. However, unlike 'The Lake Isle of Innisfree', the tone of 'When You Are Old' becomes a little more cynical and perhaps bitter as he warns the subject (believed to be Maud Gonne) that when her good looks are gone from her 'changing face', she will regret the missed opportunity of true love. This is evident in the harsher, repeated sounds of the first line in the final stanza: 'And bending down beside the glowing bars', and then in the soft, repeated 'm' and 'l' sounds of 'Murmur, a little sadly, how Love fled'.

Reflecting on your work

Think back to the work you have done in this collection: the presentations you have prepared and the texts you have written for your own Collection of Texts. Write a short paragraph for two of the questions below based on your thoughts. Where possible, refer in detail to one or more of the poems you included in your Collection of Texts.

* How the poems I read helped me to be a better writer/speaker

* How I worked with my classmates as part of my writing/speaking tasks

* What a reader/audience might enjoy most about one of my presentations/the texts in my collections

Drama Part 1 – Through the Ages

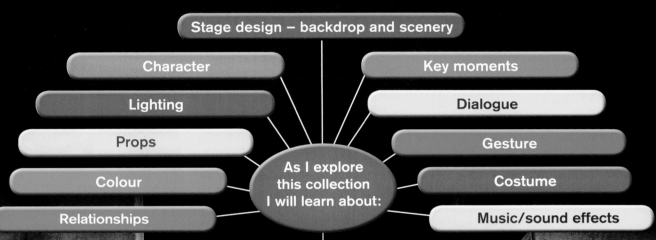

Stage design – backdrop and scenery

Character

Key moments

Lighting

Dialogue

Props

Gesture

Colour

As I explore this collection I will learn about:

Costume

Relationships

Music/sound effects

Setting, characters and emotions in an opening scene

I will relate everything I learn about drama to my **studied play**

Learning Outcomes
OL8, R2, R4, R6, R7, R8, R9, W3, W7, W8

What do you know about ... Drama?

To help you revise your drama vocabulary, fill in the missing vowels. Learn the spellings as you go along for the spelling test that follows.

The writer of drama is called a dr_m_t_st or pl_ywr_ght. The correct term for people in the story is ch_r_ct_rs.

Now rewrite the following by inserting the correct words from the list.

If I were working in the *th_____* and choosing a play for our next performance, I would ask about the *s_____* (*time and place where the story happens*). Then I would want a good *p_____* (*storyline*) and well written *d_____* (*conversation in a play*). Interesting *c_____s* (*people in a play*) and interesting *re_____ps* between them are also very important. Our audience would expect the story to lead to a powerful *c_____x* (*the moment of greatest emotion*).

For our play, we would have to design a stage *s___* and make a *b_____p* (*the design at the back of the stage*) for the back of the stage. We would also have to find *p_____s* (*moveable objects needed for this play*).

Our actors need *c_____es* (*theatre word for clothes*) to make them look like people in the time and place of the story. Each actor will perform either a *m_____* (*very important*), or a *m_____* (*smaller*) role. Actors must pay attention to the *s_____ d_____s* (*the playwright's instructions for how the lines should be spoken*).

In *r_____sal* (*practice sessions for a play*), we would discuss the *t_____* (*the central idea*) of the play with the director and *c____* (*group of actors*).

If we chose a play by Shakespeare, it would be presented in five *a_____s*, each subdivided into smaller *s_____s*. It would probably have a *s_____- p_____t* (*a secondary story running alongside the main story*).

I would have to be at my acting best when speaking a *m_____* or *s_____uy* (*a speech which says aloud what I am thinking in my deepest self*).

backdrop	plot	sub-plot	stage directions
monologue	set	theme	costumes
relationships	cast	soliloquy	major
rehearsal	setting	scenes	minor
dialogue	props	climax	
characters	theatre	acts	

Drama *n.*

Definition: Writing that is performed by actors on stage, radio or film

These are the two traditional faces of drama.

The sad face is Melpomene, the Greek inspiration for tragedy and tears.

The happy face is Thalia, the Greek inspiration for laughter and comedy.

Stages Through the Ages

Match each photograph with the correct caption.

2 A Greek amphitheatre in the 5th century BC.

3 A 21st century Royal Shakespeare theatre; audience seated on three sides of the stage.

1 A 16th century theatre. Open to the sky; covered boxes on the side for wealthy patrons; poorer people stood in the pit under the open roof; no artificial lighting.

4 A 19th century Victorian theatre, showing the curtain and framed stage.

Exam Focus

1 Imagine your studied play is to be performed on one of these four stages. Discuss with the person beside you which stage would make for the most interesting or enjoyable performance. Say where you would like to be seated in the auditorium (the place in the theatre where the audience sits).

2 Choose one of the four stages. Imagine yourself watching **one** of the following three scenes from **your studied play** on the stage you chose.

- The opening scene
- A scene of drama or great emotion
- The closing scene

Draw a rough sketch of the stage, with your suggested **backdrop/scenery** and **props** shown on it. Then write a paragraph including these points, plus any other points that you think would add to the impact of the design on the audience.

- Place the **characters** where they should be positioned on the stage.
- Design a suitable **backdrop** or **scenery** that would add to the audience's enjoyment of the scene.
- Name any **props** that should be on the stage.
- Suggest any **music** or **sound effects** that would add to the scene.

Writing About Stage Sets

A play is only words on a page until it is performed and comes to life on stage.

The pleasure for the audience is not only in hearing the words and seeing the characters, but also in seeing the costumes and the set that the stage designer and lighting designer have made for the play.

Stagecraft is the term for all the skills that go towards making the physical elements of a stage production, e.g. scenery, lighting, costumes, props, sound effects and music. Certain colours may dominate to create a particular atmosphere.

Model your sketch on this example.

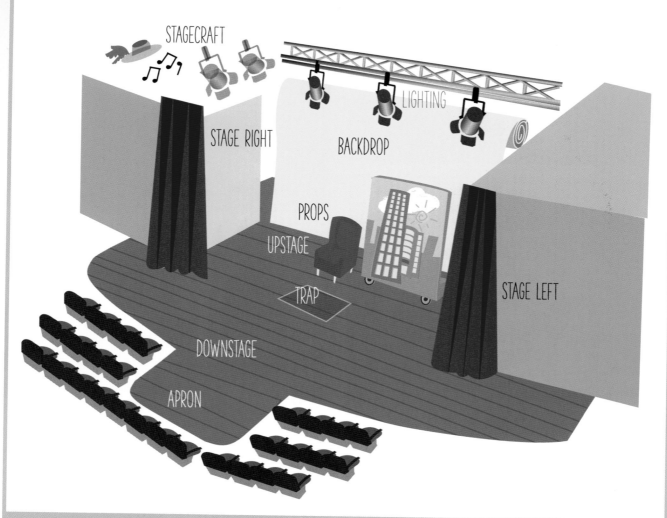

Useful vocabulary for writing about a stage set

(Labels in image: STAGECRAFT, STAGE RIGHT, BACKDROP, LIGHTING, PROPS, UPSTAGE, TRAP, STAGE LEFT, DOWNSTAGE, APRON)

Apron: part of stage or full stage that juts out into the audience area.

Backdrop: the stage background, often a painted design or curtain.

Downstage: the part of the stage that is closest to the audience.

Lighting: illumination of all or parts of the stage/actors with electric lamps and spotlights.

Props: all the moveable stage furnishings, including furniture, that are physically used by the actors.

Stage Right: the right side of the stage from the actor's point of view (facing the audience).

Stage Left: the left side of the stage from the actor's point of view (facing the audience).

Trap: an opening in the stage floor.

Upstage: the area of the stage farthest away from the audience and nearest to the back wall.

1. **Identify which play is being performed in each case from the descriptions given below.**

ANNIE by Thomas Meehan

An orphanage in New York City in 1933.

A neglected little orphan who lives in a cruel institution and dreams of finding her real parents discovers that they died when she was a baby; but all ends happily when she is adopted by Oliver Warbucks, a millionaire New York businessman.

THE SHADOW OF A GUNMAN by Seán O'Casey

A return room in a tenement house in Hilljoy Square.

During the Irish War of Independence, the poet Donal Davoren is mistakenly admired by his poor tenement neighbours as a secret IRA gunman, but when British troops find ammunition in the house, the true heroic character turns out to be young Minnie Powell.

JAMES AND THE GIANT PEACH by Roald Dahl

A giant peach in which fantastically-dressed actors can travel.

Orphaned, mistreated James Henry Trotter escapes from his cruel Aunt Sponge and Aunt Spiker, and sets off in a giant peach across the Atlantic Ocean, arriving in New York City after many fabulous adventures.

MACBETH by William Shakespeare

A desert place, thunder and lightning.
Enter three witches.

The story of a noble, brave man who commits a murder for the sake of ambition and then descends into evil until he himself is murdered.

EXPLORE

Answer these questions in relation to the stage designs and costumes in these photographs.

1. Which of the sets do you think makes the very best use of lighting and colour?

2. A stage design can sometimes be described as minimalist, i.e. the minimum amount of detail has been used. A few details, along with the lighting or colour, make the impact. This bare set design is very effective in creating a certain mood or atmosphere. Which of the four sets would you most describe as minimalist and why do you think it was used for this moment in the play?

3. *James and the Giant Peach* and *Annie* were both written for children. Which of the two photographs for these musicals do you think would most successfully appeal to a child's imagination?

4. Based on the impression you have of these four stage sets, which play would you most like to see performed? Give reasons for your answer.

Excerpt from *The Field* by John B. Keane

What I will learn:

stage directions, props, character and dialogue

PREPARE

W8.3

Read these stage directions for the opening scene of the play, *The Field*, by John B. Keane, (*pictured*) written in 1965 but set in 1950s Ireland.

```
STAGE DIRECTIONS FOR THE FIELD - OPENING SCENE

Action takes place in the bar of a public house in Carraigthomond, a small village
in the south west of Ireland.

Mick Flanagan is the owner of the public house and father to a large family of nine
children.

Leamy is his eldest son. Bird is a local cattle dealer who often comes into the pub.

Leamy Flanagan is playing pitch and toss with his younger brothers and sisters.

Enter the Bird O'Donnell.
```

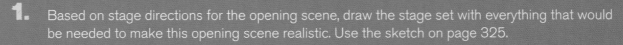

1. Based on stage directions for the opening scene, draw the stage set with everything that would be needed to make this opening scene realistic. Use the sketch on page 325.

2. Make a list of the props that would be required.

3. Decide on colours for the backdrop and the lighting.

4. Give instructions for the costumes, both the style of clothes and their colours.

READ

Now read the extract from *The Field* that follows on from these stage directions.

Excerpt from *The Field* by John B. Keane, Act 1, Scene 1

Bird: Give us a half of whiskey for God's sake, Leamy, to know would anything put a bit of heat in me. Leamy, do you hear me talking to you?

Leamy: 'Tis freezing!

Bird: 'Tis weather for snowmen and Eskimos. Where's your father? This place is getting more like Las Vegas with all the gambling going on.

Leamy: He's gone down to O'Connor's for the paper ... That'll be half a dollar.

Bird: Take your time, will you? Why aren't ye all at school?

Leamy: Still on our Easter holidays. How's trade?

Bird: Same as always ... Lousy!

(*Enter Mick Flanagan, scattering the children*)

Mick: Go upstairs, your dinner is ready. (*To Leamy*) I thought I told you to sweep out the shop!

Leamy: It's nearly finished.

Mick: You've been long enough about it. Right Nellie, up to Muddy. Good morning, Bird.

Bird: Good morning, Mick.

Mick: Did you clean out the store?

Leamy: I've done the half of it.

Mick: The half of it! – I told you to do the whole of it.

Leamy: I had to look after the kids while my mother was feeding the baby.

Mick: 'Tis too fond you are of hanging about with women and children. 'Tis a daughter you should have been, not a son.

(*Discovering another child*) And what are you doing hiding under the table, you little devil? (*To Leamy*) Go and ask your mother will the dinner be ready soon.

Leamy: Yes, Da.

Mick: And finish off that store or you'll hear about it from me.

Leamy: Yes, Da.

The playwright reveals character through dialogue, i.e. what the characters say and how they say it.

1. What quality or appearance would you look for in an actor to play **one** of the parts in this scene. If you wish, you can name a particular actor. If not, simply describe the kind of person needed.

Here is a sample answer from a student about Bird O'Donnell. Notice how the student backs up the choice of actor with quotations and references to what the character says. He also gives three pieces of evidence. He also gives three pieces of evidence for his points. Try to do the same in your answer.

SAMPLE ANSWER

I would choose X [*the student named an actor here*] a small, thin actor, to play the part of Bird. I have three reasons for my choice. First, Bird says he is feeling the cold, so I imagine him to be small and very skinny.

Second, he asks for a whiskey, so I imagine him looking like a man who doesn't eat much but drinks whiskey, so he has a blotchy, unhealthy face.

Finally, he seems impatient and cranky. He grumbles about the place being like Las Vegas and he says business is 'Same as always ... Lousy!' The actor I chose is perfect for this character. He often has a mean, cranky-looking expression on his thin, wrinkled face and he is very good at hunching his shoulders to make himself look stooped and old.

2. What is your impression of the relationship between Leamy and his father in this scene?

P I E

Perform 👥

- **Cast four characters:** Mick, Leamy, Bird and the little child.
- Discuss the **tone** and **volume** of voice that each character should use.
- Give **directions** to the actors for any **gestures** or **movements** that would suit each character.
- Give each character one **prop** or one item of **costume** that will help him to be 'in character'.
- **Perform** the scene.

Write a paragraph beginning:

I would/would not like to be Leamy Flanagan, because …

Excerpt from *Billy Elliot the Musical* by Lee Hall

character, relationships, tone and tempo

Billy Elliot, the son of a coalminer, has a gift for ballet. Unfortunately, this talent is out of place in the poor Northern English town he lives in, where the miners' strike has brought terrible hardship to families.

Mrs Wilkinson, teacher of a children's Saturday dance class, spots Billy's potential, teaches him to dance and gets him an audition for the Royal Ballet in London, who offer him a place.

Having delayed sharing the life-changing news of his acceptance, Billy now goes to the dance class to tell his teacher the good news, to thank her for believing in him, and to say his goodbyes.

This scene shows us that when we are emotionally overwhelmed by a situation we sometimes cannot express what we feel and instead say all the wrong things. We may even hide our deepest hurt in awkwardness, sarcasm and hard talk.

Excerpt from *Billy Elliot the Musical* by Lee Hall

The scene takes place in the room where Mrs Wilkinson teaches her Saturday afternoon ballet class.

Billy: Hello.

Mrs Wilkinson: Can I help you?

Billy: I just came to tell you – I got in.

Mrs Wilkinson: Oh.

Billy: My Dad thought you should know.

Mrs Wilkinson: It's alright. They sent uz a letter when it happened.

Billy: Miss, I know I should have come before to tell ya, but you know …

Mrs Wilkinson: I can imagine. Toilet break, girls! Debbie, go on.

Billy: Well, bye-bye Miss. And Miss, I just wanted to say thanks, Miss. For everything – what you did. I could never have done it without you, Miss.

Mrs Wilkinson: Yeah, well good luck then Billy.

Billy: Thanks. Well, goodbye.

Mrs Wilkinson: Goodbye then.

Billy: I'll miss you, Miss.

Mrs Wilkinson: No you won't, Billy. You'll get down there and realise what a crap little dancing school this was. What a complete second rate training I gave you. And you'll spend five years unlearning everything I taught you. It's alright, it's the way it is.

Billy: No, you don't understand, I'll come and see you every time I come back, Miss.

Mrs Wilkinson: Here's a piece of advice Billy. P___ off out of here. Start everything afresh and don't look back. There's sod all left for you here. You are very special. Now p___ off before I start to cry.

Billy: OK.

Mrs Wilkinson: And good luck, Billy.

Billy: Good luck as well, Miss.

Mrs Wilkinson: Yeah, thanks, Billy.

Mrs Wilkinson exits.

The Importance of Tone and Tempo

Tone of voice and **tempo** (the rhythm of the lines and whether they are spoken quickly or slowly) reveal emotions.

 When Mrs Wilkinson says, 'Can I help you?', how do you think she says it? Write a short paragraph describing how she should say these words. Use the words 'tone' and 'tempo' in your answer. Consider some of the following words for tone.

friendly	distant	delighted	cold	irritated
angry	astonished	jolly	tearful	hysterical

Consider some of the following words for tempo.

slowly	softly	gently
loudly	quickly	abruptly

(2) If you were the actor playing Billy, in what tone of voice would you say your 'hello'? Here are a few suggestions, but you may think of something different.

very low and gentle	loudly and cheerfully
with a question mark	musically
short and sharp	worried and nervously

 When you have chosen your tone, speak it aloud to the person beside you and compare with his or her way of saying it.

(3) Mrs Wilkinson says 'good luck' twice. Would you say there is a difference in the way she says it the first time and the way she says it the second time? Explain your answer.

(4) Mrs Wilkinson was disappointed in life. In her youth, she had hopes of being a famous dancer, but it didn't happen for her. Instead, she teaches this little Saturday class in a poor town. Do you think this may influence the way she responds to Billy's opportunity?

(5) In the speech beginning, 'No you won't, Billy', do you think Mrs Wilkinson should speak the lines slowly or quickly? What do you think she is feeling as she speaks these lines?

 Perform

Rehearse this scene aloud as a dramatic performance, experimenting with different tones of voice for each character. Imagine that you are feeling angry, sad, upset, confused, happy, or any other emotion that you think is present in this scene.

Exam Focus

Key Scenes

A **key scene** is a memorable scene of special importance or great emotion that makes a strong impact on the audience. It is the kind of moment that is used in a film trailer. It may be a scene of great drama, conflict, or development of plot or character. It could be a turning point in the action, or it may reveal the truth about characters or relationships.

Answer these questions in relation to the dramatic elements in a key scene in your studied play or in an extract from a play that you enjoyed.

(1) When and where is the key scene happening?

(2) What is happening?

(3) Who are the characters?

(4) What are the characters wearing?

(5) What props or furniture are featured in the scene or the backdrop to the scene?

(6) What are the emotions in the scene?

(7) What do you learn about the characters in the scene?

Drama Part 2 – Shakespeare

Shakespeare's life

Some of his famous characters

The Globe Theatre

Props

Blank verse

Key scenes

As I explore this collection I will learn about:

Soliloquy

Stage designs

Music and sound effects

Colour

Costume

Reading, speaking and interpreting Shakespeare's poetic dialogue

I will relate everything I learn to my studied Shakespeare play

What's So Great About Shakespeare?

W8.6 'He was not of an age but for all time.'

– Ben Jonson (17th century poet and playwright)

You might wonder, what's so great about Shakespeare? Why are his plays still performed? Why are they still studied? Here are some opinions as to why Shakespeare is considered great.

Shakespeare had a fantastic imagination and was a great storyteller. His thirty-seven plays are about honour, goodness, trust, ambition, regret, remorse, violence, feuds, murder, jealousy and greed. His comedies are about love and celebration. His tragedies are about calamity and the downfall of people who once were heroes. His histories tell stories of war, power and politics. His stories still speak to us because they are true to human nature.

Shakespeare had a great understanding of what it is to be human, and his characters display a huge range of powerful emotions: love, hate, disappointment, happiness, despair, fear, anger, sorrow, grief, hope, guilt, regret and shame. Some characters are good and noble, others are cunning and evil. No writer before him understood people the way he did.

He understood about family relationships, love and friendship. He knew that people are sometimes loyal and sometimes betray the trust of those they love.

His words, his rhythmic sentences and his expression of ideas are poetic. Nobody puts into words the things we all feel better than him.

'We are such stuff as dreams are made on, and our little life is rounded with a sleep.' (from *The Tempest*)

'I am one that loved not wisely but too well.' (from *Othello*)

'Oh beware, my lord, of jealousy, it is the green-eyed monster.' (from *Othello*)

'The course of true love never did run smooth.' (from *A Midsummer Night's Dream*)

Add another famous quote from Shakespeare that you know and that you believe to be true.

Soliloquy – An Important Dramatic Technique

The word **soliloquy** comes from the Latin *solus*, meaning 'alone', and *loqui*, meaning 'speak'. So from that you can guess that a soliloquy is when a person speaks without anyone around to hear them.

Shakespeare knew that there are intense moments in our lives when we reflect deeply on our actions, review things we have done or plan what we intend to do.

In soliloquy, a character speaks his inner mind aloud, expressing secrets, deep emotions, fears, worries and questions. Other characters don't hear, but we, the audience, do.

Shakespeare used soliloquy when he wanted us to understand or feel for a character. For example, Romeo expresses his deep love for Juliet in soliloquy. In *Macbeth*, Shakespeare uses soliloquy to make us feel sympathy for a good man who turned to evil, and now feels terrible guilt and remorse for the murders he committed.

See if you know the answer to this question.

The most famous soliloquy of all begins:

'To ___ or not to ___, that is the _____.'

It is spoken by H_____ in the play called 'H_____'.

Blank Verse

Shakespeare's characters mostly speak in **blank verse**. Blank verse is a line that can be broken down into ten syllables, in pairs of a weak sound (*x*), followed by a heavy sound (*/*).

If you tap out *I AM* five times, saying *AM* heavily, you'll get it:

x	/	x	/	x	/	x	/	x	/
I	*AM*	I	*AM*	I	*AM*	I	*AM*	I	*AM*

x	/	x	/	x	/	x	/	x	/
I	**HATE**	to	**SEE**	that	**EVE-**	ning	**SUN**	go	**DOWN**

From *Romeo and Juliet*:

x	/	x	/	x	/	x	/	x	/
But	**SOFT**	what	**LIGHT**	through	**YON**	der	**WIN**	dow	**BREAKS**

RESEARCH ZONE

W8.7

1. Using your **Show-Me Boards**, answer the following **True** or **False** questions. (You might also like to watch the short video clip, 'Shakespeare's Globe Theatre London', which features in Collection 11, *Oral Communication*, page 442.)

SHAKESPEARE	True/False	If false, what is the correct answer?
Born in 1564, died in 1616		
Place of birth: London		
Wrote seven plays		
Wrote fifty-four sonnets		
Wrote three kinds of plays: comedies, histories and musicals		

HIS THEATRE	True/False	If false, what is the correct answer?
'The World' was the most famous theatre for Shakespeare's plays.		
There were many famous actresses in the 1590s.		
Much Ado about Everything is a comedy.		
Three witches appear in the opening scene of *Hamlet*.		
One well-known play is *The Merchant of Verona*.		
Another is *A Midsummer Night's Moon*.		

2. Choose the correct number from the list below to complete these sentences.

   a) Shakespeare died at the age of _____.

   b) The word 'love' occurs a total of _____ times in his writing.

   c) He wrote _____ sonnets.

   d) His plays are set in _____ countries, from Scotland right across Europe and North Africa, into Turkey and Syria, with Italy being his favourite country in which to set his plays.

   e) He created over _____ characters in his plays.

   f) Shakespeare's plays were written between the years _____ and _____.

   g) The year 2016 is the _____ anniversary of Shakespeare's death.

2,191	900	12	1615
1590	154	52	400th

Exam Focus

Props are very important in Shakespeare's plays, for example knives or daggers in *The Merchant of Venice*, *Macbeth* and *Romeo and Juliet*. In Shakespeare's time, to give the impression of blood and bleeding, sheep's hearts would have been placed under the actors' clothing!

List **three props** that would be needed to perform your studied Shakespeare play. In which scenes would those props be needed?

Do You Speak Shakespeare?

Words and Phrases

Shakespeare had a way with words. The phrases, 'Knock, knock, who's there?' and 'What's done is done' both come from Shakespeare's play *Macbeth*. 'Good riddance' comes from *Troilus and Cressida*. 'Love is blind' comes from *The Merchant of Venice*.

You may be surprised to learn that Shakespeare made up all of the following phrases, which then became part of the English language.

as dead as a doornail	off with his head
all's well that ends well	wear your heart on your sleeve
a foregone conclusion	heart of gold
a laughing stock	lie low
a sorry sight	more fool you
cruel to be kind	neither here nor there
eaten out of house and home	vanish into thin air
fair play	the game is up
flesh and blood	heart of gold
green-eyed monster	wild goose chase
high time	brave new world
I have not slept one wink	break the ice
in stitches	for goodness' sake
what's done is done	

Match the Shakespeare line with the modern English translation.

Shakespeare

1. There's daggers in men's smiles.

2. Give every man thine ear, but few thy voice.

3. We are such stuff as dreams are made on/ And our little life is rounded on a sleep.

4. I like not fair terms and a villain's mind.

5. Let me be that I am and seek not to alter me.

6. Suspicion always haunts the guilty mind.

7. I have touched the highest point of all my greatness;/ I haste now to my setting: I shall fall/ Like a bright exhalation in the evening.

8. What's the matter,/ That you have such a February face?

9. The evil that men do lives after them/ The good is oft interred with their bones.

10. *Add another line from your studied Shakespeare play.*

Modern English Version

1. Don't try to change me. I want to be myself.

2. Guilty people always feel watched.

3. I was a famous star, but I will soon be a forgotten nobody.

4. Do more listening than talking.

5. People seem to be all charm, but behind it they are planning evil.

6. I'm very suspicious when a sly person seems to be offering a good deal.

7. People remember the awful things that someone did, they often forget the good.

8. What's wrong, why are you looking so angry?

9. Our lives are very short and fragile.

10. *Write the line you added in modern English.*

Insults

Shakespeare could combine words in ways that made for sharp, witty and quite wounding insults. In pairs, **A** and **B**, practise speaking these insults from his plays.

A. You showed your teeth like apes, and fawned like hounds

B. You ratcatcher, you fat guts, you scurvy knave

A. Thou loggerheaded maggot-pie!

B. Thou swag-bellied pignut!, cream-faced loon

A. Thou hell-hated ratsbane!

B. Thou urchin-snouted foot-licker!

A. Thou beetle-headed canker-blossom!

B. That bolting-hutch of beastliness, that swollen parcel of dropsies, that stuffed cloak-bag of guts, that roasted Manningtree ox with pudding in his belly

A. Thou clay-brained guts, thou knotty-pated fool

B. Out, you mad-headed ape, you Banbury cheese

A. Is thy name mouldy, thou ugly witch?

B. Thou cruel, ungrateful savage, poisonous hunch-back toad

A. Thou box of wrinkles, beggar, coward, son and heir of a mongrel bitch

B. Thou taffety punk, filthy bung

Tips for Speaking

- Imagine you are in a competition where the judges are wishing you well and want you to give your best performance.
- Aim to speak in an aggressive snarl, as you imagine an actor would hiss the words.
- Speak each word separately and enjoy the sounds of the words.
- Emphasise the t's, b's and d's.
- Remember that speaking slowly and in a low tone of voice can sometimes be more effective than rapid-fire shouting!

CREATE

You can create Shakespearean insults by combing his adjectives with his nouns and putting either *you or thou* in front of them. Speak what you create like an actor.

Adjectives	Nouns
boil-brained	lout
lumpish	baggage
puking	foot-licker
flap-mouthed	maggot-pie
beetle-headed	bladder
toad-spotted	scut
beslubbering	varlet
urchin-snouted	guts

Roald Dahl was surely inspired by Shakespeare when he wrote *Matilda*:

You blithering idiot! You festering gumboil! You flea-bitten fungus …
You bursting blister! You moth-eaten maggot! (*Miss Trunchbull*)

FUN FACT

In *A Midsummer Night's Dream*, Hermia calls Helena a 'painted maypole'. The comparison is appropriate because she is tall, thin, and wears a lot of colourful make-up.

Now you are ready to read and interpret a piece of Shakespeare's writing!

The Merchant of Venice

Portia and her maid, Nerissa, talk about the boys who fancy Portia.

The Italian city of Venice was considered a fashion capital in Shakespeare's time. In this scene, fabulously rich Portia is speaking to her maid, Nerissa. Portia's father has left an instruction in his will that three caskets – gold, silver and lead – must be placed before any man who wishes to marry her. Only one casket contains her portrait. If a man chooses the correct casket, he will become her husband. If not, he has to leave immediately.

This conversation between Portia and Nerissa is about the men who have travelled from all over Europe to try their luck. Portia is telling Nerissa why she despises every one of them.

The Merchant of Venice, Act 1, Scene 2

PORTIA

I pray thee, over-name them; and as thou namest them, I will describe them.

NERISSA

First, there is the Neapolitan prince.

> **Neopolitan:** from Naples

PORTIA

Ay, that's a colt indeed, for he doth nothing but talk of his horse; I am much afeard my lady his mother played false with a smith.

> **smith:** blacksmith

NERISSA

Then there is the County Palatine.

> **County Palatine:** from the Rhineland

PORTIA

He doth nothing but frown, he hears merry tales and smiles not: I fear he will prove the weeping philosopher when he grows old, being so full of unmannerly sadness in his youth. I had rather be married to a death's-head with a bone in his mouth than to either of these.

TOP TIP

When you read Shakespeare for the first time, it can seem like a jumble of strange words, but be patient. Use your imagination and try to get a 'feel' for the words and the mood – this will help you to understand what is going on, even if you don't understand every single word.

NERISSA

How say you by the French lord, Monsieur Le Bon?

PORTIA

God made him, and therefore let him pass for a man.
In truth, I know it is a sin to be a mocker: but,
he! why, he hath a horse better than the
Neapolitan's, a better bad habit of frowning than
the Count Palatine; he is every man in no man; if a
throstle sing, he falls straight a capering: he will
fence with his own shadow: if I should marry him, I
should marry twenty husbands.

> **throstle:** a little songbird

NERISSA

What say you, then, to Falconbridge, the young baron
of England?

PORTIA

You know I say nothing to him, for he understands
not me, nor I him: he hath neither Latin, French,
nor Italian, but, alas, who can
converse with a dumb-show? How oddly he is suited!
I think he bought his doublet in Italy, his round
hose in France, his bonnet in Germany and his
behaviour everywhere.

> **doublet:** buttoned-up, close-fitting jacket

> Here, Portia is jeering the English bad sense of dress

NERISSA

What think you of the Scottish lord, his neighbour?

PORTIA

That he hath a neighbourly charity in him, for he
borrowed a box of the ear of the Englishman and
swore he would pay him again when he was able.

> Scots had a fighting reputation

NERISSA

How like you the young German, the Duke of Saxony's nephew?

PORTIA

Very vilely in the morning, when he is sober, and most vilely in the afternoon, when he is drunk.

NERISSA

Do you not remember, lady, in your father's time, a Venetian, a scholar and a soldier?

PORTIA

Yes, yes, it was Bassanio; as I think, he was so called.

NERISSA

True, madam: he, of all the men that ever my foolish eyes looked upon, was the best deserving a fair lady.

PORTIA

I remember him well, and I remember him worthy of thy praise.

> Germans were said to be drinkers

Exam Focus

1 Name the suitor that best matches each description.

aggressive	
sad and gloomy	
badly dressed	
hyperactive	
drunk	
brave, intelligent and interesting	
obsessed with his horse	

2 These two images show the setting decided on by two different directors and stage designers for their productions of *The Merchant of Venice*.

A This director presented the stage as a Las Vegas casino with everyone chasing money.

B This director presented the stage with an overarching bridge reminiscent of the Rialto bridge in Venice and an exotic-looking black canopy.

Choose one of them as a stage backdrop for the Portia and Nerissa dialogue.

a) What do you like about the backdrop you chose?

b) Choose a piece of music that you would have playing as the audience sees this backdrop for the first time.

c) What kind of atmosphere do you think your chosen backdrop and music would create for the audience?

d) Write a short paragraph telling the lighting designer how to light up the stage. Choose two adjectives to describe each of the two backdrops.

3 Did you have an image in your head of Portia and Nerissa when you read the extract?

1 Here they are in the 2014 'Las Vegas' production. Portia is the blonde, glamorous prize in a TV gameshow.

2 Here they are in a 2004 film.

Compare and **contrast** the two photos using the three headings below. Add one more comparison or contrast that you notice.

Costume and jewellery	
Hairstyles and make-up	
Facial expressions or gestures	
One other comparison or contrast that you notice	

4 If you were the film or stage director, what quality or appearance would you look for in the actresses you would choose to play Portia and Nerissa? Give reasons based on what you know about the play and what you read in the scene.

5 Choose a scene from your studied Shakespeare play in which two characters are in conversation. Describe the characters, either on stage or in a film, using the following headings.

Costume and jewellery	
Hairstyles and make-up	
Your choice of actor/actress to play the roles	

Three Famous Soliloquies

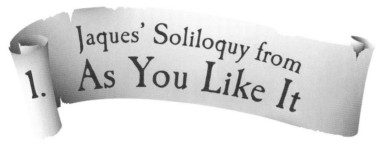

1. Jaques' Soliloquy from As You Like It

A gloomy man describes seven stages in life.

Jaques, the gloomy man in question, is a pessimistic character who in this scene gives us his view on life, from the cradle to the grave.

As You Like It, Act 2, Scene 7

JAQUES:
All the world's a stage,
And all the men and women merely players:
They have their exits and their entrances
And one man in his time plays many parts,
His acts being seven ages. At first the infant,
Mewling and puking in the nurse's arms;
Then, the whining schoolboy with his satchel
And shining morning face, creeping like snail
Unwillingly to school; and then the lover,
Sighing like furnace, with a woeful ballad
Made to his mistress' eyebrow; then a soldier,
Full of strange oaths and bearded like the pard,
Jealous in honour, sudden, and quick in quarrel,

YouTube

Look up 'Benedict Cumberbatch BBC Drama Trailer' on YouTube to hear the British actor reciting this soliloquy, accompanied by images from various BBC dramas.

The baby

The schoolboy

The boyfriend

The soldier

Seeking the bubble 'reputation'
Even in the cannon's mouth; and then the justice,
In fair round belly with good capon lined,
With eyes severe and beard of formal cut,
Full of wise saws and modern instances –
And so he plays his part; the sixth age shifts
Into the lean and slippered pantaloon,
With spectacles on nose and pouch on side,
His youthful hose well saved – a world too wide
For his shrunk shank – and his big manly voice,
Turning again toward childish treble, pipes
And whistles in his sound; last scene of all,
That ends this strange eventful history
Is second childishness and mere oblivion,
Sans teeth, sans eyes, sans taste, sans everything.

The judge

Capon judges: judges who took bribes

The elderly man

Old age and death

The speech in a nutshell

Life is a sad series of seven stages. Babies are crying, needy nuisances; young boys hate school; young men are rash and stupid; middle-aged men are fat, powerful people who become greedy and take bribes; old age is weak, pathetic and ridiculous.

Exam Focus

According to this soliloquy:

1 The baby

   a) Smiles and coos

   b) Bawls and vomits

   c) Sleeps peacefully

2 The schoolboy

   a) Hates school and whinges about it

   b) Sets off happily to school

   c) Has nothing to carry

3 The young boyfriend

   a) Is a great poet

   b) Writes stupid poems

   c) Takes it easy

4 The soldier

   a) Is humble and modest

   b) Is clean-shaven

   c) Is willing to lose his life for glory

5 The middle-aged judge

a) Is a fat, corrupt know-all

b) Eats very little

c) Has a rough beard

 6 The elderly man

a) Wears smart shoes

b) Is only a thin shadow of his former strong self

c) Has a strong, manly voice

 7 The very old man

a) Has lost his teeth and much of his senses

b) Has everything he ever wanted

c) Is full of energy

Write a letter to Jaques telling him that you either agree or disagree with his views on the stages of life.

 Perform a dramatic reading of this soliloquy. Appoint a narrator to speak lines 1–5.

Form seven small groups of three for each 'age'. One person reads the lines while the other two mime the actions.

SPEAK

 1. Re-read each of the seven ages carefully. Choose two of Jaques' opinions with which you agree or disagree. Defend your opinions with evidence and good reasons.

EXPLORE

2. Watch the BBC drama trailer once more and fill in the grid below, choosing a best moment in each case. Explain why you think this is the best moment.

Dramatic element	I think the best moment is	Because …
Costume		
Facial expressions		
Dramatic gestures		
Setting/colour/lighting		
Characters' emotions		

A man mourns the death of his friend and vows revenge.

Julius Caesar, the Roman emperor, has just been assassinated. His closest friend, Mark Antony, speaks to the assassins and pretends to accept their reasons. When they leave, he makes this speech over the body, revealing his true feelings and promising revenge.

Julius Caesar, Act 3, Scene 1

ANTONY:

O, pardon me, thou bleeding piece of earth,
That I am meek and gentle with these butchers!
Thou art the ruins of the noblest man
That ever lived in the tide of times.
Woe to the hand that shed this costly blood!
Over thy wounds now do I prophesy –
Which, like dumb mouths, do ope their ruby lips,
To beg the voice and utterance of my tongue –
A curse shall light upon the limbs of men;
Domestic fury and fierce civil strife
Shall cumber all the parts of Italy;
…
And Caesar's spirit, ranging for revenge,
With Ate by his side come hot from hell,
Shall in these confines with a monarch's voice
Cry 'Havoc', and let slip the dogs of war;
That this foul deed shall smell above the earth
With carrion men, groaning for burial.

W8.10

1. Find the lines in the soliloquy that match the modern equivalent.

a) I am soft with these thugs.

b) There will be the stench of walking, dead, unburied bodies.

c) Now I foretell the future.

d) Caesar's ghost will wander, the goddess of vengeance beside him.

e) Forgive me.

f) These killers will pay.

g) Your wounds are like red mouths asking me to avenge them.

h) Civil war will take over this country.

i) Chaos, destruction! Start the battles.

j) You were the greatest man that ever lived.

2. Imagine you are giving advice to an actor who has to perform this speech in an audition for the role. Explain clearly what the speech is about. Offer ideas on tone of voice (soft/loud); which words need emphasis; body positioning (sit/stand/kneel) and gestures. Use the words 'tone' and 'tempo' that you learned on page 331.

Exam Focus

(1) Each person writes the title of the Shakespeare play you are studying. Check each other's work, ensuring you have both used inverted commas around the play's name, have spelled it correctly and have used capital letters where necessary.

(2) Test each other on the spelling of the name, 'William Shakespeare'.

(4) Together, choose a soliloquy from your studied play and name the character who speaks it.

Briefly, **A** explains to **B** the situation that occurred just before this soliloquy. Each then write the explanation.

Briefly, **B** explains to **A** the thoughts and feelings that are expressed by the character in the soliloquy. Each then write a paragraph about these thoughts and feelings.

Then, working separately, you each write any five of its lines in modern English.

Swap your work over. You must each find the quotations in the soliloquy that match your modern English versions.

SHAKESPEARE.

3. Romeo's Soliloquy from Romeo and Juliet

Love-struck boy observes girl from a distance.

It is night time. Romeo, who has met Juliet and fallen in love with her, is hiding in the orchard below her bedroom window. She cannot sleep and comes out to stand on the balcony, not knowing that she is being watched. He looks up and quietly speaks his feelings in soliloquy.

Romeo and Juliet, Act 2, Scene 2

ROMEO:

But, soft! what light through yonder window breaks?
It is the east, and Juliet is the sun.   A metaphor: Juliet is the sun about to appear
Arise, fair sun, and kill the envious moon,   The moon is waning, the sun is rising
Who is already sick and pale with grief,
That thou her maid art far more fair than she: The moon is sad to be so outdone/outshone
Be not her maid, since she is envious;
Her vestal livery is but sick and green   In ancient times, the vestal virgins wore green
And none but fools do wear it; cast it off.
It is my lady, O, it is my love!   At this moment, he sees her
O, that she knew she were!
She speaks yet she says nothing: what of that?
Her eye discourses; I will answer it.
I am too bold, 'tis not to me she speaks:
Two of the fairest stars in all the heaven,   Two stars have disappeared for a while and want
Having some business, do entreat her eyes   her bright eyes to take their place
To twinkle in their spheres till they return.
What if her eyes were there, they in her head?
The brightness of her cheek would shame those stars,
As daylight doth a lamp; her eyes in heaven   If her bright eyes shone in the night sky, the birds
Would through the airy region stream so bright   would think it was daytime and start singing
That birds would sing and think it were not night.
See, how she leans her cheek upon her hand!
O, that I were a glove upon that hand,
That I might touch that cheek!

1. Complete this synopsis of the extract using the words from the list below.

I see a light in that _____. It's Juliet. She is the _____, shining and fabulous, brighter than the _____. Be my love! Her_____ seem to be moving but I can't hear her. I wish she knew how much I love her. Two of the brightest stars in the sky have asked for her _____ to take their place while they go away for a while. Her eyes shine brighter than the stars. Her cheek is bright and beautiful. If her eyes were in the sky they would light the world so brightly that _____ would think night was day. Look at her putting her _____ on her hand. I would love to be a _____ on that hand.

glove   cheek   sunrise   birds

eyes   lips   moon   window

2. Complete the sample answer below regarding the character of Romeo by adding quotations from the soliloquy that support the various points. Remember to place the quotations in inverted commas.

P I E

SAMPLE ANSWER

This soliloquy shows us that Romeo is dramatic and imaginative. His opening question and answer is about light breaking through the darkness: '_____ _____,'

He is a complete romantic. He is love-struck and besotted by Juliet, as can be seen in this line: '_____,'

He uses powerful, energetic verbs such as 'A_____e' and 'K_____.' He wishes that she would know how much he loves her so that she would fall as quickly in love with him as he has with her: '_____,'

His 'O's' and exclamations tell us how excited and impatient he feels. He follows her every slight movement, never taking his eyes off her: '_____ _____,'

His language is poetic, full of beautiful images of light and energy (sun, moon, stars, lamp, heaven, birds): '_____,'

He is so overcome with love that he can hardly express his feelings. He compares Juliet with the stars, but even the stars are pale in comparison with her luminous beauty: '_____,'

He is mesmerised by the beauty of her cheeks, her eyes, her hand. He is gentle and tender by nature. He wishes that he could touch her hand: '_____ _____,'

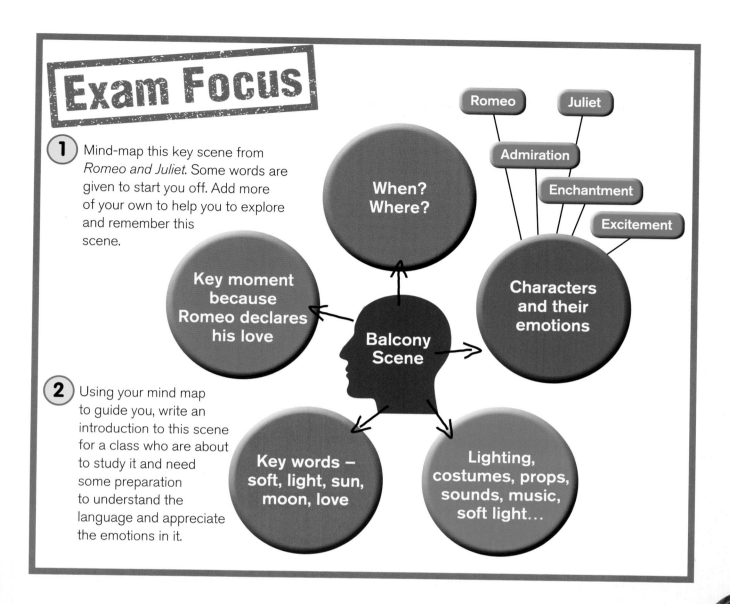

Exam Focus

1 Mind-map this key scene from *Romeo and Juliet*. Some words are given to start you off. Add more of your own to help you to explore and remember this scene.

2 Using your mind map to guide you, write an introduction to this scene for a class who are about to study it and need some preparation to understand the language and appreciate the emotions in it.

Mind map elements:

- When? Where?
- Key moment because Romeo declares his love
- Balcony Scene
- Characters and their emotions
  - Romeo
  - Juliet
  - Admiration
  - Enchantment
  - Excitement
- Key words – soft, light, sun, moon, love
- Lighting, costumes, props, sounds, music, soft light…

Henry IV Part I

A London Dad gives out to his son for his disgraceful behaviour.

Harry, Prince of Wales, is heir to the throne of England. Unfortunately, he is also the black sheep of the royal family. His father, King Henry, is exasperated with Harry's behaviour and his reputation for mixing with low-life pub crawlers around London. He has called his son to a meeting in the palace so that he can tell Harry to change his ways and make himself acceptable to the people as the future king of England.

King Henry explains how he himself was distant with his subjects and seldom seen in public. The result was that people were excited when he made his rare appearances and were in awe of him.

He compares his own gracious, dignified behaviour with the poor behaviour of the previous king, and warns Harry that he will follow in that line if he does not mend his ways.

EXPLORE

1. Looking at this photo, taken from a BBC adaptation of the play, what do you think might be happening?

2. What emotions can you see in each character?

3. What signs of wealth and/or power can you see?

4. Who do you think is doing most of the talking?

5. What does the facial expression of the young man tell you?

6. Have you ever been in a similar situation? Who was involved? What was the situation?

WATCH

Watch this scene between Prince Harry and his father. This is a brilliant performance by the actors Jeremy Irons as King Henry and Tom Hiddleston as Harry.

While you watch, look out for a number of dramatic gestures made by King Henry. The final gesture comes as a shock. It was not in the stage directions, but was rather a decision taken by the director and the actors on how to play the scene.

EXPLORE

W8.12

Fill in this grid describing the dramatic elements in the video clip of this scene.

Setting/colour/lighting	
Costume	
Voices/facial expressions	
Dramatic gestures	
Signs of conflict	
Characters' emotions	

Learn to Thought-Track

When you 'thought-track' a scene, you carefully track the thoughts and statements of the characters, noting their line of thinking as they express themselves in words and gestures.

Thought-track Henry's speech by completing the sentences given in the orange tabs, putting the lines spoken by the King into modern English.

Extract from *Henry IV, Part I*, Act 3, Scene 2

KING HENRY

The hope and expectation of thy time
Is ruin'd, and the soul of every man
Prophetically doth forethink thy fall.

> 'Everyone thinks that you ____'

Had I so lavish of my presence been,
So common-hackney'd in the eyes of men,
So stale and cheap to vulgar company,
Opinion, that did help me to the crown,
Had still kept loyal to possession

> 'When I was your age, if I had behaved as you're behaving ____'

And left me in reputeless banishment,
A fellow of no mark nor likelihood.
By being seldom seen, I could not stir
But like a comet I was wonder'd at;

> 'Because I was out and about in public so seldomly ____'

That men would tell their children 'This is he;'
Others would say 'Where, which is Bolingbroke?'
And then I stole all courtesy from heaven,
And dress'd myself in such humility
That I did pluck allegiance from men's hearts,
Loud shouts and salutations from their mouths,
The skipping king, he ambled up and down
With shallow jesters and rash bavin wits,

> 'The undignified former king behaved like a fool. He hung around with ____'

Soon kindled and soon burnt; carded his state,
Mingled his royalty with capering fools,
Enfeoff'd himself to popularity;
So when he had occasion to be seen,
He was but as the cuckoo is in June,
Heard, not regarded.
And in that very line, Harry, standest thou;

> 'And you are just like him now, because you ____'

For thou has lost thy princely privilege

With vile participation: not an eye
But is a-weary of thy common sight,
Save mine, which hath desired to see thee more;
Which now doth that I would not have it do,
Make blind itself with foolish tenderness.

PRINCE HARRY

I shall hereafter, my thrice gracious lord,
Be more myself.

'I would like _____'

'I will try to _____'

Exam Focus

W8.13

Review the grid (p. 354) you used to examine the dramatic elements of the video clip of this scene from *Henry IV, Part I*. Complete this grid in relation to one scene that you enjoyed in your studied Shakespeare play.

Romeo Kills Tybalt

A turning point in the story of Romeo and Juliet.

There are two feuding families in Shakespeare's *Romeo and Juliet* play, the Capulets (Juliet's family) and the Montagues (Romeo's family). In this scene, set on the streets of Verona, Romeo, who has secretly married Juliet, comes across a fight between young men from the Montague and Capulet clans, and tries to stop it. Tybalt, a cousin of Juliet, insults Romeo, who refuses to fight. His friend Mercutio steps in to defend Romeo's honour. Tybalt stabs and fatally wounds Mercutio. In rage and despair, Romeo stabs and kills Tybalt.

Romeo and Juliet, Act 3, Scene 1

TYBALT

Romeo, the hate I bear thee can afford
No better term than this, – thou art a villain.

Tybalt challenges and provokes Romeo

ROMEO

Tybalt, the reason that I have to love thee
Doth much excuse the appertaining rage
To such a greeting: villain am I none;
Therefore farewell; I see thou know'st me not.

Romeo will not be provoked into fighting

TYBALT

Boy, this shall not excuse the injuries
That thou hast done me; therefore turn and draw.

Tybalt tells him to draw his sword

ROMEO

I do protest, I never injured thee,
But love thee better than thou canst devise,
Till thou shalt know the reason of my love:
And so, good Capulet, – which name I tender
As dearly as my own, – be satisfied.

MERCUTIO

O calm, dishonourable, vile submission!
Alla stoccata carries it away.
Draws
Tybalt, you rat-catcher, will you walk?

Mercutio steps in and challenges Tybalt

TYBALT

What wouldst thou have with me?

MERCUTIO

Good king of cats, nothing but one of your nine
lives; that I mean to make bold withal, and as you
shall use me hereafter, drybeat the rest of the
eight. Will you pluck your sword out of his pitcher
by the ears? Make haste, lest mine be about your
ears ere it be out.

TYBALT

I am for you.
Drawing

Mercutio and Tybalt fight

ROMEO

Gentle Mercutio, put thy rapier up.

MERCUTIO

Come, sir, your passado.
They fight

ROMEO

Draw, Benvolio; beat down their weapons.
Gentlemen, for shame, forbear this outrage!
Tybalt, Mercutio, the prince expressly hath
Forbidden bandying in Verona streets:
Hold, Tybalt! good Mercutio!
TYBALT under ROMEO's arm stabs MERCUTIO, and flies with his followers

MERCUTIO

I am hurt.
A plague o' both your houses! I am sped.
Is he gone, and hath nothing?

Mercutio knows that he will die

BENVOLIO

What, art thou hurt?

MERCUTIO

Ay, ay, a scratch, a scratch; marry, 'tis enough.
Where is my page? Go, villain, fetch a surgeon.
Exit Page

ROMEO

Courage, man; the hurt cannot be much.

MERCUTIO

No, 'tis not so deep as a well, nor so wide as a
church-door; but 'tis enough, 'twill serve: ask for
me to-morrow, and you shall find me a grave man. I
am peppered, I warrant, for this world. A plague o'
both your houses! Zounds, a dog, a rat, a mouse, a
cat, to scratch a man to death! a braggart, a
rogue, a villain, that fights by the book of
arithmetic! Why the devil came you between us? I
was hurt under your arm.

Mercutio curses both families

ROMEO

I thought all for the best.

MERCUTIO

Help me into some house, Benvolio,
Or I shall faint. A plague o' both your houses!
They have made worms' meat of me: I have it,
And soundly too: your houses!
Exit MERCUTIO and BENVOLIO

ROMEO

This gentleman, the prince's near ally,
My very friend, hath got his mortal hurt
In my behalf; my reputation stain'd
With Tybalt's slander, – Tybalt, that an hour
Hath been my kinsman! O sweet Juliet,
Thy beauty hath made me effeminate
And in my temper soften'd valour's steel!
Re-enter BENVOLIO

> Romeo says Mercutio died for him

BENVOLIO

O Romeo, Romeo, brave Mercutio's dead!
That gallant spirit hath aspired the clouds,
Which too untimely here did scorn the earth.

ROMEO

This day's black fate on more days doth depend;
This but begins the woe, others must end.

BENVOLIO

Here comes the furious Tybalt back again.

ROMEO

Alive, in triumph! and Mercutio slain!
Away to heaven, respective lenity,
And fire-eyed fury be my conduct now!
Re-enter TYBALT
Now, Tybalt, take the villain back again,
That late thou gavest me; for Mercutio's soul
Is but a little way above our heads,
Staying for thine to keep him company:
Either thou, or I, or both, must go with him.

> Romeo will take revenge

TYBALT

Thou, wretched boy, that didst consort him here,
Shalt with him hence.

ROMEO

This shall determine that.
They fight; TYBALT falls

BENVOLIO

Romeo, away, be gone!
The citizens are up, and Tybalt slain.
Stand not amazed: the prince will doom thee death,
If thou art taken: hence, be gone, away!

ROMEO

O, I am fortune's fool!

> Romeo is a marked man in Verona

> Romeo knows this is a catastrophe for him

Mind Map

Mind-map this key scene in *Romeo and Juliet*. Some words are given to start you off. Add more of your own to help you to explore and remember the scene.

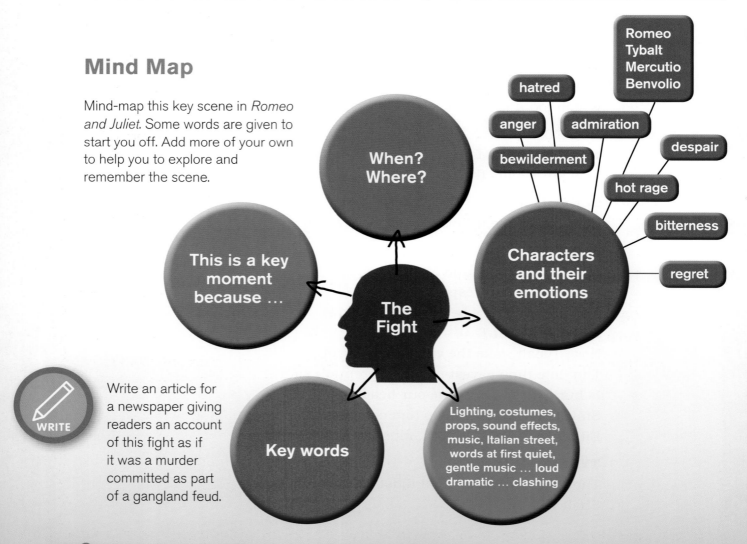

WRITE Write an article for a newspaper giving readers an account of this fight as if it was a murder committed as part of a gangland feud.

Exam Focus

W8.14

Mind-map another key scene in your studied Shakespeare play.

Create a Mind Map with the 'Title of your Play' in the centre and the following offshoots:

- Major male characters
- Major female characters
- Minor male characters
- Minor female characters
- Setting
- Three key scenes that I will mind-map (give each one a title)
- Six key quotes that I will learn

Final Exam Focus

Analysis *n.*

Definition: A careful examination, description or study of all the parts that are needed to make something

When you write as an examination candidate, you must pay special attention to accuracy in spelling and punctuation. With that in mind:

(1) Rewrite, punctuate and divide this piece into two paragraphs. Remember capital letters, full stops, commas, question marks, inverted commas and apostrophes where they are needed.

romeo and juliet a play written by william shakespeare is set in verona italy it is the story of two feuding families the capulets and the montagues and contains many famous scenes such as romeos soliloquy in the garden of juliets house its characters are many and varied romeo and juliet are romantic gentle and idealistic while tybalt is aggressive and angry when he sees romeo at the party he asks for his rapier and says he will strike him dead

(2) Based on the corrections you made to the piece above, write **five rules** on good punctuation that you would teach to examination students. Give an example for each rule. The first one has been done for you.

Names of people are always written with capital letters, e.g. Romeo.

(3) Read back over the test you completed at the beginning of the *Drama* collection (p. 322). Then write an analysis of a key scene in your studied play in which you include as many of the following words as possible:

act	scene	backdrop	plot	set	dialogue
characters	props	lighting	costumes	music	colour
gestures	soliloquy	emotions	sub-plot	theme	
facial	sound	major	minor		
expressions	effects	relationships	relationships		

A Novel Approach

Book covers and blurbs

Book advertisements

Tracking a theme

Character development

Setting

As I explore this collection I will learn about:

Key moments

Genre

Relationship development

The gothic genre

Symbolism

I will relate everything I learn about novels to my **studied novel**

Learning Outcomes
R4, R6, R7, R13, W7, W8

What do you know about ... Novels?

To help you revise what novels are all about, rewrite the following by inserting the correct words from the list.

Novels are well-developed stories featuring an _____, f_____ p_____ of c_____, _____ and r_____. The modern novel dates back to the eighteenth century and some of the first novels are thought to be *Robinson Crusoe* and *Moll Flanders*. Novels are put into different categories called _____, depending on what type of novel it is.

Novels often feature a _____ and _____ who go on a long journey to reach the end of their crisis. Authors can spend more time developing the character's personality and how they react with the people they share _____ with.

Sometimes, a novel can have the main p_____ and a sub-_____, which is another storyline running alongside the main _____ but it is not the most important one. Usually the _____ and sub-_____ are connected. Novels can afford to have endings which are c_____-h_____ as they can have a _____.

Certain novels are known as _____ because they have all the elements of great storytelling. Novels are longer in length than short stories so authors can create lots of descriptive passages featuring detailed i_____ and symbolism. This helps the reader really imagine the world that is being created.

Many of the classic films that we know were originally n_____. Directors saw potential in their compelling characters and intriguing plotlines. Films like *Jurassic Park*, *The Lord of the Rings* and *Jaws* were all based on novels.

relationships	first point of conflict
sequel	novels
imagery	cliff-hangers
antagonist	climax
genres	plot (x 5)
opening	classics
protagonist	resolution

Do Judge a Book by its Cover!

What I will learn:

to evaluate book covers and blurbs

You've heard of that old adage (a short but memorable saying): Never judge a book by its cover. However, the cover of a novel is the first point of contact with the reader. Covers will influence whether a reader buys a book or not.

Book covers feature:

- The **name** of the **author**
- The **title** of the book
- **Testimonials** – people recommending the book
- **Illustrations/photographs** – pictures are very important to catch the reader's attention – or maybe sometimes just text
- The name of the publisher
- Any extra or important information, e.g. the name of the illustrator

The **spine** of a book is the part you can see when books are stocked on a shelf. The spine also features the name of the book and the author, as it's often the only part of the book that can be seen in bookstores.

The **blurb** of a book is the short introduction/summary of the plot you can find on the back cover.

1. Examine the cover of this classic book, *Pride and Prejudice* by Jane Austen, and fill in the missing words.

- The _____ of the book is *Pride and Prejudice* and the _____ is Jane Austen.

- The black and white book cover uses an _____ of a man and woman, separated by a tree. This leads me to think that the story might be set in the countryside and that these two people might be a couple. Maybe they are arguing because they are separated by the tree and are not facing each other, or maybe they haven't met yet.

- Written above the man are the words '_____ _____', so that points to the idea that the two characters might be in a complex relationship, with one person's love for the other not being returned.

- The _____ says that the story is a 'classic tale of love and values'. It also tells me more about the book, and confirms my suspicions about this couple.

- The _____ of the book features the title of the book and the logo of the _____, which is a penguin.

- The back cover also features a _____ from Claire Tomalin saying that this book has always been one of the author's most popular books.

2. Choosing a novel you haven't read, examine its cover, referring to the features of a book cover as listed.

3. Match the following book descriptions with their book covers.

 1

This cover uses a peculiar illustration of an animal. The animal is looking out at the audience, and looks slightly sinister. He is smoking a pipe and holding an object of some sort with wires. This makes me think that this book is not just about animals, despite its title. In the background is a thunder cloud and a radio on a fence. The fence has barbed wire running through it, which suggests something prison-like.

2

This cover's illustration is an overhead shot of a boat at sea. In the sea there seems to be a variety of sea creatures of various sizes, suggesting that this story takes place in tropical waters. It is a strange illustration of a person on a boat with a tiger. This makes the reader curious, as it is a very unusual situation to have a tiger on a boat, let alone with a human! The testimonial at the top suggests that it is a powerful story that will have a profound effect on the reader. There is also a big circle on the front saying that it has won the Man Booker Prize, which makes me think that the book must be worth reading.

 3

This book cover uses black and white very effectively, with it being divided in half. This purposeful use of these particular colours suggests a theme of division and perhaps even racism. However, the fact that the black X is not mirrored by a white O, but rather an orange O, is confusing. The words 'black and white, right and wrong', suggest conflict within the story. Noughts and crosses is a children's game, so the main characters could possibly be young. One of these main characters could be 'Callum', as that character has been given their own short story within the novel. This book is part of an 'award-winning sequence', so it must be popular.

 4

This book cover uses the colours blue and green predominantly. The illustrations – a flying car and a castle in the clouds – suggest magic, so you know immediately this book will be about fantasy. The font doesn't suggest anything in particular, but it makes the name of the character the most important part of the title. The blurb tells us this is the second book in a series so we know the first must have been successful. The testimonials add to the appeal of the book.

Book Advertisements

to explore book advertisements

Look at each advertisement. The publishers have used various different formats and means to promote their books: on a poster; through a website dedicated to books; in a trailer; and in a tweet. Which do you think would be more successful in advertising a book? Explain your choice.

You can't blend in when you were born to stand out.

WONDER

R. J. PALACIO

Tips for Creating a Trailer

- Work in groups
- Use a camera and editing equipment like Windows Movie Maker
- Introduce your main character(s) with one line of dialogue
- Add suitable music
- Don't give too much away

Eeva Lancaster
@eevalancaster

Follow

#RT 🌋🌋🌋 MORIUM 🌋🌋🌋
RAW, DARK, GRIPPING TALE
booklaunch.io/s.j.hermann/mo…
#IARTG
★★★★★ MUST READ
#thriller #PDF1
#book

RETWEETS 16   LIKES 3

11:34 p.m · 8 Aug 2015

You Tube

Look up 'Wonder book trailer' on YouTube to see a video advertising *Wonder* by R. J. Palacio.

CREATE Pick one of these advertising formats to advertise a novel you have studied.

Fiction [1]

What I will learn:

to identify and track a theme throughout a novel

The novel *Chalkline* was written in 2009 by Jane Mitchell. It deals with a wide variety of powerful themes. When studying any novel, it is vital to identify the themes and issues at an early stage in the story. An author deliberately presents themes in a story in order to get the reader thinking and questioning.

  PREPARE What novels have you studied in school so far? You can think back to primary school if you wish. In groups of three, create a list of the novels you have studied and the themes you have encountered in them. From these themes, draw up a list of **recurring themes** (in other words, themes that keep popping up again and again).

 READ **Read the following blurb from the novel *Chalkline* by Jane Mitchell, which gives you a little more information about this story.**

Rafiq's turn came and he stepped up to the chalk line. It reached the top of his ear. 'This one is big enough. He goes in the truck. He's our first.'

Rafiq is only nine when Kashmiri Freedom Fighters raid his village in search of new recruits. Tall for his age, he is the first boy to cross the chalk line into a life of brutality and violence. Jameela cannot forget her brother. While Rafiq is trained to kill in the rebel camp high in the mountains, she keeps his memory alive. When finally their paths cross again, Rafiq is unrecognisable as the boy who left the village. Will Jameela know him?

 EXPLORE

1. What is the purpose of the blurb?

2. Having read the blurb, would you wish to read the novel?

3. Based on this blurb, can you suggest some of the themes that may be addressed in this novel?

STUDYING YOUR NOVEL – *Themes*

When studying your novel you will be expected to:

- **Identify** the main/central themes of the story. For example, the **main themes** in *Chalkline* are armed conflict and human rights.

- **Identify** the sub-/secondary themes of the story. For example, two of the **sub-themes** in *Chalkline* are gender roles and education.

- **Track** these themes from when they are first suggested to the resolution of the story. For example, in *Chalkline* there is rarely a chapter in the book when the main themes of armed conflict and abuse of human rights are not obvious to the reader or lurking in the back of the reader's mind.

- Explain how the theme is emphasised through **key moments**.

- **Assess** how the lives and actions of the characters are connected to the theme and affected by it.

- **Understand** the writer's view on the theme from reading the story.

TOP TIP

Themes are rarely stated by an author. They are usually **inferred** (implied) or **suggested**.

Identifying Theme

  Read the following extracts from *Chalkline*. For each section, try to identify the theme you think the author is writing about from the list on the right. Choose a **maximum** of three themes per extract.

EXTRACT	POSSIBLE THEMES
EXTRACT ONE Jameela longed to go to school, but in her village, girls didn't attend lessons. Instead they stayed at home and helped their mothers with cooking and cleaning and household tasks. Only the boys went to school, where they learned prayers and writing and reading. Rafiq was clever in school, but once it was over for the day, he threw his books aside to run and play football with his friends in the square.	• Sport • Communication • Separation • Racism • Power • Education • Family • Armed conflict/war • Gender roles • Friendships • Death and loss • Human rights

EXTRACT	POSSIBLE THEME
EXTRACT TWO Two boys next to Rafiq were crying, sobbing miserably, their arms round each other. 'We're going to die,' they spluttered. 'We'll never see our families again and we'll be killed.'	• Sport • Communication • Separation • Racism • Power • Education • Family • Armed conflict/war • Gender roles • Friendships • Death and loss • Human rights
EXTRACT THREE Back at their home Jameela's mother lit the stove and began to prepare food like she always did, except that tears kept dripping from her face and sizzling in the hot pan. Mahmoud sat in the dirt, lost about what to do now that Rafiq wasn't coming home. The baby sucked his fist and rocked in the hammock while Afrah stood holding Jameela's hand, gazing up at her, her brown eyes round and frightened. Jameela waited for a while, looking to her mother, but there was no discussion, no change in routine.	• Sport • Communication • Separation • Racism • Power • Education • Family • Armed conflict/war • Gender roles • Friendships • Death and loss • Human rights
EXTRACT FOUR The police then told them that a bus carrying pilgrims to a holy festival in a distant village had been blown up in the explosions, men and women killed and injured. The authorities said the mines had only been set that morning, and they were very interested in what the village people had to tell them.	• Sport • Communication • Separation • Racism • Power • Education • Family • Armed conflict/war • Gender roles • Friendships • Death and loss • Human rights

Developing Theme

Authors are faced with the challenge of developing a theme throughout a story. In every story there are **main themes** and **sub-themes**. A main theme will be obvious from chapter to chapter, whereas a sub-theme may only appear during certain incidents in the story. The theme is something that the author *wants* you to discuss or be informed about.

Development of a Theme in *Chalkline*

Now we will examine how the author develops the theme of gender roles throughout *Chalkline*. The following extracts are taken in chronological order (in the order they occur in the book).

> Jameela longed to go to school, but in her village, girls didn't attend lessons. Instead they stayed at home and helped their mothers with cooking and cleaning and household tasks. Only the boys went to school, where they learned prayers and writing and reading. Rafiq was clever in school, but once it was over for the day, he threw his books aside to run and play football with his friends in the square.

In this first extract, the narrator provides us with the setting and context of the story and in doing this highlights the theme of gender roles.

In this second extract the theme of gender roles is reinforced through the attitudes of a central character.

> 'Teacher says to learn something new every day, Papa', Rafiq dared to answer. 'Jameela's learning to read. She's clever. She knows her numbers already.' Jameela smiled up at her father, but he spat against the wall the red juice from the betel nut he was chewing. 'And she'll forget them quickly enough when she is married and she is busy preparing food, taking care of her husband and giving him children. Those are the skills she needs to learn.'

> They turned to Rafiq, seeking to bring him into their group, but he looked away from them. He could understand how they felt, but they shouldn't cry. It wasn't honourable behaviour and they were shaming their families by weeping in the dirt like little girls, by showing their emotions so openly. Had they no pride?

In this extract, the setting and circumstances are different, but the theme of gender roles is demonstrated powerfully through the attitude of Rafiq. He sees the crying boys as being 'like little girls', which reinforces male and female roles.

In this extract, the description of the police officer portrays him as intimidating and easily frustrated. The woman is portrayed as lacking in confidence and embarrassed. This extract is taken from later in the book and can be seen as a natural progression from the attitudes highlighted in the first extract.

> Her voice faded under the irritated glare of the police officer. He pulled out a sheaf of forms and slapped them on the counter. He snatched up a pen, which he laid on the forms, and looked at them again.
>
> 'You need to fill these in.'
>
> Her mother paused, then shook her head with shame, dropping her gaze to the counter. 'I'm sorry,' she said. 'It's not possible.'

EXPLORE

1. What type of things are women restricted from doing, according to the extracts?
2. How are men/boys expected to act in this society?
3. How do these gender roles affect the woman in the final extract?

You are in charge of giving a presentation to the Parent's Association of your school on behalf of a well-known charity who campaign for children's rights. Research the facts about child soldiers in different parts of the world. What can your school do to help?

Exam Focus

(1) Apart from the theme indicated at the beginning, what other themes arose during your reading of the above extracts from *Chalkline*?

(2) How successful was the author of your studied novel in developing either a main theme or sub-theme throughout the story?

(3) Choose a key moment that expresses the theme of your studied novel and explain how the author brought the theme to life.

W9.3

TOP TIP

You can use PowerPoint, Prezi, Vimeo and PicCollage to help you display images and text. For more details about making presentations, see Collection 11, *Oral Communication*.

Fiction [2]

to understand and explore an author's point of view

The story of Callum and Sephy in the novel *Noughts & Crosses* by Malorie Blackman (*pictured*) unfolds in an alternate society where the Noughts fight for equality with the Crosses. When you read through the extract below, consider some of the themes and issues being raised by the author. Blackman herself does not hide the fact that one of her motivations in writing the book was 'a desire to tackle the subject of racism head on'.

What major issues in the world today concern you? If you were to write a novel, what major issues would you like to highlight?

Extract from *Noughts & Crosses* by Malorie Blackman

I turned back to the sea. It shone like a shattered mirror, each fragment reflecting and dazzling. It never ceased to amaze me just how beautiful the sand and the sea and the gentle breeze on my face could be. My family's private beach was my favourite place in the whole world. Kilometres of coastline that was all ours, with just a couple of signs declaring that it was private property and some old wooden fencing at each end, through which Callum and I had made a gap. And I was here with my favourite person. I turned to look at Callum. He was looking at me, the strangest expression on his face.

'What's the matter?'

'Nothing.'

'What're you thinking?' I asked.

'About you and me.'

'What about us?'

Callum turned to look out over the sea. 'Sometimes I wish there was just you and me and no-one else in the whole world.'

'We'd drive each other crazy, wouldn't we?' I teased.

At first I thought that Callum wasn't going to answer.

'Sephy, d'you ever dream of just … escaping? Hopping on the first boat or plane you come across and letting it take you away.' There was no mistaking the wistfully wishful tone in Callum's voice. 'I do …'

'Where would you go?'

'That's just the point,' Callum said with sudden bitterness. 'This place is like the whole world and the whole world is like this place. So where could I go?'

'This place isn't so bad, is it?' I asked, gently.

'Depends on your point of view,' Callum replied. 'You're on the inside, Sephy. I'm not.'

I couldn't think of an answer to that, so I didn't reply. We both sat in silence for a while longer.

'Wherever you went, I'd go with you,' I decided. 'Though you'd soon get bored with me.'

Callum sighed. A long, heartfelt sigh which immediately made me feel like I'd failed some test I hadn't even known I was taking.

'We'd better get on with it,' he said at last. 'What's the lesson for today, teacher?'

Disappointment raced through me. But then, what did I expect? *'Sephy, I could never be bored of you, with you, around you. You're exciting, scintillating, overwhelming company!'* Yeah, right! Dream on, Sephy!!

'So what're we doing today?' Callum's voice was tinged with impatience.

'OK! OK!' I said, exasperated. Honestly! The sun was too warm and the sea was too blue to do any schoolwork.

'Callum, you've already passed the entrance exam. Why do we still have to do this?'

'I don't want to give any of the teachers an excuse to kick me out.'

'You haven't even started school yet and already you're talking about being kicked out?' I was puzzled. Why was he so cynical about my school? 'You've got nothing to worry about. You're in now. The school accepted you.'

'Being in and being accepted are two different things.' Callum shrugged. 'Besides, I want to learn as much as I can so I don't look like a complete dunce.'

I sat up suddenly. 'I've just had a thought. Maybe you'll be in my class. Oh, I do hope so,' I said eagerly. 'Wouldn't that be great?'

'You think so?'

I tried – and failed, I think – to keep the hurt out of my voice. 'Don't you?'

Callum looked at me and smiled. 'You shouldn't answer a question with a question,' he teased.

'Why not?' I forced myself to smile back.

Taking me by surprise, Callum pushed me over onto the sand. Indignant, I scrambled up to kneel in front of him.

'D'you mind?' I huffed.

'No. Not at all.' Callum smirked.

We looked at each other and burst out laughing. I stopped laughing first.

'Callum, wouldn't … wouldn't you like to be in my class …?'

Callum couldn't meet my eyes. 'It's a bit … humiliating for us noughts to be stuck in the baby class.'

'What d'you mean? I'm not a baby.' I jumped to my feet, scowling at him.

'Jeez, Sephy, I'm fifteen, for heaven's sake! In six months' time I'll be sixteen and they're still sticking me in with twelve- and thirteen-year-olds. How would you like to be in a class with kids at least a year younger than you?' Callum asked.

'I … well …' I sat back down.

'Exactly!'

'I'm fourteen in three weeks,' I said, unwilling to let it drop.

'That's not the point, and you know it.'

'But the school explained why. You're all at least a year behind and …'

'And whose fault is that?' Callum said with erupting bitterness. Until a few years ago we were only allowed to be educated up to the age of fourteen – and in the noughts-only schools at that, which don't have a quarter of the money or resources that your schools have.'

I had no answer.

'Sorry. I didn't mean to bite your head off.'

'You didn't,' I said. 'Are any of your friends from your old school going to join you at Heathcrofts?'

'No. None of them got in,' Callum replied. 'I wouldn't've got in either if you hadn't helped me.'

He made it sound like an accusation. I wanted to say sorry and I had no idea why.

Callum sighed. 'Come on, we'd better get to work …'

'OK.' I turned and dug into my bag for my school books. 'What d'you want to do first? Maths or History?'

'Maths. I like Maths.'

'Yeuk!' I shook my head. How could anyone in their right mind like Maths?! Languages were my

favourite subjects, followed by Human Biology and Sociology and Chemistry. Maths fought with Physics for the subject I liked least.

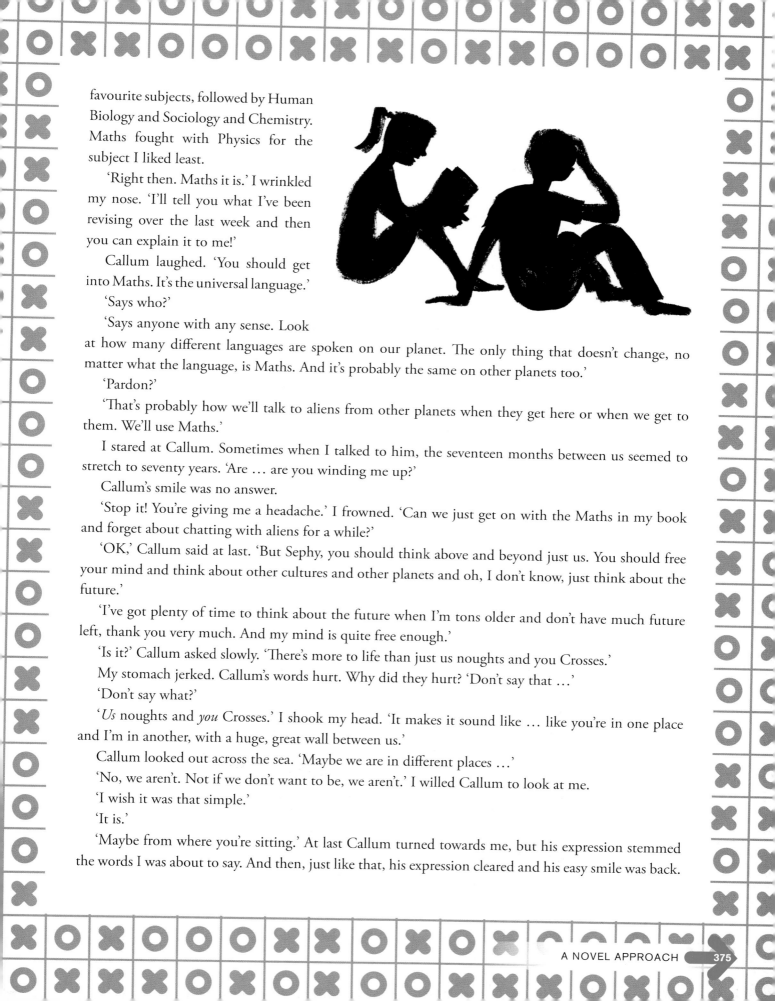

'Right then. Maths it is.' I wrinkled my nose. 'I'll tell you what I've been revising over the last week and then you can explain it to me!'

Callum laughed. 'You should get into Maths. It's the universal language.'

'Says who?'

'Says anyone with any sense. Look at how many different languages are spoken on our planet. The only thing that doesn't change, no matter what the language, is Maths. And it's probably the same on other planets too.'

'Pardon?'

'That's probably how we'll talk to aliens from other planets when they get here or when we get to them. We'll use Maths.'

I stared at Callum. Sometimes when I talked to him, the seventeen months between us seemed to stretch to seventy years. 'Are … are you winding me up?'

Callum's smile was no answer.

'Stop it! You're giving me a headache.' I frowned. 'Can we just get on with the Maths in my book and forget about chatting with aliens for a while?'

'OK,' Callum said at last. 'But Sephy, you should think above and beyond just us. You should free your mind and think about other cultures and other planets and oh, I don't know, just think about the future.'

'I've got plenty of time to think about the future when I'm tons older and don't have much future left, thank you very much. And my mind is quite free enough.'

'Is it?' Callum asked slowly. 'There's more to life than just us noughts and you Crosses.'

My stomach jerked. Callum's words hurt. Why did they hurt? 'Don't say that …'

'Don't say what?'

'*Us* noughts and *you* Crosses.' I shook my head. 'It makes it sound like … like you're in one place and I'm in another, with a huge, great wall between us.'

Callum looked out across the sea. 'Maybe we are in different places …'

'No, we aren't. Not if we don't want to be, we aren't.' I willed Callum to look at me.

'I wish it was that simple.'

'It is.'

'Maybe from where you're sitting.' At last Callum turned towards me, but his expression stemmed the words I was about to say. And then, just like that, his expression cleared and his easy smile was back.

1. How are Sephy and Callum different?

2. What type of lifestyle do you suspect Sephy has?

3. What issues cause tension between Sephy and Callum?

4. What suggestions of discrimination are made in this extract?

5. 'There is a lot of tension between the characters in this extract.'
Do you agree or disagree with this statement. **P I E**

STUDYING YOUR NOVEL –
Author's Point of View

When you are studying your novel, you may or may not realise that the author is presenting a certain **point of view**. This is not to be confused with the narrator's point of view, although they can sometimes be the same.

Authors can do this in a number of ways:

- A character may provide a **voice** for the author.
- The author may raise **themes**.
- There may be a stark **difference** between the **opening** and **resolution** of the story.

When we read a novel, we can only make **suggestions** about the writer's point of view on different issues, based on what we have read (unless, of course, we get to interview the author and ask them about their point of view!).

The following steps will help in examining any text.

'Yes! Finally a boat!'

'Yes! Finally some land!'

STEP ONE: What themes and issues are raised?

STEP TWO: Choose one of these issues and examine how the author presents it.
- When is the issue first raised?
- Does the issue influence the actions of the characters?
- Is the author trying to shock or surprise you to make you really think about the issue?

STEP THREE: Gather evidence from the story that indicates a particular stance or opinion.
- What actions do the characters take to solve the issue?
- What is the outcome – positive or negative?
- Does the protagonist reflect on the issue at the end of the story?

WATCH

Patrick Ness wrote *The Knife of Never Letting Go*, a novel about a world where everyone can hear what everyone else is thinking. Watch 'Interview with Patrick Ness' at the London Book Fair to hear him explain his point of view when writing this book.

SAMPLE QUESTION & ANSWER – *Examining point of view in a novel*

What is the author's point of view on discrimination and racism in the novel, *Noughts & Crosses*?

SAMPLE ANSWER using P I E

I suggest Malorie Blackman's own view on racism is one of anger and frustration. She clearly believes racism is an ongoing problem and one that causes obstacles for many people in the world, for example access to education.

'Until a few years ago we were only allowed to be educated up to the age of fourteen – and in the noughts-only schools at that, which don't have a quarter of the money or resources that your schools have.'

Blackman's view is very obvious by the way she creates tension between Sephy, who is a Cross, and Callum, who is a nought, despite the fact that they are friends and care about each other deeply. The source of this tension is the fact that they come from opposite sides of a racial divide. The tension is very obvious when Callum blames the Crosses for his lack of educational opportunity.

I believe the book is certainly not a celebration of discrimination; it is a criticism of it. Seeing two characters who care about each other argue bitterly over the differences between them is heart-breaking; it is also Blackman's way of highlighting what she believes is the injustice of discrimination and racism.

REMEMBER

When you write your explanation, you should try to give your own personal response. Elaborate with as much detail and opinion as possible. Your explanation should always be the longest part of the answer.

Exam Focus

1. Based on the extract from *Noughts & Crosses*, what do you think is Malorie Blackman's point of view on relationships?

2. Choose a key moment from a novel you have studied where an author's point of view is very obvious. Explain how the author presents their point of view through characters, themes and events.

Fiction [3]

What I will learn:

to revise the creation of setting; to recognise how a character is developed; to track and evaluate the development of relationships throughout a novel

You will now read two extracts from the first chapter of *Of Mice and Men*, written by John Steinbeck in 1937. Steinbeck won the Nobel Prize for Literature in 1962, and *Of Mice and Men* is one of his most acclaimed stories.

This novel follows two migrant workers in California during the 'Great Depression' of the 1930s. Thousands of people struggled to find work and were living in poverty. Many people, like the story's two protagonists, Lennie and George, had to migrate (move from one region to another) in order to find work.

California is a place very often depicted in films and TV programmes. Below are some of the following words used in John Steinbeck's opening and introduction to the setting. Try and use them in sentences to describe what you think the landscape of Steinbeck's California looks like.

deep	twinkling	recumbent (lying back or lying down)
horizontal	rocky	stilted (unnatural flow so it comes to a stop)

Extract 1 from *Of Mice and Men* by John Steinbeck

A few miles south of Soledad, the Salinas River drops in close to the hillside bank and runs deep and green. The water is warm too, for it has slipped twinkling over the yellow sands in the sunlight before reaching the narrow pool. On one side of the river the golden foothill slopes curve up to the strong and rocky Gabilan Mountains, but on the valley side the water is lined with trees – willows fresh and green with every spring, carrying in their lower leaf junctures the debris of the winter's flooding; and sycamores with mottled, white, recumbent limbs and branches that arch over the pool. On the sandy bank under the trees the leaves lie deep and so crisp that a lizard makes a great skittering if he runs among them. Rabbits come out of the brush to sit on the sand in the evening, and the damp flats are covered with the night tracks of 'coons, and with the spreadpads of dogs from the ranches, and with the split-wedge tracks of deer that come to drink in the dark. There is a path through the willows and among the sycamores, a path beaten hard by boys coming down from the ranches to swim in the deep pool, and beaten hard by tramps who come wearily down from the highway in the evening to jungle-up near water. In front of the low horizontal limb of a giant sycamore there is an ash pile made by many fires; the limb is worn smooth by men who have sat on it.

Evening of a hot day started the little wind to moving among the leaves. The shade climbed up the hills toward the top. On the sand banks the rabbits sat as quietly as little gray sculptured stones. And then from the direction of the state highway came the sound of footsteps on crisp sycamore leaves. The rabbits hurried noiselessly for cover. A stilted heron labored up into the air and pounded down river. For a moment the place was lifeless, and then two men emerged from the path and came into the opening by the green pool.

EXPLORE

1. Below you see an image of the setting of this opening scene in *Of Mice and Men*. Pick out words and phrases from the extract above that you feel have been represented in this opening scene, according to the photograph.

2. Paragraph 1 and 2 feature a lot of powerful adjectives. Write down the five best examples that describe the setting.

3. Paragraph 3 uses powerful verbs. Write down the five best examples that describe the setting.

Now you will read a second extract from the novel. Here, the two main characters are introduced. Think about how Steinbeck reveals clues about their personalities.

Extract 2 from *Of Mice and Men* by John Steinbeck

They had walked in single file down the path, and even in the open one stayed behind the other. Both were dressed in denim trousers and in denim coats with brass buttons. Both wore black, shapeless hats and both carried tight blanket rolls slung over their shoulders. The first man was small and quick, dark of face, with restless eyes and sharp, strong features. Every part of him was defined: small, strong hands, slender arms, a thin and bony nose. Behind him walked his opposite, a huge man, shapeless of face, with large, pale eyes, and wide, sloping shoulders; and he walked heavily, dragging his feet a little, the way a bear drags his paws. His arms did not swing at his sides, but hung loosely.

The first man stopped short in the clearing, and the follower nearly ran over him. He took off his hat and wiped the sweat-band with his forefinger and snapped the moisture off. His huge companion dropped his blankets and flung himself down and drank from the surface of the green pool; drank with long gulps, snorting into the water like a horse. The small man stepped nervously beside him.

'Lennie!' he said sharply. 'Lennie, for God' sakes don't drink so much.' Lennie continued to snort into the pool. The small man leaned over and shook him by the shoulder. 'Lennie. You gonna be sick like you was last night.'

Lennie dipped his whole head under, hat and all, and then he sat up on the bank and his hat dripped down on his blue coat and ran down his back. 'That's good,' he said. 'You drink some, George. You take a good big drink.' He smiled happily.

George unslung his bindle and dropped it gently on the bank. 'I ain't sure it's good water,' he said. 'Looks kinda scummy.'

Lennie dabbled his big paw in the water and wiggled his fingers so the water arose in little splashes; rings widened across the pool to the other side and came back again. Lennie watched them go. 'Look, George. Look what I done.'

George knelt beside the pool and drank from his hand with quick scoops. 'Tastes all right,' he admitted. 'Don't really seem to be running, though. You never oughta drink water when it ain't running, Lennie,' he said hopelessly. 'You'd drink out of a gutter if you was thirsty.' He threw a scoop of water into his face and rubbed it about with his hand, under his chin and around the back of his neck. Then he replaced his hat, pushed himself back from the river, drew up his knees and embraced them. Lennie, who had been watching, imitated George exactly. He pushed himself back, drew up his knees, embraced them, looked over to George to see whether he had it just right. He pulled his hat down a little more over his eyes, the way George's hat was.

George stared morosely at the water. The rims of his eyes were red with sun glare. He said angrily, 'We could just as well of rode clear to the ranch if that bastard bus driver knew what he was talkin' about. "Jes' a little stretch down the highway," he says. "Jes' a little stretch." God damn near four miles, that's what it was! Didn't wanta stop at the ranch gate, that's what. Too God damn lazy to pull up. Wonder he isn't too damn good to stop in Soledad at all. Kicks us out and says "Jes' a little stretch down the road." I bet it was more than four miles. Damn hot day.'

Lennie looked timidly over to him.

'George?'

'Yeah, what ya want?'

'Where we goin', George?'

The little man jerked down the brim of his hat and scowled over at Lennie. 'So you forgot that awready, did you? I gotta tell you again, do I? Jesus Christ, you're a crazy bastard!'

'I forgot,' Lennie said softly. 'I tried not to forget. Honest to God I did, George.'

'O.K. – O.K. I'll tell ya again. I ain't got nothing to do. Might jus' as well spen' all my time tellin' you things and then you forget 'em, and I tell you again.'

'Tried and tried,' said Lennie, 'but it didn't do no good. I remember about the rabbits, George.'

'The hell with the rabbits. That's all you ever can remember is them rabbits. O.K.! Now you listen and this time you got to remember so we don't get in no trouble. You remember settin' in that gutter on Howard Street and watchin' that blackboard?'

Lennie's face broke into a delighted smile. 'Why sure, George. I remember that … but … what'd we do then? I remember some girls come by and you says … you says …'

'The hell with what I says. You remember about us goin' in to Murray and Ready's, and they give us work cards and bus tickets?'

'Oh, sure, George. I remember that now.' His hands went quickly into his side coat pockets. He said gently, 'George … I ain't got mine. I musta lost it.' He looked down at the ground in despair.

'You never had none, you crazy bastard. I got both of 'em here. Think I'd let you carry your own work card?'

Lennie grinned with relief. 'I … I thought I put it in my side pocket.' His hand went into the pocket again.

George looked sharply at him. 'What'd you take outa that pocket?'

'Ain't a thing in my pocket,' Lennie said cleverly.

'I know there ain't. You got it in your hand. What you got in your hand – hidin' it?'

'I ain't got nothin', George. Honest.'

'Come on, give it here.'

Lennie held his closed hand away from George's direction.

'It's on'y a mouse, George.'

'A mouse? A live mouse?'

'Uh-uh. Jus' a dead mouse, George. I didn't kill it. Honest! I found it. I found it dead.'

'Give it here!' said George.

'Aw, leave me have it, George.'

'Give it here!'

Lennie's closed hand slowly obeyed.

George took the mouse and threw it across the pool to the other side, among the brush.

'What you want of a dead mouse, anyways?'

'I could pet it with my thumb while we walked along,' said Lennie.

'Well, you ain't petting no mice while you walk with me. You remember where we're goin' now?'

Lennie looked startled and then in embarrassment hid his face against his knees.

'I forgot again.'

'Jesus Christ,' George said resignedly.

'Well – look, we're gonna work on a ranch like the one we come from up north.'

'Up north?'

'In Weed.'

'Oh, sure. I remember. In Weed.'

'That ranch we're goin' to is right down there about a quarter mile. We're gonna go in an' see the boss. Now, look – I'll give him the work tickets, but you ain't gonna say a word. You jus' stand there and don't say nothing. If he finds out what a crazy bastard you are, we won't get no job, but if he sees ya work before he hears ya talk, we're set. Ya got that?'

'Sure, George. Sure I got it.'

'O.K. Now when we go in to see the boss, what you gonna do?'

'I … I … ' Lennie thought. His face grew tight with thought.

'I … ain't gonna say nothin'. Jus' gonna stan' there.'

'Good boy. That's swell. You say that over two, three times so you sure won't forget it.'

Lennie droned to himself softly, 'I ain't gonna say nothin' … I ain't gonna say nothin' … I ain't gonna say nothin'.'

'O.K.,' said George. 'An' you ain't gonna do no bad things like you done in Weed, neither.'

Lennie looked puzzled. 'Like I done in Weed?'

'Oh, so ya forgot that too, did ya? Well, I ain't gonna remind ya, fear ya do it again.'

A light of understanding broke on Lennie's face. 'They run us outa Weed,' he exploded triumphantly.

'Run us out, hell,' said George disgustedly.

'We run. They was lookin' for us, but they didn't catch us.' Lennie giggled happily.

'I didn't forget that, you bet.'

George lay back on the sand and crossed his hands under his head, and Lennie imitated him, raising his head to see whether he was doing it right.

'God, you're a lot of trouble,' said George.

'I could get along so easy and so nice if I didn't have you on my tail. I could live so easy and maybe have a girl.'

For a moment Lennie lay quiet, and then he said hopefully, 'We gonna work on a ranch, George.'

'Awright. You got that. But we're gonna sleep here because I got a reason.'

The day was going fast now. Only the tops of the Gabilan Mountains flamed with the light of the sun that had gone from the valley. A water snake slipped along on the pool, its head held up like a little periscope. The reeds jerked slightly in the current. Far off toward the highway a man shouted something, and another man shouted back. The sycamore limbs rustled under a little wind that died immediately.

'George – why ain't we goin' on to the ranch and get some supper? They got supper at the ranch.' George rolled on his side.

'No reason at all for you. I like it here. Tomorra we're gonna go to work. I seen thrashin' machines on the way down. That means we'll be buckin' grain bags, bustin' a gut. Tonight I'm gonna lay right here and look up. I like it.'

Lennie got up on his knees and looked down at George. 'Ain't we gonna have no supper?'

'Sure we are, if you gather up some dead willow sticks. I got three cans of beans in my bindle. You get a fire ready. I'll give you a match when you get the sticks together. Then we'll heat the beans and have supper.'

Lennie said, 'I like beans with ketchup.'

'Well, we ain't got no ketchup. You go get wood. An' don't you fool around. It'll be dark before long.'

Lennie lumbered to his feet and disappeared in the brush. George lay where he was and whistled softly to himself. There were sounds of splashings down the river in the direction Lennie had taken. George stopped whistling and listened.

'Poor bastard,' he said softly, and then went on whistling again.

In a moment Lennie came crashing back through the brush. He carried one small willow stick in his hand. George sat up.

'Awright,' he said brusquely. 'Gi'me that mouse!'

But Lennie made an elaborate pantomime of innocence.

'What mouse, George? I ain't got no mouse.' George held out his hand.

'Come on. Give it to me. You ain't puttin' nothing over.'

Lennie hesitated, backed away, looked wildly at the brush line as though he contemplated running for his freedom.

George said coldly, 'You gonna give me that mouse or do I have to sock you?'

'Give you what, George?'

'You know God damn well what. I want that mouse.'

Lennie reluctantly reached into his pocket. His voice broke a little. 'I don't know why I can't keep it. It ain't nobody's mouse. I didn't steal it. I found it lyin' right beside the road.'

George's hand remained outstretched imperiously. Slowly, like a terrier who doesn't want to bring a ball to its master, Lennie approached, drew back, approached again. George snapped his fingers sharply, and at the sound Lennie laid the mouse in his hand.

'I wasn't doin' nothing bad with it, George. Jus' strokin' it.'

George stood up and threw the mouse as far as he could into the darkening brush, and then he stepped to the pool and washed his hands. 'You crazy fool. Don't you think I could see your feet was wet where you went acrost the river to get it?' He heard Lennie's whimpering cry and wheeled about. 'Blubberin' like a baby! Jesus Christ! A big guy like you.' Lennie's lip quivered and tears started in his eyes. 'Aw, Lennie!' George put his hand on Lennie's shoulder. 'I ain't takin' it away jus' for meanness. That mouse ain't fresh, Lennie; and besides, you've broke it pettin' it. You get another mouse that's fresh and I'll let you keep it a little while.'

Lennie sat down on the ground and hung his head dejectedly.

TOP TIP

You will notice that some words are shortened throughout the piece whenever Steinbeck uses **direct speech**. This is to show George and Lennie's way of speaking – their **dialect**. Dialect is language spoken in a certain region.

1. Having read the entire extract, match the description to the correct character.

'The first man was small and quick, dark of face, with restless eyes and sharp, strong features. Every part of him was defined: small, strong hands, slender arms, a thin and bony nose.'

☐ George ☐ Lennie

'Behind him walked his opposite, a huge man, shapeless of face, with large, pale eyes, and wide, sloping shoulders; and he walked heavily, dragging his feet a little, the way a bear drags his paws. His arms did not swing at his sides, but hung loosely.'

☐ George ☐ Lennie

2. Pick four adjectives from each list to describe each character.

George		**Lennie**	
timid	cunning	honest	sensitive
strong	patient	independent	cruel
smart	carefree	intelligent	rational
bossy	brave	stupid	confident
funny	philosophical	rough	mature
cruel	friendly	strong-minded	childlike
ambitious	daring	weak	thoughtful
trustworthy	tough	robust	violent
kind	loveable	vulnerable	cynical

3. Steinbeck spends time developing his characters in this extract. Use the vocabulary you have picked for the two characters and write two **PIE** paragraphs showing this development. Does Steinbeck use ***Show Don't Tell*** at any point during this character development?

REMEMBER

Show Don't Tell is when the author shows us what a character is like, rather than just telling us.

4. Relationships are a vital part of storytelling. Novels have much more time to develop these relationships than short stories do. Comment on the characters' relationship at the beginning of the extract.

> The first man stopped short in the clearing, and the follower nearly ran over him. He took off his hat and wiped the sweat-band with his forefinger and snapped the moisture off. His huge companion dropped his blankets and flung himself down and drank from the surface of the green pool; drank with long gulps, snorting into the water like a horse. The small man stepped nervously beside him.
>
> 'Lennie!' he said sharply. 'Lennie, for God' sakes don't drink so much.' Lennie continued to snort into the pool. The small man leaned over and shook him by the shoulder. 'Lennie. You gonna be sick like you was last night.'

5. What is their relationship like at the end of the extract?

> He heard Lennie's whimpering cry and wheeled about. 'Blubberin' like a baby! Jesus Christ! A big guy like you.' Lennie's lip quivered and tears started in his eyes. 'Aw, Lennie!' George put his hand on Lennie's shoulder. 'I ain't takin' it away jus' for meanness. That mouse ain't fresh, Lennie; and besides, you've broke it pettin' it. You get another mouse that's fresh and I'll let you keep it a little while.' Lennie sat down on the ground and hung his head dejectedly.'

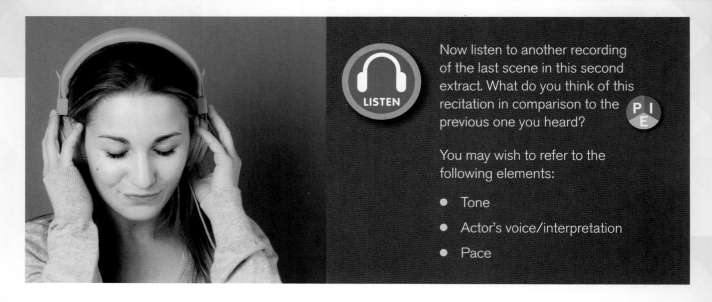

Now listen to another recording of the last scene in this second extract. What do you think of this recitation in comparison to the previous one you heard?

You may wish to refer to the following elements:

- Tone
- Actor's voice/interpretation
- Pace

STUDYING YOUR NOVEL – *Characters*

It is important that you know the **main characters** in your novel extremely well as you can be asked about any of them in the exam. Here are some tips that you can apply to your own novel.

1. Who is your protagonist/s and what do they want?

2. How would you describe them and their personality? Find key quotes and adjectives to help you talk about them. Be able to refer to things they have done and what these moments tell us about them.

3. What is their attitude to things going on around them?

4. Do they experience a change of some kind from the opening to the resolution?

5. How do they react to other characters in the novel? What does this say about them? Are their relationships complicated or simple?

Pick a character from a novel you have studied. Imagine you are that character but keep it a secret from your classmates.

- Who would the character have as their top five contacts in their phone?
- What apps would they have that might tell us something about them?
- Draw a photo they might have in their phone that highlights an important time in their life.
- Write a message to each of the top five contacts in their phone about different moments in your character's life and how he/she feels about them.

When you have finished, read out the information to the class and have them guess who you are.

STUDYING YOUR NOVEL – *Relationships*

You must be aware of the **relationships** that are present in your novel and how they develop over the course of the novel. Here are some tips to help you with this process.

- Choose a character and build a relationship tree around them.
- Are the relationships positive or negative at the start of the novel?
- What emotions do the characters in the relationship display?
- What moments best highlight the state of the relationships?
- Do the relationships change over the course of the novel?
- Do the changes in one relationship affect other relationships in the novel?
- Do the characters ever sacrifice relationships for something else?

Choose an important relationship from your studied novel. Act out a scene of dialogue based on something important that happens to the characters featured.

Lennie and George's relationship changes many times throughout the novel.

1 Choose one important relationship from a novel you have studied. Map the high moments where things are going well, and the low moments when the relationship is struggling. Draw a graph to represent these moments.

2 Present the graph to your class, explaining a key moment and why it is important in the chosen relationship.

3 Imagine you are working on the film adaptation of this novel. Make a list of all the props you would need to get in order to shoot this scene. Explain the significance of one of the props in terms of the character, the setting and the plot.

HOW TO COMPARE?

What does it mean to **compare**? To compare means to examine things for similarities and differences. You may be asked to compare your two studied novels or your studied novel with a studied film.

What if you were to compare Batman and Superman?

- You might say that Batman is moody and has a dark personality, unlike the bright and friendly Superman.

- You might also say that both characters have come from troubled backgrounds where their parents were not around. Batman's parents were killed, while Superman's parents managed to get him to safety before their planet exploded.

- You might say that both characters have the power to fight evil but they possess different types of power. Batman relies on skills and technology whereas Superman's powers are natural – they come from within him.

Here are some useful words and phrases that will help you to compare.

Similarities

- Both
- Just as
- Likewise
- In the same way
- The scene mirrors/ reminds us of/is reminiscent of
- Similarly
- As we see in the other text
- This is exactly like
- In comparison with
- It is identical to

Contrasts

- By ways of contrast
- In contrast
- While
- Although
- However
- Unlike
- On the one hand/ On the other hand
- Whereas

Compare the main character in your two chosen novels using these two headings to guide your response: 1. Personality and 2. Social Values.

SAMPLE ANSWER using P I E

The two novels that I have studied are *Of Mice and Men* by John Steinbeck and *Noughts and Crosses* by Malorie Blackman. Both novels feature a protagonist who is vulnerable or defenceless. Lennie from *Of Mice and Men* is a physically strong man with a childlike mind who gets himself into trouble because of his personality, while Sephy from *Noughts and Crosses* should be strong in her position as a Cross (a member of the ruling race), but is instead weakened by her dysfunctional family circumstances.

PERSONALITY

Lennie is a man who is extremely simple-minded and this means his personality is very docile [quiet and easy to control]. When George demands that he gives back the mouse, Lennie reluctantly but obediently agreeds. 'George snapped his fingers sharply, and at the sound Lennie laid the mouse in his hand.' Lennie's personality means that we feel sympathy for him whenever he does anything bad. He doesn't understand that he is doing anything wrong.

This is in contrast to Sephy who comes across as quite intelligent but struggles with her identity and place in the world. 'Be a good girl, study at school, study at university, get a good job, marry a good man, live a good life and they all lived happily ever after. The whole thing just makes me ... want to puke. I want something more in my life.' I found Sephy self-pitying and spoiled at different stages during the novel. Her personality shows she is rebellious, but much of this comes from the lack of affection from her parents and sister. Unlike Lennie, Sephy's strength of mind and personality helps her to overcome her problems.

SOCIAL VALUES

Lennie's social values come from his best friend, George. George looks after Lennie and tries to make him act in a responsible manner. 'An' you ain't gonna do no bad things like you done in Weed, neither.' Lennie and George are migrant workers and they don't have any stability in their lives. Lennie's stability is George, and George tries to teach Lennie the proper way to act. Obviously Lennie has done something bad in the past and George's guidance and social values are the only thing to stop Lennie from repeating the offence.

In contrast, Sephy's social values are influenced by her family situation. Her father is the most powerful Cross in the country and is happy to keep the Noughts as second class citizens. Sephy doesn't accept her father's values, unlike Lennie who is always trying to please George.

→

SAMPLE ANSWER

She befriends Callum, a Nought, and when this relationship becomes more complex, she comes into conflict with the social values of her family. She is appalled by the acts against the Noughts that she must witness because of her father. It disgusts her that her mother will not stand up to her father. 'You say they were your friends? Nothing would make me go to the hanging of one of my friends. Nothing. Not even Dad.' Sephy is more aware of her social values in comparison to Lennie, who just tries to follow George's way of life.

Both characters show their personality and attitudes towards social values in these novels. Lennie's situation is different to Sephy's because of his lack of intelligence and common sense. Both characters, however, find themselves in trouble because of their social values and personality.

Fiction [4]

What I will learn:

to understand the effectiveness of a key moment

To Kill a Mockingbird is an American classic written by Harper Lee in 1960. It was her first novel, and for fifty-five years her only novel until, amazingly, her second novel, *Go Set A Watchman*, was published in 2015. Her second novel was a prequel to her first. *To Kill a Mockingbird* is set in Maycomb, Alabama, also during the 1930s Great Depression. It is a small town with small-minded people who demonstrate searing racism and prejudice. Told through the eyes of a nine-year-old girl, Scout, we find out that a local black man has been accused of raping a white woman. Scout's father, a lawyer, ends up defending him.

Discrimination and prejudice are two strong themes in the book. In groups, think of any news story you have come across that deals with these themes. Explain why this particular news story stood out for you.

You will need eight speakers to read the following extract.

The narrator	Ms Caroline	Walter Cunningham	Child
Scout	Mr Cunningham	Atticus	Jem

Extract from *To Kill a Mockingbird* by Harper Lee

'Everybody who goes home to lunch hold up your hands,' said Miss Caroline, breaking into my new grudge against Calpurnia.

The town children did so, and she looked us over.

'Everybody who brings his lunch put it on top of his desk.'

Molasses buckets appeared from nowhere, and the ceiling danced with metallic light. Miss Caroline walked up and down the rows peering and poking into lunch containers, nodding if the contents pleased her, frowning a little at others. She stopped at Walter Cunningham's desk. 'Where's yours?' she asked.

Walter Cunningham's face told everybody in the first grade he had hookworms. His absence of shoes told us how he got them. People caught hookworms going barefooted in barnyards and hog wallows. If Walter had owned any shoes he would have worn them the first day of school and then discarded them until midwinter. He did have on a clean shirt and neatly mended overalls.

'Did you forget your lunch this morning?' asked Miss Caroline.

Walter looked straight ahead. I saw a muscle jump in his skinny jaw.

'Did you forget it this morning?' asked Miss Caroline. Walter's jaw twitched again.

'Yeb'm,' he finally mumbled.

Miss Caroline went to her desk and opened her purse. 'Here's a quarter,' she said to Walter. 'Go and eat downtown today. You can pay me back tomorrow.'

Walter shook his head. 'Nome thank you ma'am,' he drawled softly.

Impatience crept into Miss Caroline's voice: 'Here Walter, come get it.' Walter shook his head again.

When Walter shook his head a third time someone whispered, 'Go on and tell her, Scout.'

I turned around and saw most of the town people and the entire bus delegation looking at me. Miss Caroline and I had conferred twice already, and they were looking at me in the innocent assurance that familiarity breeds understanding.

I rose graciously on Walter's behalf: 'Ah – Miss Caroline?'

'What is it, Jean Louise?'

'Miss Caroline, he's a Cunningham.'

I sat back down.

'What, Jean Louise?'

I thought I had made things sufficiently clear. It was clear enough to the rest of us: Walter Cunningham was sitting there lying his

head off. He didn't forget his lunch, he didn't have any. He had none today nor would he have any tomorrow or the next day. He had probably never seen three quarters together at the same time in his life.

I tried again: 'Walter's one of the Cunninghams, Miss Caroline.'

'I beg your pardon, Jean Louise?'

'That's okay, ma'am, you'll get to know all the county folks after a while. The Cunninghams never took anything they can't pay back – no church baskets and no scrip stamps. They never took anything off of anybody, they get along on what they have. They don't have much, but they get along on it.'

My special knowledge of the Cunningham tribe – one branch, that is – was gained from events of last winter. Walter's father was one of Atticus's clients. After a dreary conversation in our livingroom one night about his entailment, before Mr. Cunningham left he said, 'Mr. Finch, I don't know when I'll ever be able to pay you.'

'Let that be the least of your worries, Walter,' Atticus said.

When I asked Jem what entailment was, and Jem described it as a condition of having your tail in a crack, I asked Atticus if Mr. Cunningham would ever pay us.

'Not in money,' Atticus said, 'but before the year's out I'll have been paid. You watch.'

We watched. One morning Jem and I found a load of stovewood in the back yard. Later, a sack of hickory nuts appeared on the back steps. With Christmas came a crate of smilax and holly. That spring when we found a crokersack full of turnip greens, Atticus said Mr. Cunningham had more than paid him.

'Why does he pay you like that?' I asked.

'Because that's the only way he can pay me. He has no money.'

'Are we poor, Atticus?' Atticus nodded. 'We are indeed.' Jem's nose wrinkled.

'Are we as poor as the Cunninghams?'

'Not exactly. The Cunninghams are country folks, farmers, and the crash hit them hardest.'

Atticus said professional people were poor because the farmers were poor. As Maycomb County was farm country, nickels and dimes were hard to come by for doctors and dentists and lawyers. Entailment was only a part of Mr. Cunningham's vexations. The acres not entailed were mortgaged to the hilt, and the little cash he made went to interest. If he held his mouth right, Mr. Cunningham could get a WPA job, but his land would go to ruin if he left it, and he was willing to go hungry to keep his land and vote as he pleased. Mr. Cunningham, said Atticus, came from a set breed of men.

As the Cunninghams had no money to pay a lawyer, they simply paid us with what they had. 'Did you know,' said Atticus, 'that Dr. Reynolds works the same way? He charges some folks a bushel of potatoes for delivery of a baby. Miss Scout, if you give me your attention I'll tell you what entailment is. Jem's definitions are very nearly accurate sometimes.'

If I could have explained these things to Miss Caroline, I would have saved myself some inconvenience and Miss Caroline subsequent mortification, but it was beyond my ability to explain things as well as Atticus, so I said, 'You're shamin' him, Miss Caroline. Walter hasn't got a quarter at home to bring you, and you can't use any stovewood.'

Miss Caroline stood stock still, then grabbed me by the collar and hauled me back to her desk. 'Jean Louise, I've had about enough of you this morning,' she said. 'You're starting off on the wrong foot in every way, my dear. Hold out your hand.'

I thought she was going to spit in it, which was the only reason anybody in Maycomb held out his hand: it was a time-honored method of sealing oral contracts. Wondering what bargain we had made, I turned to the class for an answer, but the class looked back at me in puzzlement. Miss Caroline picked up her ruler, gave me half a dozen quick little pats, then told me to stand in the corner. A storm of laughter broke loose when it finally occurred to the class that Miss Caroline had whipped me.

EXPLORE

1. How did Miss Caroline come to realise that Walter had no lunch?

2. Why did the class look at Scout to 'do the talking'?

3. According to Scout, what reason had Walter to not take the quarter?

4. Highlight one way we know that this story is not set in the modern era.

5. What impression do you get of Scout from this extract? **P I E**

6. The incident you have read is a key moment from the novel. Why?

7. Read this line from the extract again.

'Walter's one of the Cunninghams, Miss Caroline'.

a) If you were to read this sentence aloud, what word do you think you might place emphasis on?

b) Why does Scout say this?

- to explain his family name

- to show that he is different

- to make fun of him

Scout, in all her innocence, tells the teacher the way things are. The Cunninghams are different to the other children and families; they are the 'other' (meaning not part of her or the other children's world). In your opinion, how is this moment connected to the themes of racism and prejudice?

STUDYING YOUR NOVEL – *Key Moments*

Key moments are critical when discussing your novel. For your exam, you should know **at least five key moments**. This will allow you to refer to specific moments that are important to the story.

1. When does the key moment happen in the novel?

2. What characters are involved?

3. Why is the moment important to the protagonist?

4. Is the event important in establishing the theme or author's point of view?

5. What is the outcome of the moment?

Here are some key moments from *Alice in Wonderland.* Write a sentence for each picture to sum up what is going on.

(1) Imagine you are Walter Cunningham from *To Kill a Mockingbird*. Write a diary entry describing your thoughts and emotions following this incident in the classroom.

(2) Pick a key moment from your own studied novel and write about why it is important to the story.

CREATE — Make a trailer or cartoon strip featuring the key moments from your studied novel.

Fiction [5]

What I will learn:

to understand genre; to identify elements of the gothic genre

Charlotte Brontë (*pictured*) was one of three sisters who published poetry and novels during the nineteenth century. As a female writer, Charlotte was forced to publish her work under a pseudonym (an assumed name), as women found it difficult to get their work circulated during this period. *Jane Eyre* was one of her earliest publications.

Orphaned at a young age, this eponymous character (having the same name as the title of the book; say: *eh-pon-eh-mus*) is sent into the household of her Aunt Reed at Gateshead and then experiences a cruel establishment at Lowood charity school. Jane Eyre nonetheless manages to overcome her hardship and maintain her integrity. In the following extract, Jane has taken up the post of governess at Thornfield, a castle belonging to the mysterious Mr Rochester. She follows the head of house, Mrs Fairfax, on a tour of the castle.

PREPARE — Think of a book, film or TV programme that has made you feel scared or uncomfortable. What was it about your chosen text that made you feel this way?

Extract from *Jane Eyre*
by Charlotte Brontë

When we left the dining-room, she proposed to show me over the rest of the house; and I followed her upstairs and downstairs, admiring as I went; for all was well arranged and handsome. The large front chambers I thought especially grand: and some of the third-storey rooms, though dark and low, were interesting from their air of antiquity. The furniture once appropriated to the lower apartments had from time to time been removed here, as fashions changed: and the imperfect light entering by their narrow casement showed bedsteads of a hundred years old; chests in oak or walnut, looking, with their strange carvings of palm branches and cherubs' heads, like types of the Hebrew ark; rows of venerable chairs, high-backed and narrow; stools still more antiquated, on whose cushioned tops were yet apparent traces of half-effaced embroideries, wrought by fingers that for two generations had been coffin-dust. All these relics gave to the third storey of Thornfield Hall the aspect of a home of the past: a shrine of memory. I liked the hush, the gloom, the quaintness of these retreats in the day; but I by no means coveted a night's repose on one of those wide and heavy beds: shut in, some of them, with doors of oak; shaded, others, with wrought old English hangings crusted with thick work, portraying effigies of strange flowers, and stranger birds, and strangest human beings, – all which would have looked strange, indeed, by the pallid gleam of moonlight.

'Do the servants sleep in these rooms?' I asked.

'No; they occupy a range of smaller apartments to the back; no one ever sleeps here: one would almost say that, if there were a ghost at Thornfield Hall, this would be its haunt.'

'So I think: you have no ghost, then?'

'None that I ever heard of,' returned Mrs. Fairfax, smiling.

'Nor any traditions of one? no legends or ghost stories?'

'I believe not. And yet it is said the Rochesters have been rather a violent than a quiet race in their time: perhaps, though, that is the reason they rest tranquilly in their graves now.'

'Yes – after life's fitful fever they sleep well,' I muttered. 'Where are you going now, Mrs. Fairfax?' for she was moving away.

'On to the leads; will you come and see the view from thence?' I followed still, up a  very narrow staircase to the attics, and thence by a ladder and through a trap-door to the roof of the hall. I was now on a level with the crow colony, and could see into their nests. Leaning over the battlements and looking far down, I surveyed the grounds laid out like a map: the bright and velvet lawn closely girdling the grey base of the mansion; the field, wide as a park, dotted with its ancient timber; the wood, dun and sere, divided by a path visibly overgrown, greener with moss than the trees were with foliage; the church at the gates, the road, the tranquil hills, all reposing in the autumn day's sun; the horizon bounded by a propitious sky, azure, marbled with pearly white. No feature in the scene was extraordinary, but all was pleasing. When I turned from it and repassed the trap-door, I could scarcely see my way down the ladder; the attic seemed black as a vault compared with that arch of blue air to which I had been looking up, and to that sunlit scene of grove, pasture, and green hill, of which the hall was the centre, and over which I had been gazing with delight.

Mrs. Fairfax stayed behind a moment to fasten the trap-door; I, by drift of groping, found the outlet from the attic, and proceeded to descend the narrow garret staircase. I lingered in the long passage to which this led, separating the front and back rooms of the third storey: narrow, low, and dim, with only one little window at the far end, and looking, with its two rows of small black doors all shut, like a corridor in some Bluebeard's castle.

While I paced softly on, the last sound I expected to hear in so still a region, a laugh, struck my ear. It was a curious laugh; distinct, formal, mirthless. I stopped: the sound ceased, only for an instant; it began again, louder: for at first, though distinct, it was very low. It passed off in a clamorous peal that seemed to wake an echo in every lonely chamber; though it originated but in one, and I could have pointed out the door whence the accents issued.

'Mrs. Fairfax!' I called out: for I now heard her descending the great stairs. 'Did you hear that loud laugh? Who is it?'

'Some of the servants, very likely,' she answered: 'perhaps Grace Poole.'

'Did you hear it?' I again inquired.

'Yes, plainly: I often hear her: she sews in one of these rooms. Sometimes Leah is with her; they are frequently noisy together.'

propitious: giving or indicating a good chanc of success

mirthless: not amused

clamorous: noisy, loud, excited

preternatural: beyond what is normal or natural

cachinnation: a loud laugh or guffaw

The laugh was repeated in its low, syllabic tone, and terminated in an odd murmur.

'Grace!' exclaimed Mrs. Fairfax.

I really did not expect any Grace to answer; for the laugh was as tragic, as preternatural a laugh as any I ever heard; and, but that it was high noon, and that no circumstance of ghostliness accompanied the curious cachinnation; but that neither scene nor season favoured fear, I should have been superstitiously afraid. However, the event showed me I was a fool for entertaining a sense even of surprise.

The door nearest me opened, and a servant came out, – a woman of between thirty and forty; a set, square-made figure, red-haired, and with a hard, plain face: any apparition less romantic or less ghostly could scarcely be conceived.

'Too much noise, Grace,' said Mrs. Fairfax. 'Remember directions!' Grace curtseyed silently and went in.

'She is a person we have to sew and assist Leah in her housemaid's work,' continued the widow; 'not altogether unobjectionable in some points, but she does well enough. By-the-bye, how have you got on with your new pupil this morning?'

Genre *n.*

Definition: A category or type of writing, song, film, etc. Other genre categories include sci-fi, action and adventure, romance and thriller.

Gothic Fiction

Jane Eyre is considered to be a gothic novel. This means it belongs to the gothic genre.

Gothic fiction is a genre that combines horror, romanticism and the supernatural. There are some factors which help us to figure out whether or not a story belongs to the gothic genre.

Guide to Gothic Fiction

- The gothic genre can feature ghosts or the **supernatural**. Often the protagonist struggles in their acceptance of these spirits. The supernatural element makes the reader and protagonist feel on edge.

- Gothic stories are usually set in **castles**. The setting allows for an eerie atmosphere as they are usually large, cold and austere.

- The writer will create many moments of **uneasiness**. There is a build-up of tension and suspense.

- The **weather** is extremely important in establishing the mood and usually features rain, thunder and lightning.

- Characters, in particular women, have heightened **emotions** or are in distress. They experience fear, anger or sorrow and might let out a 'blood-curdling scream'.

1. Having read this 'Guide to Gothic Fiction', identify whether the extract from *Jane Eyre* includes any of these elements of gothic fiction. Write down any corresponding quotes.

2. Read back over the pieces of dialogue. Would you say that Jane is:

a) friendly

b) inquisitive

c) rude

d) *an adjective of your choice*

3. Pick two sentences or phrases from the text that you think describes a stereotypical castle.

Listen to the following excerpts from two different gothic novels. Identify the gothic elements within them.

1. Without a word he shook his reins, the horses turned, and we swept into the darkness of the pass. As I looked back I saw the steam from the horses of the coach by the light of the lamps, and projected against it the figures of my late companions crossing themselves. Then the driver cracked his whip and called to his horses, and off they swept on their way to Bukovina. As they sank into the darkness I felt a strange chill, and a lonely feeling come over me. But a cloak was thrown over my shoulders, and a rug across my knees, and the driver said in excellent German – 'The night is chill, mein Herr, and my master the Count bade me take all care of you. There is a flask of slivovitz (the plum brandy of the country) underneath the seat, if you should require it.'… Then a dog began to howl somewhere in a farmhouse far down the road, a long, agonized wailing, as if from fear. The sound was taken up by another dog, and then another and another, till, borne on the wind which now sighed softly through the Pass, a wild howling began, which seemed to come from all over the country, as far as the imagination could grasp it through the gloom of the night.

From Dracula *by Bram Stoker*

2. 'I perceived in the gloom a figure which stole from behind a clump of trees near me; I stood fixed, gazing intently; I could not be mistaken. A flash of lightning illuminated the object and discovered its shape plainly to me; its gigantic stature, and the deformity of its aspect, more hideous than belongs to humanity, instantly armed me that it was the wretch, the filthy demon to whom I had given life. What did he there? Could he be (I shuddered at the conception) the murderer of my brother? No one can conceive the anguish I suffered during the remainder of the night, which I spent, cold and wet, in the open air.'

From Frankenstein *by Mary Shelley*

MIND YOUR LANGUAGE

PUNCTUATION

Rewrite and punctuate this passage from the *Jane Eyre* extract without referring back to it. When you have finished, check your answer with the extract and highlight any punctuation corrections that you missed.

Hint: *The author uses three semi-colons, two colons, ten commas and four full stops.*

while I paced softly on the last sound I expected to hear in so still a region a laugh struck my ear it was a curious laugh distinct formal mirthless I stopped the sound ceased only for an instant it began again louder for at first though distinct it was very low it passed off in a clamorous peal that seemed to wake an echo in every lonely chamber though it originated but in one and I could have pointed out the door whence the accents issued

Exam Focus

1 Setting is one important way of establishing genre. Pick a setting from a novel you have studied and write one paragraph explaining why this setting is so important to establishing the genre.

2 Match these well-known novels and films with their correct genre.

Novel or Film	Genre
The Maze Runner	Romantic melodrama
The Fault in Our Stars	Thriller
Vampire Academy	Historical coming of age
Mean Girls	Post-apocalyptic
The Breadwinner	Comedy
War Horse	Fantasy
Coraline	Historical/mulicultural

Fiction [6]

What I will learn:

to appreciate and understand symbolism

The Outsiders by S. E. Hinton tells the story of Ponyboy Curtis, a fourteen-year-old boy who deals with struggles between right and wrong. It is set in Tulsa, Oklahoma, during the 1960s, where two separate teenage groups – the Greasers and the Socs – try to maintain control of their territory.

As you grow up, you find that you might wear certain things, follow certain teams or bands or even listen to certain music. This is part of your identity. Think of an item of clothing or a particular object that you feel says something about you and your identity.

Extract from *The Outsiders* by S. E. Hinton

WHEN I STEPPED OUT into the bright sunlight from the darkness of the movie house, I had only two things on my mind: Paul Newman and a ride home. I was wishing I looked like Paul Newman – he looks tough and I don't – but I guess my own looks aren't so bad. I have light-brown, almost-red hair and greenish-gray eyes. I wish they were more gray, because I hate most guys that have green eyes, but I have to be content with what I have. My hair is longer than a lot of boys wear theirs, squared off in back and long at the front and sides, but I am a greaser and most of my neighborhood rarely bothers to get a haircut. Besides, I look better with long hair.

I had a long walk home and no company, but I usually lone it anyway, for no reason except that I like to watch movies undisturbed so I can get into them and live them with the actors. When I see a movie with someone it's kind of uncomfortable, like having someone read your book over your shoulder. I'm different that way. I mean, my second oldest brother, Soda, who is sixteen-going-on-seventeen, never cracks a book at all, and my oldest brother, Darrel, who we call Darry, works too long and hard to be interested in a story or drawing a picture, so I'm not like them. And nobody in our gang digs movies and books the way I do. For a while there, I thought I was the only person in the world that did. So I loned it. Soda tries to understand, at least, which is more than Darry does. But then, Soda is different from anybody; he understands everything, almost. Like he's never hollering at me all the time the way Darry is, or treating me as if I was six instead of fourteen. I love Soda more than I've ever loved anyone, even Mom and Dad. He's always happy-go-lucky and grinning, while Darry's hard and firm and rarely grins at all. But then, Darry's gone through a lot in his twenty years, grown up too fast. Sodapop'll never grow up at all. I don't know which way's the best. I'll find out one of these days.

Anyway, I went on walking home, thinking about the movie, and then suddenly wishing I had some company. Greasers can't walk alone too much or they'll get jumped, or someone will come by and scream 'Greaser!' at them, which doesn't make you feel too hot, if you know what I mean. We get jumped by the Socs. I'm not sure how you spell it, but it's the abbreviation for the Socials, the jet set, the West-side rich kids. It's like the term 'greaser,' which is used to class all us boys on the East Side.

We're poorer than the Socs and the middle class. I reckon we're wilder, too. Not like the Socs, who jump greasers and wreck houses and throw beer blasts for kicks, and get editorials in the paper for being a public disgrace one day and an asset to society the next. Greasers are almost like hoods; we steal things and drive old souped-up cars and hold up gas stations and have a gang fight once in a while. I don't mean I do things like that. Darry would kill me if I got into trouble with the police. Since Mom and Dad were killed in an auto wreck, the three of us get to stay together only as long as we behave. So Soda and I stay out of trouble as much as we can, and we're careful not to get caught when we can't. I only mean that most greasers do things like that, just like we wear our hair long and dress in blue jeans and T-shirts, or leave our shirttails out and wear leather jackets and tennis shoes or boots. I'm not saying that either Socs or Greasers are better; that's just the way things are. [...]

Steve Randle was seventeen, tall and lean, with thick greasy hair he kept combed in complicated swirls. He was tacky, smart, and Soda's best buddy since grade school. Steve's specialty was cars. He could lift a hubcap quicker and more quietly than anyone in the neighborhood, but he also knew cars upside-down and backward, and he could drive anything on wheels. He and Soda worked at the same gas station – Steve part time and Soda full time – and their station got more customers than any other in town. Whether that was because Steve was so good with cars or because Soda attracted girls like honey draws flies, I couldn't tell you. I liked Steve only because he was Soda's best friend. He didn't like me – he thought I was a tag-along and a kid; Soda always took me with them when they went places if they weren't taking girls, and that bugged Steve. It wasn't my fault; Soda always asked me; I didn't ask him. Soda doesn't think I'm a kid.

Two-Bit Mathews was the oldest of the gang and the wisecracker of the bunch. He was about six feet tall, stocky in build, and very proud of his long rusty-colored sideburns. He had gray eyes and a wide grin, and he couldn't stop making funny remarks to save his life. You couldn't shut up that guy; he always had to get his two-bits worth in. Hence his name. Even his teachers forgot his real name was Keith, and we hardly remembered he had one. Life was one big joke to Two-Bit. He was famous for shoplifting and his black-handled switchblade (which he couldn't have acquired without his first talent), and he was always smarting off to the cops. He really couldn't help it. Everything he said was so irresistibly funny that he just had to let the police in on it to brighten up their dull lives. (That's the way he explained it to me.) He liked fights, blondes, and for some unfathomable reason, school. He was still a junior at eighteen and a half and he never learned anything. He just went for kicks. I liked him real well because he kept us laughing at ourselves as well as at other things. He reminded me of Will Rogers – maybe it was the grin.

EXPLORE

1. For Pony, what is so attractive about Paul Newman?
2. Why can't Pony walk home from the movie theatre by himself?
3. What happened to Pony's parents?
4. What kind of people are the 'Socials'?
5. Why can't Pony ever get involved in stealing or fights?

STUDYING YOUR NOVEL – *Symbolism*

Symbolism is extremely important when discussing your novel.

Read the following list and tick the things that make Pony feel like a 'Greaser', finding a quote to support your answer.

Item	Tick	If ticked, find a quote to support it
Eyes		I have … greenish-gray eyes. I wish they were more gray because I hate guys with green eyes.
Hair		
Lips		
T-shirt		
Shorts		
Polo neck shirt		
Leather jacket		
Blue jeans		
Boots		
Loafers		
Tennis shoes		
Leather shoes		
Singing		
Working		
Stealing		
Cars		
Drinking		

Having also read the descriptions of Steve Randle and Two-Bit Mathews, the one feature mentioned in all three descriptions is their hair.

> 'My hair is longer than a lot of boys wear theirs, squared off in back and long at the front and sides, but I am a greaser.'

> 'Steve Randle was seventeen, tall and lean, with thick greasy hair he kept combed in complicated swirls.'

> 'Two-Bit Mathews was the oldest of the gang and the wisecracker of the bunch. He was about six feet tall, stocky in build, and very proud of his long rusty-colored sideburns.'

In all three examples, the boys take great pride in their hair. It is a physical symbol of their identity and what they stand for.

A symbol is something that stands for or represents something else. When symbols appear throughout a story, it is known as symbolism.

Read this second short extract from later in the novel. Pony and his friend Johnny are on the run from the police.

> Johnny sat down and pulled out his knife. 'We're gonna cut our hair, and you're gonna bleach yours.' He looked at the ground carefully. 'They'll have our descriptions in the paper. We can't fit 'em.' 'Oh, no!' My hand flew to my hair. 'No, Johnny, not my hair!' It was my pride. It was long and silky, just like Soda's, only a little redder. Our hair was tuff – we didn't have to use much grease on it. Our hair labelled us greasers, too – it was our trademark. The one thing we were proud of. Maybe we couldn't have Corvairs or madras shirts, but we could have hair.

In this scene, the boys are forced to cut their hair. This is symbolic of them cutting ties with their identity and the gang. From this moment onwards, they have the opportunity to think and behave independently.

For your exam, you should know *at least* two symbols that the author of your **studied novel** uses. This will allow you to discuss the novel in depth.

1. List all the symbols in your studied novel.

2. Explain what they represent.

3. Do they help the character to change or do they restrict them?

Exam Focus

You have to teach the concept of **symbolism** to your class. Create a mind map using examples from your studied novel. You may also use images to aid understanding and explain why they are important to the story.

Final Exam Focus

Write about a **key moment** from your studied novel, discussing the importance of **two** of the following literary elements: theme, setting, character development, relationship development, genre, symbolism.

Fabulous Film

As I explore this collection I will learn about:

- Mise-en-scene
- Costume
- Make-up
- Special effects
- Scenes
- Music
- Sound effects
- Shots
- Camera angles
- Editing
- Animation
- Documentaries
- Lighting

I will relate everything I learn about film to my **studied film**

Learning Outcomes
OL8, R7, R9, W7, W8

What do you know about ... Film?

To help you revise what films are all about, rewrite the following by inserting the correct words from the list.

Films are another way of bringing stories to life. With huge budgets and glamorous stars, the film industry can make a story truly magical. You can watch lots of different types of films including f_____ length, short films, a_____ and d_____. Like novels, films can be categorised into g_____.

Vast amounts of money are spent on costumes, s_____, actors and s_____ e_____. In novels, you use your imagination, whereas in films, the d_____ brings his/her imagination or vision to the viewers. Directors are hugely important to the overall look of the film. It is important to pay attention to the way a director shoots the film.

Camera a_____ and s_____ are purposefully framed to create a scene. A director might want us to feel sympathy for the villain, so he/she might set up the camera frame to capture this. If the villain is wounded or dying, the m_____-_____ department will create a wound. Those looking after lighting might create a darkened room with a spotlight focusing only on the villain.

Many films are produced on sets in _____, California. It is the birthplace of cinema and home to all the major film companies such as Universal Studios and MGM. Often, studios are just waiting for a great book to be published so they can quickly make it into a film. It only took John Green's *The Fault in Our Stars* two years from its publication date for it to be released as a film.

Music is a vital component of film, with movie s_____ and soundtracks being released as albums. Famous c_____ John Williams has written music for many successful films such as *Harry Potter*, *Jurassic Park*, *Star Wars* and *Jaws*.

animation	sets	shots	genres	Hollywood
scores	angles	make-up	composer	
director	documentaries	feature	special effects	

Mise-en-Scene

You are about to explore the world of film and all the different methods filmmakers use to bring a story to life. All of these recognisable elements are summed up by the phrase *mise-en-scene*. This phrase comes from French theatre and it means to 'put into a scene'.

Imagine you have pressed pause during a film and the screen goes still: this is a frame. Look at everything in that frame. What things do you notice?

Study the still from the movie, *Thor*. You should notice the setting, the lighting, the costume, actors, props and special effects. If you were to press play, you should hear dialogue and music, see action and choreography. All of these elements come under the heading, *mise-en-scene*.

Scene *n.*
Definition: A short section of a play or movie

Frame *n.*
Definition: One of many still images that make up a moving picture (film)

Costumes in Film

What I will learn:

to assess the importance of costume, special effects and make-up in film production

Costumes worn in films or plays have a very important role to fulfil. Actors use costume to help them get into character. It can enhance the actor's performance and the audience's interpretation of the character. For example, when you think of *The Wizard of Oz*, more than likely you see Dorothy in her blue dress and sparkly red shoes, or when you think of *The Pirates of the Caribbean*, you likely picture Jack Sparrow with his red bandana and pirate hat.

FUN FACT

The Lion's costume from *The Wizard of Oz* weighed ninety pounds and was made from two real lion skins.

Look at the following characters in costume from famous films. Match them with the correct film.

Name of Film	
Batman: The Dark Knight	
Edward Scissorhands	
The Hunger Games	
Indiana Jones and the Temple of Doom	
The Fault in Our Stars	
Cinderella	

FUN FACT

In the hit musical *Grease*, Olivia Newton-John wore a costume so figure-hugging in the final scene that she needed to be sown into it every day. She couldn't even go to the toilet!

STUDYING YOUR FILM – *Costume*

When studying film and examining costume, follow these pointers:

- Describe the costume.

- What material is used and what does it suggest? For example, velvet suggests wealth, leather suggests toughness, lace suggests formality or femininity.

- Does the character wear this costume all the time? Perhaps the character wears one type of clothing at the beginning of the film but another towards the end.

- Does the costume empower or limit the character?

- Does the costume reflect the character's personality or their profession?

- Does the costume make the character appear happy or sad, or some other emotion?

Choose one costume from your studied film and write a paragraph describing why it is important to the character and plot.

Make-Up and Special Effects

A film's make-up and special effects crew are vital in bringing a character to life. Make-up artists can create the effect of flesh-eating skin diseases, gashes on a victim's head or even alien features. They work alongside the special effects team, who create prosthetic limbs, face masks and computer-enhanced features.

You Tube

Look up 'Voldermort's Makeup from Deathly Hallows: Part 1' on YouTube to see the power of special effects and make-up. In your opinion, how does the make-up and special effects enhance the character of Voldemort?

FUN FACT

The character of Gollum in *The Lord of the Rings* was digitally created using thirteen cameras pointed at different sensors attached to actor Andy Serkis' costume.

STUDYING YOUR FILM –
Make-Up and Special Effects

When studying film and examining make-up and special effects,
follow these pointers:

- Does the character wear everyday make-up and look natural?
- Is there something unusual about their appearance?
- Is the character's gender or personality altered by their make-up?
- How does the make-up enhance the character?
- Do the make-up and special effects add to the storyline?

Exam Focus

Choose one or two characters from a film you have studied and discuss the impact make-up or special
effects had on your experience of this character/these characters.

Music in Film

What I will learn:

*to comprehend a scene from a popular film; to explore the
impact of music and sound effects in film-making*

Working in groups, list five films that have a memorable score or music.

 **E.T. the Extra-Terrestrial (Steven Spielberg, dir.)**

Look up 'Ride in the Sky – ET' on YouTube. This scene is from the film *E.T. the Extra-Terrestrial*, which is a classic film about an American family who find a gentle alien living in their house. The alien – ET – is befriended by Elliot, the youngest boy in the house, who tries his best to keep him a secret. Elliot wants to help ET to 'go home'. In this particular scene, Elliot and his friends are trying to escape from the authorities, who want to take ET away and study him.

The film was directed by Steven Spielberg and the music was written by John Williams. Pay particular attention to the music.

EXPLORE

Use the following vocabulary to help you discuss your feelings about the music from the film. Does the music add anything to the scene?

composer	score	powerful	exciting	moody
creepy	original	dramatic	triumphant	atmospheric
threatening	emotional	energetic	tempo	slow
explosive	ground-breaking	passionate	magical	menacing
moving	beat	pace	sad	riveting
soft	melodic	crescendo	rhythmic	soulful

Exam Focus

From your studied film, choose a scene that uses music effectively. Write a paragraph about how it is used in the scene and how it adds to the storyline.
The following sentences will help you:

- The scene I have studied is when …
- This is a key moment in the story and adds to the storyline because …
- The music is important to this scene because …
- When I hear the music, I understand …
- The music makes me feel …

SAMPLE ANSWER

I have chosen a scene from the film *Jaws*, directed by Steven Spielberg. His long-term creative partner, John Williams, was responsible for writing the intelligent score to accompany the appearance of the villain of the piece. The music is only two notes and beats 'dun dun', which doesn't seem that exciting on paper. However, it is highly effective when used in scenes that feature the shark, Jaws, attacking the characters in the story. Williams creates creepy and atmospheric music by starting with a slow tempo. As the shark gets nearer, Williams quickens the pace to create a menacing tempo which makes the audience feel scared.

TOP TIP

Films use **theme music** and **incidental music**. Theme music is used as part of the main soundtrack, whereas incidental music is background music. Both create **ambiance** (atmosphere), but incidental music creates **realism** in a scene, for example elevator music or a band playing in a bar in the background.

FUN FACT

A certain scream has been used in over two hundred movies. It is called the Wilhelm Scream. Look up 'Wilhelm Scream compilation' on YouTube to hear a compilation of the many times it has been used.

Sound Effects

Films also feature **sound effects** to help create a realistic story. Films can feature:

- Isolated sounds, such as a car horn or dogs barking
- Speciality effects, such as the noise from a space transporter or a 'magical machine'
- Foley sounds – when sounds are replaced by louder and more enhanced sounds, such as footsteps
- Background ambiance, such as subtle talking or the sound of train tracks

FUN FACT

The noises the dinosaurs make in *Jurassic Park* are actually recordings of whales, horses and koala bears. No one knows what a dinosaur sounded like, but scientists believe they made a gurgling noise. Gurgling wasn't very exciting for a film, so sound director Gary Rydstrom changed the sounds to make them more powerful.

CREATE

Find objects to make the following sounds and record them on your phone or bring them into class.

1. Thunder
2. Rain
3. The opening of doors on a spaceship
4. A monster's roar

Shots and Camera Angles

What I will learn:

to examine the variety of shots and camera angles used by filmmakers;
to explore the process of editing in film-making

PREPARE

Study these images carefully. What differences do you notice between them?

You will notice that these photos show certain angles and shots from different films. Directors and camera operators use different types of shots and angles to help the audience to understand the story.

- Extreme close-up shot: Focuses on one detail such as a person's eyes or fingernails.

- Close-up shot: A shot that focuses on a person's face or an object.

- Medium shot: Taking a shot from a medium distance, usually featuring a full length shot of a person or object.

- Long shot: A wide shot or full view, which is taken from a great distance.

- Aerial shot: An overhead or bird's eye view.

- Low shot: Taken from a low angle facing upwards.

- High shot: Taken from a high angle facing downwards.

A shot is a frame or series of frames (images) recorded on film. An angle is the position for capturing or viewing something.

TOP TIP

Watch this video on Vimeo to see lots of different shots used in film production https://vimeo.com/72859928

W10.2

Review images 1–7 again. Match each image up with the type of shot/camera angle being used in each one.

Extreme close-up shot	Close-up shot	Medium shot	Long shot	Aerial shot	Low shot	High shot

You Tube *The Karate Kid* (John G. Avildsen, dir.)

Look up this scene from the classic film, *The Karate Kid*, on YouTube: 'Karate Kid Halloween Fight'. This film was directed by John G. Avildsen and stars Ralph Macchio as the 'karate kid' who learns to stand up to bullies by mastering the art of karate. In this scene, Daniel (Ralph Macchio) is trying to escape his enemies after playing a practical joke on them at a fancy dress party. Watch out for the director's editing of angles and shots.

Editing is the process of cutting and assembling shots to make sense of the action for the audience. Films don't shoot all their material in order. Sometimes the first scene of a film might be the last one to be shot. It is the film director/editor's job to cut and put all the scenes together in a logical manner.

EXPLORE

1. Where does this scene take place?

2. How does the setting add to the storyline?

3. Do all the bullies want to hurt Daniel?

Filmmakers often **storyboard** their film in advance of shooting any scenes. This means they draw out what scenes they want to shoot, shot by shot, so they have a brief to show the camera people, the lighting directors, as well as the actors, of how they want the shots to look.

Study this storyboard for a sequence of scenes from this clip in *The Karate Kid*. Identify the different types of shots and angles the director wants depicted in each scene. Write one-line descriptions of the shot wanted, which would be inserted below each image in the storyboard.

Karate Kid Storyboard

_____

_____

_____

_____

_____

_____

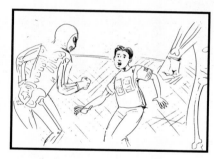

_____

_____

_____

_____

_____

_____

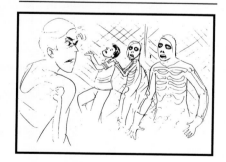

_____

_____

_____

_____

_____

_____

STUDYING YOUR FILM – *Shots and Angles*

Pick an important scene from your studied film. Track the different types of shots which are used. Explain why the director decided to film the scene in this way (editing).

- Does the sequence of shots and angles create excitement, adventure, fear, joy, etc.?

- Has the director decided to focus on something in particular, for example an aerial shot, to show how big and busy a city is, or a close-up to show a person's emotion?

- What is the order of the shots (editing)? Does the director edit the shots to feature an extreme close-up, panning out to a long shot to show a character is all alone, for example?

- Does the director choose a certain angle to reveal something to the audience, for example an overhead shot during a card game, whereby the audience knows a character is cheating but the other characters have no idea?

TOP TIP

You Tube

If you want to hear discussions, reviews or interviews about films, listen to the brilliant 'Kermode and Mayo's Film Review' podcast. You can download this podcast from BBC Radio or look up the specific clips on YouTube; for example, look up the interview with Hugh Jackman talking about his character in the film, *Pan*.

RESEARCH ZONE

Find a written or aural interview with the director of your studied film. Read or listen to their views on the film you have studied. Write down the main points based on their experience of directing their film.

Animation

  What I will learn:

to explore the process of animation in film

In groups, make a list of all the animated films that you know of.

> An animated film is a series of drawn, painted or digital scenes.

Having worked in groups to create your list, you will notice that there are lots of different types of animation.

Snow White and the Seven Dwarfs was the first ever feature-length animated film, released in 1937 by Disney. It was created using classical 2-D sketches: every image was hand-drawn and hand-painted. If *Snow White and the Seven Dwarfs* were to be made today, the team of animators would be able to use computer programmes to speed up the process considerably.

Other types of animation include what is called 'stop-motion animation', which uses clay figures that are moved only slightly and then shot, with all the frames put together to suggest continuous movement, such as is used in the *Wallace and Gromit* films; or computer-animated 3-D techniques, such as in *The Polar Express*.

THE BREAKOUT COMEDY OF THE SUMMER

You Tube The Making of *Toy Story 3*

Look up 'The making of Toy Story 3' on YouTube, and then answer the **True** or **False** statements about what is involved in making an animated film.

True or False

Statements

- Animation is when films use subtitles.
- Actors can appear on the screen as themselves.
- High-profile actors never do animated films.
- Animation is nominated as a special category at the Oscars.
- Animated films only take a couple of months to make.
- These films often use original music scores.
- Walt Disney is a company that produces animated films.
- Animated films also use particular shots and angles.
- Animated films do not use computer-generated images (CGI).
- Animated films have a director and producer just like other films.

RESEARCH ZONE

Walt Disney created the first cartoon in 1928 with Mickey Mouse starring in *Steamboat Willie*. Create a digital presentation on Walt Disney and how animation has changed since this original cartoon.

Documentary Film

What I will learn:

to brainstorm and plan for a documentary

If you were making a documentary about teenage life in your school, what would you include? What message would you like to send out? Do you feel school life is positive and full of opportunities, or negative and restrictive? Would you make a film about how teenagers act around each other? Would you want to send out a message about the pressure of exams?

> A documentary is a film or TV programme presenting facts and information rather than telling a fictional story.

Answer the following questions to help you plan a documentary about teenage life in school.

Question	Your answer
How would you describe teenage life in school?	
Who would you interview in your documentary?	
What message/information would you hope the interviewees might give?	
Name three locations you might film in.	
Would you need a voice-over? What would they say?	
What music would you have? Would it be background music or a feature song?	
What will your ending be? What is your overall message?	

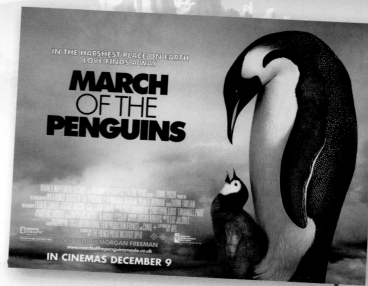

You**Tube**

March of the Penguins trailer

Look up the trailer for *March of the Penguins* on YouTube. This nature documentary was directed by Luc Jacquet and narrated by Morgan Freeman.

? EXPLORE

1. Tick the documentary techniques that you think this trailer used.

Characters	Storyline	Voice-over/ narrator	Shots and angles	Facts
Convincing points/ arguments	Interviews	Music	Lighting	Expert witness

2. Having watched the trailer, do you think this documentary will be interesting? Explain your answer.

CREATE

In groups of four, brainstorm ideas for your own documentary. Remember, documentaries tell stories too. Here are some ideas to inspire you:

- The life of a hurler
- Devoted music fans
- Youth clubs
- Putting yourself in your parents' shoes
- Making yourself independent
- Teenage life in your school

Make a two-minute documentary about one of your ideas from the brainstorm. Use different documentary elements to tell your story. You can use your phone or a camera to record. Editing software is available on iPhones or Windows Movie Maker to bring your story together.

You must always ask a person's permission to record them before actually doing so.

A Short Film

to understand the use of lighting and special effects in the film-making process

PREPARE

In pairs, make a list of any mythical or magical creatures you know of from books or movies.

WATCH

The Faeries of Blackheath Woods (Ciarán Foy, dir.)

This short film is about a young girl who stumbles across some fairies while playing in the woods. Watch out for the director's use of special effects and lighting techniques.

EXPLORE

1. How would you describe this film? Explain why you chose a particular word.

   a.) humorous   b.) disturbing   c.) exciting   d.) thrilling   e.) comforting

2. The director uses special effects in this film. Where do you see their use?

3. Do we feel sympathy for the young girl? Refer to her dialogue at the beginning of the film to support your answer.

4. How does the lighting change from one wood to another? Why has the director chosen to use certain types of lighting at a particular time? These words will help you discuss lighting.

soft	spotlight	dim	blurry
muddy	natural	black and white	sharp
dark	bright (over-exposed)	fluorescent	filters

CREATE

1. Create a collage of stills from different films that demonstrate the variety of lighting used by directors. Include a short comment on the effectiveness of the lighting used in each still.

2. Create a short film that experiments with different lighting techniques.

STUDYING YOUR FILM – *Colour*

Colour is often overlooked when we study films. We think of colour as a natural component but it is often used deliberately to show something important.

Match the colour with what it can often represent in films.

Red	Envy or jealousy
Blue	Natural elements such as soil
Green	Happy and optimistic
Yellow	Darkness and negativity
Brown	Natural elements such as the sea and sky
Black	Danger

This use of colour – to represent mood or landscape – is only one way in which colour can be used in films. Think about and consider other ways in which colour might be used. For example:

1. Is colour representing:

    - Gender (stereotypically pink for girls and blue for boys)

    - Religion (orange for Buddhism)

    - Politics (red is associated with Communism)

    - Culture (green is associated with the Irish)

2. Are certain colours being repeated?

3. Does colour help build an atmosphere or mood?

4. Are the colours being used in harmony or do do certain colours clash (not work well together)?

5. Is the film deliberately shot in black and white? If so, why?

Look at this still from *The Wizard of Oz* and describe how you think colour is being used in the scene.

Exam Focus

Find a poster for your studied film. Do the colours and use of lighting in the poster represent the film accurately? Explain your answer with reference to your poster.

Write a paragraph on the use of a particular colour in your studied film. How is it used? Does the director want to send out a certain message by using this colour?

Final Exam Focus

Pick a key moment from your studied film and discuss the use of two of the following elements: costume, shots and angles, lighting and special effects, music.

Oral Communication

As I explore this collection I will learn about:

- Choosing a topic
- Research skills
- Making a topic interesting and enjoyable
- Engaging the audience/listener
- Planning my oral communication
- The Five Golden Rules of Speech
- Choosing a style of communication or format
- Writing and organising what I have to say
- Presenting in different formats
- Modelling myself on professional communicators
- How to do interviews

Learning Outcomes
OL1, OL5, OL7, OL9, OL13, R3, W3, W5

In this chapter you will prepare for the first **classroom-based assessment (CBA 1), oral communication**. Communicating orally is a skill that you will use throughout your life. You will be glad that you mastered it during this year in school. At some time in the future, you may do an interview in which you have to speak with confidence to one or more interviewers. You may be asked to make a speech at a wedding or a family celebration. You may even choose a career in teaching, sales or in the media, where speaking clearly and confidently will be very important for you.

Oral Communication Steps

There are three areas of activity in oral communication:

1. Preparation (Plan, Research and Write)
2. Communication (Speak/Perform/Present)
3. Reflect (Draft and write a reflection; see also p. 448)

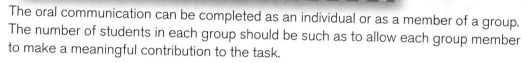

The oral communication can be completed as an individual or as a member of a group. The number of students in each group should be such as to allow each group member to make a meaningful contribution to the task.

During and after your oral communication, you must complete a written student **Reflection Note** (see sample on p. 449). Even if you collaborate with classmates, you must complete your own Reflection Note.

Preparation is as important as the communication itself, so ensure that you show this in your work.

1. Preparation

To prepare for the oral communication you will work through these steps:

1. Plan
2. Research
3. Write (Draft/Edit)

TOP TIP

You have already done a lot of preparation for oral tasks in this book. You have listened to excellent communicators in the video clips and audio recordings. Think back to the best speaker you heard. You could model yourself on him or her.

1. Plan

If you have a great interest in a certain topic (fashion, football, etc.), you can choose your **topic** first and then the style of communication, or **format** (interview, presentation, etc.). Alternatively you could choose the format you think you would prefer, then the topic.

Sample Formats

Format	Description
Presentation	You present to an audience on a topic you have prepared. You may speak with or without notes, with a prepared script or just flash cards, and you may use digital ways of presenting (e.g. PowerPoint/Prezi). You may also use photos or props in your presentation.
Interview	You interview a person of your choice. To do this you would research a person (past or present) and then write a set of questions and answers that would give listeners an understanding of this person's life. This might be a famous person or someone you know personally, or perhaps even a character from a novel being interviewed (see p. 446). The interview should be interesting and enjoyable. You can be the interviewer and the interviewee, or you can just be the interviewee and someone else (another student, the teacher) can ask you the list of pre-arranged questions.

Format	Description
Performance	You may do a scripted or unscripted performance alone or with other students, e.g. a poem, a drama, a dialogue. You need to research the topic very well (watching other performances counts as research) and rehearse in order to ensure quality in your performance. Your performance should display evidence of time spent on research and preparation. For performances, it is helpful to have an introduction and concluding comments so that you formally 'frame' the performance for your audience.
Response to stimulus material	You give a talk on something that inspired you. For example, you could choose a novel, play or film from your course. You may choose a visual, a written text or an aural text to guide and illustrate your talk. This could be a photo, an infographic, a piece of film, a short story, a poem, a song, a radio interview, etc. Be prepared to answer questions.

Sample Topics

The topic should be interesting for you, but remember you need to complete your preparation within the time allowed. Have a clear **purpose** to your communication: what is it that you want your audience to know/feel/think about at the end of the communication?

Here are some examples:

An interesting **person**, e.g. a sportsperson, writer, musician, performer or film director	An **organisation** with which you are involved, or that you support	Your favourite **hobby** or pastime	An **investigation** of a text, writer, film, etc.	One of your **activities** or interests, e.g. music, sport, fashion, reading, drama or film

Topics might involve **choosing a question and finding the answer**, e.g. which is better, the printed book or the eBook?

EXAMPLE

You may decide to talk about something that you find especially interesting, for example *fashion*. In this example, you would have chosen your **topic** first and would then need to decide on an appropriate **format**. There are many formats you can use with the topic of fashion:

You might research a famous designer and then imagine an **interview** with them.

You might ask another student(s) to wear some items you have designed yourself and then **present an illustrated talk** about what inspired you to make them, how you made them, etc. You might also write the script for a presenter at a fashion show introducing each model and outfit.

You might give a **talk** about some of the history and influences of a particular fashion item on today's society, for example, denim.

Remember some of the examples of oral communication you may have done already from this book:

1. **Friendship** p. 41: **present a photograph orally**
2. **War** pp. 74–5: write and speak a **news broadcast**
3. **Young and Old** p. 113: give a **speech** about old and young
4. **Journeys** pp. 145/147: **deliver an editorial** publicly
5. **Journeys** pp. 145/148: write a **story** to be read as an **audio recording**
6. **Journeys** p. 147: 'Success Criteria for Speaking to a Live Audience'
7. **Triumph over Adversity** p. 182: make an **oral presentation** about/do an interview with a charitable organisation
8. **Reason in Rhyme: Poetry** p. 318: prepare a **three-minute talk** about a poem

2. Research

The development of your research skills throughout the preparation will be important:

- Using key questions to shape ideas
- Searching for information
- Reading and note-taking
- Organising material
- Developing a point of view

Key Questions

The first step in any research is to ask **key questions** to help you organise your preparation and communication.

Ask basic questions about the topic using the 5Ws (who, what, when, where, why)

1. Who is involved/important/affected, etc.?
2. What is it about/for, etc.?
3. When are the important dates/timelines, etc.?
4. Where is the action/location, etc.?
5. Why is this interesting/important, etc.?
6. How much information do I need?
7. What types of information will I need: facts, opinions, analysis, research studies or a mixture?
8. What sources should I consult to find the information?
9. Are there points/examples/moments in the novels, films, poems or plays we have studied that I can quote?
10. Will I write my title in the form of a statement or a question?

Searching for Information

Research can take many forms. You may need to read, watch or listen to texts. You may also do some original investigations such as interviewing, surveying, emailing, etc. Where sources are used, you must make sure to explain the information in your own words and opinions. If you use a direct quotation, name and acknowledge the source or the person you are quoting.

There are many methods than can be used to research a topic; interviews and surveys are particularly useful.

Interviews

A great way to do research is to **interview** someone. For example, if you were making a speech about young and older people, you might interview one young person and one older person who live in the same area, asking them the same questions. Their responses would help to prepare and shape your talk. You could quote them and explore some of the points they make. For more help or if you decide to write a speech like this, go to the Oral Communication on page 113 at the end of the *Young and Old* collection.

Surveys

Another good way to gather information on a topic is to do a **survey**. For example, imagine that you decided to perform a short drama – a conversation between a woman/man and a politician on the doorstep asking for a vote. For your research, you could interview a politician about the most common questions they are asked **or** you could survey a group of your teachers or neighbours about the questions they would *like* to ask a politician or their reaction to the doorstep call (an invitation to come in, a refusal to discuss, a grilling with questions, etc.).

TOP TIP

A great way to do a survey is online using websites like Survey Monkey or Google Forms.

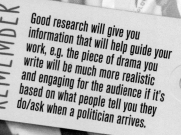

REMEMBER

Good research will give you information that will help guide your work, e.g. the piece of drama you write will be much more realistic and engaging for the audience if it's based on what people tell you they do/ask when a politician arrives.

Five Tips for Writing a Survey

1. Keep the survey **short**.

2. Keep the questions **simple**.

3. Ask yourself **what** you need to know and **tailor your questions** around that.

4. Use **closed questions** (with yes, no or specific answers that the user chooses from).

5. **Test it** by doing it yourself before you send it to anyone.

Imagine you are going to interview an Irish astrophysicist (a type of scientist) about a recent discovery of the possibility of life on Mars.

Work with another classmate or in a group to:

- **Brainstorm** the research you will do in advance of the interview (questions you would ask yourself, sources you would consult to find the information, e.g. NASA website).

- Write down **five questions** you would ask of your interviewee (the scientist) on the radio show.

TOP TIP

In *Fire and Ice 1* on pp. 105–6, you can read about the NASA discovery of a new planet and listen to two scientists explaining this discovery in a video clip. This will give you both key questions to ask and the vocabulary you need to discuss a new planet.

Mars and Water

Listen to this interview with Dr Joseph Roche, astrophysicist with the Science Gallery, Dublin, regarding the recent discovery of evidence of water on Mars. As you listen, write down the **six** questions that the radio journalist asks.

After you have finished listening, make a note of whether each question was an **open** or **closed** question. *Open* questions invite someone to speak more than a *yes* or *no* answer.

Did this interviewer ask any of the questions you would have asked?

Imagine you were going to speak in front of your class. Choose one of the topics below.

1. Walt Disney (the person, not the company)
2. New Zealand
3. American Football
4. Shakespeare

List three possible formats to present your material, e.g. a presentation, a speech, an interview, a dramatic performance, a voice-over, etc. Having decided on your topic and format, list six questions you would need to ask in order to prepare for your topic.

Reading and Note-Taking

When taking notes from sources, try not to write out the whole text again. Choose key words/phrases and try to write your own ideas about what you're reading. The more you can make your notes your own as you write, the easier it will be to translate them into a presentation.

Organising Material

Decide how you want to organise material – keep a folder for images you like, or a sheet of paper for key ideas.

Copy useful website addresses into your notes so you can find them again.

Developing a Point of View

It is very important that the audience see your point of view in what you present. Talk ideas through with friends and family to help you form and express your opinions.

3. Write

Once you have conducted your research, you are ready to start drafting. How you do this will of course depend on your chosen format. Some guidance for the following formats is given here:

- A Presentation (PowerPoint/Prezi)

- A Performance (scripting a speech/voice-over for an advertisement)

In all cases you could choose to write your own **original** piece or use an **existing work** that you enjoyed or which inspired you.

Be careful! It is very important that if you choose to perform someone else's work, you *shape* and *frame* it by writing your own **introduction** to the piece, explaining why you chose it and what you think makes it interesting. You should also write a short **conclusion**. You might also invite **questions from the audience/teacher** about the chosen piece, which would give evidence that you had done **research**.

Using the writing skills you have learned throughout this book, **plan** and **write** your **first draft**. When it is drafted, **read it aloud for yourself and edit it** (some words and phrases work well written down, but not when you read them, so you'll need to fix it accordingly).

Read it aloud for someone and get their feedback and then edit it again.

> # TOP TIP
>
> If you do a digital presentation (e.g. PowerPoint) or use props, they should help your communication. Remember: a picture (or prop) can speak a thousand words.

A Presentation

When giving a presentation, you may decide to speak directly from a script or flash cards. You could also create a PowerPoint or Prezi presentation and go through it using additional notes.

To make the presentation more interesting or enjoyable for the audience you could add illustrations, photographs or music. You are also allowed to make use of props where appropriate. Be creative in order to engage the attention of your audience.

A Performance

An oral performance can take many forms, such as:

- A speech (to revise speech-making, go to page 105/113)
- An extract from a drama
- A poem
- A story or anecdote
- A voice-over for an advertisement

There is advice and guidance on writing the scripts/text for the above types of performance throughout this book. Below we will look at the script of a speech and read some advice on how to write a voice-over script for a radio advertisement.

A Speech

When giving a speech you must be convincing and accurate about your topic. Using persuasive language as well as facts and figures can help you win over your audience.

The Girl Who Silenced the World for Six Minutes ... at the Age of 12

In 1992, twelve-year-old Severn Suzuki and three of her classmates raised the money to fly 5,000 miles (8,000 kilometres) from Canada to Rio de Janeiro to speak at the UN Earth Summit. They felt so passionately about protecting the earth that they reached out for the attention of the world's leaders.

Severn's speech became known as 'The Girl Who Silenced the World for Six Minutes' and is still watched on YouTube.

Read the text of the speech below and answer the questions that follow.

Hello, I'm Severn Suzuki speaking for ECO — The Environmental Children's Organisation.

We are a group of twelve- and thirteen-year-olds trying to make a difference: Vanessa Suttie, Morgan Geisler, Michelle Quigg and me. We've raised all the money to come here ourselves, to come five thousand miles to tell you adults you must change your ways. Coming up here today, I have no hidden agenda. I am fighting for my future.

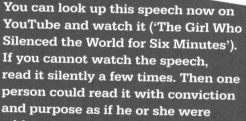

TOP TIP

You can look up this speech now on YouTube and watch it ('The Girl Who Silenced the World for Six Minutes'). If you cannot watch the speech, read it silently a few times. Then one person could read it with conviction and purpose as if he or she were addressing the international audience and attempting to convince them of this point of view.

Losing my future is not like losing an election or a few points on the stock market. I am here to speak for all generations to come.

I am here to speak on behalf of the starving children around the world whose cries go unheard.

I am here to speak for the countless animals dying across this planet because they have nowhere left to go.

I am afraid to go out in the sun now because of the holes in our ozone. I am afraid to breathe the air because I don't know what chemicals are in it.

I used to go fishing in Vancouver – my home – with my dad, until just a few years ago we found the fish full of cancers. And now we hear of animals and plants going extinct every day, vanishing forever.

In my life, I have dreamt of seeing the great herds of wild animals, jungles and rainforests full of birds and butterflies, but now I wonder if they will even exist for my children to see.

Did you have to worry of these things when you were my age?

All this is happening before our eyes and yet we act as if we have all the time we want and all the solutions.

I'm only a child and I don't have all the solutions, but I want you to realise, neither do you!

You don't know how to fix the holes in our ozone layer.

You don't know how to bring the salmon back up a dead stream.

You don't know how to bring back an animal now extinct.

And you can't bring back the forests that once grew where there is now desert.

If you don't know how to fix it, please stop breaking it!

Here, you may be delegates of your government, business people, organisers, reporters or politicians – but really, you are mothers and fathers, sisters and brothers, aunts and uncles, and all of you are someone's child.

$\longrightarrow$

I'm only a child, yet I know we are all part of a family, five billion strong; in fact, 30 million species strong, and borders and governments will never change that.

I'm only a child yet I know we are all in this together and should act as one single world towards one single goal.

In my anger, I am not blind, and in my fear, I am not afraid of telling the world how I feel.

In my country, we make so much waste, we buy and throw away, buy and throw away, and yet northern countries will not share with the needy. Even when we have more than enough, we are afraid to share, we are afraid to let go of some of our wealth.

In Canada, we live the privileged life, with plenty of food, water and shelter — we have watches, bicycles, computers and television sets. The list could go on for two days.

Two days ago here in Brazil, we were shocked when we spent time with some children living on the streets. This is what one child told us: 'I wish I was rich, and if I were, I would give all the street children food, clothes, medicines, shelter and love and affection.'

If a child on the street who has nothing is willing to share, why are we who have everything still so greedy?

I can't stop thinking that these are children my own age, that it makes a tremendous difference where you are born, that I could be one of those children living in the favelas of Rio; I could be a child starving in Somalia; or a victim of war in the Middle East, or a beggar in India.

I am only a child yet I know if all the money spent on war was spent on finding environmental answers, ending poverty and finding treaties, what a wonderful place this earth would be!

At school, even in kindergarten, you teach us to behave in the world. You teach us: to not fight with others; to work things out; to respect others; to clean up our mess; not to hurt other creatures; to share — not be greedy. Then why do you go out and do the things you tell us not to do?

Do not forget why you're attending these conferences, who you're doing this for — we are your own children. You are deciding what kind of a world we are growing up in. Parents should be able to comfort their children by saying 'everything's going to be alright, it's not the end of the world, and we're doing the best we can.' But I don't think you can say that to us anymore. Are we even on your list of priorities?

My dad always says, 'You are what you do, not what you say.'

Well, what you do makes me cry at night. You grown-ups say you love us, but I challenge you, please make your actions reflect your words. Thank you.

1. Identify the introduction, main points and conclusion of this speech.

2. Pick out at least three elements of persuasive language, with examples. For example, repetition, rhetorical questions, emotive language visual language, humour, quotes, etc.

3. Choose the three most important sentences in the speech and explain your choice.

 Working in groups, make a list of some of the most famous speeches that you know.

REMEMBER Persuasive language and writing seeks to convince others of a certain point of view; it hopes to persuade them.

A Radio Advertisement

Read the interview on the next page with Andrew McNulty, a copywriter (someone who writes copy, i.e. the words in an advertisement, written, visual or audio) from one of Ireland's leading advertising agencies, ICAN Advertising. He gives some good advice for writing an original advertisement. Notice that the interviewer asks five open-ended questions that allow Andrew to tell listeners about his work.

You can also listen to an advertisement from the agency when looking at voice-over on page 443.

Interview with Andrew McNulty, ICAN Advertising

Q: What does a good radio advertisement need?

A good script and a clear simple idea that will create a picture in the listener's mind. Listening to radio dramas can really help you with techniques and learning. Humour can be a powerful tool.

Q: What would your advice be to anyone writing a radio ad?

Know your product. Make sure you have all the information at hand (do your research). Write the way people talk. Capture the cadence [rise and fall of the voice] and flow of real speech. Use sound effects to catch your listener's attention and imagination. Never cram too much in. Give your actors time to deliver their scripts. Writing is a process. Be prepared to edit and do many versions to make it as simple and good as you can get it. I edit some radio scripts about fifteen times.

Q: What's the most important consideration when picking someone to do the voice-over?

Actors bring so much to your script. Choose someone who can do the accents you need and is happy to take your direction. Listen to your actor's suggestions and be willing to tweak the script to suit their delivery or ideas.

Q: What's the hardest thing about your job?

Having ideas that are creatively interesting yet still sell a brand, service or business can be tough. You're trying to serve both art and business at the same time. Get it right, and it's very satisfying.

Q: Any advice to someone who wants to become a copywriter?

Be prepared to work hard. Copywriting is a process. You might not get it right first time. The important thing is to start. Keep editing and shaping your work into something you're happy with it. You never know what ideas could be a big hit for your clients. And deliver those sales!

TOP TIP

Notice how Andrew is willing to write many versions of a text before he gets it right. This is what you will also be doing in your second CBA, i.e. your Collection of Texts.

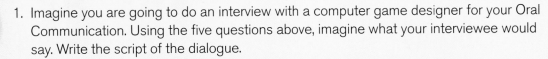

1. Imagine you are going to do an interview with a computer game designer for your Oral Communication. Using the five questions above, imagine what your interviewee would say. Write the script of the dialogue.

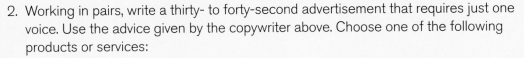

2. Working in pairs, write a thirty- to forty-second advertisement that requires just one voice. Use the advice given by the copywriter above. Choose one of the following products or services:

- A computer game
- A mobile phone with a battery life of one week
- An outdoor summer cinema
- A new theme park for teenagers

Some Practical Tips

1. When you are preparing, imagine that you are in the audience – what would you like to know about this topic? What would you be interested to hear? Would music, photographs, diagrams, etc., help to inform you and keep your attention?

2. Your title should reflect your purpose.

3. You must have a clear structure: an introduction, two or three main points and a conclusion. Use PIE to guide you.

4. Always draft and redraft your work to ensure it reads well and is accurate.

2. Communication

Speak/Perform/Present

Now it is time to present your topic in whatever format you have chosen. **Practise** until you know it almost **off by heart**. Think about where to **pause** for effect, when to **raise** your voice, when to **lower** it, when to **speak quickly** and when to **slow down**.

Practise in front of a **mirror** or **record yourself** and make any last minute adjustments.

Whatever you are doing, a talk, speech, performance, etc., always remember the **Five Golden Rules of Speech**.

Five Golden Rules of Speech

1. Clarity

2. Tone

3. Enthusiasm

4. Pace

5. Eye contact

1. Clarity

To speak with clarity means to speak clearly, so people can hear and understand you. Listeners should never have to ask you to repeat words because you spoke carelessly.

In pairs, **A** and **B**:

Test how good you are at speaking each word clearly by saying the **tongue twisters** on the next page for each other.

Listen carefully to your partner so you can give them two stars (two positive things) and a wish (one thing that could improve) for their pronunciation.

Whether the weather is warm, or whether the weather is hot, we have to put up with the weather, whether we like it or not.

Peter Piper picked a piece of pickled pepper, Where's the piece of pickled pepper Peter Piper picked?

She sells sea-shells on the sea-shore. The shells that she sells are sea-shells I'm sure.

Betty Botter had some butter, 'But,' she said, 'this butter's bitter. If I bake this bitter butter, it would make my batter bitter. But a bit of better butter — that would make my batter better.'

So she bought a bit of butter, better than her bitter butter, and she baked it in her batter, and the batter was not bitter.

2. Tone/Cadence

The **tone** of a voice is a quality that expresses the speaker's feelings or thoughts. The **cadence** is the rise and fall of the voice. It is important to vary your tone and cadence to avoid sounding monotonous, i.e. a boring, unchanging tone where you can't be bothered being enthusiastic, and put zero energy into what you say.

In pairs, **A** and **B**, take turns to speak the following **weather forecast**, slowly, clearly and carefully, as if you were the forecaster. You could model yourself on one particular weather forecaster you think is good. Take notes as you listen to each other and give feedback to help your partner.

And now for today's weather forecast.

It will be a cloudy start to the day. By mid-morning, heavy,

thundery showers will start moving across the country. This is due to this area of low pressure. Most areas will have heavy rain before this evening.

Better news for the sunny southeast.

Temperatures there are expected to reach the low twenties.

Tomorrow, early morning fog is expected in the midlands. There will also be misty patches in the east. These will soon burn away to give

a bright day in most places. The outlook for the rest of the week is for hazy sunshine, with light breezes and very little rain.

3. Enthusiasm

Enthusiasm is infectious, so if you seem excited about your topic, then your audience will be more likely to be attentive and interested too. Be yourself, but with about 20% extra!

In pairs, **A** and **B**, take turns to practise speaking this **promotion** for a local GAA club which is looking for new members. Read it a few times until you have the gist of it. Then speak it. It can be spoken in your own words, adding anything you think will make it better. Take it in turns to give one another feedback.

> **Come and join us at your local GAA club! We provide Gaelic football for boys and girls of all ages, starting at pre-school and going all the way through to adult men and women. It's a great way to get fit, keep fit and make friends!**
>
> **We're just beside the bus stop on the Old Conna Road, with big pitches and a brand new sports hall raised by funds from our parishioners over the last five years. We'll give you coaching at all levels. You can learn at your own pace with our relaxed, friendly teams.**

4. Pace

Listeners need time to absorb the information you are giving them. You must pause at commas and full stops and match the pace with the content.

In pairs, **A** and **B**, take turns to practise speaking these **Premier League results**. Read them aloud a few times until you have the gist. Then speak it. It can be spoken in your own words, adding anything you think will make it better. Take it in turns to give one another feedback.

> **Hello and welcome to our live coverage of match results from this afternoon's Premier League fixtures.**
>
> **Manchester United and Newcastle finished in a scoreless draw, ending Newcastle's wretched record of nine successive away defeats.**
>
> **Meanwhile, Arsenal prove that their recent losing streak might have been just a blip as they defeated Liverpool 4-1 in their first victory of the campaign.**
>
> **Over at Selhurst Park, there are four minutes remaining, with the score Crystal Palace 2, Aston Villa 1.**
>
> **Keep up to date with Galaxy News.**

5. Eye Contact

If when reading you look down at your notes all the time, you are not making the best connection with your audience. By making eye contact with members of the audience, you look more confident and trustworthy. Watching the audience's reaction helps you to better pace yourself; it can slow you down if you are speaking too quickly.

Bad Habits

Do you have any bad habits when you speak? Like, saying 'like' every five seconds!

We often repeat ourselves or use particular words and phrases without even realising it. When this kind of language creeps into formal situations, it can sound inappropriate.

Think about the way that people speak and make a list of **five** unnecessary words or phrases that are used regularly in everyday conversation, e.g. 'you know?'

'Like' by Joseph O'Connor

Now listen to the author, Joseph O'Connor (*pictured*), talk about words and phrases that annoy him.

As you listen, make a list of those words that he repeats. Are there any in common with the ones you had on your list? For the next week, make a conscious effort to remove three unnecessary words or phrases that you use.

Delivery

How well you deliver your performance/presentation will depend on your use of the five golden rules, but also on how you stand, your facial expressions, hand gestures and much more. You can see some examples of good delivery in the following excerpts relating to:

- Story
- News item
- Radio advertisement

Storytelling

A great resource for **hearing people tell stories** is the RTÉ Radio 1 programme, *Sunday Miscellany*. You can listen back to many of these stories as podcasts on the RTÉ website. If you wish to submit your story to *Sunday Miscellany*, their submission guidelines can be found on the website.

For **inspiration**, listen to some fantastic storytellers available on websites like The Moth www.themoth.org or This American Life www.thisamericanlife.org. There are great **storytelling tips** on The Moth website.

For **storytelling techniques**, go to page 129.

LISTEN

Listen to the story 'My First Valentine' written by Gerry Moran (*pictured*) and read by him on the RTÉ Radio 1 programme, *Sunday Miscellany*.

EXPLORE

1. Did the story keep you interested? Why?

2. What would you say about the speaker's tone, pronunciation and delivery?

3. Which storytelling techniques did the speaker use?

CREATE

Research and write a story that you could tell in about three minutes.
You can **research** by listening to 'My First Valentine' again or by listening to other stories on *Sunday Miscellany*, The Moth or other similar podcasts. Listen to how the story is crafted and delivered, and take notes on your favourite ones. What do they do that you could try?

• **News Item** • **News Item** • **News Item** • **News Item** •

A formal news or documentary item requires a very different delivery to a story or anecdote.

WATCH

Shakespeare's Globe Theatre London

Watch this four-minute clip in which a professional communicator encourages visitors to visit the new Globe Theatre in London and gives them lots of information about Shakespeare.

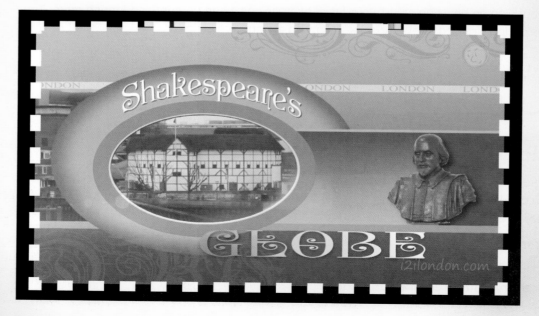

Comment on the performance of the speaker in the clip by copying and completing this grid.

	Agree	Disagree	Reasons/examples for my answer
The **title** is **clear** and **well chosen**			
There is evidence that **research** was done when the script was being planned and written			
Key questions were asked in order to give information in the presentation			
The presenter used **diagrams/props/objects** to explain the information that she was presenting			
She showed **good knowledge** of her subject			
There was **energy and enthusiasm** in her voice and she made it interesting			
The **tone** of her voice was **varied**			
The **pace** of speaking was **good**, neither too fast nor too slow			
The **music was appropriate** for the topic and made the presentation more enjoyable			
She **arranged** the presentation **in a clear way**, with a good introduction, middle and conclusion			

• **News Item** • **News Item** • **News Item** • **News Item** •

Radio Advertisement

Radio adverts are delivered by **voice-over** artists. You probably recognise some of the same voices on radio stations. These artists are skilful when it comes to delivering the message.

'How Do You Know a Website is Irish?'

You read an interview with the copywriter Andrew McNulty about his process for writing an advert on page 437. Now listen to the advert and think about how the voice-over artist delivered it.

1. Rate the aspects of the advertisement on a scale of 1 to 5 (with 5 being the best score) and give reasons for your answers.

The advertising copy (how the advertisement is written)				
	Poor ⟶			Excellent
Entertaining	1	2	3	4	5
Informative	1	2	3	4	5
Persuasive	1	2	3	4	5

The voice-over (how he speaks)					
	Poor ⟶ Excellent				
Clarity	1	2	3	4	5
Tone/pitch	1	2	3	4	5
Enthusiasm/energy	1	2	3	4	5
Pace	1	2	3	4	5
Acting quality	1	2	3	4	5

2. Point out two good things about this advertisement, one referring to how it is spoken, and the other to the content.

3. Mention one thing that would improve or make this a stronger advertisement.

Now you try!

Form groups of three to write and speak about these three topics:

- Introduce a famous sportsperson or entertainer as if you were a talk show host.
- Choose a hobby (sport, pastime, club) you enjoy and speak about it.
- Speak a YouTube clip recommending a book you have studied in class.

Each person in the group should choose a different topic and write a thirty second speech. When it is ready, speak it aloud to the other two people in the group.

Group members will complete the grid below as they listen to each person.

Peer Assessment

	Very well done	Quite well done	Suggestion for a next attempt
Focus on the task			
Interesting points and knowledge of the topic			
Volume of voice			
Cadence (the rise and fall of a voice, just as in singing a song)			
Spoke neither too fast nor too slow			
Confident posture and gestures			
Eye contact			
Energy/enthusiasm			

Some Practical Tips for a Great Presentation

1. Don't be afraid to try something new – sing, dance, bring props – with guidance from your teacher. Make it lively and interesting. Consider what you will wear. Don't be afraid to be your own prop!

2. Think about how you will present. You don't have to stand up – you can sit down if it suits your style of presentation. If you do stand up, think about how you'll stand.

3. Rehearse aloud to yourself in the mirror and notice your body language, posture and voice projection.

4. Speak your presentation to a friend or family member and ask for honest feedback.

5. As part of your practice, try to speak your presentation simply, without reading it off the page.

6. Look at people who present the news and notice how they sometimes stand with notes in their hands.

7. Get a good night's sleep the evening before and arrive in a state of relaxed alertness to do your oral communication task.

8. On the day of your oral communication, don't forget to **stand straight** (if you choose to stand), **speak clearly** and **smile**!

3. Reflect

Filling in the Reflection Note

In preparation for the assessment, you must fill in a **Student Reflection Note**. In this note, you explain the part you played in the preparation, particularly in the box headed:

'The part I played in the communication and preparation, including material used/accessed'

See the guidelines and sample Reflection Note in the *Assessment Focus* chapter on pages 448–9.

It is important that you do some discussion, thinking and rough drafts before you fill in the official template.

Sample Oral Communication Task

After studying *To Kill a Mockingbird*, imagine that you and another student wanted to speak about life in small-town Alabama during the 1930s Depression in the United States. You might do this by imagining an interview between a talk show host and one of the main characters.

Here is a flowchart to show how you might research, prepare for and perform/present this oral communication.

1. Plan
- Choose topic from the list on page 428:
  'An investigation of a text, or writer, or film' – *To Kill a Mockingbird*
- Define purpose: 'to show that the book gives a true picture of life in America during the Depression'"
- Choose specific title to give focus:
  'Life in small-town Alabama during the Depression as shown by Harper Lee'
- Choose appropriate format from CBA list (see p. 427/428).
  'Response to stimulus material/an interview/a performance'

2. Research
- Watch examples of interviews by Oprah Winfrey.
- Write some open questions that Oprah might ask Scout e.g.
  What was good about living in a small town?
  How did you feel when the people in the courtroom said, 'Miss Jean Louise, stand up. Your father's passin''?
  What were the differences between your life and the life of other children?
  Describe a typical day for a family in small-town Alabama.
- Seek out different sources to find answers:
  Text: Re-read key moments to find out about life in Alabama.
  Film: Watch *To Kill a Mockingbird* (film)
  Books: Take notes from library books on the Depression
  YouTube: Watch footage of the deep South during the Depression.
- You might also do a survey/ interview if you know people with who are knowledgeable about this topic.

3. Draft/Write
- Write the autocue* script for Oprah's introduction.
- Write a rough draft of the interview script (include relevant quotes from the book)
- Compose one question that will be asked by a member of your audience (this could be done by someone in the class as if this was live television).
- Write a conclusion, thanking the audience and your interviewee.
- This conversation should seem natural but show evidence of research.
- Choose support materials. For example you could create a PowerPoint that, when clicked, has the autocue for Oprah's introduction, main questions and conclusion. You could also include photographs/stills from the film or music from that era.

*Autocue
a TV screen with the words of the script so the presenter can read it.

4. Perform/Present
- Practise this together. Perform it for another group and get their feedback.
- Learn as much of the script as possible.
- Make sure that everything is ready the night before your presentation
- Perform the interview in front of your audience on the day. Your teacher may ask you questions after the performance about what you did to prepare and what you learned.

5. Reflect on the task, writing up the Reflection Note.

CREATE

Choosing another text as stimulus material, work with a partner to create a plan similar to the one above.

W11.9

Assessment Focus

ORAL COMMUNICATION

REFLECTION NOTE

Classroom-based Assessment (CBA) **1**: 2nd Year

THE COLLECTION OF STUDENT'S TEXTS

REFLECTION NOTE

Classroom-based Assessment (CBA) **2**: 3rd Year

ASSESSMENT IN ENGLISH

ASSESSMENT TASK

In-class formal written task related to CBA2: 3rd Year

FINAL WRITTEN EXAMINATION

Formal two-hour exam at the end of 3rd Year

Learning Outcomes

CBA 1/ CBA 2 OL1, OL5, OL7, OL9, OL13, R3, W3, W5

Final Written Examination OL8, OL12, R1, R2, R3, R4, R6, R7, R8, R9, R11, R12, R13, W1, W3, W4, W6, W7, W8, W9, W10, W11, W12

This chapter will help you to prepare for your various stages of assessment in English, right up to your final examination.

Assessment in English

Your work and progress in English will be assessed at various stages through second and third year. The diagram above gives you a quick overview of the types of assessment you will have to undertake. They will be explained in greater detail later in this chapter.

CBA 1: Oral Communication

During your English classes you will learn how to communicate orally and you will have many opportunities to practise and have fun speaking and performing. This is a very important life skill, one that you will be glad you mastered in school. You will need it on many occasions throughout your lifetime.

At the end of second year, you will be ready to do your first CBA (classroom-based assessment) in **Oral Communication**. Before the assessment, you will choose a **FORMAT** and **TOPIC**. You will then research the topic and prepare for communication. You will speak for three minutes on your topic and your task will be to show how well you can communicate as a speaker in the chosen format.

As part of your Oral Communication CBA, you will fill in a **Reflection Note** sheet. In this note you will reflect on the process of the preparation and the things you learned. A sample has been completed on the next page.

CBA 1: Oral Communication

Choose your topic/format

Research your topic (asking key questions, taking notes, recording sources etc. and reflecting on your work as you progress*)

Reflect regularly on your work/progress*

Speak for 3 minutes

Complete Reflection Note

*Reflection is a very important process. You should regularly think about your work, i.e. after each stage of the process is complete. This will help you to become better at oral communication.

Oral Communication – Student Reflection Note

SCHOOL	STUDENT
TITLE	

The part I played in the communication and preparation, including material used/ accessed

Personal reflection on the Oral Communication

One important thing I learned from doing the task	Things I would change or try to improve on

Student	Teacher	Date

12

REMEMBER All you need to know about preparing and delivering your Oral Communication task can be found in the Oral Communication chapter.

448 FIRE AND ICE 2

Sample Reflection Note for an Oral Communication Task

SCHOOL Fire and Ice Academy

STUDENT Mark Jones

TITLE The LauraLynn Children's Hospice and My Family

The part I played in communication and preparation, including material used/accessed

I chose this charity because my cousin is ill and she stays there sometimes. To prepare, I did some online research and later, face-to-face interviews. I used a number of key questions to guide my research. I went to the charity's website and got a lot of information there. I still had a few unanswered questions so my auntie brought me to the hospice. I interviewed some staff and asked my cousin, auntie and uncle questions about how it has helped their family. I got some great photos of my cousin with her hospice friends.

When I had all the information, I divided my speech into three parts (the history of the charity, how the hospice is funded and how they have helped my family). I did a rough plan on paper under these headings and then organised the information in Prezi. To communicate clearly I put my title on the front and key words on each slide. To make my talk interesting, I included colourful screenshots of the website, a scanned brochure, some photos and quotes from my interviews. My final slide summed up how important this organisation is to my family to link back to the title of my talk. I practised it in front of my friends and they gave me feedback which I used to edit the talk. I also practised at home. On the day, I tried to speak slowly and clearly but I rushed a little. Everybody was really interested – they asked me questions at the end and I was able to answer all of them as I had done so much research and preparation.

Personal reflection on the Oral Communication

One important thing I learned from doing the task

I learned that good researching takes time and that there are many ways to do it. I tried Wikipedia but the information wasn't very good so I went to the official website for the charity which was much better. Face-to-face interviews were the best part of my project because I saw the emotions in the faces of the people I spoke to — it showed me what a difference this charity makes. I could never have learned that from a website or email.

Things I would change or try to improve on

When I heard that I would be speaking in front of the class for three minutes I was very nervous. I practised a lot but there was a lot to remember. I rushed a little and forgot what I was going to say twice. The next time I'll speak more slowly. I will also make flash cards with key words to remind me of my main points and I will also turn around and glance at the presentation as I noticed some students did. This will help me to relax as I will know that I have a something to look at if I forget what I'm saying.

Student

Mark Jones

Teacher

Ms Farrelly

Date

X X 20XX

CBA 2: My Collection of Texts

Writing is a skill that is developed over time. Like any skill, it needs lots of practice. Over your three years in Junior Cycle English, you will develop a voice and style that is all your own!

To help develop your writing:

- **Read, read, read**! You can't expect to write well if you haven't read any good examples.

- **Keep pieces of writing that you like** and think about what it is about these pieces that you admire.

- **Try new things** and always read them aloud to hear how they sound.

- **Use feedback** from your teacher and peers to help you improve.

From the beginning of Year Two, you will be putting together a **Collection of Texts**.

CBA 2: Collection of Texts

Build your collection of texts

Keep all drafts

Choose your best four texts in four different genres

Complete a Reflection Note on each text

TOP TIP

Keep all drafts of your pieces of writing in a well-organised folder. This will make choosing your final pieces much easier. It will also allow you to refer back to great ideas that you want to use again.

Guidelines for the Collection of Texts

1. Create and keep **at least four pieces of work in four different genres (short story, poem, speech, advert, etc.).** This means that you must have one example from each category; for example, you cannot pick two short stories or two speeches. You can place these in your *My Collection of Texts* folder, given with this book, for safekeeping.

2. Include a **first draft, final draft and Reflection Note**. (You may have more than two drafts of each piece.)

3. Choose **two** of these texts for assessment.

4. Just as with Oral Communication, you will have to complete a **Reflection Note** for each piece of work included in your **Collection of Texts**.

Checklist

✓ **Re-read your work** one last time before you fill in the official **Reflection Note**.

✓ Write a brief, thoughtful answer to the questions below that are relevant to your text. This preparation is to **make sure you've done your best work** before you hand it in. The sample questions refer to four particular types of text, but you can change the questions to suit your genres. Ask yourself good questions to test if you've done your best. **Some sample answers are given to help you get started.**

1. Will someone reading my **story** say that I did what my title promised?

Yes ☐   No ☐
Could do it better ☐

My aim was to write a promising title, give my readers a good story and to tell it as well as I could. I wanted my opening sentence to make a reader curious and interested enough to read more. I aimed to write a short last paragraph that sounded like an ending and made the reader think.

2. Did you write an interesting **review**?

Yes ☐   No ☐
Could do it better ☐

I wrote an interesting review of a film/book/concert. I wanted it to be interesting and give good information to a person who hadn't read it or seen it but wanted to know if it was worth their while to read it or go to see it.

3. Did you back up your **argument/debate points** with evidence?

Yes ☐   No ☐
Could do it better ☐

I wrote a good argument, making interesting points about my subject, giving evidence to back up what I said. I showed that I hadn't written off the top of my head, but instead I did reading and research and put thought into expressing my ideas.

4. Did you plan, write and conduct an interesting **interview**?

Yes ☐   No ☐
Could do it better ☐

I wrote an interview that asked thoughtful, open questions based on the research I had done and therefore I got interesting answers that revealed a lot about the person being interviewed. I showed enthusiasm for the person I was interviewing. I encouraged them to open up to me and be honest and thoughtful in their answers.

5. Did you use **an interesting and varied vocabulary** (maybe with the help of a dictionary or thesaurus) to avoid repetition and always get the right expression? Pick out one or two words, phrases, or sentences that you are particularly happy with and that you think show you at your best as a writer.

Yes ☐   No ☐
Could do it better ☐

6. Did you **read what you wrote out loud** either to yourself or for someone else to hear? As you come to the end of each paragraph, make it a habit to read what you write out loud. Then read the whole thing out loud at the end. This is the test to hear if it all flows well and sounds right.

Yes ☐   No ☐
Could do it better ☐

7. **Were you creative?** Were you imaginative? Did you give this task the time it needed to make it interesting, thoughtful and enjoyable to read?

Yes ☐   No ☐
Could do it better ☐

8. Have you been careful and precise about **punctuation, capital letters and paragraphs**? Read your work with a red pen in your hand as if you are an examiner underlining mistakes. Keep checking and correcting until there are no more red marks to be made.

Yes ☐   No ☐
Could do it better ☐

✓ Now **imagine that it was not you who had written this piece**. Read it first silently and then read it aloud as if you are seeing it for the first time. How does it sound? Do you enjoy listening to it? What impact does it make on you? Does it inform you? Does it interest you?

✓ Now you are ready to fill in the official **Reflection Note** and feel confident that you are handing in your best work.

Sample Reflection Note for Collection of the Student's Texts

The sample given here was completed by a student who had written a short story.

SCHOOL Fire and Ice Academy	**STUDENT** Jane Dickens

TITLE/GENRE 'Vanished' A mystery short story

I chose this genre because …

I enjoyed Roald Dahl's mystery story 'The Landlady', which is about Billy Weaver who goes on a journey and disappears in very strange circumstances. I wanted to write a mystery about someone who disappears but is then discovered many years later.

In fact, there are many true, unsolved disappearances in Ireland and around the world, so I read some news articles for ideas. I also read the novels 'Girl Stolen' and 'Girl Missing' so I realised that readers love a mystery story about people who vanish. I also enjoy listening to stories and reading novels, so I wanted to write something that would be enjoyable for someone else to read.

My assessment of my work …

What I learned from creating this text

I learned that it's good to use the planner at the start. It's also good to write a few paragraphs at first and then leave them for a while, then come back to them later and read them aloud to hear how they sound. I learned that you can get good ideas from true stories in the news as well as from reading novels and short stories. I made a diagram of the story by drawing the four-part planner from my English book [p. 72]: Opening — Start the action — Build to a dramatic climax — Resolution. I learned how to create an atmosphere of suspense by describing the winter weather, the cold streets he passes through and the sinister character who kidnaps him.

What I would do differently next time

I would get a little notebook and make a collection of words and sentences from stories I read so that I build up a better vocabulary. Sometimes I repeat myself when I can't find a different word. I would like to get better at writing the last paragraph. I think that's the hardest thing to get right in a short story. I read the last paragraphs of the stories in my English book to give me ideas. I intend to read more stories to see how other writers do it so I will improve my style. I intend to study how different writers use the 'twist in the tail' technique, which is very clever but hard to do. I think a short, sharp sentence works best, like a curtain falling at the end of a play, or a character walking away from the camera at the end of a film.

Student	**Teacher**	**Date**
Jane Dickens	Mr. O'Brien	1 X 20XX

The Assessment Task

When you have completed **CBA2: My Collection of Texts** (p. 450), you will then do the **Assessment Task** (AT). The AT is a formal written task completed during class time which is submitted to the State Examinations Commission for marking along with the Final Assessment for English.

It will be in two parts:

Part 1. You will be expected to **engage** with, **discuss** and **reflect** on a **piece of stimulus material** (for example, a poster or a radio/TV/film clip)

Part 2. You will be expected to respond in **writing** to the questions asked in the assessment task booklet using your experiences as someone who has written texts

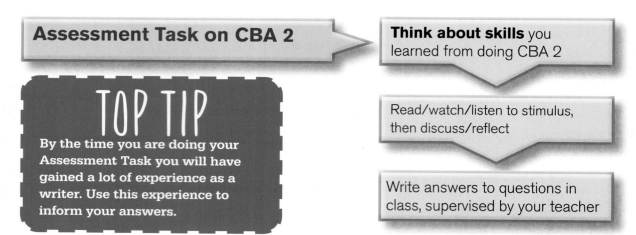

Assessment Task on CBA 2

Think about skills you learned from doing CBA 2

Read/watch/listen to stimulus, then discuss/reflect

Write answers to questions in class, supervised by your teacher

TOP TIP
By the time you are doing your Assessment Task you will have gained a lot of experience as a writer. Use this experience to inform your answers.

Below is a sample Assessment Task to show you what the task will involve. The content and format may change from year to year.

Sample Assessment Task

Time allowed: approximately two class periods

 **Stimulus material:** Look up 'Rick Riordan: Three Tips for Young Writers' on YouTube.

Part 1: Engage with, discuss and reflect on the stimulus material

When you have watched the video, discuss it in relation to the process of creating texts. Here are some questions that might guide a discussion on the video content:

1. What are the main points that Rick Riordan makes?

2. Do you agree with these points, based on your own experience of the writing process (for your Collection of Texts)?

3. What, in your view, is the best piece of advice Rick Riordan gives to young writers? Give one reason for your choice.

4. Based on what you learned from the process of writing your own Collection of Texts, what tip would you give to young writers?

Part 2: Reflect upon and write about your experiences as someone who has written texts (in your Collection of Texts)

(A)

1. List the two texts from your collection that you consider to be your best and identify the genre of each.

2. Select an **extract** (e.g. paragraph/passage/verse) from one text in your Collection of Texts. Copy the extract into the answer booklet.

Answer either 3 or 4

3. Explain how **two** features of the extract you have chosen are typical of its genre.

OR

4. Identify **one** change that you made in the course of writing this text that you think improved it and explain how it improved the text.

Sample Answer

1. Text 1: The Glass Palace; Genre: Short Story

Text 2: Journey into the Unknown; Genre: Non-literary Text, a blog entry

2. Sample paragraph from Text 2:

'So, you arrive home from a hard day's work at school waiting for your routine, freshly brewed cup of tea and the comforting "How was your day?", an invitation to rant about the egotistical Mr Jones. However, the grey head barely looks up from her iPad these days, the slightly wrinkly finger has found The Great British Bake-off app – there is certainly a role-reversal happening these days between the old and young. Frequently the youth of today are scolded for being too focused on technology and I do agree that this does happen to a certain level, but what I find fascinating is that adults are just as guilty. Being obsessed with technology is not just confined to a particular age group. Next time I should threaten to ground my nanny when she won't listen to me because she is buried in her iPad.'

3. Two features which are typical of this genre are informal language, for example 'an invitation to rant', and humour, 'I should threaten to ground my nanny when she won't listen to me'.

4. When I reflected on my first draft, I realised that I hadn't used any great variety of tone and it was pretty boring. I had written a very bland account of seeing my nanny using her iPad when I visited her. I introduced some humour by referring to my 'hard day's work at school' and 'the egotistical Mr. Jones' and I decided to joke about grounding my nanny. I think this helped make the blog more personal and appealing.

(B)

Thinking about the process of writing/compiling your Collection of Texts, write a short paragraph on two of the following:

1. How the things I read helped me to be a better writer.

2. The different kinds of writing included in my collection.

3. How I worked with classmates as part my writing.

4. What a reader might enjoy most about one of the texts in my collection.

5. How my writing has changed over the past two years.

6. How I edited my writing to make it better for a reader

7. How a specific piece of feedback was useful to me.

8. How I hope to use my writing skills in the future.

Sample Answers (1–6)

1. How the things I read helped me to be a better writer.

I learned three important things from short story writers. First, how to hook the reader with a clever first sentence. For example, in Langston Hughes' story, 'Thank You, M'am':

'She was a large woman with a large purse that had everything in it but a hammer and nails.'

So I started a story with:

'She was a small old woman with a raggy little dog that she carried in a tattered blanket.'

Second, from Roald Dahl, I learned how to describe interesting personal details:

'. . . she had small, white, quickly moving hands and red fingernails' ('The Landlady').

From Washington Irving, I learned how to describe setting:

'. . . the Kaatskill Mountains clothed in blue and purple, in the last rays of the setting sun' ('Rip Van Winkle').

From Liam O'Flaherty in 'The Sniper', I learned how to create tension by describing a scene as if it was a little film:

'The blood was oozing through the sleeve of his coat. His hand trembled with eagerness.'

Finally, I tried to imitate good endings. Roald Dahl goes for the shocking twist-in-the-tail ending:

'No my dear, only you' ('The Landlady').

So does Liam O'Flaherty:

'The sniper turned over the dead body and looked into his brother's face' ('The Sniper').

I recognised how writing can be very powerful. For example, in 'Guests of the Nation', Frank O'Connor is very deep and solemn. His character looks at the night sky feeling 'very lost and lonely like a child astray in the snow'.

'And anything that happened to me afterwards, I never felt the same about again.'

My ambition is to write an ending like that myself. I know that by reading lots of different short stories, I will learn how to write like this.

2. The different kinds of writing included in my collection

I have studied various types of writing and genres. I tried so many different things but I can really only focus on my favourite ones.

For my blog entry, I used an informal and humorous tone as I am used to reading and hearing conversational language on social media and YouTube. I read 'How to Stay Young', written by The Cranky Old Man, and I found it quite funny. It reminded me of my granny giving out. It inspired me to write a humorous blog about the difference between old and young people. I had to make sure I used great vocabulary and capital letters (because sometimes I forgot to use these). My opening was:

'So, you arrive home from a hard day's work in school waiting for your routine, freshly brewed cup of tea and the comforting "How was your day?", an invitation to rant about the egotistical Mr Jones. However, the grey head barely looks up from her iPad these days, the slightly wrinkly finger has found The Great British Bake-off app – there is certainly a role-reversal happening these day between the old and young.'

In comparison, I didn't really like writing newspaper articles at first. I enjoyed reading them but found it difficult to express my opinion clearly. So, I focused on writing a strong and eye-catching starter sentence.

'Beijing's awful smog cloud has lifted the fog from China's vision regarding the international climate crisis.'

It was important to write my opinion because that's what journalists do.

'It is unacceptable for China to ignore the problem even though it is visible and real in the grimy soot that covers a person's clothes if they are forced to go out in it.'

Another style of writing that really appealed to me was scriptwriting as I love being creative. However, I learned that I needed to be brief and to the point in delivering characters' lines.

'Martin: Jade, will ya ever get down the stairs so we can open the pressies!'

In scriptwriting, stage directions are the only way to communicate certain things to your actors.

You can't put in stage directions everywhere, so when you do, they are important to the story and performance.

'Jade: (shaking the empty box) And what is this? Is this some kind of joke, Martin? After all I have done for you, you lazy fool.'

My experience of writing different genres has been helpful to my overall approach to English and my writing has improved.

3. How I worked with classmates as part of my writing.

I have always liked working with my classmates, but in the last two years I have realised how much we can all learn from one another. My favourite piece of work is a persuasive speech I wrote and then delivered to the class. I never thought that this would be the case as writing and delivering speeches has always been very difficult for me, but I really improved by working with a classmate.

I spent a lot of time working on it because I was very nervous. I thought about the speeches we had read and listened to, especially the one by Chris O'Dowd. I checked the success criteria this time and I used the RAFT structure and thought about my audience.

Our teacher asked us to work in pairs and to do a peer assessment. I had to listen to a classmate's speech as he read it aloud and then I read it. As I listened to him reading it, I realised that my classmate had used a lot of elements of persuasive language like rhetorical questions and some good examples, which I had forgotten to do. I was really surprised that listening to another person's speech would help me to improve my own. I was also able to help my classmate because I noticed that his sentences were too long, so it was difficult to understand his points. I then read my speech aloud to my friend and he gave me a lot of great feedback, which helped to increase my confidence. He also pointed out that I had included an example, which is an element of persuasive speech, so I was really happy with that as I was worried that mine was really bad.

When we swapped work and read one another's speeches, we both realised that our punctuation wasn't great, so we took out our proof-reading wheels and fixed the mistakes (we had both forgotten some capital letters and full stops). My final draft was much better and finally I felt like I was improving. I realised that getting feedback from another student can be really helpful. My partner was also really nice about my mistakes and didn't make me feel embarrassed about it. This reminded me of something our teacher says: 'Honesty without sensitivity is brutality.' I agree because taking feedback can be hard enough, but when someone is nice about it, it's much easier!

4. What a reader might enjoy most about one of the texts in my collection.

It may not be the most obvious choice, but I believe a reader would enjoy my email to a local businessman outlining why he should support my chosen charity. I carefully wrote out the 'To:', 'From:' and 'Re:' so my reader would understand why I was writing the email.

In order to persuade the businessman, I highlighted the important work the charity carries out throughout the country.

> 'Homelessness is a difficult issue and it is hard to find a solution. Yet, Focus Ireland works to support those living on the streets or in emergency accommodation. They provide housing services, shelters and employment assistance.'

I had to provide information about this serious problem because I was trying to convince a businessman to give me money. I made sure to include statistics so the businessman could see how the problem was growing.

> 'Focus Ireland estimate that at any one time, five thousand people are homeless.'

It was important to use persuasive vocabulary and emotive language. I learned to use words such as 'atrocious', 'implore' and 'startling'. The persuasive language was also backed up with details of how the money was going to be spent.

> 'Your money will have tremendous results; it will buy twelve new beds and bedding to allow homeless people to take shelter from the rough streets.'

I feel that an email was an unusual way to convince an audience, but I think a reader would enjoy learning about the work of a charity in this way.

5. How my writing has changed over the past two years.

Over the past two years, I tried out different kinds of writing. At first, I only wrote stories, but then I added blogs, diary entries, letters, reviews, emails and speeches to my portfolio.

I start by brainstorming, jotting down words and random ideas. Then I write an opening paragraph and I read it out loud to hear how it sounds. I have a notebook where I collect words and sentences from good stories.

I have improved three things: first, I read a lot to get ideas for plots and characters; second, I write an interesting opening sentence that makes a reader curious to read on; third, I write good descriptions of people and places.

My best story is about a character who goes on a journey and then goes missing. Years later, a young news reporter solves this mysterious disappearance. My story's opening sentence imitates a short story I read. I think it's my best.

> 'When Oliver Woodward turned the corner from the station that evening, downy flakes of snow were falling on the sign that said B & B.'

I also made progress when creating atmosphere in a story.

> 'The air was deadly cold and the wind was like a flat blade of ice on his cheeks.'

I always stop writing and re-read my story before I write the last paragraph. I was very happy with this ending.

> 'So ended the mystery of the strange disappearance of Oliver Woodward whose short life ended in the home of a pale old lady who kept stuffed creatures in her house of death.'

6. How I edited my writing to make it better for a reader.

Over the last two years I have learned how to improve my work by editing. Before that I thought that the first version should be perfect so I only did one draft and handed that up. I always felt quite disheartened when I got my work back in primary school because it had a lot of mistakes. I really wanted to make it enjoyable for a reader but I didn't know how.

The first time I really learned how to improve my work by editing was at the beginning of second year when I wrote a film review. I regularly read film reviews online but I had never written one before then. I wrote my first draft using the success criteria from my English book [p. 40]. When we had finished writing, our teacher asked us to do a self-assessment by writing down two things we did well and one thing we could improve on. She also asked us to check the success criteria and to make sure we had done all of the 'must' parts and attempted at least one thing from each of the 'should' and 'could' sections.

When I did this I realised that I had done most of the 'must' parts but I hadn't used the RAFT structure so I hadn't actually considered who my target audience was (students reading a school magazine). When I edited my review, I changed my language slightly so that it was appropriate for secondary school students. I hadn't done any of the 'should' criteria so I decided to give the film a star rating. I think this definitely made it much better for a reader as they could see that I really liked it.

I now believe that it is much better for a reader when I draft and edit my work before handing it up.

The Final Assessment

At the end of third year you will sit your **Final Assessment**. Separate examinations, each two hours in length, are set for Higher and Ordinary Level. The layout may vary from year to year. You may be asked to write for various purposes, for example to show your appreciation and understanding of your studied texts; to show your knowledge of appropriate vocabulary for stories, plays, film and poems; to write in response to a variety of texts which you are seeing for the first time.

Final Assessment

June of 3rd Year
Separate Higher and Ordinary Levels
One **2-hour written exam** at each level

Content and format of examination papers may vary from year to year

Linked to learning outcomes marked for the final examination (p. 447)

TOP TIP

Use the texts and skills from your genre chapters (Short Story, Poetry, Drama, Novel, Film) to help in preparing for your final examination. Read the cloze test at the beginning of each genre chapter to revise the skills you have learned from your genre chapters.

Exam Focus Vocabulary

Certain words are repeatedly used in examination questions. Follow our exam vocabulary page to help you understand instructions.

A
Analyse:
study something closely in order to understand or explain it

Appropriate:
suitable, right or proper in the circumstances

Assess:
judge something to evaluate its stage of progress

C
Characteristics:
qualities or features that are typical of something

Clarify:
make something clear

Compare:
examine people or things for similarities

Content:
the main subject, ideas, information in a text

Compose:
create, produce or put things together

Contrast:
examine people or things for differences

Convey:
to communicate, share ideas, information, response or feelings

Corresponding:
similar to or in agreement with something else

Criteria:
principles or standards by which something may be judged or decided

D
Describe:
explain or create a picture of something with words

Discuss:
talk about something

E
Elements:
the basic units that make up a bigger idea

Engaging:
pleasing, attracting attention

Evaluate:
consider something carefully and judge it on its importance or quality

Examine:
study something in detail

F
Footnotes:
extra piece of information at the bottom of the page

J
Justify:
defend, give reasons or evidence for your opinions

O
Outline:
give the most important facts or points about something

P
Prompt:
something that inspires or causes a reaction

R
Reflect:
think seriously and say something thoughtful

Respond:
react to something

S
Screenshot:
an image taken from a computer screen

Style:
a particular way of doing, designing, writing, speaking, shaping something

T
Task:
a piece of work to be done

Exam Preparation: Practical Tips

Preparation for the Final Exam

Revise **key scenes** from your *studied texts*
- The setting, where and when?
- What happens?
- Who is involved?

Practise writing **titles** and **authors**
- Correct spelling
- Correct punctuation

Quote **key lines** from your *studied texts*
- Who is the speaker?
- What is said?
- Why is it important?

Review the **main characters** from your *studied texts*
- Role
- Characterisation
- Relationships
- Development through the text

Reflect on **opening and closing moments** from your *studied texts*
- What makes them interesting or appealing?
- Can you compare or contrast them?

Look at **advertising** in newspapers, on radio, and on screen
- Who is the target audience?
- What do you find interesting or appealing?

Use **PIE** in your answers
- Point
- Illustrate
- Explain

Re-read the **short stories** you enjoyed
- What made them enjoyable?
- What were your favourite moments?
- What themes did they explore?

Revise your **studied poems**
- Learn memorable quotations
- Be familiar with the authors/poets
- What themes did they explore?

Remember **RAFT** when planning your writing
- Role of the writer
- Audience
- Format
- Topic

Read and **listen** to the news in newspapers, on radio, and on screen
- Know what is happening in the world today
- Have interesting things to tell the examiner
- Refer to issues in the news

Revise the different types of **non-literary texts**
- Who is the target audience?
- What did you find interesting or appealing?

Acknowledgments

Digital Permissions

'A Poem for a Best Friend' by Emma Ronan, recorded by kind permission of the poet • *Lamb* directed, written and produced by Emma Freeman, included by kind permission of Emma Freeman • *Sunday Miscellany*, 'Picturing the Past', read by Barbara McKeon (8 March 1998) is courtesy of RTÉ Archives and the author • 'Base Details' and 'The General' are copyright Siegfried Sassoon by kind permission of the Estate of George Sassoon • 'On Turning Ten' from *The Art of Drowning*, by Billy Collins © 1995. Recorded by permission of the University of Pittsburgh Press • *Drama on One*, RTÉ Radio 1, *Infancy* by Maeve Binchy (2012) is courtesy of RTÉ Archives, Christine Green on behalf of Gordon Snell and the Estate of Maeve Binchy, and the Lisa Richards Agency on behalf of Mikel Murfi • 'Welcome to My Channel' vlog from Donal Skehan's YouTube channel, used with permission of Donal Skehan • 'Mid-Term Break' by Seamus Heaney recorded by kind permission of Faber and Faber • 'Stopping by Woods on a Snowy Evening' from the book THE POETRY OF ROBERT FROST edited by Edward Connery Lathem. Copyright © 1923, 1969 by Henry Holt and Company, copyright © 1951 by Robert Frost. Reprinted by permission of Henry Holt and Company, LLC. All rights reserved • 'The Listeners' by Walter de la Mare, from *The Complete Poems of Walter de la Mare* (1975), is reprinted by permission of the Literary Trustees of Walter de la Mare and the Society of Authors as their representative • *Documentary on One*, 'Small Lives and Great Reputations' (2014) is courtesy of RTÉ Archives • *Drama on One*, RTÉ Radio 1, *Yardstick* written and directed by Joe O'Byrne (2013) is courtesy of RTÉ Archives, Joe O'Byrne, MacFarlane Chard Associates on behalf of Saoirse Ronan, James Killeen is courtesy of The Independent Theatre Workshop, and the Lisa Richards Agency on behalf of Amy Huberman • 'Join Our Family', video about the School of St Jude, Tanzania, used by permission of Gemma Sisia • *New Boy*, directed by Steph Green, is used by permission of the producer, Tamara Anghie at Zanzibar Films • Interview with Patrick Ness (2012), from the London Book Fair YouTube channel, is used with permission • 'Introduction to Poetry' by Billy Collins, from *The Apple that Astonished Paris* (1988). Permission by Chris Calhoun Agency © Billy Collins • 'Head Lice' by Terry McDonagh, from Boxes (2006) is reprinted by kind permission of the poet • 'OnaMaTaPia' by Spike Milligan from *Unspun Socks From a Chicken's Laundry*. By kind permission of Norma Farnes • 'Little Red Riding Hood' by Roald Dahl, from *Revolting Rhymes*, published by Jonathan Cape Ltd & Penguin Books, is recorded by permission of David Higham agent • 'Back in the Playground Blues' by Adrian Mitchell, from *For Beauty Douglas* (1982), is reproduced by permission of United Agents on behalf of the poet • 'Night Feed' by Eavan Boland from *New Collected Poems* reprinted by permission of Carcanet Press (2005) • 'Timothy Winters' by Charles Causley, from *Collected Poems 1951–2000* published by Macmillan, is reprinted by permission of David Higham agent; 'Timothy Winters' by Charles Causley recording © The Poetry Archive, used by permission of The Poetry Archive • 'When all the others were away at Mass', from 'Clearances', by Seamus Heaney is reprinted by kind permission of Faber and Faber Ltd; 'When all the others were away at Mass', from 'Clearances', by Seamus Heaney recording courtesy of RTÉ Archives • 'Inniskeen Road: July Evening' by Patrick Kavanagh is reprinted from *Collected Poems*, edited by Antoinette Quinn (Allen Lane, 2004), by kind permission of the Trustees of the Estate of the late Katherine B. Kavanagh, through the Jonathan Williams Literary Agency • 'Cinderella' by Sylvia Plath reprinted by kind permission of Faber and Faber Ltd • 'Same Love' written by Ben Haggerty, Ryan Lewis and Mary Lambert. © Published by Inside Passage Music. Administered by Kobalt Music Publishing Ltd • 'The Road Not Taken' from the book THE POETRY OF ROBERT FROST edited by Edward Connery Lathem. Copyright © 1923, 1969 by Henry Holt and Company, copyright © 1951 by Robert Frost. Reprinted by permission of Henry Holt and Company, LLC. All rights reserved • *The Faeries of Blackheath Woods*, written and directed by Ciarán Foy, is used by permission of Ciarán Foy • *Morning Ireland*, 'Is there life on Mars?', Dr Joseph Roche (29 September 2015) is courtesy of RTÉ Archives • *Drivetime*, 'Like' by Joseph O'Connor is courtesy of RTÉ Archives • *Sunday Miscellany*, 'My First Valentine Card', by Gerry Moran (14 February 2016) is courtesy of RTÉ Archives and Gerry Moran • © 'Shakespeare's Globe Theatre, London: All the World's a Stage' reproduced by permission of i2iTravel YouTube Channel (https://www.youtube.com/channel/UChxfTENPzqfsl4fOl89-Rqw)

Text Permissions

'A Poem for a Best Friend' by Emma Ronan, reprinted by kind permission of the poet • Extracts from *We Are All Completely Beside Ourselves* by Karen Joy Fowler reprinted by kind permission of Profile Books, 3 Holford Yard, Bevin Way, London • *Big Hero 6* review reprinted by kind permission of Tara Brady • Extracts from *The Apple Tart of Hope* by Sarah Moore Fitzgerald reprinted by kind permission of Orion Children's Books • 'Women and Armed Conflict' infographic reproduced by kind permission of UN Women, 2015 (unwomen.org) • 'Base Details' and 'The General' are copyright Siegfried Sassoon by kind permission of the Estate of George Sassoon • 'Guests of the Nation' by Frank O'Connor reprinted by permission of Peters Fraser & Dunlop (www.petersfraserdunlop.com) • 'How to Stay Young' from the Cranky Old Man blog reprinted by kind permission of Joe Hagy ▪ 'I Don't Want to Grow Up Because' by Konni Kim reprinted by kind permission of the writer ▪ 'On Turning Ten' from *The Art of Drowning*, by Billy Collins © 1995. Reprinted by permission of the University of Pittsburgh Press ▪ Text from *Lord of the Flies: Acting Edition* by Nigel Williams reprinted by kind permission of Faber and Faber ▪ 'A Twist in the Tale' by Michael Somers is reprinted by kind permission of the author ▪ 'Mid-Term Break' by Seamus Heaney is reprinted by kind permission of Faber and Faber ▪ 'Give Peace a Chance – Run With Youth' by Ettie Higgins, reprinted by kind permission of Ettie Higgins, UNICEF ▪ 'Stopping by Woods on a Snowy Evening' from *The Poetry of Robert Frost*, edited by Edward Connery Lathem, published by Jonathan Cape. Reprinted by permission of The Random House Group Limited; 'Stopping by Woods on a Snowy Evening' from the book THE POETRY OF ROBERT FROST edited by Edward Connery Lathem. Copyright © 1923, 1969 by Henry Holt and Company, copyright © 1951 by Robert Frost. Reprinted by permission of Henry Holt and Company, LLC. All rights reserved ▪ 'The Listeners' by Walter de la Mare, taken from *The Complete Poems of Walter de la Mare* (1975), is reprinted by permission of the Literary Trustees of Walter de la Mare and the Society of Authors as their representative ▪ 'The Landlady' by Roald Dahl, from *Kiss Kiss* published by Penguin Books is reprinted by permission of David Higham agent ▪ 'Reunion', from *Collected Stories* by John Cheever, published by Jonathan Cape. Reprinted by permission of The Random House Group Limited ▪ © Martin McDonagh, 2013, *The Cripple of Inishmaan*, Bloomsbury Methuen Drama, an imprint of Bloomsbury Publishing Plc ▪ 'The Sniper' by Liam O'Flaherty from *Spring Sowing* reprinted by permission of Peters Fraser & Dunlop (www.petersfraserdunlop.com) on behalf of the estate of Liam O'Flaherty ▪ 'The Hero of Drumree' by Derek Landy, from *Beyond the Stars* by Sarah Webb. Reprinted by permission of HarperCollins Publishers Ltd © (2014) Derek Landy ▪ 'Humming Through My Fingers', from *Love Hurts* by Malorie Blackman, published by Corgi Children's, 2015. Reprinted by permission of The Random House Group Limited ▪ 'Fall' by Emma Donoghue from *Three and A Half Deaths*. Copyright © Emma Donoghue, 2011. Reprinted by permission of Picador ▪ 'Mother and Mrs Everington' by Melvin Burgess. Reprinted by permission of A.P. Watt at United Agents on behalf of Melvin Burgess ▪ *Teapot Therapy* by A.J. Poyiadgi is reproduced by kind permission of the artist ▪ 'Introduction to Poetry' by Billy Collins, from *The Apple that Astonished Paris* (1988). Permission by Chris Calhoun Agency © Billy Collins ▪ 'Head Lice' by Terry McDonagh, from *Boxes* (2006) is reprinted by kind permission of the poet ▪ 'OnaMaTaPia' by Spike Milligan from *Unspun Socks From a Chicken's Laundry*. By kind permission of Norma Farnes ▪ 'Little Red Riding Hood' by Roald Dahl, from *Revolting Rhymes*, published by Jonathan Cape Ltd & Penguin Books, is reprinted by permission of David Higham agent ▪ 'Back in the Playground Blues' by Adrian Mitchell, from *For Beauty Douglas* (1982), is reproduced by permission of United Agents on behalf of the poet ▪ 'Night Feed' by Eavan Boland from *New Collected Poems* reprinted by permission of Carcanet Press (2005) ▪ 'Timothy Winters' by Charles Causley, from *Collected Poems 1951–2000* published by Macmillan, is reprinted by permission of David Higham agent ▪ 'When all the others were away at Mass', from 'Clearances', by Seamus Heaney is reprinted by kind permission of Faber and Faber Ltd ▪ 'Inniskeen Road: July Evening' by Patrick Kavanagh is reprinted from *Collected Poems*, edited by Antoinette Quinn (Allen Lane, 2004), by kind permission of the Trustees of the Estate of the late Katherine B. Kavanagh, through the Jonathan Williams Literary Agency ▪ 'Cinderella' by Sylvia Plath reprinted by kind permission of Faber and Faber Ltd ▪ 'Same Love' written by Ben Haggerty, Ryan Lewis and Mary Lambert. © Published by Inside Passage Music. Administered by Kobalt Music Publishing Ltd ▪ 'I am the song' by Charles Causley, from *Collected Poems 1951–2000* published by Macmillan, is reprinted by permission of David Higham agent ▪ 'The Road Not Taken' from *The Poetry of Robert Frost*, edited by Edward Connery Lathem, published by Jonathan Cape. Reprinted by permission of The Random House Group Limited; 'The Road Not Taken' from the book THE POETRY OF ROBERT FROST edited by Edward Connery Lathem. Copyright © 1923, 1969 by Henry Holt and Company, copyright © 1951 by Robert Frost. Reprinted by permission of Henry Holt and Company, LLC. All rights reserved ▪ 'Memory of My Father' by Patrick Kavanagh is reprinted from *Collected Poems*, edited by Antoinette Quinn (Allen Lane, 2004), by kind permission of the Trustees of the Estate of the late Katherine B. Kavanagh, through the Jonathan Williams Literary Agency ▪ Text © 2009 Jane Mitchell from CHALKLINE by Jane Mitchell. Reproduced by permission of Walker Books Ltd, London SE11 5HJ www.walker.co.uk ▪ Extracts from *Noughts & Crosses* by Malorie Blackman, published by Corgi Children's, 2006. Reprinted by permission of The Random House Group Limited ▪ Extract from *To Kill a Mockingbird* by Harper Lee, reprinted with permission of Andrew Nurnberg Associates ▪ Extracts from *The Outsiders*, copyright © 1967 by S.E. Hinton. Copyright renewed 1995. Published in *The Outsiders* by S.E. Hinton. Reprinted by permission of Curtis Brown, Ltd ▪ 'For Word' from FUNKY CHICKENS by Benjamin Zephaniah (Viking, 1996) Copyright © Benjamin Zephaniah, 1996 ▪ 'Fire and Ice' from *The Poetry of Robert Frost*, edited by Edward Connery Lathem, published by Jonathan Cape/The Random House Group Limited; 'Fire and Ice' from the book THE POETRY OF ROBERT FROST edited by Edward Connery Lathem. Copyright © 1923, 1969 by Henry Holt and Company, copyright © 1951 by Robert Frost. Henry Holt and Company, LLC. All rights reserved.

For permission to reproduce photographs, the authors and publisher gratefully acknowledge the following:

© 20th Century Fox: 174; © A.J. Poyiadgi: 247-250; © Adventurous Kate: 77BR; © Alamy: 5, 7C, 16, 28, 44BL, 44BC, 44BR, 47, 60T, 88, 89, 116TL, 116TC, 116TR, 117TR, 180T, 180B, 257, 263, 275B, 276, 279T, 279B, 287, 289, 291, 296, 311, 313, 322CB, 334T, 339, 344R, 351, 363B, 365CR, 365CL, 367, 370, 371, 372, 378, 390, 394TL, 394TR, 394CR, 394CL, 394B, 395, 401, 405, 409T, 409C, 409B, 410TL, 410TC, 410C, 410CR, 410TR, 410B, 410CL, 413, 415TC, 415TR, 415CL, 415C, 415BL, 419C, 419CR, 419B, 420T, 422, 424, 430, 435; © ArenaPal: 91, 326TR; Courtesy of Barbara McKeon: 38B; © BBC Photo Library: 326TL; © BBC Worldwide Ltd / Neal Street Productions: 354; Courtesy of beyondblue (beyondblue.org.au): 150; © Bloomsbury Publishing Plc: 365BR; Reproduced by permission of the Charles Causley Trust / National Portrait Gallery: 275T; © Ciarán Foy: 423 © Collins Agency: 90; Courtesy of the Concord Players (concordplayers.org): 144T; © Dalmdad Landscape Photography: 379; © Dara Munnis: 15BR, 23BL; © Debora Robinson / South Coast Repertory: 326BL; © Emma Freeman: 27; © Gemma Sisia: 164T; Courtesy of Gerry Moran: 42; © Getty Images: 7B, 8, 17BL, 46, 48, 56, 57, 58, 59, 60B, 77, 83, 115R, 115L, 117TL, 179, 185, 259, 261t, 265T, 270T, 285, 300, 308, 309, 322T, 323BL, 337, 418, 420BL; © Goodreads Inc: 366CL; © i2iTravel: 442; © Irish Times: 29TL, 327L, 327R; © Jenni Milton: 364; Joe Cocks Studio Collection © Shakespeare Birthplace Trust: 343R; © Kobal / Picture Desk: 116BL, 388R; Courtesy of Konni Kim: 71; © Mary Evans Picture Library: 363T; © Mashable: 77BTR; Courtesy of Michael Somers: 100; © Michelle Tiger Heath / Scholastic: 366T; © NASA / JPL-Caltech: 431; Published by arrangement with Random House Children's Publishers UK, a division of The Random House Group Limited: © Quentin Blake: 265B; 365BL; Artwork © Tad Carpenter: 366CR; Photograph by Richard Gibbs (richardpgibbs. org): 302; © Press Association: 7T, 152; © Profile Books: 17BR; © REX Shutterstock: 44T, 104, 144B, 305, 322B, 322CT, 323CR, 330, 344L, 356, 388L, 415CR, 415BC, 417, 420BR; © rollingnews.ie: 441; © Royal Shakespeare Company: 343L; © RTÉ Stills Library: 272, 278, 283; © Shane Scollard / The Everyman, Cork: 323BR; © So Sue Me: 77BCL; © Temple Street Children's Hospital / iCan: 165; © TMZ: 77BL; © Topfoto: 129; Tricycle Theatre Production. Directed by Dominic Dromgoole / Designed by Michael Taylor / Lighting by Mark Doubleday / photo © Mark Doubleday: 326BR; © Trip Advisor: 22; © UN Women, 2015 (unwomen.org): 49; © UNHCR: 118T; © UNICEF: 167; © Zanzibar Films: 174.

Additional images supplied by the authors, iStock, Shutterstock, Twitter, YouTube and Wikipedia.

The authors and publisher have made every effort to trace all copyright holders, but if any have been inadvertently overlooked we would be pleased to make the necessary arrangement at the first opportunity.